QUEER READINGS OF
THE CENTURION AT CAPERNAUM

BIBLE AND ITS RECEPTION

Robert Paul Seesengood, General Editor

Editorial Board:
Brennan Breed
Stephen R. Burge
Siobhan Dowling Long
J. Cheryl Exum
Michael Rosenberg

Number 5

QUEER READINGS OF THE CENTURION AT CAPERNAUM

Their History and Politics

Christopher B. Zeichmann

Atlanta

Copyright © 2022 by Christopher B. Zeichmann

All rights reserved. No part of this work may be reproduced or transmitted in any form or by any means, electronic or mechanical, including photocopying and recording, or by means of any information storage or retrieval system, except as may be expressly permitted by the 1976 Copyright Act or in writing from the publisher. Requests for permission should be addressed in writing to the Rights and Permissions Office, SBL Press, 825 Houston Mill Road, Atlanta, GA 30329 USA.

Library of Congress Control Number: 2022947677

Cover photo: Attic red-figure stemmed pottery cup depicting a courting scene, fifth century BCE. AN1896-1908.G.279. © Ashmolean Museum.

Contents

Acknowledgments vii
Abbreviations xi

Introduction 1

1. A Homophile Centurion and the Legality of Love:
   Continental Europe, 1950–1990 27

2. A Centurion and His Partner at the Altar:
   The United States, United Kingdom, and
   Australia, 1985–2010 67

3. Military Occupation and Sexual Abuse in Roman Galilee:
   Homoerotic Counterreadings, 2000–Present 95

4. Whose Interpretation Is Legitimate? 141

5. Did the Centurion at Capernaum Have
   Intercourse with the Pais? 169

A Disappointing Conclusion 217

Appendix 1: Text and Translation of the Passage in
   Matthew, Luke, John, and Reconstruction of Q 225

Appendix 2: Chronology of Homoerotic
   Readings 1950–1989 229

Appendix 3: Military Presence in Capernaum 249

Bibliography 253
Ancient Sources Index 289
Modern Authors Index 299
Subject Index 305

Acknowledgments

It will surprise no one that a book requiring archival investigation was only possible with the aid of many. To start with the most obvious, I extend my gratitude to Rhonda Burnette-Bletsch, Robert Seesengood, Nicole L. Tilford, Bob Buller, and the editorial board of the Bible and Its Reception series for seeing this book to fruition. The two anonymous peer reviewers offered helpful comments—whoever they are, their work is appreciated. This is not to mention other staff and workers at SBL Press whose names are unknown to me, despite their important contributions. The present volume would not exist if not for their collective support and labor.

Dozens of archives and libraries also proved vital in this project, though a few stand out as particularly important. Invaluable help of various sorts was provided by The ArQuives, Académie Gay et Lesbienne, ONE National Gay and Lesbian Archives, the LGBTQ Religious Archives Network, Lesbian Herstory Archives, and the interlibrary loan staff at the University of Toronto.

Numerous colleagues provided feedback on drafts of specific chapters, including Leif E. Vaage, Caryn Tamber-Rosenau, Joseph Marchal, Jimmy Hoke, Scott E. Gunther, Jennifer Glancy, Ronald Charles, Emma CushmanWood Ceruti, and Paul CushmanWood Ceruti. The volume is far stronger thanks to the expertise they brought to their comments. Halvor Moxnes, Kevin McGinnis, Michiko Bown-Kai, and Morgan Bell are all incredible people for reading a draft of the entire book and indulging me in long exchanges about it; the book is more cohesive thanks to their thoughtful reading, benefiting from the very different experiences they incorporated into their feedback. Readers will notice the name Morgan Bell in several footnotes, especially in chapter 1. He has offered valuable assistance by translating French texts into smoother English than my capability permits; though his research interest in Karl Barth is a significant character flaw, he is otherwise a loyal and valued friend. Jordan

Balint also did fantastic work on the indices for the present volume, labor that has been immensely helpful.

Other colleagues who contributed in noteworthy, if less direct, ways include Ralph Carl Wushke, Kieren Williams, Natalie Wigg-Stevenson, Nathanael Romero, Rhiannon Graybill, and John Egger. Many other friends and acquaintances helped in the research, though my own memory fails me. If you are among such people and feel a tinge of pain because you don't see your name listed here, please reassure yourself with the knowledge that I almost certainly resent my own forgetfulness more than you do. In fact, one such friend just came to mind: Ellen Burch was the first to inform me that this pericope was mentioned in an episode of Queer Eye. Thanks, Ellen!

Though these things often appear perfunctory to those unaware of the circumstances, I cannot overstate the support offered by various loved ones in the production of this book. Given that this book was largely produced in solo quarantine (living alone with mandatory stay-at-home orders for about a year), their encouragement was particularly meaningful. My parents entertained me with supportive discussions, perhaps humoring me in their mind, but their conversations were productive and deeply appreciated. Laura Zeichman and Jim Walsh also generously hosted me for a few weeks while I edited this manuscript, a rejuvenating break from pandemic isolation. My family has always provided unconditional support. I offer my thanks once again to Emma and Paul CushmanWood Ceruti, whose care and friendship proved all the more vital during my year in solitude; likewise with Christine Perri and her family, whose tomfoolery is always a delight to experience. Among those who know Luba, no one will be surprised she was particularly important to the writing process, as she has ensured I get fresh air more regularly than I otherwise would during a Canadian winter midst lockdown.

I have benefited from opportunities to present parts of this book at different venues, including the LGBTI/Queer Hermeneutics and Ideological Criticism sections at the Annual Meeting of the Society of Biblical Literature, the Queering Biblical Studies Workshop at the annual Queer and Transgender Studies in Religion conference, along with presentations hosted by Toronto Metropolitan University's Student Christian Movement, Huron College at Western University, the Toronto OC, and Urbs & Polis. My thanks go to the organizers for providing an outlet to discuss my research and to the attendees for their feedback. These opportunities were particularly valuable, given how severely the pandemic curtailed my contact with academic colleagues.

While none of the following chapters has been previously published, some sections of the present monograph rework and remix ideas I have articulated elsewhere. Thus, there are instances where a few consecutive paragraphs are very similar to things I have said in an earlier publication. This book includes brief overlaps with the following publications:

Zeichmann, Christopher B. "Gender in Biblical Studies after the Forgery of The Gospel of Jesus's Wife." *BibInt* 26 (2018): 391–412.

———. "Gender Minorities in and under Roman Power: Respectability Politics in Luke–Acts." Pages 61–73 in *Luke–Acts*. Edited by James Grimshaw. Texts@Contexts. London: Bloomsbury, 2018.

———. "Same-Sex Intercourse Involving Jewish Men 100 BCE–100 CE: Sources and Significance for Jesus' Sexual Politics." *Religion and Gender* 10 (2020): 13–36.

———. "Rethinking the Gay Centurion: Sexual Exceptionalism, National Exceptionalism in Readings of Matt 8:5–13 // Luke 7:1–10." *BCT* 11.1 (2015): 35–54.

———. "X-Men Films and the Domestication of Dissent: Sexuality, Race, and Respectability." Pages 175–97 in *Supersex: Sexuality, Fantasy, and the Superhero*. Edited by Anna F. Peppard. World Comics and Graphic Nonfiction. Austin: University of Texas Press, 2020.

Readers who enjoy the present book may wish to seek them out for further discussion of related issues.

Toronto Metropolitan University's History Department and the Canadian Union of Public Employees 3904 (Units 1 and 2) have reimbursed some of the expenses incurred while researching and writing this book. Toronto Metropolitan is exemplary in its support of contingent workers. I am grateful for their recognition that the neoliberal university is predicated upon precarious labor and offer an exceptional level of support for their contract lecturers.

I would like to dedicate this book, as unceremoniously as his humility would demand, to Nathanael P. Romero. His conversations have been the genesis of this study, and for that I cannot adequately articulate my gratitude.

Abbreviations

Ab urbe cond.	Livy, *Ab urbe condita*
Abr.	Philo, *De Abrahamo*
ABRL	Anchor Bible Reference Library
Acts Andr.	Acts of Andrew
AE	*Année épigraphique*
Ages.	Xenophon, *Agesilaus*
AGJU	Arbeiten zur Geschichte des antiken Judentums und des Urchristentums
Agr.	Cato the Elder, *De agricultura*
A.J.	Josephus, *Antiquitates judaicae*
Anab.	Arrian, *Anabasis*; Xenophon, *Anabasis*
ANF	Roberts, Alexander, and James Donaldson, eds. *The Ante-Nicene Fathers: Translations of the Writings of the Fathers Down to A.D. 325.* 10 vols. Buffalo: Christian Literature Company, 1885–1887.
Ann.	Tacitus, *Annales*
Anth. pal.	Palatine Anthology
ASAE	*Annales du Service des antiquités de l'Egypte*
ASP	American Studies in Papyrology
ASV	American Standard Version
Att.	Cicero, *Epistulae ad Atticum*
Aug.	Suetonius, *Divus Augustus*
Autol.	Theophilus, *Ad Autolycum*
b.	Babylonian Talmud
B. Bat.	Bava Batra
BAR	*Biblical Archaeology Review*
BBB	Bonner biblische Beiträge
BBE	Bible in Basic English
BBR	*Bulletin for Biblical Research*
BCT	*Bible and Critical Theory*

BDAG	Danker, Frederick W., Walter Bauer, William F. Arndt, and F. Wilbur Gingrich. *Greek-English Lexicon of the New Testament and Other Early Christian Literature*. 3rd ed. Chicago: University of Chicago Press, 2000.
BECNT	Baker Exegetical Commentary on the New Testament
Bib hist.	Diodorus Siculus, *Bibliotheca historica*
BibInt	*Biblical Interpretation*
Bell. cat.	Sallust, *Bellum catalinae*
B.J.	Josephus, *Bellum judaicum*
BT	*The Bible Translator*
BTB	*Biblical Theology Bulletin*
C.Ap.	Josephus, *Contra Apionem*
C. Gent.	Athanasius, *Contra gentes*
Carm.	Horace, *Carmina*
Cat. Maj.	Plutarch, *Cato Major*
Cels.	Origen, *Contra Celsum*
Chaer.	Chariton, *Chaereas and Callirhoe*
Chron.	George Hamartolos, *Chronicle*
CIIP	*Corpus Inscriptionum Iudaeae/Palaestinae*
CIL	*Corpus Inscriptionum Latinarum*
Claud.	Suetonius, *Divus Claudius*
Cod. Iust.	Codex Iustinianus
Congr.	Philo, *De congressu eruditionis gratia*
Contempl.	Philo, *De vita contemplativa*
Contr.	Seneca the Elder, *Controversiae*
CPJ	Tcherikover, Victor A., ed. *Corpus Papyrorum Judaicarum*. 3 vols. Cambridge: Harvard University Press, 1957–1964.
CPL	Cavenaile, Robert, ed. *Corpus Papyrorum Latinarum*. Harrassowitz: Wiesbaden, 1958.
CQ	*Classical Quarterly*
CurBR	*Currents in Biblical Research*
De gub. Dei	Salvian, *De gubernatione Dei*
Decal.	Philo, *De decalogo*
Decl.	Quintilian, *Declamationes*
Descr.	Pausanias, *Graeciae descriptio*
Dig.	Digesta
Disc.	Musonius Rufus, *Discourses*

DMIPERP	Database of Military Inscriptions and Papyri of Early Roman Palestine
Dom.	Suetonius, *Domitianus*
Ecl.	Vergil, *Eclogae*
ELH	English Literary History
Ep.	Jerome, *Epistulae*; Pliny the Elder, *Epistulae*; Pseudo-Diogenes, *Epistulae*; Seneca, *Epistulae*
Eph.	Xenophon of Ephesus, *Ephesian Tale*
Epig.	Martial, *Epigrams*
Euch.	Paulinus of Pella, *Eucharisticus*
ExAud	Ex Auditu
ExpTim	Expository Times
Fab.	Phaedrus, *Fabulae*
Fact.	Valerius Maximus, *Facta et dicta memorabilia*
FHAR	Front Homosexuel d'Action Révolutionnaire
G&R	Greece and Rome
Galb.	Suetonius, *Galba*
Git.	Gittin
GLQ	*GLQ: A Journal of Lesbian and Gay Studies*
GNT	Good News Translation
Hell.	Xenophon, *Hellenica*
Herm. Sim.	Shepherd of Hermas, Similitudes
Hipp. Epid.	Galen, *Hippocratic Epidemics*
Hist.	Polybius, *Historiae*; Tacitus, *Historiae*
Hist. Aug. Ael.	Historia Augusta, Aelius
Hist. rom.	Dio Cassius, *Historiae romanae*
HNT	Handbuch zum Neuen Testament
Hom. 1 Cor 7:2	John Chrysostom, *In illud: Propter fornicationes autem unusquisque suam uxorem habeat*
Hom. Matt.	John Chrysostom, *Homiliae in Matthaeum*
Hom. Tit.	John Chrysostom, *Homiliae in epistulam ad Titum*
Hypoth.	Philo, *Hypothetica*
Id.	Theocritus, *Idylls*
IEJ	Israel Exploration Journal
IG	Gaertringen, Fridericus Hiller von, et al., eds. *Inscriptiones Graecae*. Editio Minor. Berlin: de Gruyter, 1924–.
IGBulg	Mihailov, Georgi, ed. *Inscriptiones Graecae in Bulgaria repertae.* 4 vols. Sofia: Academiae litterarum Bulgaricae, 1956–1970.

IKyme	Engelmann, Helmut, ed. *Die Inschriften von Kyme*. Bonn: Habelt, 1976.
ILind	Blinkenberg, Christian, ed. *Inscriptions*. Vol. 2 of *Lindos*. Berlin: de Gruyter, 1941.
Incomp. nupt.	Augustine, *De incompetentibus nuptiis*
Inst.	Lactantius, *Divinarum institutionum*
Ios.	Philo, *De Iosepho*
JAAR	*Journal of the American Academy of Religion*
JBL	*Journal of Biblical Literature*
JECS	*Journal of Early Christian Studies*
JGRChJ	*Journal of Greco-Roman Christianity and Judaism*
JH	*Journal of Homosexuality*
JHSex	*Journal of the History of Sexuality*
JIWE	Noy, David. *Jewish Inscriptions of Western Europe*. 2 vols. Cambridge: Cambridge University Press, 2005.
JQR	*Jewish Quarterly Review*
JR	*Journal of Religion*
JRE	*Journal of Religious Ethics*
JRS	*Journal of Roman Studies*
JSHJ	*Journal for the Study of the Historical Jesus*
JSJ	*Journal for the Study of Judaism in the Persian, Hellenistic, and Roman Periods*
JSP	*Journal for the Study of the Pseudepigrapha*
Jub.	Jubilees
Ketub.	Ketubbot
KJV	King James Version
LCL	Loeb Classical Library
Leg.	Plato, *Leges*
LNTS	The Library of New Testament Studies
LSJ	Liddell, Henry George, Robert Scott, Henry Stuart Jones. *A Greek-English Lexicon*. 9th ed. with revised supplement. Oxford: Clarendon, 1996.
LXX	Septuagint
m.	Mishnah
Mem.	Xenophon, *Memorabilia*
Metam.	Apuleius, *Metamorphoses*
Mil. glor.	Plautus, *Miles gloriosus*
MTSR	*Method and Theory in the Study of Religion*
NAMBLA	North American Man/Boy Love Association

NKJV	New King James Version
Noc. Att.	Aulus Gellius, *Noctes Atticae*
NRTh	*La Nouvelle revue théologique*
NTS	*New Testament Studies*
OBT	Overtures to Biblical Theology
Or.	Dio Chrysostom, *Orationes*
Or. Graec.	Tatian, *Oratio ad Graecos*
P.Oxy.	Grenfell, Bernard P., et al., eds. *The Oxyrhynchus Papyri*. London: Egypt Exploration Fund, 1898–.
Paed.	Clement of Alexandria, *Paedagogus*
Phaen.	Aratus, *Phaenomena*
Phil.	Cicero, *Orationes philippicae*
Quaest. conv.	Plutarch, *Quaestionum convivialum libri IX*
Quaest. rom.	Plutarch, *Quaestionum romanae et graecae (Aetia romana et graeca)*
Qidd.	Qiddushin
Prot. Jas.	Protevangelium of James
Protr.	Clement of Alexandria, *Protrepticus*
P.W.	Thucydides, *Peloponnesian War*
R&T	*Religion and Theology*
Rep.	Cicero, *De republica*
Res gest.	Ammianus Marcellinus, *Res Gestae*
Rhet. Her.	Rhetorica ad Herennium
RIBLA	*Revista de Interpretación Bíblica Latinoamericana*
RSV	Revised Standard Version
Rust.	Columella, *De Re Rustica*
Sanh.	Sanhedrin
Sat.	Horace, *Satirae*; Juvenal, *Satirae*; Petronius, *Satryicon*
SB	Preisigke, Friedrich, et al. *Sammelbuch griechischer Urkunden aus Aegypten*. Vols. 1–21. Wiesbaden: Harrassowitz, 1915–2002.
SCI	*Scripta Classica Israelica*
SCJ	Studies in Christianity and Judaism
SEÅ	*Svensk Exegetisk Årsbok*
SEG	Supplementum epigraphicum graecum
SemeiaSt	Semeia Studies
SFSHJ	South Florida Studies in the History of Judaism
SIG	Dittenberger, Wilhelm, ed. *Sylloge Inscriptionum Graecarum*. 4 vols. 3rd ed. Leipzig: Hirzel, 1915–1924.

Silv.	Statius, *Silvae*
SJ	Studia Judaica
SJT	*Scottish Journal of Theology*
SPhiloA	*Studia Philonica Annual*
Spec.	Philo, *De specialibus legibus*
SR	*Studies in Religion*
t.	Tosefta
T. Jos.	Testament of Joseph
T. Jud.	Testament of Judah
Tab. Vindol.	Vindolanda tablets
TAM 4.1	Dörner, Friedrich Karl, ed., with the assistance of Maria-Barbara von Stritzky. *Tituli Asiae Minoris, IV: Tituli Bithyniae linguis Graeca et Latina conscripti, 1. Paeninsula Bithynica praeter Chalcedonem; Nicomedia et ager Nicomedensis cum septentrionali meridianoque litore sinus Astaceni et cum lacu Sumonensi.* Vienna: Academiam Scientiarum Austriacam, 1978.
TDNT	Kittel, Gerhard, and Gerhard Friedrich, eds. *Theological Dictionary of the New Testament.* Translated by Geoffrey W. Bromiley. 10 vols. Grand Rapids: Eerdmans, 1964–1976.
Tg. Ps.-J.	Targum Pseudo-Jonathan
Trad. ap.	Traditio apostolica
TSAJ	Texte und Studien zum antiken Judentum
Tusc.	Cicero, *Tusculanae disputationes*
UTQ	*Union Theological Quarterly*
Var. hist.	Aelian, *Varia historia*
Verr.	Cicero, *In Verrem*
Vit. Const.	Eusebius, *Vita Constantini*
WBC	Word Biblical Commentary
WEB	World English Bible
WGRWSup	Writings from the Greco-Roman World Supplement series
WUNT	Wissenschaftliche Untersuchungen zum Neuen Testament
y.	Jerusalem Talmud

Introduction

During an episode of the makeover reality show *Queer Eye*, the "Fab Five" refashion the wardrobe and home of a Philadelphia man named Noah Hepler.[1] Hepler, a parish minister in the Evangelical Lutheran Church in America (a denomination that affirms the full inclusion of queer people), identifies as gay but grew up attending a homophobic Baptist congregation. When Hepler begins chatting with the Fab Five's interior designer Bobby Berk during a car ride, the conversation eventually turns toward their childhood experiences of Christian hostility when discovering their own sexuality. Although Berk continues to resent Christianity, Hepler relates the tensions he has negotiated as a gay man and committed Christian:

> The faith has been used against us, and it should not have been. There are a lot of stories in the Bible. They're in there, and they're not told. For example, there's one where the centurion goes to Jesus and says, "My slave is ill, and I want you to heal him." The Greek word that is used there is "beloved." If you take into account historical distance, it means "boyfriend." And Jesus doesn't say anything about that; he just heals the guy.

When Berk responds with a combination of surprise and bewilderment, Hepler offers a concise statement of the pericope's importance: "It's a very short story, but it's very powerful. It's like, *there we are*. But the story has been told in a way that leaves us out. I would like the rest of the Lutheran world to see that." Berk's reaction was undoubtedly shared by many of the *Queer Eye*'s viewers: Why is Jesus's affirmation of a same-sex couple news to *me*?

---

1. Mark Perez, dir., *Queer Eye: More Than a Makeover*, season 5, episode 1, "Preaching Out Loud," aired 5 June 2020 on Netflix.

Queer bodies are almost intrinsically marginal, but their mistreatment has been particularly egregious within Christian contexts. For most of the twentieth century, the best that queer Christians and their allies could claim was Jesus never broached the topic of same-sex intercourse. In a 1974 monograph on sex in the Bible, gay theologian Tom Horner stated unequivocally, "Jesus Christ never said anything about homosexuality—one way or the other."[2] There was a sense that although Jesus never directly encouraged acceptance of queer people, neither did he say anything that would authorize harm against them. Although some biblical authors seem to have promoted homophobia, Jesus's silence rendered him a tentative ally. But more recently, many have come to doubt that Jesus and the evangelists were so neutral, thanks to the slow introduction of queer theory and hermeneutical considerations. Interpreters have identified traces of queer people in the gospels with varying explicitness: the discussion of eunuchs in Matt 19:12 extols the virtues of gender nonconformity, the Secret Gospel of Mark describes Jesus loving a young man who was nude except for a linen cloth, Jesus's affections toward the beloved disciple invites a homoerotic reading, and so on.

Such interpretations excavate queer-sympathetic readings from the Bible, a corpus that has long authorized hostility toward nonconforming sexual and gender practices. Such readings emerged at a point when the increasingly prominent presence of queer folk within Christian social life warranted biblical justification; understandable, given the widespread sense of incompatibility between homosexuality and Christianity. Indeed, most Christian denominations regarded same-sex intercourse as sinful and did not recognize gay marriage until the early twenty-first century, with many still holding such positions. Beyond such apologetic purposes, these readings provide biblically sanctioned models of queer discipleship and same-sex relationships—what might it mean to be a Christian in a same-sex relationship or to practice Christianity as a queer person more broadly?

Even though such interpretations have proliferated, they rarely gather traction among academics, instead mostly circulating among lay readers who are already invested in queer theology. Few people with a PhD in the New Testament argue, for instance, that Jesus had sex with either the beloved disciple or the young man mentioned in Secret Mark. That said,

---

2. Tom M. Horner, *Sex in the Bible* (Rutland: Tuttle, 1974), 92.

a homoerotic reading of one pericope has found modest support among New Testament scholars: the instance discussed by Hepler above, when Jesus healed a centurion's boy.

The Exegetical Basis

The pericope known as "The Healing of the Centurion's Slave" is attested in Matt 8:5–13 and Luke 7:1–10, with a loose parallel in John 4:46–54 (see appendix 1 for Greek texts and English translations). Scholars supporting the Two-Source Hypothesis agree that the pericope derives from the Sayings Gospel Q. While Matthew and Luke differ on important points in their telling of the story, both depict a scene in the Galilean village of Capernaum featuring a centurion whose young man became ill. The centurion, seeking aid for him, requested Jesus restore him to health, albeit from a distance. Jesus did so with enthusiasm because the centurion revealed a greater degree of faith than Jesus had encountered in Israel.

At first glance, there is little to warrant a homoerotic reading: after all, there is no explicit language of romance, sex, gender norms, or anything else of the sort. Homoerotic readings of this pericope are built upon three of the story's features: the specific Greek word designating the "young man" (i.e., παῖς), Luke's characterization of the young man as "dear" (ἔντιμος) to the centurion, and commonplace homoeroticism in the Roman army. The details of these three arguments are worth exploring in depth, being presented here as sympathetically and persuasively as possible.[3]

To start, the centurion's dialogue features two distinct Greek words for slaves. δοῦλος refers to slaves in general (Matt 8:9; Luke 7:8), but the word παῖς is reserved for the young man who is ill. παῖς is the *only* term that Matthew uses for the young man (8:6, 8, 13), whereas Luke once refers to him as a παῖς (7:7) and otherwise indicates he was enslaved (7:2, 3, 10). Even so, whenever Luke refers to the sick young man as a δοῦλος, it is either the narrator's characterization or indirect discourse, since the centurion exclusively refers to the young man as his παῖς.

---

3. As noted above, this pericope has multiple textual performances, though readers have tended to harmonize them out of interest in a single biblical/historical story. This loose historical/literary method only began to adopt some methodological rigor upon the intervention of academic interpreters into the conversation. This is a topic to which we will return.

The term παῖς referred not only to youth and slaves but also junior partners in sexual relationships between two men. Literary evidence of this usage abounds. I quote here from the discussion of Theodore Jennings and Tat-siong Benny Liew to give a sense for how pervasively ancient writers imbued the word with homoerotic connotations.

> Marilyn B. Skinner describes the "conventional" παῖς καλός (a "fair" or "lovely boy") as "the toast of the gymnasium, acclaimed by suitors who thronged his doors and decked his house with garlands."[4] Correspondingly, David Fredrick suggests that Callimachus (the chief librarian of the library at Alexandria [third century B.C.E.]) not only writes about the παῖς as an object of desire, but presents the παῖς as the embodiment of "desired poetic qualities."[5] We can see this meaning of παῖς from Callimachus's *Epigrams* (an example that will also partly illustrate Skinner's and Fredrick's claims): "Fill the cup and say again 'to Diocles!'And Achelous knows not of his sacred cups. Fair is the boy, O Achelous, and very fair (καλὸς ὁ παῖς, Ἀχελῷε, λίην καλός): and if any denies it, may I alone know how fair he is!" (31). Similar word forms—with or without expressions of beauty and/or desire—are used by Thucydides to refer to the (former) boy-love or boy-favorite of the Spartan king Pausanias (παιδικά ποτε, 1.132.5), as well as by Xenophon to talk about the reason behind many "battles" of and among Greek soldiers ("a handsome boy ... that he [a soldier] had set his heart upon" [παιδὸς ἐπιθυμήσας ... τῶν εὐπρεπῶν, *Anab.* 4.1.14]; "his son, who was just coming into the prime of youth ... Episthenes, however, fell in love with the boy" [τοῦ υἱοῦ ἄρτι ἡβάσκοντος ... Ἐπισθένης δὲ ἠράσθη τοῦ παιδός, *Anab.* 4.6.1–3]; "Was it in a fight over a boy?" [ἀλλὰ περὶ παιδικῶν μαχόμενος, *Anab.* 5.8.4–5; "Episthenes ... was a lover of boys, and upon seeing a handsome boy, just in the bloom of youth and carrying a light shield ... threw his arms around the boy and said: 'It is time, Seuthes, for you to fight it out with me for the boy" [Ἐπισθένης ... παιδεραστής, ὅς ἰδὼν παῖδα καλὸν ἡβάσκοντα ἄρτι πέλτην ἔχοντα ... περιλαβὼν τὸν παῖδα εἶπεν· Ὥρα σοι, ὦ Σεύθη, περὶ τοῦ δέ μοι διαμάχεσθαι, *Anab.* 7.4.7–11]; "there was a boy of Oreus, an extremely fine lad too" [τινος τῶν Ὠραιτῶν παιδός ... μάλα καλοῦ τε κἀγαθοῦ, *Hell.* 5.4.57]; "he [Agesilaus] loved Megabates, the handsome son of Spith-

---

4. Marilyn B. Skinner, "*Ego Mulier*: The Construction of Male Sexuality in Catullus," in *Roman Sexualities*, ed. Judith P. Hallett and Marilyn B. Skinner (Princeton: Princeton University Press, 1997), 136.

5. David Fredrick, "Reading Broken Skin: Violence in Roman Elegy," in Hallett and Skinner, *Roman Sexualities*, 174–75.

ridates" [Μεγαβάτου τοῦ Σπιθριδάτου παιδὸς ἐρασθέντα, ὥσπερ ἄν τοῦ καλλίστου, *Ages.* 5.4–5]).[6]

Examples beyond these are innumerable. That the word παῖς often referred to younger lovers is not controversial, as it even forms part of the compound word παιδεραστία (pederasty). Though the word *pederasty* tends to denote pedophilia today, in Greco-Roman societies it designated sexual relationships between a mature and a younger man. These sexual relationships comprised initiation rituals into political life in Greek contexts, though in Roman contexts they were less socially important, being more concerned with satisfying sexual urges. In both Greek and Roman settings, such interactions were a matter of course.

Homoerotic readings of the pericope interpret the word παῖς in one of two ways. Either the centurion's slave was also his sexual partner or the wording in Matthew is deemed more original than that of Luke, meaning that the young man was not a slave at all but simply the centurion's *eromenos*—a freed or freeborn sexual partner.[7]

The quotation from Jennings and Liew above gives a sense of how often the term homoerotically referred to freeborn youth, but even if Luke's phrasing is preferred (i.e., the young man was enslaved), ancient sources are clear that masters and slaves were commonly sexual partners. The character Trimalchio—a Jewish freedman in Petronius's novel *Satyricon* (75.11)—is forthright about his sexual experiences with his former master: "For fourteen years I pleasured him; it is no disgrace to do what a master commands." The poet Horace is also direct:

When your prick swells, then,

---

6. Theodore W. Jennings Jr. and Tat-siong Benny Liew, "Mistaken Identities but Model Faith: Rereading the Centurion, the Chap, and the Christ in Matthew 8:5–13," *JBL* 123 (2004): 473–74. In the original article, Jennings and Liew note the following: "Unless indicated otherwise, all English translations of Greco-Roman texts are taken from the Loeb Classical Library." All brackets and ellipses are in Jennings and Liew's publication; footnotes from the original are partially retained but reformatted for consistency.

7. It is generally agreed among Q scholars that Matthew's phrasing of παῖς more likely reflects Q's phrasing than Luke's δοῦλος. The Greek text of Q and its English translation are found in appendix 1. On Q's wording here, see Steven R. Johnson, ed., *Q 7:1–10: The Centurion's Faith in Jesus' Word*, Documenta Q (Leuven: Peeters, 2002), 167–84.

and a young slave girl or boy's nearby you could take
at that instant, would you rather burst with desire?
Not I: I love the sexual pleasure that's easy to get. (*Sat.* 1.2.116–119)⁸

This is a common theme in Roman literature: the epigrams of Martial, the comedies of Plautus, and many, many other texts indicate that masters and slaves often had intercourse, regardless of the slave's gender.⁹ Intercourse with slaves was widespread and discussed in writings that range from the lowbrow (e.g., the graffito *CIL* 4.1863: "Take hold of your slave girl [*servam*] whenever you please, it's your right!") to those at the apex of Roman literature (e.g., Vergil, *Ecl.* 2).

Sex between masters and slaves was sufficiently pervasive that Romans took it for granted without moral judgment. Gaius Sempronius Gracchus, returning to the city of Rome following his post as a magistrate in Sardinia, proudly asserted, "I spent two years in the province; if any [female] prostitute came into my home or if anyone's slave-boy [*servulus*] was accosted for my sake, you can think of me as the basest and most worthless person in the world. Considering that I so chastely kept myself from their slaves, you can reflect on how you think I treated your children" (Aulus Gellius, *Noc. Att.* 15.12.13).¹⁰ Craig Williams detects two important assumptions within Gracchus's speech. First, when Gracchus boasted about his chastity, he was conspicuously silent about intercourse with his own slaves, clearly implying that he had sex with them. Gracchus assumed this was socially acceptable behavior. Second, Gracchus implied that *even*

---

8. Translation by A. S. Kline. tument tibi cum inguina, num, si ancilla aut verna est praesto puer, impetus in quem continuo fiat. malis tentigine rumpi? non ego; namque parabilem amo Venerem facilemque.

9. This has been discussed extensively, but see Craig A. Williams, *Roman Homosexuality*, 2nd ed. (Oxford: Oxford University Press, 2010), 31–40; Beert C. Verstraete, "Slavery and the Social Dynamics of Male Homosexual Relations in Ancient Rome," *JH* 5 (1980): 227–36; Jerzy Kolendo, "L'esclavage et la vie sexuelle des hommes libres à Rome," *Index* 10 (1981): 288–97; Joseph A. Marchal, "The Usefulness of an Onesimus: The Sexual Use of Slaves and Paul's Letter to Philemon," *JBL* 130 (2011): 749–70; Christian Laes, "Desperately Different? *Delicia* Children in the Roman Household," in *Early Christian Families in Context: An Interdisciplinary Dialogue*, ed. David L. Balch and Carolyn Osiek (Grand Rapids: Eerdmans, 2003), 298–324; Keith Hopkins, "Novel Evidence for Roman Slavery," *Past and Present* 138 (1993): 3–27.

10. Translation and discussion from Williams, *Roman Homosexuality*, 20–21, brackets in original but Latin added.

if he had slept with another person's slave, it would not have been a serious offense. Rather, Gracchus intended to show that he was particularly well behaved and did not even indulge in slightly less acceptable arenas of sexual intercourse, such that no one need worry about more grievous offenses involving Roman citizens. This outlook was not limited to pagans, as the Hebrew Bible also depicts conjugal slavery as normal and explicitly authorized its practice (e.g., Exod 21:7–11; Lev 19:20–22; Num 31:7–8; Deut 21:10–14; Judg 21:10–24).

A second argument for the homoerotic interpretation is that Luke 7:2 declares that the slave was ἔντιμος for the centurion, meaning something like "precious" or "honored." In this pericope, ἔντιμος designates either the usefulness of the slave to the centurion or some other special bond between the two. Between the two options, there is overwhelming support for the latter, since the centurion elsewhere exhibits concern for others (*humanitas*, φιλανθρωπία) by supporting the local synagogue. Many translations thus render the word ἔντιμος into English as "dear," including the ASV, GNT, KJV (along with NKJV), RSV, and WEB; the BBE goes a step further and renders it "very dear." Biblical scholars often agree: commentators who espouse no interest in the homoerotic reading find "dear" to be a compelling translation. Darrell Bock, for instance, prefers "dear" to translations emphasizing the slave's utility, and John Nolland observes that there is "a quite unusual degree of concern shown by this centurion for his slave."[11] If heteronormative readings recognize that ἔντιμος signifies a special relationship between centurion and the young man, it is hardly a stretch to infer a romantic or even sexual subtext. The word ἔντιμος thus forms an important part of Donald H. Mader's famous argument for a homoerotic reading of the pericope, as he contends that "Luke, in introducing [the word ἔντιμος], was recognizing that the centurion's actions displayed a depth of feeling which was over and above that of an ordinary master-slave relationship."[12]

---

11. Darrell L. Bock, *Luke*, BECNT, 2 vols. (Grand Rapids: Baker Academic, 1996), 1:636; John Nolland, *Luke 1–9:20*, WBC 35A (Dallas: Word, 1989), 316–18.

12. Donald H. Mader, "The *Entimos Pais* of Matthew 8:5–13 and Luke 7:1–10," *Paidika* 1.1 (1987): 33; repr. Mader, in *Homosexuality and Religion and Philosophy*, ed. Wayne R. Dynes and Stephen Donaldson, Studies in Homosexuality 12 (New York: Garland, 1992), 229. In this volume, citations will refer to the reprinted version.

Finally, there is extensive evidence of homoerotic activity involving members of the Roman army.[13] The homosocial environment of the military predictably led to casual homoeroticism, so it is significant that the slave's master is not only gentile but a military officer in particular. Roman legionaries were prohibited from marrying while serving, and same-sex intercourse between two male Roman citizens (and thus between legionaries) was criminal, so soldiers commonly found liaisons among civilians living in or near their garrison. Roman writers often commented on military men's proclivity towards same-sex intercourse in such relationships. Martial, for instance, composed two epigrams about a centurion named Pudens and his beloved slave Encolpus, the first of which concerns the slave's hair and is quoted here.

> These locks, all he has from crown down, does Encolpus, the darling of his master the centurion [*centurionis*], vow to you, Phoebus, when Pudens shall attain the rank of chief centurion [*praemia pili*] which he wants and deserves. Cut the long tresses as soon as may be, Phoebus, while no down darkens his soft cheeks and flowing locks grace his milk-white neck. And so that master and lad may long enjoy your bounty, make him soon shorn, but late a man. (*Epig.* 1.31)[14]

Valerius Maximus (*Fact.* 6.1.10) reports that a centurion named Caius Cornelius was executed because he paid a young man for sex—the crime was not homosexual intercourse but sexual penetration of a Roman citizen; had the centurion slept with a noncitizen, their sex would have been unremarkable. Plautus's play *Pseudolus* likewise depicts characters teasing Harpax, an officer's slave, for sleeping with his master: "When the soldier went to keep watch at night and you were going with him, did his sword fit into your scabbard?" (1180–1181).[15] One might also refer to the passages quoted by Jennings and Liew above that discuss Greek and Roman soldiers.

---

13. See the discussion in Sara Elise Phang, *The Marriage of Roman Soldiers (13 B.C.–A.D. 235): Law and Family in the Imperial Army*, Columbia Studies in the Classical Tradition 24 (Leiden: Brill, 2001), 262–95; on legionaries' sexual intercourse with male slaves, see pages 266–75.

14. Translation by Shackleton Bailey (LCL, lightly revised); cf. 5.48, where Pudens's vow is fulfilled.

15. Translation by Wolfgang De Melo (LCL, lightly revised): noctu in vigiliam quando ibat miles, quom tu ibas simul, conveniebatne in vaginam tuam machaera militis?

Beyond literary texts, a number of epitaphs for slaves who acted as sexual partners for soldiers survive. These inscriptions refer to soldiers' slaves as *delicia*, a term usually bearing sexual connotations; if these texts do not use the word *delicium* itself, words within its semantic domain are found in its stead.[16] This is not to mention other evidence of military homoeroticism, such as soldiers being clients of male sex-workers (including a possible male brothel near the Roman fortress at Vindolanda) and contemporaries' jokes about their indiscriminate sexual preferences.[17] Evidence suggests same-sex intercourse was sufficiently widespread that Roman writers *presumed* their audience was aware that soldiers were sexually involved with slaves. Why would the gospels be any different? Moreover, would not Jesus himself presume the same?

While no one of these three arguments *proves* that a sexual or romantic relationship underlies the pericope, many have proposed that the whole is greater than the sum of these parts, cumulatively suggesting a relationship between the centurion and the young man. The fact that Jesus says nothing about same-sex intercourse may imply his tacit acceptance of their relationship.

Interpreting Interpretations

Many interpreters have celebrated the centurion as an archetype of queer discipleship: he risks humiliation by approaching Jesus on behalf of his lover, only to be commended for the excellence of his faith. Jesus's phrasing ("Among no one in Israel have I found such faith!" in Matt 8:10; cf. Luke 7:9) indicates that even though Jesus had low expectations of the centurion, the Roman officer nevertheless practiced his teachings in an exemplary fashion. Thus, John McNeill: "Here we have the most direct

---

16. See, e.g., *AE* 1929.106, 1929.193, 1977.762; *CIL* 6.3221; *CPL* 120.

17. On the Vindolanda brothel, see Carol Van Driel-Murray, "Gender in Question," *Theoretical Roman Archaeology Journal* 1992 (1995): 19; Simon James, "Engendering Change in Our Understanding of the Structure of Roman Military Communities," *Archaeological Dialogues* 13 (2006): 34–35, citing Tab. Vindol. 2.255 (referring to a centurion's six *delicia*). On indiscriminate sexual preferences, see, e.g., Plautus, *Mil. glor.* 1102–1114; Sallust, *Bell cat.* 51.9; Cicero, *Phil.* 3.31. On male sex-workers see, e.g., Cato *apud* Polybius, *Hist.* 31.25.5; Diodorus Siculus, *Bib. hist.* 31.24, 37.3.6; Plutarch, *Quaest. conv.* 668b–c, *Cat. Maj.* 8.2; Tacitus, *Hist.* 3.40; cf. much later Salvian, *De gub. Dei* 7.88.

encounter of Jesus Christ with someone who today would be pronounced 'gay' and Christ's reaction is acceptance of the person without judgment and even eagerness to be of assistance to restore the *pais* to health."[18] The gospels seem to invite readers to regard the centurion as a model for Christian living. All of this renders the centurion a particularly appealing figure for authorizing unconditional queer participation in Christianity—if Jesus was okay with it, who are Christian homophobes to disagree?

Beyond apologetics, it may be helpful to think of this reading as a contribution to the queer Christian archive. Alexis Waller describes queer archives as "evidence that might be foundational for alternative narratives of desire, expressions of gender, or queer community."[19] Within the queer Christian archive, the centurion is placed alongside Ruth and Naomi, Jonathan and David, the Ethiopian Eunuch, and others as biblical characters intelligible as queer. This archive contributes to a reimagined history of Christianity, one that does not envision queer people as later intrusions upon a heteropatriarchal institution but present at the religion's formative moments. The present book is an effort to understand the emergence and consolidation of this pericope within the queer Christian archive.

But for all the enthusiasm that lay readers express for this interpretation, such zeal is rarely found among academic readers, as scholarly support remains modest. Thomas Hanks attributes this academic neglect to "heterosexist male advocacy scholarship," while Jennings and Liew more generously observe that queer methods and theories have only recently taken hold in cognate fields such as classics.[20] There is undoubtedly truth to both explanations, as the homoerotic interpretation is consistently

---

18. John J. McNeill, *Freedom, Glorious Freedom: The Spiritual Journey of Fullness of Life for Gays, Lesbians, and Everybody Else* (Boston: Beacon, 1995), 132.

19. Alexis G. Waller, "The 'Unspeakable Teachings' of The Secret Gospel of Mark: Feelings and Fantasies in the Making of Christian Histories," in *Religion, Emotion, Sensation: Affect Theories and Theologies*, ed. Karen Bray and Stephen D. Moore, Transdisciplinary Theological Colloquia (New York: Fordham University Press, 2020), 148. On such archives, see the pioneering work of Ann Cvetkovich, *An Archive of Feelings: Trauma, Sexuality, and Lesbian Public Cultures*, Series Q (Durham: Duke University Press, 2003); Jack Halberstam, *In a Queer Time and Place: Transgender Bodies, Subcultural Lives*, Sexual Cultures (New York: New York University Press, 2006), 22–46; Charles E. Morris III, "Archival Queer," *Rhetoric and Public Affairs* 9 (2006): 145–51.

20. Tom Hanks, "Matthew and Mary of Magdala: Good News for Sex Workers," in *Take Back the Word: A Queer Reading of the Bible*, ed. Robert E. Goss and Mona West (Cleveland: Pilgrim, 2000), 195; Jennings and Liew, "Mistaken Identities," 473 n. 16.

disregarded in New Testament scholarship. Only three serialized Bible commentaries even mention it: Mikeal Parsons (Paideia) dismisses it as "unlikely," with a similar reaction from Amy-Jill Levine and Ben Witherington III (New Cambridge), though Barbara Reid and Shelly Matthews (Wisdom) regard it more seriously.[21] Jennings and Liew's article in the *Journal of Biblical Literature* remains the only article-length work in a major biblical studies journal to advocate the homoerotic reading, but even so, it received a terse rejoinder in a subsequent issue of that same journal.[22]

The homoerotic interpretation tends to find far more sympathy among popular rather than academic audiences, among theologians than biblical scholars, among MDiv's rather than PhD's, and among activists rather than academics priding themselves on disinterest. This disconnect seems to engender even greater suspicion among biblical scholars, who find further reason to disregard it as the eisegesis of wishful thinking: those without proper training merely see what they want to see in the Bible.

Although the history of interpretation has steadily gained importance within biblical studies, the history of queer biblical interpretation remains entirely neglected. Those of us interested in queer hermeneutics remain unfamiliar with the giants upon whose shoulders we stand, not

---

21. Mikeal C. Parsons, *Luke*, Paideia (Grand Rapids: Baker Academic, 2015), 118: "Despite this semantic ambiguity [of the word ἔντιμος], it is unlikely that Luke intends through the use of the word to indicate a sexual dimension (some form of pederasty) in the relationship between the centurion and his slave." Amy-Jill Levine and Ben Witherington III, *The Gospel of Luke*, New Cambridge Bible Commentary (Cambridge: Cambridge University Press, 2018), 198 discuss at some length and then reject a strawman homoerotic interpretation (see the discussion below). The discussion in Barbara E. Reid and Shelly Matthews, *Luke 1–9*, Wisdom Commentary 43A (Collegeville: Liturgical, 2021), 223–25 is much better attuned to the contours of this interpretation. Occasionally nonserialized commentaries mention the interpretation (e.g., Ronald E. Long, "Introduction: Disarming Biblically Based Queer Bashing," in *The Queer Bible Commentary*, ed. Deryn Guest, Robert E. Goss, Mona West, and Thomas Bohache [London: SCM, 2006], 16–17; Sean McDowell, *CSB Apologetics Study Bible for Students* [Nashville: Holman, 2017]), 1182), though these tend to be more theological in orientation and do not reflect the *status quaestionis* of academic biblical scholarship.

22. Jennings and Liew, "Mistaken Identities"; Denis B. Saddington, "The Centurion in Matthew 8:5–13: Consideration of the Proposal of Theodore W. Jennings, Jr., and Tat-siong Benny Liew," *JBL* 125 (2006): 140–42. For other endorsements of the homoerotic interpretation in peer-reviewed journals, see below.

to mention changes to the texture of such interpretations before the most recent decades—at best, most of us can perform a literature review that accounts for tectonic academic shifts around issues of gender and sexuality in biblical interpretation. Consequently, there is a pervasive ignorance of nonacademic works that performed groundwork essential for the more scholarly interpretations that we find ourselves regularly citing. Discussion of nonspecialists tends to focus upon big names like Oscar Wilde and Jeremy Bentham, such that one overlooks the obscure individuals who performed the vast majority of this intellectual labor. The names Dinos Christianopoulos, James Kepner, and Michel Mayer may be unknown to most biblical scholars or queer theologians, but it is difficult to overstate their contributions to homoerotic interpretation of the pericope, as their works provided necessary precursors to articles like Jennings and Liew's or even Hepler's discussion on a popular television show. That said, these men (and we will see that such interpreters have overwhelmingly been *men*) were largely unfamiliar with each other as well. Shortly after World War II, a time when same-sex desire sat outside the realm of respectability, these interpreters partook in loose networks of intellectual exchange—what I will characterize as "queer shadow scholarship"—communicating with each other via homophile magazines, reading groups, and local conferences. These networks of shadow scholarship tended to be highly regionalized (e.g., Arcadie in France, the ONE Institute in Southern California, Weg in West Germany) but were pivotal in the development of the queer Christian archive.[23]

This localization was hardly incidental. The politics that have animated these exegetical projects are inseparable from the specific legal situation of queer folk within a jurisdiction. These interpretations are often caught up in the legal particulars of the interpreter's context, as the law forms a key part of how queer recognition has been sought.[24] Even

---

23. Indeed, their role in developing the queer archive was sometimes literal: James Kepner founded what is now known as the ONE National Gay and Lesbian Archives in Los Angeles.

24. I use *recognition* here in the sense of Charles Taylor, "The Politics of Recognition," in *Multiculturalism: Examining the Politics of Recognition*, ed. Amy Gutmann (Princeton: Princeton University Press, 1994), 25–74, especially on the quest for "equality of dignity." See, e.g., the explicit invocation of Taylor's recognition alongside the homoerotic interpretation of the passage in Theresa Murray and Michael McClure, *Moral Panic: Exposing the Religious Right's Agenda on Sexuality*, Listen Up! (London: Cassell, 1995), 10–11, 55–56.

within the modest omnibus of homoerotic interpretations of the centurion at Capernaum, one is struck by how much these readings differ in the implications they extrapolate from the pericope. This should be expected; the means by which queer bodies have experienced criminalization and discrimination in, say, Germany differed from how this was experienced in the United Kingdom, Poland, Argentina, Philippines, South Korea, Canada, and other nation-states. We will see that French interpreters were delighted to conclude that the centurion was a pederast, whereas American interpreters preferred to imagine the centurion and his beloved as partaking in a prototype of same-sex marriage. The two interpretations are incompatible, operating with irreconcilable conceptions of sexual consent, same-sex love, legal recognition, social power, and their sanction within the Bible.

Homoerotic interpretations of the pericope not only have political subtexts but carry a specifically *legal* inflection. The link between law and biblical interpretation is vital to the ensuing discussion. One of this book's prevailing themes is that legal systems function as productive forces in both producing subjects and constituting socially acceptable forms of (homo)sexuality.[25] That is to say, the legal regulation of sexuality is not merely epiphenomenal, as though it merely reflects and codifies dominant cultural prejudices. The law often does this, but it also forms the primary rubric through which queer recognition comes to be achieved. Whether through the abolition of sodomy laws, the recognition of same-sex marriages, enlistment in the military, or the introduction of hate-crimes legislation, the state confers legitimacy in a manner that exceeds its strictly legislative bounds of distinguishing the legal from the illegal. Instead, the law produces—even reifies—social difference: whatever prejudices may have existed against gay men, sodomy laws condemned those engaging in same-sex intercourse as criminal subjects; whatever expectations of gender conformity prevail, bathroom bills hail transgender people as predatory subjects; whatever the positive media representation of same-sex couples, marriage equality welcomed queer bodies as family subjects; whatever pronouns loved ones employ for a transgender person, gender-identity legislation recognizes people as socially gendered rather than biologically gendered subjects; and so on.

---

25. Paraphrasing Joseph J. Fischel, *Sex Harm in the Age of Consent* (Minneapolis: University of Minnesota Press, 2016), 27. See also Carl F. Stychin, *Governing Sexuality: The Changing Politics of Citizenship and Law Reform* (Oxford: Hart, 2003).

Due in part to such shifts, the legal position of queer bodies in the North Atlantic has trended in a specific direction in recent decades. The law increasingly confers rights and responsibilities upon queer subjects, granting admission to progressively deeper levels of social acceptability through its (slow, uneven, and inconsistent) incorporation of queer bodies into the state. Bodies once deemed sinful, pathological, criminal, or perverted are now being produced as provisional citizens. The *provisional* nature of these gestures is important, as it has contributed to significant social differentiation within queer subcultures. Those who were once allies become liabilities, and former enemies become newfound allies. Consider the shifting relationship between the military and queer bodies, how queer people—once banned from service—now proudly identify as patriots on account of their enlistment. Or consider the shifting position of transgender people, how "gender-critical" feminism celebrates lesbianism but actively excludes transgender women. Or consider the shifting position of drag culture, which was once niche and socially marginal but increasingly rewards those positioned to commodify it for widespread consumption. Though queer culture was never monolithic, the provisional acceptance of some queer bodies has led many to leave other queer folk waiting outside in the rain, with the former eager to claim a spot at the table of recognition and respectability at the expense of those others.

The foundational supposition of the present study is that biblical interpretation is a site of social negotiation, that when someone interprets the Bible, they also engage their social world. Discussion of the Bible can figure into the forging of alliances and disrupting of tensions into fragmentation, where good queers can be separated from problematic queers; where some marginalized bodies can be reclaimed as worthy of recognition and respect but others left to continue their struggle; where one biblical figure can be read as emblematic of one social type, to be firmly distinguished from another social type. We will see that interpreters do not read the pericope as offering blanket legitimacy for all queer people but parcel the Bible's blessings out as the interpreter's social interests mandate, with differences largely intelligible through the interpreter's legal situation—Jesus's acceptance of the centurion legitimizes *this* type of queerness, not *that* type.

These acts of social differentiation are significant because the tensions between various homoerotic interpretations rarely receive comment. Advocates for the homoerotic interpretation tend to downplay internal disagreement in service of a unified front against homophobia; likewise, those who reject the reading paint it with a broad brush, as though all homoerotic interpretations are saying the same thing. What might we find if, instead of glossing over these differences, we peer into such fissures and inquire as to the distinct politics animating these varied interpretations? What insights might we gain about the developing relationship between same-sex desire and New Testament interpretation in the twentieth and twenty-first centuries? It will be necessary to engage in some theoretical promiscuity to make sense of how this process has occurred.

A single question governs the present book: how did the sex-life of the centurion at Capernaum become meaningful in different contexts? This question takes up Vincent Wimbush's contention that "the primary focus [of biblical scholarship] should be placed *not upon texts* per se (that is, upon their content-meanings), but upon textures, gestures, and power— namely, the signs, material products, ritual practices and performances, expressivities, orientations, ethics, and politics associated with the phenomenon of the invention and uses of 'scriptures.'"[26] The present study is historiographic, not in the sense that it is propelled foremost by an historical-critical inquiry into the events possibly underlying a biblical episode, but insofar as it traces shifting patterns in the interpretation of Christian Scriptures. It is an effort to describe and theorize the intellectual labor of biblical interpreters interested in the question of the centurion's homosexuality. The present monograph therefore focuses less on biblical characters and more on the meanings that interpreters have creatively extrapolated from such characters' stories.[27]

The supposition that interpreters merely project their own desires onto the text both oversimplifies and mischaracterizes. Interpreters instead deploy a set of complex hermeneutical maneuvers to render the

---

26. Vincent L. Wimbush, "TEXTureS, Gestures, Power: Orientation to Radical Excavation," in *Theorizing Scriptures: New Critical Orientations to a Cultural Phenomenon*, ed. Vincent L. Wimbush, Signifying (on) Scriptures (New Brunswick: Rutgers University Press, 2008), 3, emphasis in original.

27. See the similar approach of James E. Harding, *The Love of David and Jonathan: Ideology, Text, Reception*, BibleWorld (London: Routledge, 2016), which examines interpretations favoring and opposing a homoerotic subtext in the relationship of Jonathan and David and ascertains the different claims to find meaning in their hetero- or homosexuality. Likewise, Nyasha Junior, *Reimagining Hagar: Blackness and Bible*, Biblical Refigurations (Oxford: Oxford University Press, 2019) offers an account of Hagar's blackness in the history of interpretation. Numerous other studies could be cited.

historical situation of the centurion comparable to their own: analogous relationships, ancient figures drawn proximate to contemporary ones, evoking sentiments of affinity, among other means. Sara Ahmed observes that feelings often stick to certain bodies (be they modern, ancient, or entirely fictional)—through repeated contact, bodies become associated with one or another disposition.[28] Some bodies are not only read as prejudiced, loving, repressed, giving, or queer, among a host of other possibilities, but even the mere invocation of such bodies can draw to mind an entire network of relations. This notion of stickiness is particularly useful when thinking about the history of interpretation, as roughly 1900 years of biblical interpretation has entailed the ready invocation of distinct affective resonances upon naming various characters. Pharisees, to take a familiar example, have long been read as emblematic of worldly legalism by Christian interpreters, bearing upon then-contemporary analogues—Roman Catholics in various Protestant traditions, institutional religion in anticlerical discourse, fundamentalists in progressive circles, among other bogeymen. While the specific referent varies, there is a shared sense of the values and dispositions that Pharisees represent. Indeed, much Jesus-within-Judaism scholarship is intelligible as an attempt to redirect the disgust and contempt that Pharisees have evoked in light of the Holocaust. As for the present project, one might inquire: What, precisely, is brought to mind when one names the centurion, his boy, the Jewish residents of Capernaum, or Jesus himself? What emotions, discourses, and bodies are proximate to and distant from same-sex intercourse? By what interpretive logic are these figures positioned relative to each other? What histories (both recent and ancient) are summoned to mind when interpreting the pericope?

Those reading the present book hoping for an unadulterated celebration of queer exegesis will find this wish disappointed. The present study is critical in its orientation, which occasionally leads to unflattering portraits of interpreters, interpretations, social movements, and their politics. Whatever noble aims may have guided queer activism, it often did not take long for activists to become sidetracked (some would say coopted) into less worthy political causes, the centurion remaining an ally through the thick and thin. To avoid the game of "spot the problematic interpreter,"

---

28. Most famously, Sara Ahmed, *The Cultural Politics of Emotion* (Edinburgh: Edinburgh University Press, 2004).

this book will limit focus on individuals and discuss instead interpretive trends (with the exception of two particularly horrendous interpretations discussed in chapter 1); interpretations are the primary focus, not interpreters. Thus, this study will not linger too long on any single interpreter, except insofar as the details of their argument are salient. Hopefully, the reader will recall that despite the sometimes-critical discussion of homoerotic readings, this monograph is anything but a condemnation of queer biblical interpretation.

Outline of the Book

This book proceeds with a roughly chronological discussion of interpretations, jumping around the globe from chapter to chapter. This geographic scope acts as part of a broader effort at decentering the United States in histories of biblical interpretation following WW II: to the extent that queer history is ever considered in biblical scholarship, there is a tendency to correlate everything with specifically *American* moments (e.g., the Stonewall Riots, Lawrence v. Texas, Defense of Marriage Act). Rather, we will see that not only did this interpretation first emerge elsewhere, but historical events pivotal for the interpretation of the passage often have little relation to what was happening in the United States; for instance, the codification of article 334 of the French penal code in 1942 and its revision in 1982 played a far more significant role in the interpretation of the pericope than did the Stonewall Riots. If the story of queer biblical interpretation is to be told, it is best to do so in a manner that does not simply regurgitate narratives that center on American experiences.[29]

---

29. The present project bears some similarities in its geographic reorientation about the study of religion in Canada found in Aaron W. Hughes, *From Seminary to University: An Institutional History of the Study of Religion in Canada* (Toronto: University of Toronto Press, 2020), quoting here from pages 5–6: "It would be a mistake to assume, however, that the American story was standard, let alone normal. Instead, I would suggest that the American story is precisely that, a story that developed out of a set of idiosyncratic concerns unique to that country. We could similarly argue that how the study of religion came to be—indeed, how it continues to be configured in places such as Britain, France, Italy, Germany, Belgium, Switzerland, Austria, Greece, and so on—is the direct product of those countries' own distinct and often idiosyncratic legal, theological, denominational, judicial, and social frameworks, all of which have been, and continue to be, forced to deal in some way, shape, or form with religion

The book is far from comprehensive in scope: three exegetical sites have been selected to the exclusion of many others. The selection of these sites was tricky, as they are not neatly divisible in terms of their data. The following chapters discuss overlapping populations and the complex politics of social differentiation that animate their readings of the pericope; a given interpretation might sit at the nexus of multiple contexts. This book presents a simplified typology of intricate historical processes, reducing them to a linear narrative for comparative purposes—what Jonathan Z. Smith called a "disciplined exaggeration in service of knowledge."[30] There is much more to be said about Spanish, Latin American, Eastern European, and even Roman Catholic interpretation of the pericope, for instance, all of which receive short shrift in the following pages.[31]

By proceeding in a rough chronological sequence, we are positioned to understand how the *status quaestionis* on the topic came to emerge. For readers primarily interested in historical-critical and related issues (e.g., did the centurion have same-sex intercourse? did any biblical authors presume a homoerotic relationship in composing this pericope?), this may feel like an extended detour, but I would insist that it is nonetheless necessary: it is only through the history of interpretation that one can ascertain why these specific historical issues have become pivotal to the pericope's interpretation. Readers are advised that sexual violence is discussed throughout this book, but at particular length in chapters 1, 3, and 5.

---

broadly conceived." To be sure, academic and quasi-academic biblical interpretation has largely found its center of gravity in the United States since WW II, but the effects of this position are often overstated.

30. Jonathan Z. Smith, *Drudgery Divine: On the Comparison of Early Christianity and the Religions of Late Antiquity*, Jordan Lectures in Comparative Religion 14 (Chicago: University of Chicago Press, 1990), 52.

31. For instance, Catholic and ex-Catholic commentators commonly note the irony of the phrase *Domine, non sum dignis* ("Lord, I am not worthy"; Vulgate Matt 8:8; Luke 7:6), offered by Catholic congregations before receiving the Eucharist, being uttered by a man in a same-sex relationship. E.g., Patrick S. Cheng, "Domine, Non Sum Dignus: Theological Bullying and the Roman Catholic Church," in *More than a Monologue: Sexual Diversity and the Catholic Church. Volume II: Inquiry, Thought, and Expression*, ed. J. Patrick Hornbeck II and Michael A. Norko, Catholic Practice in North America (New York: Fordham University Press, 2014), 172; Robert E. Goss, "Luke," in Guest, Goss, West, and Bohache, *The Queer Bible Commentary*, 538; John J. McNeill, *Sex as God Intended: Reflection on Human Sexuality as Play* (Maple Shade: Lethe, 2008), 90. For more on the homoerotic interpretation in Spanish, Latin American, and Eastern European contexts, see the brief discussion below.

Chapter 1, "A Homophile Centurion and the Legality of Love: Continental Europe, 1950–1990," is divided into two parts. The first provides context for early homoerotic readings of the centurion, highlighting especially Dinos Christianopoulos's poem Εκατόνταρχος Κορνήλιος ("The Centurion Cornelius," 1950). Christianopoulos was the first to assert a romantic relationship between the centurion and his slave, doing so in the form of a poem. Though rarely cited within biblical scholarship, it laid important groundwork for later homoerotic exegesis. The second part of the chapter discusses the first substantial engagement with the homoerotic reading through formal biblical interpretations, France in the 1960s and 1970s, where—in a manner that prompts alarm—homophile activists emphasized the youthfulness of the beloved slave. Several writers used this reading of the pericope to authorize a lower age of majority for same-sex intercourse in France (where same-sex intercourse was partially criminalized through an unusually high age of consent at twenty-one years), a position advocated by many well-known intellectuals, such as Jacques Derrida, Louis Althusser, Jean-Paul Sartre, Simone de Beauvoir, and Michel Foucault. Thus, a homophile writer could claim, without irony or shame, that the centurion was "a pederast officer" (*un officier pédéraste*). The chapter concludes by observing how this pederastic legacy proves a liability, with homophile interpretations resembling recent efforts by ancient historians to destigmatize adult-adolescent intercourse, not to mention the tendency to forgive-and-forget acts of sexual violence within the biblical academy.

Chapter 2, "A Centurion and His Partner at the Altar: United States, United Kingdom, and Australia, 1985–2010," examines the fallout of the homophile reading and its transition into turn-of-the-millennium interest in gay rights. The constellation of discourses prompting the French homophile reading was so specific to its context—not least of which was the viability of a pederast as a point of identification—that one might wonder how it could be adopted among Anglophone interpreters at all. The first part of this chapter examines how the homophile interpretation was adapted for a different legal context, drawing particular attention to efforts to depict the centurion and his slave as peers. Gay interpretations depict the slave as a consenting adult, emphasizing the couple's cohabitation and mutual love so as to render their relationship a precursor to same-sex marriage. Over this period, homoerotic exegesis began identification with the state, attending to the shifting position of same-sex desire within Anglophone societies. To use the language of Foucauldian biopolitics, it was during this period that queers were being left to die with decreasing frequency (the decline of, e.g., the AIDS epidemic, sodomy laws) and increasingly made to live through participation in major institutions of the state (e.g., military inclusion, marriage). This becomes apparent in an emphasis on the military career of the centurion, such that he becomes a figure for contemplating the US armed forces' "Don't Ask, Don't Tell" policy. The second part of the chapter examines writings opposed to homoerotic readings of the pericope. Heteronormative opposition to the reading frequently objected that insofar as Jesus was Jewish, he was unlikely to have a favorable opinion about same-sex relationships. These heteronormative interpretations are sometimes linked to homophobic politics, responding negatively to calls for gay rights. Rather than construing this as a tension between pro-gay and antigay interpretations, we might understand this within a larger mobilization of the sexual in recent politics.

Chapter 3, "Military Occupation and Sexual Abuse in Roman Galilee: Homoerotic Counterreadings, 2000–Present," examines homoerotic interpretations operating with a different approach and thus marking a turning point within the history of interpretation. The readings discussed in previous chapters usually connect the homoerotic interpretation with the rights and recognition of queer folk, along with its inverse: criticism of the homoerotic interpretation often entailed opposition to such political projects. This relationship becomes complicated upon consideration of a counterreading that regards the pericope as tantamount to a text of terror. How might queer-sympathetic readers understand the prospect of sexual violence in this pericope, along with its connection to the enslavement of human beings and state violence? This chapter locates such counterreadings within two traditions. The first places it alongside abolitionist criticism of biblical slavery before the American Civil War. Many abolitionists noticed that biblical texts espouse a positive view of slavery, including the pericope under consideration. Rather than attempting to reconcile or reclaim these texts, many saw fit to jettison them from their own canon. Second, various interpreters situate the homoerotic reading of the pericope alongside American abuses of racial Others in a manner particularly salient after 9/11 and amid the occupations of Iraq and Afghanistan. The counter interpretation is helpfully read alongside recent historians of the Roman army who draw attention to this same phenomenon over the course of the late Republic and early Empire. Noting that "consent" was not part of Roman slaves' vocabulary, the counterreading drastically reframes the pericope and ponders a provocative question: did Jesus restore an abusive relationship when he healed a slave whose body served to sexually please his owner?

It is here the history of interpretation ends and consideration of its implications for biblical scholars begins. Chapter 4 asks, "Whose Interpretation Is Legitimate?" When reading the preceding chapters, one may notice a fault-line between credentialed biblical scholars who tend to ignore or deride the homoerotic interpretation and nonspecialists who enthusiastically promote it. Drawing upon Amy Richlin's work on queer "shadow scholarship," this chapter pursues the tension between academic and shadow scholarship as adjacent fields in asymmetrical competition for legitimacy. Although queer shadow scholars place considerable weight on academic research to establish the validity of their historiography, credentialed biblical scholars adopt an indifferent stance toward the enterprise, disregarding it as an instance of activist hermeneutics. Academics' glib dismissals of queer biblical historiography are acts of social differentiation, since the disavowal of direct interest in one's exegetical/historical conclusions remains integral to the academic field of biblical scholarship.

Chapter 5, "Did the Centurion at Capernaum Have Intercourse with the Pais?," addresses the historical question lingering over the book and directs our attention to the biblical texts themselves. Does the evidence favor or oppose the homoerotic interpretation of the pericope? The answer to this question is complicated and requires detours through Greek, Roman, Jewish, and Christian social history before assessing John, Luke, Matthew, and the Sayings Gospel Q individually. The distinctive literary features of the gospels (including their wording and sexual politics) lead to contrasting assessments of homoeroticism in each gospel: though untenable for the pericopes in the Gospels of John and Luke, the stories presented in the Gospel of Matthew and the Sayings Gospel Q are viably read as homoerotic.

Following chapter 5 is a brief conclusion and three appendices. The conclusion offers a tentative reflection on the difficult emotional terrain encountered in this book. It suggests this disappointment might be productively directed toward the reforming of the biblical academy in its capacity to enable sexual violence. Appendix 1 includes the Greek text and my own English translation of the pericope from Matthew, Luke, and John, and the Critical Edition of Q for reader convenience. Appendix 2 attempts a chronological bibliography of all homoerotic interpretations before 1990. When excerpts are sufficiently brief, they are quoted in full—those originally published in another language are translated into English.

Appendix 3 provides a table outlining the military presence in the village of Capernaum in the early Roman period, 66 BCE—135 CE, as its military history is more complicated than usually acknowledged.

Notes on Terminology

The gospels disagree on whether the παῖς in this pericope was enslaved (so Luke) or free (so John), with his status entirely unclear in both Matthew and Q. Though most assume that the Greek word παῖς refers to a slave in this narrative, some interpreters suggest that the young man may have been free, drawing upon Matthew's ambiguity and the lexical range of the word παῖς. The meaning of the word παῖς is of paramount importance to the homoerotic interpretation, as the present book largely examines how different people have attempted to resolve the ambiguity of this specific word. To avoid mischaracterizing various interpreters' arguments, this unnamed character in Q 7:1–10, Luke 7:1–10, Matt 8:5–13, and John 4:46–54 will henceforth be called "the Pais" with capitalization and no italics. The term is shared by Matthew, Luke, Q, and John and thus will act as a neutral designation that does not prefer any gospel's depiction over another. When referring to the broader phenomenon of ancient homoeroticism, a junior partner will be termed *pais* in lower case and italics—this usage is synonymous with *eromenos* for present purposes. In sum, the Pais was located in Capernaum, but Martial, Hadrian, and others each had one or more *pais* of their own.

Some terms that may appear synonymous operate with important distinctions in the following pages. This book distinguishes between three different homoerotic readings of the pericope: the *homophile* reading discussed in chapter 1, the *gay* reading discussed in chapter 2, and the *counter*reading discussed in chapter 3. This book will argue that there is a reactive relationship between these readings, such that they are productively understood as developing sequentially. These readings are unified in their imagination of a sexual relationship between the centurion and the Pais and thus represent *homoerotic* readings, an umbrella term that includes all three interpretations; that is, the homophile, gay, and counterreadings all agree that there might be something homoerotic going on in the pericope even if they disagree about its significance. These homoerotic readings will sometimes be contrasted with *heteronormative* readings that either presume or explicitly argue that the centurion and the Pais never had intercourse. This is the prevailing interpretation that one finds in biblical commentaries or academic articles on the pericope. This includes readings that are both explicitly opposed to the homoerotic interpretation and also those more casually assuming without comment that there is nothing sexual going on. These terms are used in a stipulative and heuristic capacity, being afforded greater precision in the relevant chapter. *Queer*, by contrast, is used loosely to designate gender and sexually nonconforming people, politics, interpretations, and so on, generally referring to those of the twentieth and twenty-first centuries.

Readers may notice that the word *homosexual* rarely refers to a person's orientation in this book. Though it may seem clinical, phrases like *same-sex intercourse* are preferred with respect to sexual acts, given that sexual orientation and related identities (the "homosexual," "bisexual," or "heterosexual" subject, for instance) are recent historical developments, whereas the wordier phrasing presumes nothing about sexual preferences or subjectivity—this is not to mention that the term homosexual is itself becoming antiquated! Given that accusations of anachronism figure prominently into debates about the interpretation, the characterization of homoerotic feelings and practices warrants precision.[32] Romans and Greeks distinguished sharply between penetrator and penetrated in sexual acts. In Roman contexts, the penetrated partner was properly some combination of enslaved, freed, sex-working, *peregrinus*, recently conquered, low social status, of younger age, female, eunuch, or otherwise compromised with regards to gender norms. The act of sexual penetration both replicated and was replicated by Roman social hierarchies: insertion served as a synecdoche for the existing relationship of dominance and was an act of further domination itself. Romans had various words to designate men who were sexually penetrated by other men in transgression of these norms, such as *cinaedus* and *pathicus* for anal intercourse and *fellator* for oral sex. There was no Greek or Latin word for

---

32. Here I refer to the well-known argument of Michel Foucault, *The History of Sexuality: An Introduction*, trans. Robert Hurley (New York: Pantheon, 1978) and further developed by many others: that *the homosexual* only emerged during the late nineteenth century and earlier sexual subjectivities and morphologies are not intelligible under the rubric of *sexual orientation*. See more on this below. Bibliography on the matter is extensive, but the most compelling counterarguments to this thesis vis-à-vis Roman antiquity are to be found in Amy Richlin, "Not before Homosexuality: The Materiality of the *Cinaedus* and the Roman Law against Love between Men," *JHSex* 3 (1993): 523–73.

homosexual for the simple reason that Greco-Roman discourse marked the penetrator-penetrated distinction as crucial, rather than the preferred gender(s) of one's sexual partners.[33] This is not to mention the problem of how exactly one would ascertain the sexual preferences of the centurion and the Pais, who died about two millennia ago (if they existed in the first place). These matters are unknowable. Indeed, how many queer people today misrepresent their sexual preferences to save face, because of personal uncertainty, or due to fear of violence? When *homosexuality*, *homosexual*, or similar words refer to a sexual orientation of someone in antiquity, these are always either another interpreter's characterization or my own understanding of another interpreter's claims; this phrasing does not imply agreement with their supposition that sexual orientation existed in antiquity. Following the prejudices of writers both ancient and modern, the following pages largely operate with a cisnormative understanding of sexual intercourse; the matter deserves far more space than can be allotted in the present volume.

Obvious typos from quotations have been silently corrected throughout the book (e.g., spelling errors, duplicate or missing words). Given that many interpretations were self-published, content for low-budget newsletters, or otherwise distant from the processes of academic publication, I would feel uncomfortable retaining the original typos, since this might impress a sneering tone, with a condescending "[sic]" found whenever there is evidence an author was unable to afford an editor to thoroughly proofread the product of their labor. The exception to this generosity is in appendix 2, which reproduces all excerpts exactly and retains nonstandard formatting to the extent that it is possible.

This book's scope is limited to sexual and romantic readings of the pericope. This entails the exclusion of commentary that treats the centurion or Pais as *analogously* queer: some argue that insofar as Jesus welcomed a pagan gentile, so also should Christians treat the marginalized

---

33. One recalls the famous Teratogenic Grid and the related Priapic Protocol: Roman sexual vocabulary did not denote foremost the gender of the person with whom one had sex but the particular orifice penetrated and whether one was penetrating it or penetrated *in* it. It should be noted that the normativity of this framework is sometimes overstated, especially in homoerotic contexts. See Joseph A. Marchal, "Bottoming Out: Rethinking the Reception of Receptivity," in *Bodies on the Verge: Queering Pauline Epistles and Interpretations*, ed. Joseph A. Marchal, SemeiaSt 93 (Atlanta: SBL Press, 2019), 209–38.

of their own society with kindness, including queer people.[34] Such reasoning often operates on a nonerotic understanding of the pericope, such that the centurion's social position is merely analogous to that of queer folk. These readings are omitted from the present book, even if there is some type of queering going on.

Finally, *sexual intercourse* is construed broadly throughout the book. Though current Anglophone usage usually limits the word *intercourse* to penetrative sexual acts, the term will be used in a way that includes other varieties of sexual contact (e.g., intercrural sex, fondling). There are many reasons for this choice, but the most practical is that it is rarely possible to know the specific type of sexual contact between two people in antiquity, and, rather than listing all possibilities, it is expedient to lump them all under the umbrella term intercourse. Beyond convenience, restricting one's understanding of sex to penetrative acts reinscribes particular sexualities as normative (usually, cis-heterogenital): such an understanding of sex, on the one hand, leaves little conceptual space for sexual activities between women or involving transgender people and, on the other hand, can downplay certain types of sexual violence as instances of mere touching. For these reasons, the following pages do not differentiate too much between various sexual activities (e.g., oral, anal, manual stimulation). There is much more to be said on the topic, and I would refer readers to Maia Kotrosits's remarkable article addressing these issues for the study of Christian origins.[35]

---

34. See, e.g., Paul Moore, *Take a Bishop Like Me* (New York: Harper & Row, 1979), 183: "Some feel that the modern revolution in sexuality contains a freer way of living out the Commandment of love, a way more consistent than ever before with the gospel of incarnate love.... Indeed, Jesus was wont to point to a Samaritan or a Roman centurion, who lived in the world outside the Church, as an image bearer for the Kingdom." Many, many other examples could be cited.

35. Maia Kotrosits, "Penetration and Its Discontents: Greco-Roman Sexuality, the *Acts of Paul and Thecla*, and Theorizing Eros without the Wound," *JHSex* 27 (2018): 343–66. Cf. Kotrosits, *The Lives of Objects: Material Culture, Experience, and the Real in the History of Early Christianity*, Class 200 (Chicago: University of Chicago Press, 2020), 124–44.

1
A HOMOPHILE CENTURION AND THE LEGALITY OF LOVE: CONTINENTAL EUROPE, 1950–1990

> The French homosexual movement of the 1950s has been little studied, in large part because of the widely held opinion that the homophile militancy of the period was not radical enough and, therefore, not worth a detailed examination. This attitude has been due largely to the influence of the revolutionary homosexual groups that developed in France after May 1968, which had nothing but contempt for their predecessors.
> —Olivier Jablonski, "The Birth of a French Homosexual Press in the 1950s"

When did the centurion at Capernaum come out of the closet, as far as the history of interpretation is concerned? The question is difficult to answer definitively. In the sixteenth century, Christopher Marlowe suggested that Jesus partook in a romantic or sexual relationship with the beloved disciple, an idea repeated by such luminaries as Jeremy Bentham and Oscar Wilde.[1] None of them, however, remarked upon the centurion at Capernaum. Although commentators have long observed the care that the centurion shows for the Pais, there had been little doubt that the centurion was simply a kind-hearted military officer. John Watson, for example, remarked in 1882 that "most men cared little for their slaves. How different the centurion!"[2] Far from suggesting any special relationship, Watson and most other interpreters took this care as evidence of

---

1. Richard Baines in "Accusations against Christopher Marlowe by Richard Baines and Others," f. 185v; Jeremy Bentham, *Doctrine*, in *Not Paul, but Jesus*, vol. 3 (London: Bentham Project, 2013), 177–97; Oscar Wilde, *Le Chant du cygne: Contes parlés d'Oscar Wilde* (Paris: Mercure de France, 1942), 112–14.

2. John Watson, *Lessons on the Miracles and Parables of Our Lord* (London: Church of England Sunday School Institute, 1882), 17.

the centurion's high moral standing—consistent with his remarkable faith in Jesus's word and positive relationship with the Jewish populace of the town.

Decades earlier, however, Wilhelm Reinhard published a German novel titled *Lenchen im Zuchthause* ("Little Helen in Prison"; 1840), which hinted at the centurion's queer desires.[3] The novel *purportedly* narrates a lightly fictionalized account of abuses typical in German women's prisons as an effort to expose this injustice. At a time when Elizabeth Fry, Dorothea Dix, and others advocated reform of penal institutions in Anglophone contexts, activists were also scrutinizing prisons in the German Confederation for their cruelty. *Lenchen im Zuchthause* situates itself alongside such activism. Readers, however, need barely read between the lines to ascertain that the book's pretense of condemning the punitive flogging was merely a façade for indulging in sado-masochistic fantasy. The fetish appeal is obvious throughout: the novel's protagonist describes in detail the aroused expression on witnesses' faces, the variously sized buttocks and thighs, the different hues of skin, and the numerous forms of bondage restraining such women while being struck by both male and female prison guards. Unsurprisingly, the book included twelve illustrations of young women in various states of undress undergoing some sort of flogging. *Lenchen im Zuchthause* was translated into English in 1900 with a title that made its crypto-pornographic contents clear to anyone who might be perusing a book-distributor's catalogue: *Nell in Bridewell: Description of the System of Corporal Punishment (Flagellation) in the Female Prisons of South Germany*.[4] The translators, Alfred Allinson and

---

3. Wilhelm Reinhard, *Lenchen im Zuchthause* (Karlsruhe: Bielefeld, 1840). Though the book was first published in 1840, Edward Shorter claims that it was "evidently written in the late eighteenth century." See Edward Shorter, *Written in the Flesh: A History of Desire* (Toronto: University of Toronto Press, 2005), 290 n. 23. Shorter clarified his reasoning via personal communication: "Torture was abolished in Bavarian prisons in 1806, also in that period for the other South German states (Baden 1767, Württemberg 1806). To the extent that the events described in Reinhard's account did not come entirely from his imagination, they must have been situated before that time."

4. Wilhelm Reinhard, *Nell in Bridewell: Description of the System of Corporal Punishment (Flagellation) in the Female Prisons of South Germany*, trans. W. Charles Costello and Alfred R. Allinson (Paris: Society of British Bibliophiles, 1900), the subtitle adapted from German editions beginning 1848 (*Lenchen im Zuchthause: Schilderung des Strafverfahrens (Flagellantismus) in einem Süddeutschen Zuchthause*

Charles Costello, were known for translating publications with sadomasochistic themes into English, ranging from French erotic novellas to pseudo-anthropological inquiries into foreign rituals.⁵

Many North Atlantic countries had established antiobscenity laws banning pornographic publications (e.g., Comstock laws in the United States, Campbell's Act in the United Kingdom, various laws in the German Confederation), which predictably led to an underground market for such literature. Many authors and publishers maneuvered this obstacle so as to provide a veneer of legitimacy for their books' content—or at least plausible deniability that such books promoted one or another vice. In this case, Reinhard composed his novel under the noble aegis of prison reform. True to form, the novel never mentions the act of intercourse, even though illicit sex lingers just beneath the surface of its pages.

Though it may seem odd for an erotic novel, the Christian faith of the narrator-protagonist ("Helen") is a major theme in *Lenchen in Zuchthause*. The book consistently depicts Christianity as a benevolent force. Helen lays her hopes upon the church amid the horrors she experiences, regularly praying for deliverance. One episode relates to the present study, wherein she recounts the prison matron's threats of violence.

> I came here, my dear prison-companion, fully resigned, having given up everything which others look to in earthly life. Like the centurion's men [*Leuten*] at Capernaum I went wherever I was told to go, I took the place, the work appointed to me, I laid me down to rest where I was told to. Everything was indifferent to me; I could not bring myself to bear physical pain on skin and flesh.⁶

---

vor 1848: Ein Beitrag zur Sittengeschichte). In a shrewd business move, the publishers noted that if English readers desired the illustrations included in the German version of the novel, they needed to purchase them separately via mail order. Beginning 1967, English editions included updated art that was even more sexually explicit and featured a revised subtitle that more directly evoked the book's erotic appeal (*Nell in Bridewell: Horrors of Female Flagellation; The Famous Confessions of a Young Girl Imprisoned for Love*).

5. On Allinson and Costello, see Rod Boroughs, "Oscar Wilde's Translation of Petronius: The Story of a Literary Hoax," *English Literature in Translation* 38 (1995): 34–35.

6. Reinhard, *Nell in Bridewell*, 71. From the German original: "ich ging, gleich den Leuten des Hauptmanns zu Kapernaum, mohin man mich gehen hies" (Reinhard, *Lenchen im Zuchthause*, 61).

Helen's obedience to the prison matron evokes the centurion's words (Matt 8:9; Luke 7:8), "Because I am also a man under practicing authority, having soldiers under me. I say to this one, 'Go' and he goes; and to another, 'Come' and he comes; and to my slave, 'Do this' and he does it." Particularly striking is the mirrored homoeroticism within this passage: just as Helen is hierarchically subordinate to and homoerotically disciplined by the prison matron, so also were male soldiers by the centurion at Capernaum. Unlike subsequent readings of the pericope, Reinhard does not eroticize the relationship between the centurion and the Pais, but instead he alludes to a relationship between the centurion and his *military* subordinates. The excerpt is tame in comparison to the book's other sadomasochistic musings, but the centurion is nevertheless a sexualized figure, if only implicitly. The implication is subtle, so it is unsurprising that this book has been entirely neglected in subsequent homoerotic interpretation of the passage.

The centurion peeked out of the closet on occasion in subsequent decades. For instance, when Dr. Lilian Cooper passed away in 1947, her lifelong, cohabitating companion Josephine Bedford donated a double stained-glass window depicting the centurion and the Pais to the Warriors' Chapel of St. Mary's Anglican Church at Brisbane, Australia in her memory.[7] Cooper was the first woman to become a physician in Queensland, which proved a difficult life. Cooper had been rejected from both the Australian and English armies during World War I, as they refused to accept a female doctor into their ranks. She ended up serving with the Scottish. Male colleagues regularly commented on her gender nonconformity and unmarried state, to which she had several clever replies prepared. Cooper and Bedford were regular worshippers at the Warriors' Chapel, and the two were eventually buried next to each other at the Toowong Cemetery in Brisbane. Their former house was donated to serve as a local hospice center. It is easy to see why the centurion provided a meaningful site of reflection for the two women: the biblical story sits at the nexus of same-sex love, Christian healing, feelings of foreignness, and military service.

---

7. This discussion draws especially upon Deborah Jordan, *Centenary of Queensland Women's Suffrage 2005* (Brisbane: University of Queensland Press, 2005), 11–13. For more on Cooper and Bedford, see Clive Moore, *Sunshine and Rainbows: The Development of Gay and Lesbian Culture in Queensland* (Saint Lucia: University of Queensland Press, 2001), 81–83. Whether Cooper and Bedford partook in a Boston Marriage of platonic or another character can only be the object of speculation.

Even though it would take over a century after the initial publication of *Lenchen im Zeuthause* for the next homoerotic reading of the passage to see print, the pericope was already identified as a tool for claiming a queer space within a context of patriarchy and heteronormativity.

The rest of this chapter will explore homoerotic interpretations of the centurion at Capernaum under the aegis of "homophile readings," mostly emerging from Continental Europe. The key term here may be unfamiliar to Anglophone readers, as it fell out of use several decades ago. The word *homophile* was coined in 1924 by the German physician Karl-Günther Heimsoth for those experiencing same-sex desire, but without pathological or deviant connotations that other terms bore.[8] The word was commonly used from the 1940s to the early 1970s, as it lacked the clinical and carnal connotations of *homosexual*. Its use quickly declined after the Stonewall riots in 1969 (United States), Operation Soap in 1970 (Canada), the unrest of May 1968 (France), and other events catalyzed the nascent gay rights movement, as there had been a significant political divide between the younger and more radical gays and the older, more conservative homophiles.[9] While not every interpreter discussed in this chapter identified as homophile, most of them did, and those who did not nevertheless supported the homophile subculture's causes. Thus, even though some readings discussed in the present chapter were published at

---

8. Karl-Günther Heimsoth, "Hetero- und Homophilie: Eine neuorientierende An- und Einordnung der Erscheinungsbilder, der 'Homosexualität' und der 'Inversion' in Berücksichtigung der sogenannten 'normalen Freundschaft' auf Grund der zwei verschiedenen erotischen Anziehungsgesetze und der bisexuellen Grundeinstellung des Mannes" (PhD diss., Universität Rostock, 1924). Heimsoth self-identified as homophile but was an outspoken anti-Semite and member of the Nazi Party. Homophile dignity and anti-Semitism were clearly linked in his writings: "[Die] männerheldische heroische Freundesliebe [bleibt] in der Idee und Verständnismöglichkeit dem Judengeiste fremd." See Heimsoth, "Freundesliebe oder Homosexualität: Ein Versuch einer anregenden und scheidenden Klarstellung," *Der Eigene* 10 (1925): 415–25. Heimsoth eventually abandoned the Nazi Party following their increased persecution of homosexual men and joined the Communist Party in 1931, whereupon he began acting as an anti-Nazi informant, before being executed extrajudicially by the SS in 1934.

9. For a concise discussion of the homophile movement's decline in the United States, see Elizabeth A. Armstrong, *Forging Gay Identities: Organizing Sexuality in San Francisco, 1950–1994* (Chicago: University of Chicago Press, 2002), 56–80. Its decline in France is the topic of the present chapter. Note that cognates and derivatives of homophile remain the standard terms for same-sex attraction in a few languages (e.g., Norwegian "homofil").

a point when few people still used the word homophile as a self-descriptor, these readings embraced the political causes that had concerned homophile writers in the preceding decades.

After discussing a seminal poem by the Greek poet Dinos Christianopoulos, we will see that homophile readers deployed the centurion as a way of intervening in debates about the legality of same-sex intercourse. The primary issue at stake was the homosexual age of consent, which differed from the age of consent for heterosexual intercourse. Particularly curious is how the centurion's homophilia became inseparable from his pederasty in France during the 1960s–1980s. While many of these interpretations simply proposed equal treatment under the law, this chapter will conclude with two exceptionally troubling readings that came from this time, one of which has been remarkably influential. Before we arrive in France, we must take a brief shore leave in Greece with an eye toward the 1950s.

The Poetry of Greek Love

The centurion was first identified as out (if not exactly proud) within the poetry of Dinos Christianopoulos (Ντίνος Χριστιανόπουλος; 1931–2020)—the pen-name of Konstantinos Dimitriadis—one of Greece's most highly regarded poets.[10] Christianopoulos gained the attention of English-speakers thanks to translations by Kimon Friar and Nicholas Kostis.[11] Christianopoulos's poetry adopts an emphatically *provincial* style, mirroring his own life: he lived his entire life in Thessaloniki, travelling to Athens or islands only for poetry readings. His poem titled "The Centurion Cornelius" (1950) contains the earliest instance of an unambiguously homoerotic relationship between the centurion and the Pais. This poem, quoted here in full via the translation of Kimon Friar, elaborates upon a

---

10. For more on his background, see Kimon Friar, "The Poetry of Dinos Christianopoulos: An Introduction," *Journal of the Hellenic Diaspora* 6 (1979): 59–67; Dinos Christianopoulos, *Poems*, trans. Nicholas Kostis (Athens: Odysseas, 1995), xiii–xix.

11. Friar: Willis Barnstone, ed., *Modern European Poetry* (New York: Bantam, 1966), 264–68; Dinos Christianopoulos, "The Poetry of Dinos Christianopoulos: A Selection," *Journal of the Hellenic Diaspora* 6 (1979): 68–83. Kostis: Christianopoulos, *Poems*; Christianopoulos, *The Naked Piazza: Poems*, trans. Nicholas Kostis (Peania: Bilieto, 2000).

romantic relationship between the centurion at Capernaum (the titular "Cornelius") and his enslaved Pais named Andónios.[12]

> Lord, do not wonder at my great faith;
> it is love that dictates my faith.
> I do not beg you for Nikítas or for Harílaos,
> nor for Nikólaos who has not had time yet to be bored with prayer.
> Only make Andónios well, Andónios;
> this is all so painful for me—
> when he was young and a free man
> he also concerned himself with letters and the arts;
> he was conversant with ancient Greek and loved to play the accordion
> on nights when the sky slept and the drowsy moon
> leaned her head on the house with the lilac bushes.
> But now he is my slave—do not ask me how.
> I have authority over him to bind or to free.
> I can do with him whatever I please;
> I can even set him free, though this would be most painful for me;
> besides, he works efficiently with his great strength.
> For these reasons, Lord, and for many others,
> make Andónios well, slave of your slave.
> If need be, I can even turn Christian.
> Only make him well, all I ask of you, nothing else.
> Anything else I might dare ask of you would be immoral.

The poem depicts Andónios as a young aristocrat fascinated with intellectual pursuits and emotionally involved with the centurion Cornelius. Though the circumstances are unstated, Andónios became Cornelius's slave and eventually fell ill. Cornelius then petitioned Jesus that he might heal the slave, for whom he held affection marked by longing and guilt. The poem fills in a number of narrative gaps of the biblical tale, inviting an implicitly homoerotic reading of the centurion Cornelius and the Pais Andónios. It relies heavily upon insinuation, as even the romantic nature of their relationship is only implied. One is also struck at how chaste the poem depicts the men, as we will see that interpretations soon after come

---

12. Dinos Christianopoulos, Εποχή των ισχνών αγελάδων [*Season of the Lean Cows*] (Thessaloniki: Kochlias, 1950), 9. The English translation here was first published by Friar as Dinos Christianopoulos, "The Centurion Cornelius," in Barnstone, *Modern European Poetry*, 267–68. This translation has been reprinted on occasion; see below.

to emphasize their sexuality. The two lines, "I can do with him whatever I please / I can even set him free, though this would be most painful for me," are the closest to anything explicitly sexual—or even romantic—in their relationship. Sexuality remains oblique throughout, with obvious homoeroticism that is never named directly. Longing, rather than love itself, takes center stage.

The illicit nature of same-sex love is implied throughout: Cornelius's erotic desire for Andónios is a source of shame and guilt, prompting repentance (μετάνοια) and prayer (προσευχή). It would surprise few readers to learn that same-sex intercourse was illegal in Greece at the time it was published, being decriminalized shortly afterwards in 1951. The emphatically *Christian* nature of the poem is noteworthy as well; even the author's penname Christianopoulos translates as "son of Christ."[13] The poem sits at the nexus of two of his recurring themes: sexuality and sainthood. Emmanouil Doundoulakis observes that when these themes overlap in Christianopoulos's works, they consistently provide oblique references to the saint's own feeling that their sexual desires are sinful.[14] Christianopoulos devoted poems to similarly sinful saints such as Mary Magdalene, Sebastian (the unofficial patron saint of gay men),[15] Mary of Egypt, and Agnes—saints whose sexuality figures prominently in their popular imagination. He represents these figures as experiencing a combination of repressed desire, regret, and melancholic longing for divine pleasures. These themes should be understood alongside, though certainly not reduced to, Christianopoulos's own situation as a sexually inexperienced young man who desired the affection of other men; as Kimon Friar notes, "in symbolic and metaphorical terms he embodies

---

13. Friar, "Poetry of Dinos Christianopoulos."

14. Emmanouil Doundoulakis, "Saints and Sanctity in the Poems of Greek 'Unconventional' Poets during the Twentieth and Twenty-First Century: The Cases of C. P. Cavafy and D. Christianopoulos," in *The 2015 West East Institute International Academic Conference Proceedings: Prague* (Prague: West East Institute, 2015), 12–18; cf. Friar, "Poetry of Dinos Christianopoulos," 60, who translated the poem quoted above: "the erotic element [in Christianopoulos's poems] is inextricably linked to the religious." One would be hard-pressed to find a reader who disagrees.

15. See, e.g., the discussion of Sebastian in Richard A. Kaye, "Losing His Religion: Saint Sebastian as Contemporary Gay Martyr," in *Outlooks: Lesbian and Gay Sexualities and Visual Cultures*, ed. Peter Horne and Reina Lewis (New York: Routledge, 1996), 86–105.

the agony of erotic privation intensified by what is hinted at as some sort of sexual anomaly."[16]

Another noteworthy element of the poem is the rich internal life of the Pais. Unlike the biblical tale that names neither the centurion nor the Pais and nearly eliminates the latter from the narrative, Christianopoulos reflects upon the plight of the Pais, whom he named Andónios. We will see that whereas most interpreters approach the pericope from the centurion's perspective, Christianopoulos is an important exception: slavery is never romanticized. The implications of Andónios's lost freedom are afforded vivid specificity, no longer having a life marked by opportunities for carefree reflection, having been reduced to a strong body for manual labor—the joy he lost is evident to his friend-turned-master Cornelius. Whatever affection Cornelius has for Andónios, their relationship is inextricable from the power relations of their master-slave dynamic. This reflects an important theme in Christianopoulos's works, namely, his doubt that institutions of power can ever be benevolent. For instance, when awarded the 2012 Grand State Prize for Literature by the Greek Ministry of Culture, Christianopoulos refused the award, quoting a different poem of his own as an explanation: "Nor will I show up, nor will I stretch my hand to take it / I want neither their prizes, nor their money."[17] As Alexandra Boutopoulou observes:

> Christianopoulos made very clear through his poetry that he is against all awards because they diminish human dignity, something he expressed in the first issue of *Diagonal* [of the year 1979]. For Christianopoulos, giving an award means to recognize the value of somebody who is my inferior; and according to him, we should cast off the need to be approved by big bosses of any kind. Receiving an award means that I do accept intellectual bosses and, at some point, we should dismiss those bosses from our lives.[18]

---

16. Friar, "Poetry of Dinos Christianopoulos," 60.

17. Anonymous, "Ο Ντίνος Χριστιανόπουλος αρνήθηκε το Μεγάλο Βραβείο Γραμμάτων" [Dinos Christianopoulos refused the Grand State Prize for Literature], *Naftemporiki*, 23 January 2012, https://tinyurl.com/sbl6705a. The poem is titled Εναντίον ("Against").

18. Quoted in An Xiao, "On the Origins of 'They Tried to Bury Us, They Didn't Know We Were Seeds,'" *Hyperallergic*, 3 July 2018, https://tinyurl.com/sbl6705b. Christianopoulos himself founded the journal Διαγώνιος (*Diagonal*): Dinos Christianopoulos, "Συνέντευξη" [Interview], Διαγώνιος 79.1 (1979): 3–4.

A similar suspicion of power operates in his poem "The Centurion Cornelius," such that the centurion, though a sympathetic and thoughtful narrator, is hardly innocent: Cornelius *could* free Andónios, but he benefits too greatly from his enslavement and remains too preoccupied with his own sinfulness to do so. He holds a morally complex position, one that nevertheless conjures the reader's compassion.[19]

One might contrast "The Centurion Cornelius" with James Kirkup's infamously raunchy poem, "The Love That Dares to Speak Its Name."[20] Kirkup's poem has been banned in the United Kingdom under its blasphemy laws—the very last instance of prosecution under this legislation—thanks to a lawsuit initiated by Mary Whitehouse, founder of the conservative watchdog group National Viewers and Listeners Association. Kirkup's poem describes the lust of the centurion at the cross for the deceased body of Jesus (Matt 27:54; Mark 15:39; Luke 23:47, an entirely distinct centurion from the one at Capernaum). The poem describes the corpse of Jesus in crudely pornographic language, purporting that Jesus had intercourse with his disciples, John the Baptist, Pontius Pilate, and other men. Kirkup admitted that "The Love That Dares to Speak Its Name" was not particularly good poetry and primarily deployed homoeroticism for provocation.[21] This contrasts with Christianopoulos's approach, which preferred understatement and oblique insinuation, thereby prompting the reader's reflection on two minor biblical characters.

---

19. Cf. Nikolaides Anastasios, "Πάθος και Ήθος στο έργο του Ντίνου Χριστιανόπουλου" [Pathos and ethos in the work of Dinos Christianopoulos] (PhD diss., Aristotle University of Thessaloniki, 2011), 28–31. For a contrasting interpretation of the poem, which contends that Christianopoulos therein eliminates class distinctions, see Ioanna Skordi, "The 'Regiment of Pleasure': Cavafy and His Homoerotic Legacy in Greek Writing" (PhD diss., King's College London, 2018), 265–67.

20. James Kirkup, "The Love That Dares to Speak Its Name," *Gay News* 96 (1976): 26, notably evoking the famous phrase of Lord Alfred Douglas's 1892 poem "Two Loves." Kirkup's was hardly the first homoerotic poem evoking the centurion at the cross; see Geoffrey Deamer, "The Dead Turk," in *Lads: Love Poetry from the Trenches*, ed. Martin Taylor (London: Constable, 1989), 166, initially published in 1918.

21. Kirkup acknowledged that "The Love That Dares to Speak Its Name" was "not aesthetically a successful work" and expressed regret that such a frivolous piece loomed so large over his literary reputation: Anonymous, "James Kirkup," *The Telegraph*, 12 May 2009, https://www.telegraph.co.uk/news/obituaries/culture-obituaries/books-obituaries/5314221/James-Kirkup.html.

Christianopoulos's poem was innovative and presents a complex portrait of the centurion and the Pais, but it had little direct influence on how the pericope was read. "The Centurion Cornelius" was translated into English in 1966 but has remained of interest only to queer readers and literary critics specializing in Greek poetry. The inclusion of the poem in the anthology *Modern European Poetry*, edited by Willis Barnstone, marks an early and particularly visible English-language articulation of the homoerotic reading. The English translation of the poem was occasionally reprinted in queer literary venues, which pushed it further into the public eye, but also ensured its relegation to the status of queer lit and thus outside the standard purview of most biblical interpreters.[22] This poem has only been cited by one subsequent biblical interpreter, Donald H. Mader, who briefly noted its "poetic enthusiasm."[23] Even so, Christianopoulos announces as possible the homoerotic interpretation of this biblical text, a possibility pursued by innumerable commentators since. Though no reader would mistake Christianopoulos's poem for historiography, it nevertheless exists in conversation with more formal biblical interpretation and draws upon the poet's own practical sense of Mediterranean intimacies and experimentations.

This Pederast Officer

Because Christianopoulos's poem exerted little influence on biblical interpreters, it is hardly surprising that subsequent homoerotic readings went an entirely different route. A number of Continental writers from the 1950s to 1990s reflected on the pericope, a surprising portion of which highlighted a pederastic element within the Healing of the Centurion's

---

22. See, e.g., Dinos Christianopoulos, "The Centurion Cornelius," *Gay Sunshine Journal* 47 (1982): 170; Dinos Christianopoulos, "The Centurion Cornelius," in *Gay Roots: Twenty Years of Gay Sunshine; An Anthology of Gay History, Sex, Politics, and Culture*, ed. Winston Leyland, trans. Kimon Friar, vol. 1 (San Francisco: Gay Sunshine, 1991), 673, using Kimon Friar's translation and accompanied by a short note from the translator. See also Kostis's translation in Christianopoulos, *Poems*, 5, with a short note from the translator on page 147.

23. Mader, "*Entimos Pais*," 233 n. 6. It is possible that the anonymous author of "How Dare You Presume These Are Heterosexual!," *Oregon Liberator* 5.1 (1975?): 6 was aware of Christianopoulos's poem as well, given that it refers to the centurion as "Cornelius."

Pais.²⁴ Lest one think this is alarmist overstatement, a few examples might demonstrate this propensity. The earliest explicit mention of homosexual intercourse between the centurion and the Pais is found in a brief footnote in a 1959 article published in *ONE Institute Quarterly: Homophile Studies*. James Kepner asserts with an almost cavalier tone, "Luke 7:2 uses a term which was used for the boy love-slaves of well-to-do Roman soldiers."²⁵ A

---

24. While some interpretations discussed in this chapter were produced outside Continental Europe, we will see that the genesis of this reading makes sense only as a product of Continental social historical issues. Moreover, even when interpreters are American, they are best understood in a Continental context.

25. James Kepner Jr., "World Religions and the Homophile: An Introduction," *ONE Institute Quarterly* 7 (1959): 130 n. 35, based on classes he had been teaching on "the homophile and world religions" since 1956. When, precisely, the centurion first appeared in his courses is not clear from his lecture notes or syllabi. Kepner's discussion is so little-known that Mader, Mader, "*Entimos Pais*," 233 n. 6, despite his comparatively thorough bibliography, mistakenly claims that Parker Rossman (*Sexual Experience between Men and Boys: Exploring the Pederast Underground* [New York: Association, 1976], 99) provided the earliest English interpretation. Jennings and Liew, "Mistaken Identities," 473 n. 16; Robert E. Shore-Goss, "Gay Liberation," in *The Oxford Encyclopedia of the Bible and Gender Studies*, ed. Julia O'Brien (Oxford: Oxford University Press, 2014), 259, and others incorrectly claim that Tom M. Horner (*Jonathan Loved David: Homosexuality in Biblical Times* (Philadelphia: Westminster John Knox, 1978), 122) was the first in English. See the genealogy of citations in figure 2 below. Many of these early discussions went unnoticed by sympathetic would-be readers and preceded the better-known interpretations by several years. On Kepner's use of antiquity for grounding his claims about homophile rights, see Amy Richlin, "Eros Underground: Greece and Rome in Gay Print Culture 1953–65," *JH* 49.3–4 (2005): 421–61. As an aside, the designation of *earliest* throughout this chapter is entirely provisional. These early publications were not part of the social mainstream and thus were not likely to be archived (let alone subsequently digitized) with the same rigor as, say, academic or denominational literature. Moreover, these ideas often circulated orally before they were put to paper: the authors discussed here regularly mention conversations, papers delivered to obscure and now-defunct organizations, and other poorly documented means of discussing the homoerotic interpretation of the pericope. E.g., Rossman, *Sexual Experience between Men and Boys*, 99 cites the author's conversation with an anonymous monk; J. Martignac, "Le centurion de Capernaüm," *Arcadie* 255 (1975): 117–28 was initially presented as a paper at a meeting of Groupe des Chrétiens Homophiles de Marseille in May 1974; McNeill (*Freedom, Glorious Freedom*, 201) cites "an unpublished manuscript by a Franciscan biblical scholar" later revealed to be Jack Clark Robinson (see Jack Clark Robinson, "Author's Reply," *Gay and Lesbian Review Worldwide* 15.1 [2008]: 6). But this problem of documentation is best represented by R. H. Crowther, "Sodom: A Homosexual Viewpoint," *ONE Magazine* 3.1 (1955): 26,

far more substantial discussion can be found a few years later in the homophile journal *Arcadie*, published by the premier homophile organization in France of the same name. In a 1965 issue, Michel Mayer wrote a piece of historical fiction about the centurion and the Pais and appended it with an exegetical analysis of the passage concluding, "the Son of the living God did not condemn the adulterous woman and did not look away from the sinner of Magdala. Why would he who ceaselessly repeated 'I desire mercy, not sacrifice' condemn the only lover of a boy (*garçon*)?"[26] J. Martignac, writing an exegetical article about the pericope for *Arcadie* a decade after Mayer, straightforwardly refers to the centurion at Capernaum as a "pederast officer."[27] Raymond Lawrence, declares likewise: "Readers or hearers of the story in the first century would unquestionably conclude, given the language that is used, that the centurion was a pederast and his boy a catamite."[28] Several other examples could be cited.[29] Indeed, only a few homoerotic readings of the passage from 1950–1985 *avoided* the issue of pederasty, and this strain of interpretation lingered for several years afterward with diminishing prevalence.

---

which quotes an anonymous letter to the editor, the letter itself quoting and translating from memory an article published in another language from a magazine whose name the letter-writer cannot recall and may not have existed at all (see appendix 1).

26. Michel Mayer, "Le procurateur de Judée: Suite à la manière d'Anatole France," *Arcadie* 134 (1965): 71. Translated by Morgan Bell.

27. Martignac, "Le centurion de Capernaüm," passim: "officier pédéraste."

28. Raymond J. Lawrence Jr., *The Poisoning of Eros: Sexual Values in Conflict* (New York: Augustine Moore, 1989), 70–71; cf. Lawrence Jr., "The Fish: A Lost Symbol of Sexual Liberation?," *Journal of Religion and Health* 30 (1991): 315.

29. See, e.g., J. Duncan M. Derrett, "Law in the New Testament: The Syro-Phoenician Woman and the Centurion of Capernaum," *NovT* 15 (1973): 174; Marcel Eck, *Sodome: Essai sur l'homosexualité* (Paris: Fayard, 1966), 266; Ronald M. Enroth and Gerald E. Jamison, *The Gay Church* (Grand Rapids: Eerdmans, 1974), 56–57; Michael Gray-Fow, "Pederasty, the Scantinian Law and the Roman Army," *Journal of Psychohistory* 13 (1986): 457; Mader, "*Entimos Pais*"; Rossman, *Sexual Experience between Men and Boys*, 99; Larion Gyburc-Hall, "Legende," *Der Kreis* 31.4 (1963): 14–22; William R. Stayton, "Pederasty in Ancient and Early Christian History," in *Human Sexuality: An Encyclopedia*, ed. Vern L. Bullough and Bonnie Bullough, Garland Reference Library of Social Science 68 (New York: Garland, 1994), 439. Cf. Tom M. Horner, "Jesus," in *Encyclopedia of Homosexuality*, ed. Wayne R. Dynes (New York: Garland, 1990), 639; Thomas Martin and B. Newman, "Guilt and the Homosexual," *ONE Magazine* 8.12 (1960): 13; Martin and Newman, "Guilt and the Homosexual," *ONE Magazine* 14.11 (1966): 13.

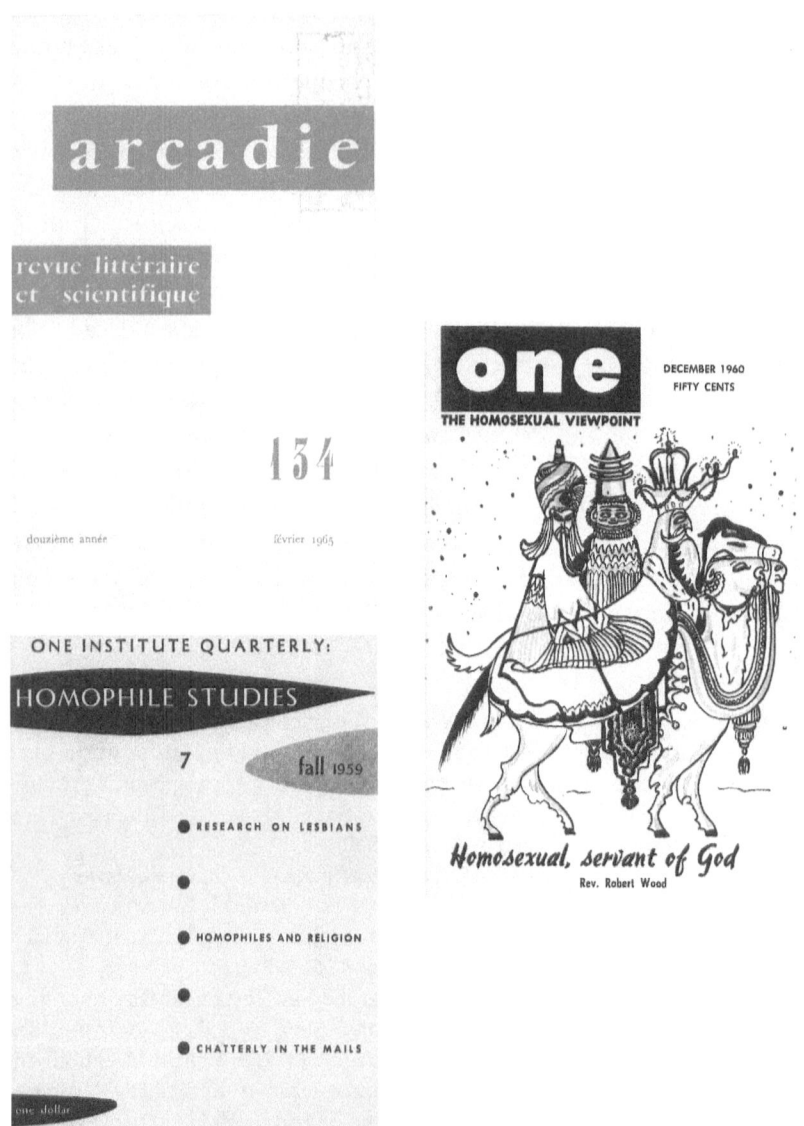

Figure 1. Covers of various homophile periodicals publishing the homoerotic interpretation. *Arcadie* 134 features Michel Mayer's 1965 short story and exegesis; *ONE Magazine* 8.12 features Thomas Martin and B. Newman's 1960 brief reference; *ONE Institute Quarterly* 7 features James Kepner's 1959 footnote. The covers are representative of the periodicals' contents and politics: the high-minded solemnity of *Arcadie*, the playful populism of *ONE Magazine*, and the aspirations of academic legitimacy of *ONE Institute Quarterly*. Thanks to the ArQuives for assistance with these scans.

This sexualization of the slave's juvenility is shocking, to say the least. Homophile readers put heavy emphasis on the word παῖς (Matt 8:6, 8:8, 8:13; Luke 7:7), which not only denoted *younger* partners in homosexual intercourse but often male *adolescents* in sexual relationships more specifically. Despite the alarming nature of this phrasing, the term *pederast* carried specific connotations in France at the time, attending a constellation of distinctive discourses. Though the word pederast connotes the sexual abuse of children today, the word meant something quite different for these interpreters. Rather, the centurion's designation as a pederast should be understood within France's peculiar legal situation, which criminalized much homosexual intercourse by imposing an oddly high age of consent. In short, age of sexual majority laws were de facto sodomy laws. It will become clear that homophile activism against such laws was a complicated affair: while it served the noble purpose of undermining the criminalization of queer bodies, this campaign eventually sought to legalize forms of sexual predation as well—the dividing lines between these causes is not always clear.

After situating French readings of the passage within their legal context, this chapter will look at two particularly distressing readings of the centurion at Capernaum, namely, those of Donald H. Mader and Parker Rossman, reflecting changing intonations of the term pederasty both within and outside Continental Europe. For present purposes, homophile interpretations are marked by a preoccupation with the adolescent youthfulness of the Pais before gay rights groups almost universally removed age of consent reduction/abolition from their platform in the 1990s, a topic that will be addressed in chapter 2.

The Centurion Ships Out to the Gallic Provinces

Although there were cursory references to the centurion's homophilia in the 1950s and 1960s, the first two instances of formal homoerotic exegesis were published in France, namely, the articles published in *Arcadie* by Michel Mayer (1965) and Martignac (1975).[30] Mayer's article consists of two parts. The first comprises historical fiction, presenting a conversation between Pontius Pilate and a Cappadocian centurion named Manlius stationed at Capernaum. Pilate, having forgotten who Jesus even was, is

---

30. Martignac, "Le centurion de Capernaüm"; Mayer, "Le procurateur de Judée."

reminded by Manlius, who recounts an instance wherein Jesus saved the life of his Bithynian Pais. The second part of Mayer's article concisely presents the exegetical basis for extrapolating a same-sex relationship from the pericope. Martignac's article is more straightforwardly devoted to social-historical and exegetical reasons for inferring the centurion's homophilia, foregrounding the theological implications of the homoerotic reading:

> In Jesus's eyes, this event simply underlies everything that signifies a certain kind of love; a love that, through Jesus, melds the love of neighbour with the love of the Father. The relationship between a man and a young boy was the occasion that permitted [Jesus] to bring this to light for the first time. It may well have been a homosexual relationship. Let us simply bless the fact that the centurion permitted Jesus to show that homophilia or heterophilia made no difference, and equally, that the churches are mistaken in establishing and practicing a so-called Christian morality—in reality, hardly derived from the Gospels—which banishes and persecutes homophilia.[31]

Far from arguing from a position of theological convenience, Martignac admits that it is best to avoid extrapolating too much about Jesus's opinions on same-sex intercourse from an abstruse passage, instead emphasizing that the centurion's love—in all its ambiguity—is paramount.

These two were hardly the only ones in France to advocate the reading. Psychiatrist Marcel Eck assented to this interpretation in a 1966 monograph on homosexuality: "the centurion's servant was, in fact, his *eromenos*."[32] Eck further observed that the relationship between *erastes* and *eromenos* was characterized by an "*a priori* shocking disparity in ages."[33] Also noteworthy are the comments of Rossman about a conversation he had with a "gnostic pederast monk" about the passage. The monk claimed that "Jesus evidently blessed the pederast and his adolescent lover with one of his rare miracles because of the quality of their love."[34] Though Rossman does not explicitly state where the monk lives, his footnote concerning the exchange only cites French literature—presumably readings suggested by the monk, given that

---

31. Martignac, "Le centurion de Capernaüm," 127. Translated by Morgan Bell.
32. Eck, *Sodome*, 266: "le serviteur du centurion n'était autre que son éromène." Eck's phrasing and extensive familiarity with *Arcadie* make it almost certain that he draws upon Mayer, "Le procurateur de Judée," even though he never cites it directly.
33. Eck, *Sodome*, 47: "disparité des âges, quelque chose qui est a priori choquant."
34. Rossman, *Sexual Experience between Men and Boys*, 99, with 230 n. 14.

Rossman garbled the citations badly enough that he clearly did not have access to the readings and merely scrawled notes. The monk likely participated in one of the French *églises gnostiques* that saw a resurgence in popularity during the 1960–1970s. Indeed, the homoerotic reading of the pericope was so well known that queer theorist Guy Hocquenghem's 1980 travel guide for French homophiles casually mentioned it![35]

Given present-day apprehensions about the term pederast, it is striking that the designation was deployed so flippantly—even positively. While it might sound bizarre to modern readers, its usage is readily contextualized within French age of majority/consent laws. Although such legislation is usually presented as a means of protecting youth from sexual exploitation and abuse, this was not the case in postwar France, where these laws singled out homosexual populations for criminal prosecution. At least in the French cultural context, one might want to differentiate between activists that contested age of consent laws in service of homophile political emancipation and activists that sought consequence-free intercourse with children.

The French had used the word pederast as a legal term for classifying various sexual crimes from the July Monarchy through the Second Empire (1830–1871). French police records likewise used the word *pédéraste* (pederast) when describing men who had sex with other men, even if both parties were adults. The designation had nothing to do with age.[36]

---

35. Guy Hocquenghem, *Le gay voyage: Guide et regard homosexuels sur les grandes métropoles* (Paris: Michel, 1980), 48. Sometimes another French discussion is cited as an early interlocutor, namely, Émile Gillabert, *Saint Paul: Ou Le Colosse aux pieds d'argile* (Marsanne: Métanoïa, 1974). The attribution of this interpretation to Gillabert is based on a misunderstanding. Rossman (*Sexual Experience between Men and Boys*, 230 n. 14) lists a single source (i.e., Martignac) for the homoerotic interpretation of the pericope, but because Rossman's discussion involved a conversation with a gnostic monk, he cited the work of Gillabert as a discussion of neo-Gnosticism for those interested in that particular topic. Those who mistakenly interpreted Rossman's citation of Gillabert as a discussion of the centurion include Horner, *Jonathan Loved David*, 122 n. 24; Mader, "*Entimos Pais*," 233 n. 6. I am aware of other French interpretations that I have been unable to procure due to a combination of the global pandemic and the obscurity of some of the publications. For instance, the Catholic communist periodical *Masses Ouvrières* printed a letter to the editor favoring the homoerotic interpretation from a priest around this time.

36. Though gender identification practices have changed immensely since then, many of those arrested might be thought of as precursors to transgender women or drag queens—temporarily dressing in feminine clothing and adopting a feminine

For instance, a police report claimed that a knight of the imperial guard named Monsieur Cabanier "had [sexual] relations with other *pédérastes* who were known by women's names," that he "often came to the Hôtel de l'Alma, and that in asking about the civilian *pédérastes* who frequented the place, [Cabanier] would often say, 'Isn't there a single one here tonight?'" The report ultimately concluded, "Cabanier is a *pédéraste*."[37] One criminologist of the time, François Carlier, used the term to describe adult men performing oral sex at urinals in Paris: "When the pederasts had adopted this as a meeting place, they drilled little holes in the partitions that allowed those in neighboring stalls to commit acts of public indecency."[38] Carlier's book, of course, explicitly promoted the legal prohibition of same-sex intercourse, with an intended readership of police officers.

As this period came to an end, the legal language of pederast slowly gave way to the medical terminology of *sexual inversion* and eventually *homosexual*.[39] That is to say, same-sex desire had previously been classified as a strictly *criminal act* but came to be understood as a deviant *pathology* that might be diagnosed and studied to save the afflicted individual. As Daniel Borrillo notes, "the doctor was no longer solely the judge's ally in assessing the reality of the offence in order to punish it, but took on the mission of better understanding, better defining, even curing, and at least, protecting society from the scourge that threatened it."[40] Concomitant with Germans thinking similarly about "der Homosexuell" and Anglophones "the homosexual," France saw the emergence of a combined medical and criminal discourse on "l'homosexuel" during the

---

persona at such venues. See Halberstam, *Queer Time and Place*, 47–75 for helpful thoughts on characterization of the trans past.

37. Translation from Scott Gunther, *The Elastic Closet: A History of Homosexuality in France, 1942–Present* (Basingstoke: Palgrave Macmillan, 2009), 19.

38. François Carlier, *Études de Pathologie Sociale: Les Deux Prostitutions* (Paris: Dentu, 1887), 304. Translation from Julian Jackson, *Living in Arcadia: Homosexuality, Politics, and Morality in France from Liberation to AIDS* (Chicago: University of Chicago Press, 2009), 23.

39. Patrice Corriveau, *Judging Homosexuals: A History of Gay Persecution in Quebec and France*, trans. Käthe Roth, Sexuality Studies (Vancouver: University of British Columbia Press, 2011); Corriveau also notes that the legal terminology of pederast itself replaced earlier theological terminology of sodomite, each reflecting changing interests and subjectivities associated with same-sex desire in France.

40. Daniel Borrillo, *L'homophobie*, Que sais-je? (Paris: Presses Universitaires de France, 2001), 65. Translation from Corriveau, *Judging Homosexuals*, 62.

Third Republic (1875–1940).[41] This focus on innate features of the psyche proved influential and would become integral to the present-day notion of sexual orientation; today, the act of intercourse is deemed secondary to questions of identity: a man can, say, identify as bisexual even if he remains entirely chaste, or a woman may realize she is a lesbian despite only having slept with men to that point. One's sexual experiences have no inherent connection to sexual identities under the rubric of orientation that prevails today.[42] The notion that sexual preferences might be innate (and thus a matter of identity) has its genesis in this period's transition away from largely criminal understandings of homoeroticism toward medical discourses.[43]

---

41. The following discussion relies heavily upon the excellent work of Gunther, *Elastic Closet*, 1–65; Jackson, *Living in Arcadia*; Corriveau, *Judging Homosexuals*; Julian Bourg, *From Revolution to Ethics: May 1968 and Contemporary French Thought*, 2nd ed. (Montreal: McGill-Queen's University Press, 2017), 204–23; Jean Bérard and Nicolas Sallé, "The Ages of Consent: Gay Activism and the Sexuality of Minors in France and Quebec (1970–1980)," *Clio* 42 (2015): 99–124.

42. This, of course, does not preclude sexual subjectivities in earlier times. I quote here the somewhat dated narrative of David M. Halperin, *One Hundred Years of Homosexuality and Other Essays on Greek Love* (New York: Routledge, 1990), 8–9: "A certain identification of the self with the sexual 'self' began in late antiquity; it was strengthened by the Christian confessional. Only in the high middle ages did certain kinds of sexual acts start to get identified with certain specifically sexual types of person: a 'sodomite' begins to name not merely the person who commits an act of sodomy but one distinguished by a certain type of specifically sexual subjectivity which includes such a person to commit those acts; nonetheless, sodomy remains a sinful act which any person, given sufficient temptation, may be induced to commit. In London and Paris, in the seventeenth and eighteenth centuries, there appear—evidently for the first time, and in conjunction with the rise of companionate marriage—social gathering-places for persons of the same sex with the same socially deviant attitudes to sex and gender who wish to socialize and to have sex with one another. In London, these are the so-called molly-houses, where men dress as women and assume women's names. This phenomenon contributes to the formation of the great nineteenth-century experience of 'sexual inversion,' or sex-role reversal, in which some forms of deviance are interpreted as, or conflated with, gender deviance. The emergence of homosexuality out of inversion, the formation of a sexual orientation independent of relative degrees of masculinity and femininity, takes place during the latter part of the nineteenth century and comes into its own only in the twentieth." Only after WW II did sexual orientation become the predominant rubric for classifying homoerotic desires.

43. To provide a concrete example, the Roman Catholic Church has long banned priests from partaking in same-sex intercourse, even beyond its broader policy of

The shift from legal classification of "the pederast" to medical classification of "the homosexual" was slow, and the two understandings of homoerotic desire coexisted for some time. A cottage industry of French medico-criminologists drew upon a variety of in-vogue sciences (e.g., psychiatry, morphology) to identify and regulate the subjects of their analysis. Ambroise Tardieu wrote the following assessment, rivaling the self-assured incredulity of his contemporaries in the field of phrenology.

> The characteristic signs of passive pederasty, which we will look at in succession, are the excessive development of the buttocks, the infundibular (funnel-shaped) deformation of the anus, the relaxation of the sphincter.... It is on the virile member that we expect to find the mark of active habits. The dimensions of the penis on individuals who participate as the active partner in sodomy are either very spindly or very voluminous.[44]

Tardieu's works were widely cited and provided the legal framework for much of the following period.

But despite the terminological shift from pederast to the more neutral designation homosexual, the period leading up to and including the Second World War was marked by widespread insistence that homosexual men corrupted French youth. Such claims commonly cited the nation's fall to the Germans as evidence that effeminate young men were symptomatic of the French nation-state's fallen stature, having been seduced by queer predators. Thus, when the novelist Robert Brasillach was arrested for soliciting a young man, the police chief told Brasillach that his kind was

---

sexual celibacy; the fourteenth canon of the Fourth Lateran Council (1215) put in place a policy that defrocked any priest who held Mass after committing unchastity, "especially that on account of which the anger of God came from heaven upon the children of unbelief committed," which is to say, the so-called sin of Sodom. However, more recent Catholic policy has shifted away from focus on individual acts of sexual misconduct and toward identities marked by sinful desires. The 1961 papal document *Instruction on the Careful Selection and Training of Candidates for the States of Perfection and Sacred Orders* 30.4 articulated a significantly different policy, one that barred "those who are afflicted with evil tendencies to homosexuality" from priesthood, regardless of whether or not they ever performed any act of same-sex intercourse; orientation and identity became prioritized over actions. Chapter 2 discusses similar shifts of interest from actions to identities in American military policies.

44. Ambroise Tardieu, *Étude médico-légale sur les attentats aux moeurs*, 6th ed. (Paris: Baillère, 1873). Translation from Gunther, *Elastic Closet*, 20–21.

responsible for the defeat.[45] Jean-Paul Sartre likewise wrote an article about French collaborators, wherein he claimed that "one will find throughout their articles curious metaphors presenting the relations between France and Germany under the guise of a sexual union where France plays the role of the woman.... It seems to me that there is in all this a curious mixture of masochism and homosexuality. The homosexual milieu of Paris has moreover provided numerous and brilliant recruits to collaboration."[46] While Sartre's rhetoric contested Nazi claims of masculine virility, it was abetted by a deep homophobia.

Despite widespread contempt for homosexual men, there had been no legal distinction between heterosexual and homosexual intercourse in France since 1791—what was legal between a man and a woman had been legal between two men or two women since before Napoleon's reign. This changed in 1942, when Philippe Pétain, chief of state in Nazi-occupied Vichy France, unilaterally imposed new regulations regarding the age of majority (Article 334 of the French penal code). No doubt aware that French sensibilities required there be a victim for any act to constitute a crime, Pétain did not directly criminalize homosexual intercourse but instead drew upon this widespread sense that French youth were victims of predatory homosexuals. Pétain thus specified the age of consent as twenty-one years of age for homosexual intercourse, distinct from thirteen years for heterosexual intercourse (raised to fifteen years in 1945). Two matters make clear that this was a pretense to criminalize homosexuality and not a sincere effort to protect children from sexual abuse. First, vague phrasing of the law meant that *any* deed that could be construed as "indecent or unnatural" constituted a crime. Second, and more importantly, this law dictated the age of all sexual partners involved: even if *both* partners were younger than twenty-one years of age, they were guilty of statutory rape. Consequently, any Frenchman who had sex with, say, a twenty-year-old man after 1942 was deemed a pederast, *even if he himself was twenty years old.*

This is significant: whereas today discourse on pederasty and pedophilia tends to focus on relationships marked by sexual exploitation or

---

45. Jackson, *Living in Arcadia*, 39–43. Cf. Michael Sibalis, "Homophobia, Vichy France, and the 'Crime of Homosexuality': The Origins of the Ordinance of 6 August 1942," *GLQ* 8 (2002): 301–18.

46. Jean-Paul Sartre, "Qu'est-ce qu'un collaborateur," *Situations* 3 (1949): 58. Translation from Jackson, *Living in Arcadia*, 42. Decades later Sartre would adopt a much more friendly stance to queer people.

abuse (i.e., adult-child intercourse), French calls to legalize pederasty often focused on the right of peers to engage in sexual intercourse. The demands of the radical youth organization Front Homosexuel d'Action Révolutionnaire (FHAR), for instance, included "rights for minors to freedom of desire and its fulfillment."[47] Whereas those who want to lower the age of consent today largely comprise adults who make no secret about their desire to have sex with children below the current legal age (and thus teenage or even prepubescent children), the matter was pointedly different in postwar France: (1) youth were significant participants in protests against age of consent laws because such legislation rendered intercourse with people their own age illegal; (2) at least initially, there was little discussion about lowering the already-low heterosexual age of consent, as activism concerned the legality of same-sex intercourse.

French homophile readings of the centurion at Capernaum are most productively understood in this legal context. The act of designating the centurion a pederast was a political move that tapped into a variety of overlapping sentiments. There is much to be said, but there were four particular ways the centurion proved a valuable ally in this crusade.

First, the term pederast reappropriated an outdated term of abuse specific to French culture from the nineteenth century as a self-identifier. Pederasty was already proximate to homophiles due to the Vichy legislation; homophile men claimed ownership of the term in order to diffuse its polemical value and imbue it with a more positive meaning. French homophiles were hardly the only ones to do so, as one thinks of English reclamation of the word *queer*, a term that had long been derisive, as a point of identification. This reappropriation proclaims, "this is how they see us," with its corollary "but we are not ashamed of ourselves."

The term pederast also hearkened to imagined precursors from antiquity, including Socrates, Hadrian, Theognis, and other renowned men of yore. While many homophile writers considered themselves hellenophiles, this frequent look to the past proved a point of contention, especially within the pages of *Arcadie*, the venue where Martignac and Mayer published their readings of the pericope.[48] On the one hand, the

---

47. Quoted in Neil Miller, *Out of the Past: Gay and Lesbian History from 1869 to the Present* (New York: Vintage, 1995), 393.

48. For more on Greco-Roman antiquity as a means of authorizing homophile politics, see Richlin, "Eros Underground"; Maria Wyke, "Herculean Muscle! The Classicizing Rhetoric of Bodybuilding," *Arion* 3/4.3 (1997): 51–79.

very title of the journal hearkened to the mythical Arcadia, the utopic land of pastoralism and harmonious life with nature in the Greek Peloponnese. *Arcadie* framed itself as a "literary and scientific review" on the cover;[49] contributors could thus safely assume that readers were not only conversant in classical history but literate in the languages of Greece and Rome. Mayer thus included the pericope in its Koine Greek and Latin Vulgate forms in his article, some of which was left untranslated.[50] Many other articles in *Arcadie* excavated homoeroticism from ancient literature, so in some sense the articles of Mayer and Martignac were unremarkable. On the other hand, many readers found this preoccupation with antiquity frustrating: one *Arcadie* contributor asserted that classical pederasty was "in no way similar to what we mean today by that word."[51] Another contributor to *Arcadie* was more direct and claimed, "it is absurd every time one falls in love with a boy to call classical Greece to the rescue."[52] This is not to mention how *Arcadie* adopted a policy of religious and political neutrality; theological topics were usually outsourced to the Christian homophile journal *David et Jonathan* (founded 1973), which is somewhat surprising given that the founder of *Arcadie*, André Baudry, was himself a former Catholic seminarian.[53] Thus, although the topics of religion and

---

49. "Revue Littéraire et Scientifique." This subtitle was used from the journal's inception in 1954 until August 1975. See figure 1.

50. See especially Mayer, "Le procurateur de Judée," 70–71.

51. Pierre Nedra, "'L'amour grec' et 'Eros socraticus,'" *Arcadie* 84 (1960): 707. Translation from Jackson, *Living in Arcadia*, 118.

52. Franco Cerutti, "L'homosexualité dans les lettres italiennes contemporaines," *Arcadie* 67–68 (1959): 411. Translation from Jackson, *Living in Arcadia*, 117.

53. Baudry articulated his complicated feelings about his time in seminary thus: "There are in Arcadie a considerable number of former seminarians (former priests as well).... He who has left the seminary because of his homophilia will always keep at the bottom of his heart a nostalgia for what he had believed to be his destiny.... I have always found among homophiles who have lived in the very special atmosphere of the seminary a fundamental inaptitude in adapting to the homophile life." André Baudry, "L'homophile catholique," *Arcadie* 142 (1965): 421. Translation from Jackson, *Living in Arcadia*, 58. Little has been written in English about David et Jonathan (another combination journal-organization). On its history, see Mickaël Durand, "From Tension to Reconciliation: A Look at the History and Rituals of the French Organization David et Jonathan," in *Diversidad sexual y sistemas religiosos: Diálogos trasnacionales en el mundo contemporáneo*, ed. Martín Jaime Ballero (Lima: Centro de la Mujer Peruana Flora Tristán, 2017), 155–80. Cf. Hélène Buisson-Fenet, *Un sexe problématique:*

ancient history were touchy within the pages of the journal, the centurion permitted another antique precursor for homophile readers.

Second, the centurion provided an anchor for a specific type of homophile subculture within French queerdom, one serving the distinctive interests of *Arcadie*. The 1960s and 1970s saw the fragmentation of queer subcultures that were no longer mutually constitutive but in many ways only overlapping and often even antagonistic. The shared interests that had previously bound together homophile, lesbian, drag, trans, sex-worker, cruising, and other subcultures became increasingly distinct, such that many homophiles sought to distance themselves from seemingly less respectable queer bodies for political expediency. Some homophiles saw an opportunity to gain legal and social recognition by distancing themselves from queers they deemed a liability, instead claiming affinity with the mainstream heterosexual culture. The articles published in *Arcadie* did not merely reflect this fragmentation but actively facilitated these divisions. The editorial staff of the journal insisted on political neutrality and traditional understandings of dignity, entailing a default conservatism. Particularly important to *Arcadie* was cultivating an understanding of masculinity as self-mastery; Baudry, for instance, sought to distance homosexuals from the "mannered, rouged, squealing boys who too much exemplified homophilia before the last war."[54] Effeminacy was a particular blight on the homophile cause according to Arcadians, who charged that such lack of self-respect impeded social acceptance of same-sex desire. This chauvinism was hardly confined to *Arcadie*; though the journal and its founder was particularly insistent on the matter, Julian Jackson observes that the same sentiment was fully articulated in other French homophile journals like *Juventus* and *Futur*, not to mention homophile publications abroad like the American *Mattachine Review* and the German *Der Kreis*.[55]

L'église et l'homosexualité masculine en France, 1971–2000, Culture et Société (Saint-Denis: Presses universitaires de Vincennes, 2004).

54. André Baudry, "Comiques ou martyrs," *Arcadie* 69 (1959): 465. Translation from Jackson, *Living in Arcadia*, 125; Jackson observes that contributors commonly expressed such sentiments.

55. Jackson, *Living in Arcadia*, 125–26, with citations. However, Martin Meeker argues that such respectability politics merely served as a façade "to deflect the antagonisms of its many detractors" for the *Mattachine Review* and cautions against overstating the radicalism or conservatism of pre-Stonewall homophile organizations. See Martin Meeker, "Behind the Mask of Respectability: Reconsidering the Mattachine Society and Male Homophile Practice, 1950s and 1960s," *JHSex* 10 (2001): 78–116.

So strict were the gender norms at *Arcadie* that when it opened a clubhouse, kissing was banned from the dance floor. Public displays of affection signaled a failure to embody the self-discipline that Baudry deemed essential to the homophile cause.

Many French queers resented Arcadie's enforcement of patriarchal gender norms. FHAR, for instance, gathered a chorus to sing a song to the tune of the French Christmas carol "Il est né, le divin Enfant" in 1971. The lyrics mocked the Arcadian promises of "paradise" and instead presented FHAR as a new movement with more progressive gender politics: "Let us sing, queers, let us play, pansies."[56] FHAR was founded earlier that year by lesbians frustrated with the masculinist politics of *Arcadie* and the system of respectability that the group sponsored. The politics of gender were contentious within French queerdom, and the image of a centurion was easily incorporated into the understanding of masculinity and homosexuality that *Arcadie* sought to cultivate.

The matter can be pressed even further: the nascent feminist inflection of French gay discourse put a strong emphasis on the category of rape, something that proved inimical to homophile celebration of pederasty.[57] Homophiles tended to deride *consent* as a contractual term that mischaracterized participation in physical passion, whereas feminists often pointed to an inseparable mix of violence, power, and sexualization when it comes to the exploitation of children. Representative of this controversy is an exchange at a 1977 television roundtable between Michel Foucault and feminist activists Marine Zecca and Marie-Odile Faye, wherein Foucault advocated the abolition of both age of consent laws and rape as a legally distinct form of assault.

> Foucault: One can always hold to the theoretical discourse of saying: "sexuality cannot be in any case an object of punishment." And to say that it is nothing more than an assault, and nothing else: that one shoves his fist in someone's mouth,

---

56. For the original French and a translation of the full song, see Frédéric Martel, *The Pink and the Black: Homosexuals in France Since 1968*, trans. Jane Marie Todd (Stanford: Stanford University Press, 1999), 62. For discussion of French reaction to the Stonewall Riots and nascent gay-rights movement, see Keith Harvey, *Intercultural Movements: American Gay in French Translation*, Encounters 3 (London: Routledge, 2014).

57. See especially the discussion of the matter in Bourg, *From Revolution to Ethics*, 204–23.

	or his penis in someone's privates, that does not make a difference. But first, I'm not sure that women would agree.
Zecca:	Not so much, no. Not at all, even.
Foucault:	So you admit there is a "strictly sexual" offense.
Zecca:	Ah, yes.
Faye:	For all the little girls who have been assaulted, in a public garden, in the subway, in all these experiences of everyday life, at eight, ten, or twelve years; very traumatizing.…
…	
Foucault:	I'm tempted to say: from the moment that the child doesn't refuse, there is no reason to punish any act.[58]

While Foucault cannot be reduced to a mouthpiece for homophile politics,[59] his reductive understanding of sexual violence speaks to a significant division between feminist and homophile sexual/gender politics.

The centurion may be understood as serving a function within queer debates about gender practices in light of these tensions. Martignac offers the following characterization of the centurion at Capernaum:

> When one sees him walking down the main thoroughfare, he radiates the power of the immense empire. One both reveres and fears him. But

---

58. Translation combining those of Marta Soler-Gallart, *Achieving Social Impact: Sociology in the Public Sphere*, SpringerBriefs in Sociology (Berlin: Springer, 2017), 54 n. 10; Bourg, *From Revolution to Ethics*, 215, edited for clarity. Foucault continued to make assertions in the vein of rape-apologetics during that same exchange, such as claiming that it was impossible to make a child "do what he or she doesn't really want to." Note also the recent accusation that Foucault paid Tunisian boys for sex; Matthew Campbell, "French Philosopher Michel Foucault 'Abused Boys in Tunisia,'" *The Sunday Times*, 28 March 2021.

59. Foucault's apathy toward feminism and tendency to overlook feminist critique of his own work has been discussed extensively. Despite Foucault's reputation for provocation and sympathies for FHAR, he was on good terms with Arcadie. Martel, *Pink and the Black*, 110–11, 395; David Macey, *The Lives of Michel Foucault: A Biography* (New York: Pantheon, 1994), 362–64 both note Foucault's affinities for Arcadie; among them: Foucault participated in Arcadie's twenty-fifth anniversary congress, when asked why he never joined Arcadie he responded that he had been "wrong not to do so," he was friends with its founder André Baudry (having dined together several times), and he wrote a gentle (though pseudonymous) reflection about the magazine/organization after it folded in July 1982, comparing Baudry to Moses in the process (see its reprint and discussion in Didier Eribon, *Michel Foucault et ses contemporains* [Paris: Fayard, 1994], 274–79).

he also elicits admiration and a certain affection. Like [Joseph] Gallieni in Madagascar or [Hubert] Lyautey in Morocco, this great colonial authority—with an intelligent paternalism—takes an active interest in those whom he governs. Respecting their customs, he similarly encourages their religion. Both the civil and religious authorities of the village are grateful to him, we are told, because "he loves our nation and it is he who built us our synagogue." ... His authority is reinforced, his "dignity" confirmed: a true sovereign in the eyes of the citizens.[60]

The description of the centurion's masculinity sounds suspiciously like the self-description of Arcadians: he is a man of letters, quiet dignity, and self-respect. Indeed, his closest analogues are themselves great men of the French military. There is little doubt that the author of the article conceived of himself in such terms: the author's pseudonym, "J. Martignac," points to Jean-Baptiste de Martignac, a French military officer who served at the turn of the nineteenth century.

In all of this, though, the state hardly warrants any positive feelings and does not elicit unconditional allegiance. At its best, the state has the (failed) capacity to confer dignity. Accordingly, no homophile interpretations of the centurion express interest in the contemporary military. The military *had been* a site of French excellence where noble men of olden times made their careers. Indeed, there is an implicit antagonism toward the state in most of his discussion, usually understanding it as another homophobic institution. Mayer's centurion comments on how "the law" (*la loi*) in the region where he is stationed forbids his love of the Pais.[61] Notably, *la loi* is lowercase throughout Mayer's article and never mentioned alongside Moses: it is not a proper noun denoting Torah or anything religious but functions in a strictly legal-criminal sense. Martignac is more direct, seeing a clear analogy to the 1968 French riots, a period of unrest marked by widespread worker-strikes, riots, and police violence, nearly culminating in another revolution.

> It is stunning and scandalous for all the witnesses. First, he confesses this strange agitator as "Lord!" A further outrage: [the centurion says to Jesus] "I am not WORTHY that you should enter under my roof!" From the potentate to the vagabond! From the domineering soldier to a preacher! What a reversal of their respective social positions.... Keep-

---

60. Martignac, "Le centurion de Capernaüm," 120–21. Translated by Morgan Bell.
61. Mayer, "Le procurateur de Judée," 67.

ing things proportionate, let's imagine [French Prime Minister Georges] Pompidou, in May '68, calling out to [student activist Daniel] Cohn-Bendit "Lord" or "Master, I am not worthy that you should enter under my roof!"[62]

It is striking that Martignac identifies Jesus analogically with an anarchist who served as the public face of the 1968 riots and speaks to the lingering hostility between the state apparatus and homophiles. Even though there is little to indicate that Martignac was sympathetic to the protests, this image nevertheless confronts the reader with Martignac's resentments against the French legal system.

A third point concerns the appeal of a *pagan* homophile. This non-Christian and non-Jewish centurion was convenient for French secularity (*laïcité*). That France, a country proud of its secular norms, was nevertheless beholden to religious sexual mores is a clear subtext: why would those who pride themselves on their enlightenment render themselves beholden to the worst rules that religion has to offer? Thus, Martignac:

> Fearing that Jesus was still entrenched in legalistic and ecclesiastical moralism, [the centurion] senses that this "Lord" is not abolishing the Law [*la Loi*—note capitalization], but is fulfilling it by transcending it in love. He believes that Jesus is capable of overcoming all the "taboos" of his own religion and of acting miraculously, even at the request of a pagan, and—scandalously—of a pederastic pagan without the least social acceptance.[63]

Martignac seems to push the point even farther: why should this religious legalism impede those have no such scruples, if no one is being harmed? Martignac suggests that religion in its truest form liberates rather than restricts physical expressions of love.

---

62. Martignac, "Le centurion de Capernaüm," 123. Translated by Morgan Bell. Note that Cohn-Bendit, now a German politician, published multiple texts in the 1970 and 1980s wherein he claimed to have had sexual interactions with young children; he now asserts that these stories were nothing more than "obnoxious provocation" and do not describe actual events. See Christian Füller, "Danys Phantasien und Träume," *Frankfurter Allgemeine Zeitung*, 29 April 2013; Anonymous, "Pedophilia Accusations Haunt Green Politician," *Deutsche Welle*, 4 May 2013.

63. Martignac, "Le centurion de Capernaüm," 126. Translated by Morgan Bell.

Homophile interpreters were disproportionately non-Christian or at least publishing in venues whose tenor was not identifiably Christian. Homophile interpreters frequently framed themselves like they do the centurion: outsiders to Judeo-Christianity, seeking only the end of discrimination by those deemed more religious. In effect, saying to homophobic Christians: isn't it queer that your own Bible depicts Jesus healing a homophile without judgment? Jesus does not *endorse* their relationship in French interpretations, unlike later readings. Rather, French homophile interpretations regard as sufficient that Jesus does not care one way or another.

Finally, and most complicated, is that because French law dictated an unreasonable age of majority of twenty-one, there was widespread disagreement on what a sensible age should be. The egregiously discriminatory law had prompted a public debate about the age of consent in France, albeit without an obvious solution. France reduced the age of consent for homosexual intercourse to eighteen in 1974, but the matter was sufficiently contentious that it remained the subject of civic concern. Three Frenchmen—Bernard Dejager, Jean-Claude Gallien, and Jean Burckardt—confessed to having intercourse with boys and girls aged thirteen–fourteen years in 1973 and were jailed for three years while awaiting trial. Foucault said the case revealed the tensions within the French legal system: children thirteen years old were legally incapable of consenting to sexual intercourse but were permitted to purchase contraceptives and regarded as legally culpable for their own actions.[64] Many influential French intellectuals signed a series of petitions calling for the abolition of age of consent laws. Signatories included names that will be familiar even to those with no knowledge of French political activism: Foucault, Roland Barthes, Jacques Derrida, Louis Althusser, Jean-Paul Sartre, Simone de Beauvoir, Gilles Deleuze, Félix Guattari, Jean-François Lyotard, and *Arcadie* founder André Baudry, among dozens of others, signed on. The signatures of two theologians—a Lutheran pastor of modest importance within Paris named G. Berner and a former Prior of the Boquen Abbey named

---

64. Michel Foucault, "Sexual Morality and the Law," in *Politics, Philosophy, Culture: Interviews and Other Writings 1977–1984*, ed. Lawrence D. Kritzman, trans. Alan Sheridan (London: Routledge, 1988), 271–85, an interview that aired on the French television program *Dialogues* in 1978. Foucault's interest in the matter, perhaps predictably, concerned how age of consent laws produce both criminal subjects and children incapable of agency.

Jean-Claude Besret—were present alongside the aforementioned luminaries. Notably, Guy Hocquenghem, who briefly discussed the homoerotic interpretation, was also among the signatories.[65] These petitions were published in *Le Monde*, the French newspaper of record.[66] Although age of consent abolitionists did not win the day, the age of majority was reduced to fifteen years in 1982, creating parity between heterosexual and homosexual ages of consent.

Returning to French interpretations of the pericope, one notices how different interpretations depict the Pais's age. Marcel Eck was careful to note the shocking nature of the age disparity between the centurion and the *eromenos* Pais was merely a priori, as in fact these younger lovers were *jeunes éphèbes*—young ephebes—denoting males at the lower end of seventeen–twenty years old.[67] Martignac, by contrast, determines that the Pais was barely an adolescent: "The three evangelists agree in seeing him as 'a young boy' [*jeune garçon*], we would say: an adolescent [*adolescent*], at the beginning rather than the end of adolescence."[68] Mayer is most specific, narrating in his fictional episode that the centurion "brought back a boy from a trip to Bithynia, about fifteen years old and of incomparable beauty."[69] Rossman translated his monk's phrasing into English, only describing the Pais as "adolescent," presumably corresponding to its French cognate.[70] These discrepancies, regardless of their grounding in different understanding of biblical and social-historical evidence, are intelligible within this conversation about the appropriate age of consent for homosexual intercourse: Eck tending toward seventeen or so, Mayer explicitly stating fifteen years, Rossman's monk a youth between thirteen and sixteen years, and Martignac depicting the Pais youngest, imagining someone around thirteen–fourteen years old. Martignac's interpretation is particularly striking, as it corresponds to the ages of the children exploited by the three French-

---

65. Hocquenghem, *Le gay voyage*, 48.

66. Anonymous, "À propos d'un procès," *Le Monde* 26 January 1977; Anonymous, "Un appel pour la révision du code pénal à propos des relations mineurs-adultes," *Le Monde*, 23 May 1977.

67. Eck, *Sodome*, 47, 266. Eck also distinguishes between pederasty (a teaching relationship between an experienced lover and someone of this age) and pedophilia (which targets prepubescent children).

68. Martignac, "Le centurion de Capernaüm," 123. Translated by Morgan Bell.

69. Mayer, "Le procurateur de Judée," 66. Translated by Morgan Bell.

70. Rossman, *Sexual Experience between Men and Boys*, 99.

men (i.e., Dejager, Gallien, and Burckardt) whose then-recent arrest prompted the petitions noted above. The varying age of the Pais speaks to the different perspectives on the limits of acceptable pederasty and where the law might properly delimit the age of consent.

This final point should direct our attention to a shift occurring within discourse on pederasty over the course of the 1970s and 1980s: as the age of consent reduced, youth-oriented activism (involving, e.g., university students, FHAR) declined, and discussions of pederasty increasingly took the form of adults pleading for the decriminalization of their own efforts to have sex with children. That is to say, eighteen- to twenty-year-olds understandably protested against laws that criminalized their same-sex intercourse when the age of consent was twenty-one, but it is harder to imagine large numbers of fifteen- to seventeen-year-olds finding this a political cause worthy of their time after the age of consent was reduced to eighteen. Much less so when it finally reached its nadir with fifteen. At that point, there is no evidence of youth under the age of consent involved in such protests, even though self-identified pederasts insisted that age of consent laws were an infringement upon children's rights. Though the idea of a *pederast* centurion and his love for the underage Pais was politically expedient for many homophiles in the 1960s and early 1970s, he came to serve increasingly narrow interests as the age of same-sex consent lowered. Indeed, the interests the pederast centurion came to serve warrant not only our suspicion, but unequivocal condemnation.

Figure 2 (following page). Citation Genealogy for Homophile Readings of the Pericope. The chart is tiered by decade of an author's initial reference to the centurion's homoerotic relationship and indicates sources used in their first publication on the topic, along with language of initial publication. Dotted lines indicate an author stated that they had not personally read the source but cited it for further reading. The diagram includes nearly all references to the homoerotic reading of the passage until 1985 as well as a few post-1985 readings that are usefully characterized as homophile. See appendix 2 for bibliographic references and relevant excerpts of most of these texts.

58 THE CENTURION AT CAPERNAUM

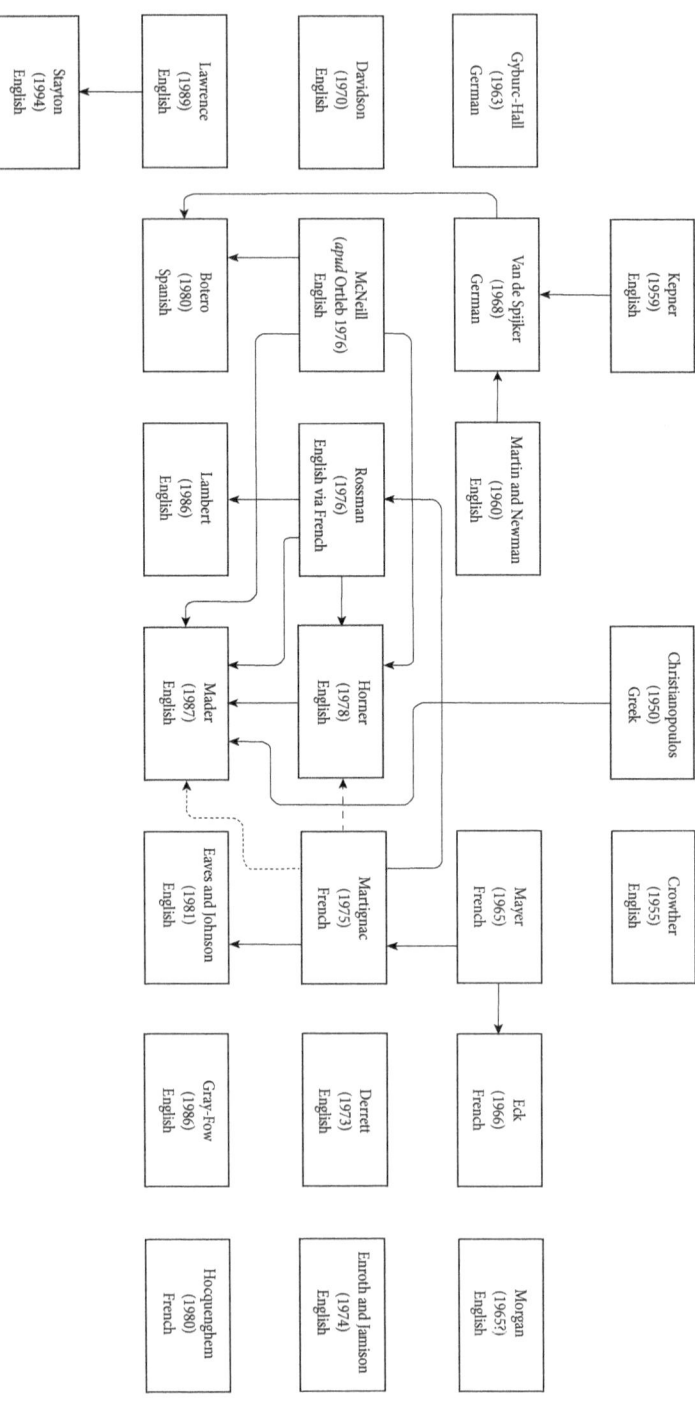

Two Contemporaneous Readings by Americans, at Home and Expatriated

The legal and cultural specificity of the French homophile reading was sufficiently particular that most early homoerotic readings of the passage in English consistently sidestep this pederastic subtext. For instance, in 1978 Tom Horner cited Martignac's and Rossman's interpretations but said only:

> There are, in fact, two hints in the Gospels which indicate that [Jesus] would not have been hostile. The first is the possible homosexual motif in the story of the healing of the centurion's servant (Matthew 8:5–13 and Luke 7:1–10). It has always seemed to me that it was more than an ordinary concern that this Roman official displayed in this case for a mere slave. Luke uses here the word *doulos*, "slave." This has not at all the same connotation as in Matthew. In either case, however, Jesus made no note of it, which means that if the homosexual element were present, he was not disturbed by it. Instead, he was overwhelmed by the man's faith, which is clearly the paramount element in the story.[71]

The absence of the category of pederasty, vital to both of the secondary sources that Horner cites, is conspicuous. In an interview with the New York magazine *Christopher Street*, John McNeill similarly observed in 1976: "There is one curious story of the Roman centurion whose boy servant is ill. Jesus is asked to cure him. It is said that the centurion loved the boy very deeply; one could read into it a homosexual relationship."[72] Notably, Horner and McNeill were apparently unaware of the pericope's homoeroticism when writing their earlier—and extensive—monographs discussing homosexuality and the New Testament.[73] Both Horner and McNeill first encountered this reading of the passage through homophile writers who foregrounded the issue of pederasty, even if Horner

---

71. Horner, *Jonathan Loved David*, 122, 143 n. 24.

72. Quoted in Charles Ortleb, "God and Gays: A New Team," *Christopher Street* 1.4 (1976): 27.

73. Horner, *Sex in the Bible*; John J. McNeill, *The Church and the Homosexual* (Boston: Beacon, 1976). McNeill would later cede that "the Greek words used for the relationship are the same words, so a scholar friend of mine claims, as those used in Greek culture for the love of an older man for a younger man." John J. McNeill, "Positive Messages from the Bible," *Advent: Lutherans Concerned/San Francisco* 11.4 (1989): 10–11, possibly referring to Mader as the friend in question. McNeill eventually shied away from this pederastic subtext once again, as we will see in chapter 2.

and McNeill ignored or downplayed this topic. Donald H. Mader, who also emphasized a pederastic subtext, claimed the personal suggestion of McNeill as the impetus for publishing his influential 1987 article on the pericope.[74] Other English-language interpreters who refer to the centurion's pederasty treat it as something distinctive to cultures of antiquity and discourage any tacit endorsement of its practice in the present.[75] We will see in chapter 2 that the emphasis on youthfulness created further complications in Anglophone contexts.

There are, however, two English-language interpretations wherein the authors not only insist that the centurion engaged in pederasty but advance a normative politics of pedophilic acceptance within a modern context. That is to say, the homophile failure to consider matters of power when interpreting this pericope was not merely relegated to the realm of erotic fantasy or legal possibility but demonstrably connected to disturbing actions in two instances.

First is the single most widely cited article advocating a homoerotic reading of the passage, Mader's article "The *Entimos Pais* of Matthew 8:5-13 and Luke 7:1-10." Mader's article is best known from the reprint anthology *Homosexuality and Religion and Philosophy*, edited by Wayne R. Dynes and Stephen Donaldson.[76] The article was initially published in the inaugural issue of a journal named *Paidika: Journal of Paedophilia*, even if the reprint in the less-scandalously-titled volume is more commonly cited. Lest one speculate about the journal's purpose, its blurb asserted that the periodical is a sustained effort "to examine the range of cultural, historical, psychological, and literary issues pertaining to consensual adult-child sexual relationships and desires." Though the journal presented itself as academic, the advertisements within its pages left no doubt about the interests of its intended readership. Mader is an ordained minister who has been an outspoken advocate for "boylove" and founded a publishing house that specialized in such literature called "Entimos Press," the name of which

---

74. Mader, "*Entimos Pais*," 233 n. 6.
75. Stayton, "Pederasty in Ancient and Early Christian History," 439. Cf. Gray-Fow, "Pederasty," 457, who places the gospels among a wide range of attitudes toward the practice of pederasty in the early Roman Empire; Lawrence, *Poisoning of Eros*, 73 clarifies, after noting this and other possibly sexual elements within the gospels, that "all this sensuous attention to the body does not quite add up to a modern American orgy."
76. Mader, "*Entimos Pais*."

refers to the *entimos* Pais of the centurion at Capernaum. An American expatriate to the Netherlands, he was the first person arrested on the country's strengthened laws about child pornography. Around the time Mader moved to the Netherlands, a legal loophole rendered child pornography legal across that nation; Mader cited the country's open-mindedness about sexuality as the reason for his immigration. This loophole closed, and newspapers report that Mader has been repeatedly arrested for taking and exhibiting nude portraits of boys, with one incident concerning a collection of over two thousand nude photographs.[77] Following each instance of arrest, to be clear, Mader was acquitted, or his conviction was overturned.

There seems to be a pervasive lack of awareness about the sexual politics of Mader's article, as it hard to imagine that this article would be regularly cited if its advocacy of boylove were seriously acknowledged. While Mader concedes that "this passage will not allow us to reach any sweeping conclusions about Jesus' attitudes toward paederasty,"[78] the article's closing words adopt a prescriptive tone.

> The issue is not, however, whether historically there were positive, nurturing relationships—which there surely were—or destructive, dehumanizing ones—which there also surely were—nor even in what proportion they existed. With the discovery of a New Testament passage which suggests an attitude of toleration toward a non-exploitive, caring paederastic relationship, the focus must move back to where it always should have been: that it is not homosexuality, or paederasty, or any other specific sexual relationship that Christian ethics condemns, but dehumanization and exploitation of another person in any relationship, heterosexual or homosexual, intragenerational or intergenerational.[79]

---

77. See Anonymous, "Kinderfoto's Mader: Kunst of Porno?," *Nieuwsblad van het Noorden*, 17 March 1992, p. 19; Anonymous, "Foto's van Don Mader als pornografisch in beslag genomen," *Nieuwsblad van het Noorden* 3 June 1994, p. 13; Anonymous, "Pornograaf vrijgesproken," *Nieuwsblad van het Noorden*, 31 March 1992, p. 7; Anonymous, "'Porno-foto's' retour," *Nieuwsblad van het Noorden*, 15 June 1994, p. 13; Anonymous, "Expositie Mader volgens hof geen kinderporno," *De Volkskrant*, 31 March 1992, p. 9; Frans Bosman, "Rechtszaak om naaktfoto's van jongens," *Het Parool*, 13 December 1990, p. 7; Aldert Schipper, "Rechter buigt zich over pornografisch karakter van foto's Amerikaan Mader," *Trouw*, 12 December 1990, p. 9. Mader was arrested for three separate incidents.

78. Mader, "*Entimos Pais*," 231.

79. Mader, "*Entimos Pais*," 232. Mader seems to be particularly invested in undermining what he understands to be religious prejudices against the practice in this

There is only the smallest of gaps between the pederasty that Mader sees the centurion practicing and the notion of boylove he openly advocates. That Mader's article can be credited with popularizing the homoerotic interpretation among English speakers is particularly noteworthy, as the vast majority of Anglophone scholarship depends either directly or indirectly upon this publication.

Rossman's interpretation is even more distressing. Rossman was a Disciples of Christ minister and associate professor at Yale Divinity School, teaching there over the period 1958–1964. Rossman's book *Sexual Experience between Men and Boys* (1976) purported to reveal the practices and ideologies of pederasts across the world in a disinterested fashion. The book was marketed as a resource for those working with youth and published by the YMCA's press. The book summarized a conversation Rossman had with an anonymous "gnostic pederast monk."

> When Jesus told his followers go the second mile, the monk asks, did he not know that to command one to carry his cloak was a common way for a soldier to solicit sex of a boy? Also, the monk reports, this tradition contains the view that the Roman centurion who pleads with Jesus for help in curing his slave boy was a pederast—for why else would such a high official go to such trouble for an adolescent slave? Further, the centurion came to Jesus apologetically, for he knew that the Jews around Jesus would be horrified that Jesus would even speak to a pederast. Yet, said the monk, "Jesus evidently blessed the pederast and his adolescent lover with one of his rare miracles because of the quality of their love. Do we have evidence here of another experiment that failed?"[80]

Though Rossman's discussion was brief and is presented as a second-hand interpretation by a possible eccentric, it proved surprisingly important. James Lambert reviewed Rossman's book for the British magazine *Gay Christian*, commenting, "the gem of the book is a report of the early Christian view that the Roman centurion who pleads with Jesus for help

---

article: "Because this condemnation often arises from religious strictures, we are even less willing to consider the possibility that there might be non-judgemental references to such practises in scripture" (Mader, "*Entimos Pais*," 227). This understanding of liberal subjectivity—the belief that social institutions repress otherwise free human subjects—is a pervasive subtext in homoerotic interpretations of the passage.

80. Rossman, *Sexual Experience between Men and Boys*, 99.

in curing his slave was apparently a pederast."[81] Though the discussion of the Bible throughout Rossman's book totals little more than a single page, Horner noted that "there is some good material on the Roman background of the New Testament references" to same-sex intercourse, in apparent reference to this interpretation.[82]

Whatever the monk may have meant with this interpretation, it served a very specific purpose in the context of Rossman's project. Rossman's book was researched and written while he was on trial for his role in a sex-trafficking ring based in Long Island, New York (charged in November 1972). Rossman and other men employed approximately fifteen boys to pose as Christmas tree salesmen as a front for underage sex-work.[83] Rossman was a particularly active member of the ring, as he had "published a newsletter for members of the ring and had tailored a 'bill of rights'" for pederasts, according to the district attorney's spokesperson. The ring trafficked boys as young as nine years old, brought in from as far away as Puerto Rico.[84] Rossman eventually pled guilty to a reduced charge of attempted sodomy and sentenced to three months probation and mandatory therapy.[85] Rossman had already written extensively about possibility of worthwhile pederasty but composed two books on the topic while awaiting trail: in addition to *Sexual Experience*, Rossman also wrote a children's book titled *Pirate Slave* about a white boy taken as a slave by Arabian pirate; the protagonist eventually buys a slave of his own, whom he marries at age fourteen.[86] Rossman died in 2013.

---

81. James Lambert, review of *Sexual Experience*, by Parker Rossman, *Gay Christian* 41 (1986): 31. Lambert's review proved a liability. Lesbian and Gay Christian Movement, the organization publishing *Gay Christian*, was evicted from its residence in a London church due to the review and leaflets advertising Rossman's book: a television documentary about child abuse (*Childwatch*) mentioned the presence of the book in the organization's office. The organization was accused of condoning "illegal paedophile practices" on this basis, leading to tabloid scrutiny (e.g., Iain Walker, "Scandal of Gay Clergy," *Mail on Sunday* 10 July 1988, pp. 12–15) and a lawsuit.

82. Tom M. Horner, *Homosexuality in Biblical Times: An Annotated Bibliography* (Location unknown: Self-published, 1977), 3.

83. Anonymous, "Minister Denies Vice Ring Guilt," *Bridgeport Telegram*, 22 November 1972, p. 10.

84. David A. Andelman, "8 Indicted in 'Boys-for-Sale' Ring," *New York Times*, May 4 1973, p. 44. News reports are not unanimous, sometimes claiming that the Puerto Rican boy was ten years old.

85. Anonymous, "Probation Set in Morals Case," *Bridgeport Post*, 16 February 1974, p. 25.

86. Parker Rossman, *Pirate Slave* (Nashville: Nelson, 1977).

The connections between Rossman's biblical interpretation and his personal actions are disturbing. His insinuation that Jesus's command to carry one's cloak (a muddled reference to Matt 5:40–41) was a means of soliciting the service of young sex-workers has a disturbing resonance with Rossman's own exploitation of children as part of a sex-for-pay ring.[87]

Some Extrapolations

Though this chapter has focused on calls to reduce the same-sex age of consent, this cannot be plausibly construed as evidence that queer folk are prone to pedophilia. Indeed, one could easily compile a similar study about calls to reduce the heterosexual age of consent under the auspices of biblical authority.[88] We have seen, moreover, that French calls to abolish the age of consent made no distinction between heterosexual and homosexual intercourse. Queer people are no more inclined to sexually abuse children than those identifying as heterosexual.[89] It is nevertheless a rhetorical commonplace in homophobic discourse, especially *Christian* homophobic discourse, to suggest that queer people are more likely to engage in pedophilia than cis-heterosexuals (recall, e.g., bathroom bills, "Don't Say Gay," Hungarian and Russian anti-LGBT laws).[90] There is, of course, no reason to take this suspicion seriously. Demonizing one's political opponents as pedophiles is a common ploy, evidenced

---

87. The topic of adolescent males soliciting intercourse from adult men for pay was a recurring interest of his in academic writings as well. E.g., Parker Rossman, review of *Adolescent Sexuality*, by Robert Sorensen, *Journal of Sex Research* 10 (1974): 165–71, where Rossman astoundingly attributed the murder of nearly thirty boys hitchhiking around Houston, Texas on the purported prevalence ("tens of thousands") of adolescent sex-workers who sought clients via hitchhiking. Rossman consistently depicted male youth as conniving schemers who lured adult men into intercourse.

88. See, e.g., John Witte Jr. "Honor Thy Father and Thy Mother? Child Marriage and Parental Consent in Calvin's Geneva," *JR* 86 (2006): 580–605.

89. There was a considerable panic on the issue in the 1980s and 1990s, especially in North America, with Anita Bryant being a famous proponent of this myth, and it seems to be making a return with current discourse on queer visibility as a form of grooming. Several quasi- or pseudo-academic studies attempted to legitimize, perpetuate, or even stoke such fears; these studies have been discredited, usually on methodological grounds.

90. See Mark D. Jordan, *Recruiting Young Love: How Christians Talk about Homosexuality* (Chicago: University of Chicago Press, 2011).

recently in the baseless Pizzagate and QAnon conspiracy theories. Proponents of these conspiracy theories frame their activities as an effort to save children, but in most instances such accusations are merely ad hoc frames for dismissing one's opponents via sexual slander. To wit: when one right-wing news commentator declared Joe Biden victor in the 2020 American presidential election, he alienated many of his QAnon fans to the extent that they immediately concocted evidence that he was part of the left-wing cabal of sex-traffickers. In such cases, the accusation of pedophilia serves less as evidence of sober investigation of sexual abuse and more as a speech-act that expels one's adversary from certain arenas of public discourse.

There are, however, efforts by ancient historians to destigmatize pederasty both ancient and, more alarmingly, modern. However heady their historiography may be, such writings contribute net harm to the public discourse. It hardly needs to be stated that young people are particularly vulnerable to sexual exploitation and that calls to normalize pederasty almost exclusively represent the interests of adults seeking intercourse with children—this is not a cause championed by young people. Indeed, those who were formerly in such relationships instead tend to describe such sex as abuse or exploitation. Also disturbing are more recent instances of biblical scholars and ancient historians being convicted of possessing child pornography or otherwise implicated in the sexual exploitation of children. Most famous in this regard is Holt Parker, whose work on Roman sexuality remains influential.[91] These concerns are all the more timely given the academy's demonstrable tendency to forgive and forget such acts: the Society of Biblical Literature, for instance, posted a celebratory obituary of Richard Pervo, a scholar who was convicted of possessing child pornography in 2001. Only after the outrage following the conviction of Jan Joosten for similar crimes in June 2020 was Pervo's 2017 obituary removed from the Society's website. We will return to these issues at the book's conclusion.

---

91. See the thoughtful discussions of Holt Parker's legacy in Lynn R. Huber, "Interpreting as Queer or Interpreting Queerly?," in *Bodies on the Verge: Queering the Pauline Epistles*, ed. Joseph A. Marchal, SemeiaSt 93 (Atlanta: SBL Press, 2019), 318–19; Sarah Scullin, "Making a Monster," *Eidolon*, 24 March 2016, https://tinyurl.com/https-tinyurl-com-SBL0699e/.

2
A Centurion and His Partner at the Altar: The United States, United Kingdom, and Australia, 1985–2010

> The privacy-in-public claims and publicizing strategies of [earlier queer activists] are rejected in favor of public recognition of a domesticated, depoliticized privacy. The democratic diversity of proliferating forms of sexual dissidence is rejected in favor of the naturalized variation of a fixed minority arrayed around a state-endorsed heterosexual primacy and prestige.
> —Lisa Duggan, "The New Homonormativity"

> I believe Jesus would approve of gay marriage.
> —Former US President Jimmy Carter

The sexual politics of the homophile interpretation were so specific to its legal context that it is surprising Anglophone readers salvaged much from it. French frustrations with age of consent laws might be contrasted with the situation in the United States, where such laws have historically been framed as protecting feminine purity; through the 1980s, many age of consent laws only applied when the always-female victim was "of chaste character," and only recent legislative emendations have added provisions for same-sex intercourse.[1] The homophile interpretation was a particularly Continental reading, and pederasty tended to warrant comparatively brief mention in other contexts.

This chapter will explore the move from the homophile exegesis discussed in chapter 1 to what will be characterized as gay readings,

---

1. See the state-by-state overview in Richard A. Posner and Katharine B. Silbaugh, *A Guide to America's Sex Laws* (Chicago: University of Chicago Press, 1996), 44–64.

specifically examining how these exegetical shifts corresponded to the Anglophone terrain from which these gay interpretations sprouted.[2] The first part of this chapter will argue that whereas homophile readings focused on the legality of intercourse, gay readings around the turn of the millennium instead mobilized the centurion and the Pais in service of a different politics of assimilation and respectability. These readings were driven by two issues of particular importance within Anglophone gay activism, namely, the legalization of same-sex marriage and the presence of "out" soldiers in the military. These interests betray an increasing identification with the state apparatus within gay political activism, quite distinct from the self-consciously outsider status of homophile politics. Given that public opposition to same-sex marriage and an inclusive military centered upon so-called Christian values, the centurion and the Pais were convenient figures for gay writers encouraging others to reconsider these matters. The second part of this chapter will explore negative responses to homoerotic readings (heteronormative interpretations), readings insisting that the relationship between the centurion and the Pais was neither sexual nor romantic. Particularly important to these counterarguments is the insistence that Jews abstained from same-sex intercourse.

Gay Readings of the Centurion at Capernaum

Homophile interpretations explored concerns about the legality of same-sex intercourse, but the state of the discourse proved considerably different in Anglophone countries in the following decades. Many homophile interpretations emphasized the youthfulness of the Pais as a means of highlighting disparities in age of consent laws and providing a biblical grounding for revising them toward parity: indeed, we saw in the previous chapter that Martignac unironically endorsed the centurion as a pederast

---

2. Though it is somewhat misleading, I will characterize the readings in this chapter *Anglophone*. Nearly all publications discussed in the present chapter were initially published in English (or at least most popular in their English translation). More importantly, the characterization as Anglophone gives an undue preference to a small set of such countries, namely, the United Kingdom, Ireland, the United States of America, and Australia. This omits the vast majority of Anglophone biblical readers (most often in the Global South), where there is much less interest in the homoerotic interpretation.

officer to demonstrate that even though the French government prohibited intercourse between an adult man and a teenager, Jesus had not.³ The homophile reading was myopic in its goals, and this created problems for gay interpretations in the following decades. The homophile suggestion of pederasty proved a liability for gay readers who, on the one hand, had few other resources to draw upon for this pericope, but, on the other hand, had little desire to contest age of consent laws.

Thus, despite the multiplicity of political issues that we will see animated the gay interpretation, such readings were unified in their concerted effort to push the age of the Pais into adulthood. Consider the interpretation proffered by McNeill, whose comments on the pericope shift emphasis from those during the homophile period.

> The words used in the Greek original of these texts for the centurion's servant are *entimos* and *pais*. These words could be translated as "my beloved boy" and would have clearly indicated to Jesus that he was dealing with two men in a loving homosexual relationship. Jesus expressed astonishment at the faith of the centurion and obviously moved by his love for his "beloved boy" heals the young man.
>
> A Roman Centurion was not allowed to marry during his period of service. Given the all-male nature of a Roman legion, the slave would have been the one to see to the physical comfort of the centurion himself. Slaves were not infrequently at the beck and call of the sexual pleasure of their master and it was not unusual for the relationship of a master and slave to grow into one of love.
>
> Here we have the most direct encounter of Jesus with someone who would today be pronounced "gay" and Jesus' reaction was acceptance of the person without judgment and even eagerness to be of assistance to restore the "*pais*" to health, and by implication to fully restore the loving relationship of the two, making possible the renewal of any sexual activity they would have enjoyed together prior to the illness.⁴

---

3. Martignac, "Le centurion de Capernaüm."

4. McNeill, *Freedom, Glorious Freedom*, 89–90. See similar arguments by Jeff Miner and Tyler Connoley: "The term *boy* can also be used as a term of endearment. For example, Jeff's father often refers to his mother as 'his girl.' He doesn't mean that she is a child, but rather that she is his 'special one.' The term *boy* can be used in the same way, as in 'my boy' or 'my beau.' In ancient Greek, *pais* had a similar range of meanings." Jeff Miner and John Tyler Connoley, *The Children Are Free: Reexamining the Biblical Evidence on Same-Sex Relationships* (Indianapolis: Jesus Metropolitan Community Church, 2002), 48.

While McNeill's interpretation resembles those of the homophile period in its evidentiary argument, a number of exegetical moves betray a considerably different understanding of the passage and its significance. Most significant may be the subtle elision from "my beloved boy" to "young man" to a "loving relationship between the two" that transforms the Pais from a boy to the centurion's peer over the course of three paragraphs. Theodore Jennings—the late professor of the New Testament at Chicago Theological Seminary—found a lexical and social-historical basis for maturing the Pais.

> Within the Greek-speaking world the term *pais* was regularly used of the male beloved in a same-sex relationship. The conventional ideal beloved for a man was a younger male, but this convention was not always honored. The situation is somewhat similar to the way in which it was customary, until recently, to refer to even older women as "girl"; or to refer to the female object of affection as "girlfriend" and the male object of affection as "boyfriend," no matter the age of the beloved. Thus in the Hellenistic world, despite the literal connotation of "boy," the "beloved" referred to in this way would not normally have been a minor.[5]

Though historical assessment of these claims must wait until chapter 5, Jennings's interpretation received extensive attention because it came from a prominent New Testament scholar. His interpretation nevertheless

---

5. Theodore W. Jennings Jr., *The Man Jesus Loved: Homoerotic Narratives from the New Testament* (Cleveland: Pilgrim, 2003), 133–34. Compare, e.g., the earlier arguments of Horner, "Centurion's Servant": "Even with Matthew's reading, however, don't think of the 'boy' as a child. The context here does not indicate that. The word is often used in Greek, ancient and modern, to refer to a young man. *Paidia*, in the plural in modern Greek, can refer to young men in their twenties." Erik Koepnick, "The Historical Jesus and the Slave of the Centurion: How the Themes of Slavery, Sexuality, and Military Service Intersect in Matthew 8:5–13," *Oshkosh Scholar* 3 (2008): 89: "However, the pais as a lover, just like the pais as a slave, was referred to as such even when he was an adult displaying adult characteristics (i.e., facial hair, height)."

Jennings later adopted a neutral stance toward pederasty in his own normative statements on the pericope, disputing that "pederastic relationships are inherently oppressive" and arguing that "pederastic relationships, like any other type of relationship, should be judged by specific practices" rather than larger generalizations: Jennings and Liew, "Mistaken Identities," 590 n. 58. Cf. Theodore W. Jennings Jr., *An Ethic of Queer Sex: Principles and Improvisations* (Chicago: Exploration, 2013), 182 n. 65, which cites his work on this pericope as a resource for thinking about pederasty apart from a sex-panic mentality.

bespeaks the problem of the age disparity between the centurion and the Pais in earlier homophile readings. Indeed, the word παῖς is itself a liability, given its etymological connection to pedophilia and pederasty.

This emphasis on the mutual love and similar age of the centurion and the Pais served two distinct purposes. First, it obviated slippery-slope rhetoric common among homophobes. Same-sex marriage, in simplest terms, legally redefines marriage so that the institution is no longer limited to a relationship one man and one woman but takes no consideration of gender. This redefinition led many opponents to declare that the malleability of marriage as a concept meant that there was little legal reason to prevent, say, a man from marrying a cow, polygamous marriage, or (in this case) marriage between a man and a boy. If the definition of marriage could change to permit nonheterosexual relationships, there was little to prevent it from changing again to accommodate one or another inappropriate relationship, until anything was permissible. Gay insistence on the adulthood of the Pais served as a statement of intent directed toward sympathetic or mildly trepidatious heterosexuals: gay activists have limited goals, seeking only slight redefinition of marriage to a gender-neutral legal bond between two loving adults.

Second, the emphasis on the maturity of the Pais marked an important distinction within queer activism. The 1990s saw a considerable amount of media attention directed toward the North American Man/Boy Love Association (NAMBLA), a propedophilia organization that advocated, inter alia, the legalization and normalization of sex between men and boys. Though the group was marginal in its membership numbers and influence, it proved a common reference point within homophobic moral panic at the time, leading various queer-advocacy groups to actively distance themselves from NAMBLA for fear of losing funding or support for their own causes. Indeed, explicit disavowal of NAMBLA was sometimes a prerequisite for funding eligibility—this social differentiation was grounded in very direct and very material concerns. In 1994, the Director of Communications for the Human Rights Campaign stated in no uncertain terms: "NAMBLA is not a gay organization.... They are not part of our community and we thoroughly reject their efforts to insinuate that pedophilia is an issue related to gay and lesbian civil rights."[6] Insistence

---

6. Gregory King *apud* Joshua Gamson, "Messages of Exclusion: Gender, Movements, and Symbolic Boundaries," *Gender and Society* 11 (1997): 178–99. Gamson's

on the Pais's adulthood served to distance one's activism from anything that might be construed as sympathy for child molestation. Indeed, this is the period when sex-offender laws first came about, producing social difference between the law-abiding homosexual and sex-offender pederast/pedophile. The maturity of the Pais in gay readings resulted from a deliberate exegetical maneuver that not only rendered their relationship similar to gay marriage, but also triangulated against the specter of homosexual pedophilia. This triangulation is particularly evident in the politics of citation surrounding Mader's article, which was the first robust articulation of the homoerotic interpretation in English. Although Mader's article was originally published in the journal *Paidika: Journal of Paedophilia*, subsequent Anglophone interpreters almost always cite its reprint in a collection of essays with the much more acceptable title *Homosexuality and Religion and Philosophy*.[7]

If the homophile readings discussed in chapter 1 presumed a certain acceptance of queer people's outsider status—adopting a position to the effect of "we do not require full participation in mainstream heterosexual culture, but we affirm your values and only ask you not punish us for having sex with people the same age as those you do"—then Anglophone gay readings saw a greater shift toward a politics of assimilation. The gay radicalism that had facilitated the decline of the homophile movement softened in the following decades and eventually came to participate in a similar business-as-usual conservatism, albeit responding to the distinct political issues of its day.

---

article offers an insightful discussion of boundary-drawing in 1990s queer activism around the topic discussed here.

7. Mader, "*Entimos Pais*." Though the original publication in *Paidika* may not have been particularly accessible (one assumes the journal had a small print run, and WorldCat indicates that research libraries largely refrained from subscribing to it), readers of the reprint in *Homosexuality and Religion and Philosophy* were hardly unaware of the article's origins: the reprint was merely a photocopy of the original in *Paidika* (as opposed to new typesetting), thereby retaining its page numbers and formatting, albeit with the header of *Paidika* removed. Mader himself has avoided naming the original publication venue in recent years. In Donald H. Mader, "To the Editor," *Gay and Lesbian Review Worldwide* 15.1 (2008): 6, he never names *Paidika*, obliquely referring it to as an "obscure European journal" and instead encourages readers to seek out the reprint of his article in the *Homosexuality and Religion and Philosophy* anthology, even though that collection had long been out-of-print.

A Wedding between the Centurion and the Pais

Though interpreters wanted to render the centurion and Pais's relationship analogous to same-sex marriage, a number of exegetical obstacles needed to be overcome in order to construct a reading that was both plausible historically and compelling politically. One of the more fanciful interpretations is noteworthy due to its laser-focus on relevance and its historiographic credulity.

> It was common practice for some homosexual centurions, in order to have their same-sex union legally recognized, to "purchase" their lover … their so called *entimos doulos* or "special servant." It was essentially the common method of choice on which to legally establish what today would be akin to a gay "civil partnership"—to where the partnership was not in fact a slave versus master relationship, but rather a legally-binding and lawfully protected homosexual relationship—this being the only way to officially solidify such a joining of two men in the Roman-ruled part of the world two thousand years ago.[8]

There is, for instance, no evidence to support the author's central contention that a Roman would purchase another man to form a sort of civil union. Nor are there any Greek texts featuring the phrase ἔντιμος δοῦλος at all. It is not even found in Matthew or Luke.[9] The point here is not to

---

8. M. W. Sphero, *The Gay Faith: Christ, Scripture, and Sexuality* (New Orleans: Herms, 2011), 100–1.

9. See Christopher B. Zeichmann, "The Slave Who Was ἔντιμος: Translation and Characterization in Luke 7:2," *BT* 74 (forthcoming); see also chapter 5 of the present book for more on the word ἔντιμος as applied to slaves. Sphero seems to draw upon Thomas C. Ziegert, "Blessed and Challenged by Jesus: Where We Get the Chutzpah to Do Our Own Ethics," *Open Hands* 13.4 (1998): 14. Ziegert anticipates large parts of Sphero's argument (with a somewhat more plausible historical scenario) by over a decade: "With the additional knowledge gained by John Boswell's research, that Roman men of prestige adopted males whom they loved and counted as their mates for the purpose of sharing their property, we can see the true relationship between the centurion and his adopted son. (There is not necessarily an age difference implied by the adoption.)" Ziegert in turn draws upon John Boswell, *Same-Sex Unions in Premodern Europe* (New York: Vintage, 1994), 98–99, whose argument also stretches credulity at times (e.g., Boswell's overstated claim that "'adopt a brother' was a specific imperial expression for establishing a relationship with a homosexual lover," citing oblique references of Paulus in Dig. 17.2.63, 28.5.59; Juvenal *Sat.* 5.135–140; Horace, *Carm.* 1.7.54–55; *CIL* 2.498). On marriages involving enslaved people (*contubernia*) during

ridicule the author but rather to observe that creative exegetical maneuvers were sometimes implemented to evoke the analogue of gay marriage.

A particularly important reading of the passage can be found in a novel written by New Testament scholar Gerd Theissen. The book—which mostly narrates a fictionalized account of Jesus's life from the perspective of a contemporary named Andreas—was originally published in German in 1986 but was translated into English within a year. The following scene involves a conversation between a rabbi named Gamaliel (who disapproves of Jesus) and Andreas. Gamaliel begins:

> "One day a Gentile centurion living here in Capernaum came to him. He asked [Jesus] to heal his orderly. Of course you have to help Gentiles. But why this one? Everyone knows that most of these Gentile officers are homosexual [Jeder weiß, daß diese heidnischen Offiziere meist homosexuell sind]. Their orderlies are their lovers. But Jesus isn't interested in that sort of thing. He didn't ask anything about the orderly. He healed him—and the thought didn't occur to him that later someone might think of appealing to him in support of the view that homosexuality is permissible."
>
> "Are you certain that the centurion was a homosexual?"
>
> "Of course not, but everyone must have their suspicions. Jesus wasn't at all bothered. I would have advised more caution."[10]

Though certainly not presented with the rigor of a peer-reviewed article, Theissen's book is noteworthy in that it not only represents the first substantial engagement with the homoerotic reading by a biblical scholar but a clear *endorsement* of such a reading.[11] Theissen's narrative indicates

---

Roman antiquity, see Jonathan Edmondson, "Slavery and the Roman Family," in *The Cambridge World History of Slavery: Volume 1. The Ancient Mediterranean World*, ed. Keith Bradley and Paul Cartledge (Cambridge: Cambridge University Press, 2011), 337–61.

10. Gerd Theissen, *The Shadow of the Galilean*, trans. John Bowden (Minneapolis: Augsburg Fortress, 1987), 106; Theissen, *Der Schatten des Galiläers: Historische Jesusforschung in erzählender Form* (Munich: Kaiser, 1986), 150. Theissen proffered a more formally exegetical reflection on the pericope in Theissen, *Erlösungsbilder: Predigten und Meditationen* (Kaiser: Gütersloh, 2002), 77–81.

11. The operative word here is *substantial*. More than a decade before Theissen's book was published, J. Duncan M. Derrett briefly remarked that the Pais "could have been a 'dolly boy' whom the centurion loved the more deeply for having conquered desire." Derrett refused to commit to the Pais being a son or a slave ("Law in the New Testament," 174, 186). Endorsements of the homoerotic reading of the passage remain

another significant difference between gay and earlier homophile, namely, an emphasis on the *sexual orientation* of the centurion. Gamaliel declares that the centurion is homosexual and reacts accordingly, simply assuming that the centurion was homosexual on account of his own prejudices. The earlier homophile readings tended to concern the legality and social acceptance of the centurion's actions rather than his identity. As was often the case with arguments favoring same-sex marriage, an emphasis on identity and orientation made clear that the centurion was born this way and his feelings were not a matter of choice.

In addition to emphasizing the centurion's sexual orientation, gay readings of the pericope also evoked same-sex marriage by stressing the shared love between the centurion and the Pais. While homophile interpretations were interested in sexual acts, gay interpretations eschewed this focus in favor of more family-friendly subtexts, most especially the idea of an enduring and romantic relationship between the centurion and the Pais. Thus, Daniel Helminiak:

> It was common that Roman householders would use their slaves for sex. It was also common for soldiers far from home to have a male sexual companion with them. The centurion and the slave boy were probably sexual partners. In this particular case, as often happened, the centurion probably fell in love with the young man. The most likely explanation of the centurion's behavior is that the young slave was the centurion's lover.[12]

Helminiak carefully deploys qualifiers ("probably," "most likely"), but his argument only works if one imagines mutual adoration between the

---

rare in peer-reviewed biblical studies or even theological journals, especially high-profile ones. For other exceptions, see Ian K. Duffield, "The Clear Teaching of the Bible? A Contribution to the Debate about Homosexuality and the Church of England," *ExpTim* 115 (2004): 114–15; Jennings and Liew, "Mistaken Identities"; William Stacy Johnson, "Finding Our Way Forward," *SJT* 62 (2009): 89; Lawrence, "Fish," 301; James A. Sanders, "God's Work in the Secular World," *BTB* 37.4 (2007): 149. Three of these articles either respond to or received critical remarks in the pages of the same journal, specifically singling out the homoerotic interpretation of this pericope, see Saddington, "Centurion in Matthew"; Ron Cassidy, "The Clear Teaching of the Bible on Homosexual Practice: A Response to Ian K. Duffield," *ExpTim* 115 (2004): 301. More complex exceptions to scholarly silence will be discussed in chapter 3.

12. Daniel Helminiak, "Jesus and the Centurion's Slave Boy," *White Crane Journal* 47 (2000): 7–8; cf. his earlier arguments in Helminiak, "Scripture, Sexual Ethics, and the Nature of Christianity," *Pastoral Psychology* 47 (1999): 264.

centurion and the Pais. This marks another point of contrast with earlier homophile readings, written in a context where the prospect of legally sanctioned same-sex marriage was nigh unimaginable.

The Roman Army Did Not Discriminate

Various gay interpretations intervened in the issue of queer people serving in the military. The most salient point of reference here was the US military's policy of "Don't Ask, Don't Tell." Like many other countries, the United States banned same-sex intercourse among members of the military for much of the twentieth and early twenty-first centuries. Article 93 in the 1920 revisions to the *Articles of War of 1916* had codified this ban as official policy: "Any person subject to military law who commits ... sodomy ... shall be punished as a court-martial may direct." Sodomy was listed alongside crimes like manslaughter, mayhem, arson, and burglary. The shift from criminal to medical-psychiatric rubrics for classifying same-sex attraction (as discussed in chapter 1) were active in military regulations. The criminalization of individual acts of same-sex intercourse while enlisted thus transformed into a much broader ban on people identifying or identified as homosexuals in the following decades: military doctors set up undercover operations to ascertain who in the ranks were prone to such "perversions," who were then court-martialed and sentenced to five or six years' imprisonment.[13] Shortly after the United States became involved in WWII, various branches of the military hired psychiatrists to develop techniques to ascertain which aspiring recruits might be homosexual in order to prevent their enlistment. In 1942, doctors advised that men "habitually or occasionally engaged in homosexual or other perverse sexual practices [were] unsuitable for military service." Intercourse was not the only grounds for dismissal but admitted homoerotic feelings—or even suspicion of homosexuality by a recruiter—was sufficient to preempt or dishonorably end a military career.

Negotiating between calls for gay inclusion and recalcitrance among military chiefs, the administration of then-president Bill Clinton achieved a compromise in 1993. Unable (or unwilling) to overturn the absolute ban

---

13. Allan Bérubé, *Coming Out under Fire: The History of Gay Men and Women in World War II*, 20th anniv. ed. (Chapel Hill: University of North Carolina Press, 2010), 8–33.

on queer people in the military, Clinton called for a policy that prohibited direct inquiry into the sexual orientation of those enlisted but kept in place a ban on homosexual acts, which still entailed court-martial and dishonorable discharge. The policy, known as "Don't Ask, Don't Tell," retained the ban to placate conservative elements but created space for queer military personnel who were both cis-hetero-passing and closeted to serve with honor. The problems with this policy are numerous, as it tacitly condoned surveillance and harassment of suspected queer folk, even if the policy officially banned such intimidation. Few activists on either side found "Don't Ask, Don't Tell" satisfactory. The policy was nullified when erstwhile president Barack Obama signed into law the *Don't Ask, Don't Tell Repeal Act of 2010*, which eliminated much of the military code that discriminated against queer servicemembers. Other Anglophone countries had enacted similar policies in the preceding years: the United Kingdom lifted its ban on gay military members in 2000, Australia and Canada in 1992, and Ireland in 1993.

Insofar as the gay reading posits that the centurion was a homosexual army officer, it is unsurprising that he was commonly summoned to support queer participation in the military. Tobias Haller, after noting that the centurion and the Pais may have been in a sexual relationship, observes that their relationship "hardly seem[s] to be the point of the story, and whatever the relationship between the master and servant it appears irrelevant to Jesus. He doesn't ask and the centurion doesn't tell."[14] The connection is not particularly subtle in Haller's phrasing, but others are even more direct with it. Thomas Hanks rehearses the arguments for the homoerotic reading before concluding, "Perhaps Alexander the Great was right after all, and gays can be good soldiers!"[15] The specifically *military* career of the centurion thus receives contemplation, presenting him as an ensign of Roman wealth and might: "This proud representative of the military might of Rome had humbled himself out of love to beg a favor from an itinerant Jewish preacher."[16] The military is far from neutral in these readings; it elicits respect and even awe. This is a significant contrast with

---

14. Tobias Stanislas Haller, *Reasonable and Holy: Engaging Same-Sexuality* (New York: Seabury, 2009), 137.

15. Hanks, "Matthew and Mary of Magdala," 192.

16. McNeill, *Freedom, Glorious Freedom*, 90. It is unclear whether this phrasing is intended to evoke gay pride.

homophile readings of the centurion, which tended to either ignore the military altogether or at most were interested in the dignity it conferred.[17]

The Centurion and the Nation-State

Both of these reference points—same-sex marriage and gays in the military—betray an increasing identification with the state apparatus among queer folk, an identification that was negligible in homophile interpretations.[18] Numerous factors contributed to this shift, but particularly important for present purposes are how this change corresponds to the transforming biopolitical situation of many queer people. Foucault characterized biopower as "the power to make live and let die."[19] This power is often exercised through use of various metrics (e.g., mortality rates, life expectancy, birth rates, income levels among various populations) to channel resources (e.g., education, healthcare, research, legal funding) in order to optimize life for some populations and neglect others to the point of death. The data generated by these metrics justify the allocation of resources, at once determined by and determining the prevailing politics of respectability: namely, identification of productive citizens worthy of life. Biopower is often distinguished from the historically prior use of sovereign power in the eighteenth century and earlier: the power to make die (via, e.g., execution, civilian death in warfare) and let live.

There is little doubt that queer folk were among those biopolitically left to die from the 1970s through the 1990s, perhaps most apparent in the management of the HIV/AIDS epidemic.[20] The tacit denial of the AIDS crisis in

---

17. See, for instance, two homophile readings where the "centurion" seems to be a civilian with no obvious military connection: Gyburc-Hall, "Legende"; Crowther, "Sodom," 26.

18. There are other ways gay readings participated in ongoing political controversies beyond the same-sex marriage and military inclusion. Tom Hanks, *The Subversive Gospel: A New Testament Commentary of Liberation*, trans. John P. Doner (Cleveland: Pilgrim, 2000), 14, for instance, declares that "Jesus does not pry into the privacy of the relationship nor even dispatch them to a priest for a bit of 'ex-gay torture,' but simply heals the youth with a word from a distance." In different vein, James E. Miller ("Letters," *The Door* 136 [1994]: 4–5) suggests that the pericope "speaks directly to how Christians should respond to the sexually transmitted disease known as AIDS."

19. Michel Foucault, *"Society Must Be Defended": Lectures at Collège de France 1975–76*, trans. David Macey (New York: Picador, 2003), 239–64.

20. Classic discussions include Leo Bersani, "Is the Rectum a Grave?," *AIDS* 43 (1987): 197–22; Judith Butler, "Sexual Inversions," in *Foucault and the Critique*

the United States by the presidential administrations of both Ronald Reagan and George H. W. Bush contributed significantly to the death-toll: Reagan first mentioned the virus only when a reporter asked in September 1985. By that time, over ten thousand Americans had died. The populations most affected by HIV in the United States (i.e., queer men, African Americans, drug-users) were already biopolitically marginalized, and this marginality compounded due to the AIDS crisis: little by way of resources were used to educate, provide healthcare, engage in research, or offer other forms of public support for those who had contracted HIV—an entirely predictable move, as these were populations the US government had already been left to die within its own borders. Similar comments might be made about the administration of Margaret Thatcher in the United Kingdom or that of Garret FitzGerald in Ireland, among others. Jasbir Puar observes how queer activists at the time named this with precision.

> During the U.S. AIDS crisis, the charge of [activist group] ACT UP activists was "You are killing us!," the "you" being the state, understood as responsible for addressing the crisis and providing care to its citizens (and noncitizens). The "you" is also the social and the political, the broader social and political contexts within which homosexual bodies could be sacrificed to such indifference and neglect.[21]

The position of queer and black folk within the American biopolitical matrix during the AIDS crisis was entirely consistent with the position they held in the period leading up to that epidemic; one thinks, for instance, of legal codes that specifically targeted black and queer men (e.g., sodomy laws, public indecency laws, punitive discrepancies for crack vs. cocaine

---

of Institutions, ed. John Caputo and Mark Yount, Greater Philadelphia Philosophy Consortium (University Park: Pennsylvania State University Press, 1993), 81–98; Jeff Nunokawa, "*In Memoriam* and the Extinction of the Homosexual," *ELH* 58 (1991): 427–38; Eve Kosofsky Sedgwick, *Epistemology of the Closet* (Berkeley: University of California Press, 1990). To be clear, the devastating effects of the AIDS epidemic has continued long after the 1990s. The point here is that it became less important to queer political organizing in the Anglophone North Atlantic as time went on, even if it continues to ravage Sub-Saharan Africa.

21. Jasbir K. Puar, *The Right to Maim: Debility, Capacity, Disability*, Anima (Durham, NC: Duke University Press, 2017), 7–9. ACT UP is an acronym for AIDS Coalition to Unleash Power.

possession, various factors contributing to homelessness, refusal to enact harm-reduction policies).

Much of the interpretive work discussed above was produced in this changing context, which Puar describes as "a transition ... in how queer subjects are relating to nation-states, particularly the United States, from being figures of death (i.e., the AIDS pandemic) to becoming tied to ideas of life and productivity (i.e., gay marriage and family)."[22] Particularly significant for Puar is the incorporation of queers into consumer-markets that granted provisional access to liberal institutions of multicultural tolerance and diversity. For instance, the 1990s saw the birth of the gay tourism industry, corporate sponsorship of Pride events, the founding of massive queer-centric media companies, queer-oriented branding by major corporations, and so on. All of these were significant forces in interpellating queer subjects as contributing members of the neoliberal nation-state. The concomitant rise of respectable and productive queer subjects facilitated public reconsideration of policies like gay marriage and sodomy laws.

To push the matter further, market participation, the visage of respectability, and biopolitical affirmation do not merely overlap but may be understood as mutually constitutive. The steady incorporation of queer bodies into global capital resulted in the shift described by Puar: the Anglophone state, having once left queers to die, now invites queers to participate in its program of benevolent protection. The military is a particularly noteworthy component of this purportedly benevolent protection, as it offers not only safety from imagined foes noteworthy for their homophobia and refusal to participate in global capital, but also an alibi for one's patriotism. This patriotic alibi is important, considering the precarious situation of queers within the nation-state, thanks to the frequent supposition of queer counterculturalism (e.g., nonmonogamy, peace movements, anticapitalism, gender nonconformity). To rephrase, the rhetoric of patriotism can gesture toward one's successful interpellation as a citizen subject, identifying with the national project, even if one hesitates regarding some of its stated goals ("I support the troops but not the war"). The increasing enlistment of queer folk in the military provides evidence of this shifting biopolitical situation and should inform a history of interpretation of the pericope under consideration.

---

22. Jasbir K. Puar, *Terrorist Assemblages: Homonationalism in Queer Times*, 10th anniversary ed., Next Wave (Durham, NC: Duke University Press, 2017), xii.

It may be helpful to understand gay interpretations as promoting what Lisa Duggan terms *homonormativity*, which she characterizes as "a politics that does not contest dominant heteronormative assumptions and institutions—such as marriage, and its call for monogamy and reproduction—but upholds and sustains them while promising the possibility of a demobilized gay constituency and a privatized, depoliticized gay culture anchored in domesticity and consumption."[23] Homonormative discourse emerged in the 1990s with the rise of third-way politics in the North Atlantic, rebuffing the perceived excesses of queer counterculture. Since then, various gay (and, less often, lesbian or transgender) groups have been founded on principles that reject both the homophobia of the right and the radicalism of the left. Duggan cites the guiding principles of the Independent Gay Forum as an example, some of which are quoted here.

- We share a belief in the fundamental virtues of the American system and its tradition of individual liberty, personal moral autonomy and responsibility, and equality before the law. We believe those traditions depend on the institutions of a market economy, free discussion, and limited government.
- We deny "conservative" claims that gays and lesbians pose any threat to social morality or the political order.
- We equally oppose "progressive" claims that gays should support radical social change or restructuring of society.[24]

Homonormativity is often presented as a third way between threats on the left and right. This deploys a rhetorical framework commonly termed the horseshoe theory of politics: the far right and far left are ideologically closer to each other than they are to reasonable centrists ("I condemn both Nazis and antifa"). Within the horseshoe theory, all critique of the liberal-democratic status quo can be reduced to the category of extremism, regardless of that opposition's character; antiracist, anticapitalist, and other forms of activism are morally equivalent to ideologies characterized by bigotry or

---

23. Duggan, "New Homonormativity," 179. Though there has much been written on homonormativity, perhaps the most important critique can be found in Holly Lewis, *The Politics of Everybody: Feminism, Queer Theory, and Marxism at the Intersection* (London: Zed, 2016).

24. Independent Gay Forum, "About IGF CultureWatch," *Independent Gay Forum*, https://tinyurl.com/sbl6705c.

unjust distribution of resources. By presenting itself as postideological, this framework's deployment of whiteness is partially concealed through its disavowals of identity politics: gays indeed deserve rights, but queerness should not threaten prevailing systems of global capitalism.

Homonormativity is deeply preoccupied with the respectability of queer folk, albeit with a different inflection than the homophile Arcadians discussed in chapter 1. Respectability politics locate the solution to injustices in a population's adherence to dominant social norms; those who fail to adhere to respectable norms are responsible for any injustices they experience. Recent examples are numerous, but one might think of recent juxtapositions of Black Lives Matter with the ostensibly more respectable protests of Martin Luther King Jr. Within such contrasts, King's choice to wear suits is often compared with more recent fashion choices ("pull up your pants"); King's diction is praised in comparison with current African American Vernacular English; King's strict adherence to nonviolence is contrasted with recent confrontations with state authorities; and so on. The differences between respectable and unrespectable bodies are not only used to explain their experience of injustice, but to also to discredit their protests and efforts at rectification. Activists must inhabit a respectable body before being taken seriously.

Though the concept of respectability politics was initially formulated to describe the experiences of black women,[25] many queer people experience it via homonormativity. Respectability politicians frame good queer folk as educated, productive, monogamous, and consumer subjects who would contribute more to global capital if given the chance. Homonormative discourse is often preoccupied with enhancing the capacity of queer folk to act within the prevailing social order, focusing activism mostly on achieving political recognition. In the homonormative framework, queer activism should be most concerned about *inclusion* within hegemonic systems.

While homonormativity's appeal may be obvious, so are its problems. One consequence is that queer folk who are incapable of achieving or not desiring such respectability become further marginalized; sex work, housing insecurity, HIV/AIDS and other precarious healthcare situations, gentrification, minimum wage, and mental illness become tangential or irrelevant to queer liberation, despite their disproportionate relevance to

---

25. Evelyn Brooks Higginbotham, *Righteous Discontent: The Women's Movement in the Black Baptist Church, 1880–1920* (Cambridge: Harvard University Press, 1993).

queer folk, especially queer people of color. The homonormative framework downplays these concerns on the grounds that those suffering on such account do so because they inhabit unrespectable bodies whose obstinance prevents their interpellation as citizen subjects (in effect, supposing that such queer folk *choose* to be marginalized). These respectability politics entail a disavowal of radical politics of liberation as well; queer critiques of the state have diminished since the 1990s, largely due to the mainstreaming of queer discourse concomitant with the rise of such respectability politics. Rather, the state comes to be understood as an agent of potential liberation. Hence, support for the legalization of same-sex marriage (queers as productive citizens), opposition to "Don't Ask, Don't Tell" (queers as patriotic soldiers), ensuring normalized relations with gay-friendly countries (queers as consumer tourists), and so on.

The biopolitical shifts that occurred during this period deepened significant fault lines in queer politics. For instance, some activists have argued that the prevailing quest for equality in queer discourse is myopic in its failure to consider the intersecting issues at play. Yasmin Nair observes that same-sex marriage was long a tertiary concern to queer activists, until wealthy whites became involved.

> When the secret history of gay marriage is finally written, it will reveal that gay marriage was foisted upon a community with few resources, held hostage by a wealthy few. The mid-90s onwards saw the rise of out gay men and women, mostly men and mostly white, who were powerful and wealthy and wanted a way to ensure that their aspirations to be seen as just like everyone else would be fulfilled and that their wealth would stay in their families and continue to enrich the financial interests they had so carefully nurtured. The secret history of gay marriage is that it has never been about "equality" in any real sense, but about ensuring that a small section of gay men and women are able to hold on to their wealth.[26]

---

26. Yasmin Nair, "The Secret History of Gay Marriage," 25 June 2015, https://tinyurl.com/sbl6705d. The point has been argued many times. To quote a few of the more incisive summaries, David L. Eng, *The Feeling of Kinship: Queer Liberalism and the Racialization of Intimacy* (Durham, NC: Duke University Press, 2010), 3 observes, "Paradoxically, prior historical efforts to defy state oppression and provide a radical critique of family and kinship have given way to a desire for state legitimacy and for the recognition of same-sex marriage, adoption, custody, inheritance, and service in the military." Similarly, Michael Warner, "Normal and Normaller: Beyond Gay Marriage," *GLQ* 5 (1999): 120–21: "No one is more surprised by the current language of gay politics than many veterans of earlier forms of gay activism, to whom marriage

Nair further observes that the rise of queer nonprofits focused upon marriage had a negative impact on funding for organizations working on HIV/AIDS issues and outreach programs for queer youth. Because same-sex marriage was widely presumed to be the ultimate desideratum of queer activism, the concerns of vulnerable queer populations were often neglected in the quest for same-sex marriage.[27]

These shifts in queer politics and subject-positioning are particularly evident in the emphases and subtexts in gay interpretations of the centurion and the Pais. Namely, the implicit antagonism towards the state found in homophile readings—especially its criminalization of same-sex intercourse—was exchanged for a politics of inclusion and assimilation in gay interpretations. We have already seen that these politics were distinct from homophile readings in defining same-sex relationships not by the carnal act of intercourse but by the more respectable goal of marriage. This point can be pressed further on the topic of the military. Homophile interpretations had little interest in the military of their own day, largely seeing the armed forces as a magnet for the literate men of a bygone era. By contrast, gay interpretations envisioned the military not as an agent of state violence but as a point of entry to legal recognition, with hopes of achieving the full rights already afforded to heterosexual citizens.

Even if shifts in interpretation are largely attributable to a politics centered on inclusion and assimilation, there were other important factors in such changes. For instance, homophile readings were rarely Christian in any meaningful sense: these ideas were usually published in homophile venues (e.g., *Arcadie*, *ONE Magazine*), and authors rarely spoke in a distinctively Christian register. In homophile readings, Jesus's approval was more etic

---

seems both less urgent and less agreed-on than such items as HIV and health care, AIDS prevention, the repeal of sodomy laws, antigay violence, job discrimination, immigration, media coverage, military antigay policy, sex inequality, and the saturation of everyday life with heterosexual privilege. Before the election of Bill Clinton in 1992, marriage was scarcely a blip on the horizon of queer politics; Paula Ettelbrick and Tom Stoddard's debate on the issue in 1989 seemed simply theoretical. Many gay activists abroad are equally baffled by the focus on marriage in the United States."

27. For example, Empire State Pride Agenda disbanded after the Supreme Court legalized gay marriage across the United States in 2015, citing "fulfilment of its mission." Though not necessarily making this same exact point, see the similar claims in, e.g., James Kirchick, "The Struggle for Gay Rights Is Over," *The Atlantic*, 28 June 2019, https://tinyurl.com/sbl6705e; Andrew Sullivan, "The End of Gay Culture," *The New Republic*, 24 October 2005, https://tinyurl.com/sbl6705f.

than emic: Jesus approved a pagan relationship in antiquity, and insofar as Jesus was a broadly authoritative figure, his commendation of the centurion served less for legitimizing Christian participation in same-sex relationships than contesting Christian objections to same-sex intercourse. Matters had changed by the 1990s, when out queer folk comprised a substantial portion of mainstream Christians, however marginal queer folk may have remained in a broader sense. The Metropolitan Community Church—a denomination comprised almost entirely of queer-identifying congregants and their families—proved a significant force, along with sporadic instances of affirming congregations in other denominations, claiming queer space within Christian social life that had long remained derelict. Christian publishers became increasingly comfortable publishing queer-sympathetic volumes and likewise queer publishers with Christian content. One consequently finds an explosion of popular homoerotic interpretations of this passage during the 1990s and 2000s, ranging from self-published books to denominational pamphlets to church sermons.[28] The centurion's sexuality became a common point of reference within gay theological circles and made common incursions into secular gay periodicals.[29]

---

28. Pamphlets and newsletters discussing the pericope are plentiful. E.g., Nancy Wilson, *Homosexuality: Our Story Too; Lesbians and Gay Men in the Bible* (San Francisco: UFMCC, 1992); Dale Gunthorp, *I'm Gay and God Loves Me: What the Bible Says* (London: Metropolitan Community Church of East London, 2003), 9; Elizabeth Stuart, "For God's Sake Stop Pretending!," *LGCM News* June 1993, p. 4; Anonymous, "Words of the Centurion," *Integrator: The Newsletter of Integrity Toronto* 93.5 (1993): 1; Michael McClure, "The Sermon," *Lesbian and Gay Christian Movements's Roman Catholic Caucus: Newsletter* 16 (1994): 5–7. The interpretation is occasionally mentioned in church publications for denominations that are not affirming of full inclusion of queer folk: e.g., McClure, "Is the Homosexual Movement to Be Condemned?," *Month* 27 (1994): 435 in a Jesuit periodical and Gordon Fell, "Is It Better to Do What's Right or What's Wrong in Our Own Eyes?," *The Journal: News of the Churches of God* 157 (2013): 7 in a Grace Communion International (then Worldwide Church of God) periodical. Self-published books on gay theology and history are numerous and frequently discuss the pericope, see, e.g., George S. E. Hopper, *Reluctant Journey: A Pilgrimage of Faith from Homophobia to Christian Love* (Leeds: University Printing Services, 1997), 39; James Kepner, Jr., *Becoming a People: A Four Thousand Year Gay and Lesbian Chronology*, 3rd ed. (Hollywood: National Gay Archives, 1996), 3; Rick Brentlinger, *Gay Christian 101: Spiritual Self-Defense for Gay Christians; What the Bible Really Says about Homosexuality* (Pace: Salient, 2007), 193–221.

29. E.g., Helminiak, "Jesus and the Centurion's Slave Boy"; Alan Page, "Jesus Was Not Anti-Gay," *Gay and Lesbian Humanist* 13.4 (1994): 30; Anonymous, "United

Heteronormative Readings and Homophobic Jews

But with every action, there is an equal and opposite reaction. As queer people were afforded increasingly visible forms of recognition by the state, some culture warriors interpreted this as an attack on a familiar way of life, mobilizing in support of atavistic heteronormativity. With respect to the pericope under consideration, many interpreters began to express suspicions about its historical plausibility or its normalization of queer Christianity. Whoever the Pais may have been, he was *not* the centurion's sexual liaison.

It is better to speak of opponents of the homoerotic reading as engaged in a heteronormative hermeneutic (i.e., without *necessarily* advancing a queer-hostile politics), rather than an outright homophobic one (i.e., advancing queer-hostile politics), even if many heteronormative interpretations are explicitly grounded in homophobia.[30] Heteronormative readings are more commonly published by biblical scholars in academic or academic-adjacent venues than homoerotic readings are.

Church of Christ Professor Says Jesus Was Actively Gay," *Gay and Lesbian Times* 805 (2003): 27; J. Falsch, "Gay Love," *Wisconsin Light* 10.22 (1997): 4; Derek Rawcliffe, "The Centurion's Faith," *The Pink Paper* 23 December 1994, p. 6. Especially noteworthy is Jack Clark Robinson, "Jesus, the Centurion, and His Lover," *Gay and Lesbian Review Worldwide* 14.6 (2007): 22–24, which prompted several letters to the editor that were published in a subsequent issue. This is not to mention mainstream news venues publishing about the homoerotic reading on occasion, such as Jerry Bartram, "A Sacred Gift from God," *The Globe and Mail*, 11 June 1994, p. D4.

30. I construe *homophobia* broadly, characterizing *any* politics grounded in phobic reactions toward homoeroticism (repulsion, horror, disgust, etc.). A significant example was the firestorm surrounding Tat-siong Benny Liew, who coauthored an article on the topic (Jennings and Liew, "Mistaken Identities"). An independent student journal at Liew's home institution of College of the Holy Cross initiated a campaign against him: Elinor Reilly, "New Ways in Theology at Holy Cross," *Fenwick Review* 25.5 (2018): 5–7. The journal's editorial directive is to "take pride in defending traditional Catholic principles and conservative ideas, and do its best to articulate thoughtful alternatives to the dominant campus ethos." The article decrying Liew's queer biblical interpretation (including his article on the centurion) was widely reported in conservative American media, including multiple articles in the *National Review*: George Weigel, "March Madness at the College of the Holy Cross," *The National Review*, 29 March 2018, https://tinyurl.com/sbl6705g; Weigel, "Defending the Indefensible at Holy Cross," *The National Review*, 5 April 2018, https://tinyurl.com/sbl6705h.

Exegetical objections to the homoerotic interpretation are numerous, but typical are those of Robert Gagnon, the most compelling of which may be summarized as follows.³¹ First, Gagnon disputes the historicity of the story as narrated by Matthew and Luke, where a sexual partner or slave (παῖς and/or δοῦλος) is healed. Rather, Gagnon contends that the parallel in John 4:46–54, which depicts a Jewish official requesting that his son (υἱός) be healed, is an earlier version of the Matthew/Luke/Q pericope and consequently more likely to be historical. If the Pais is his son, questions of same-sex intercourse are moot at the historical level.³² Second, even if the centurion and the Pais had sex, Jesus's silence on the matter does not imply he condoned it. Gagnon observes that Jesus's association with "tax collectors and sinners" (Mark 2:16) does not mean that he endorsed their activities either. Finally, Jews were hostile to same-sex intercourse, making it unlikely that Jesus or the Jewish elders at Capernaum (Luke 7:3–5) would have praised someone who was known to engage in such acts.

Gagnon is hardly alone in his heteronormative objections. Wendy Cotter proffers the longest and most thoughtful criticism of the homoerotic interpretation of the pericope, which cannot be rehearsed in full here. As with Gagnon, Cotter's primary counterarguments contest the plausibility of Jesus *qua* Jew supporting same-sex intercourse: "The problem with their research is that it does not present the Jewish abhorrence of sexual aberrations, which certainly included pederasty."³³ Stephen Voor-

---

31. Robert A. J. Gagnon, "Did Jesus Approve of a Homosexual Couple in the Story of the Centurion at Capernaum?," 24 April 2007, http://www.robgagnon.net/articles/homosexCenturionStory.pdf; cf. Gagnon, "Notes to Gagnon's Essay in the Gagnon-Via Two Views Book," 2 October 2003, http://www.robgagnon.net/2Views/HomoViaRespNotesRev.pdf, which serves as the footnote for the body text of Dan O. Via and Robert A. J. Gagnon, *Homosexuality and the Bible: Two Views* (Minneapolis: Fortress, 2003), 68. Gagnon at one time expressed his intention to write a monograph on the Healing of the Centurion's Pais (see the citation of a forthcoming monograph on the topic by then-departmental-colleague: Dale C. Allison Jr., *The Intertextual Jesus: Scripture in Q* [Harrisburg, PA: Trinity Press International, 2000], 254), though this project seems to have been abandoned. Similar arguments are enumerated in Joe Dallas, *Speaking of Homosexuality: Discussing the Issues with Kindness and Clarity* (Grand Rapids: Baker, 2016), 180–83.

32. More nuanced homoerotic interpretations avoid prematurely attributing this position to the historical Jesus. For instance, Jennings and Liew, "Mistaken Identities" discuss the pericope within the context of Matthew's literary features and Mader, "Entimos Pais" is interested in "early Christian attitudes."

33. Wendy Cotter, *The Christ of the Miracle Stories: Portrait through Encounter* (Grand Rapids: Baker Academic, 2010), 124–25. A particularly bizarre heteronorma-

winde expresses similar objections: "It stretches credulity to the limit to suggest that the centurion, who may have been a God-fearer, would have enjoyed such a good reputation in the Jewish community at Capernaum had he been known as a sexual predator."[34] Likewise Andrew Perriman: "It is hard to believe that [the centurion] would have been on such good terms with the conservative elders of the synagogue in Capernaum if it was known that he used his slave for sexual gratification."[35] The merits and problems of these counterarguments await consideration in chapter 5, but their place within the texture of the discourse is noteworthy in its own right.

Most peoples of the Roman Empire—whether Greek, Roman, Syrian, or something else—tolerated same-sex intercourse. There is a common supposition that Jews disapproved of homosexual relations, and, because his Judaism is not in doubt, Jesus must have also condemned the practice. Jews, unlike others of the Mediterranean who generally accepted homo-eroticism, abided by the commandments in Torah, notably the prohibition of sex between men as regulated in Lev 18:22 and 20:13. These commandments remained important to Jews throughout antiquity, including those of the Hellenistic and Roman periods. Thus, when the topic of intercourse between two men arises in late Second Temple literature, it uniformly condemns the practice as incompatible with Judaism. Operative in this narrative is an assumption that the uniqueness of Jewish sexual mores ultimately denotes their *moral* distinction from gentiles. That is, good rep-

---

tive discussion can be found in Levine and Witherington, *Gospel of Luke*, 198. Levine and Witherington claim "some New Testament scholars" argue that the centurion sexually abused the Pais, culminating in psychosomatic hysteria that left the Pais paralyzed. The centurion attempted to prevent Jesus's arrival at his home to keep the abuse secret, which resulted in Jesus healing the Pais from a distance. I am unaware of any publication that has argued for this reading (and they cite none), as it seems to conflate elements from incompatible interpretations of the pericope. Levine and Witherington then proceed to refute this peculiar interpretation even though it is no more than a straw man of their own creation.

34. Stephen Voorwinde, *Jesus' Emotions in the Gospels* (London: T&T Clark, 2011), 18. Cf. Michael Wolter, *Das Lukasevangelium*, HNT 5 (Tübingen: Mohr Siebeck, 2008), 269–70: "Die Behauptung, dass der Text eine päderatische Beziehugn des Centurio zu seinem Sklaven nahelegt, is abwegig. Sie steht in eklatantem Widerspruch zu dem Zeugnis, dass die jüdischen Presbyter ihm ausstellen."

35. Andrew Perriman, *End of Story? Same-Sex Relationships and the Narratives of Evangelical Mission* (Eugene: Cascade, 2019), 120.

utation among Jews is mutually exclusive with the same-sex intercourse typifying Romans.

Heteronormative interpretations usually argue that Jesus must have condemned same-sex intercourse for the simple reason that he was Jewish; ergo, Jesus's silence cannot be read as a neutral or favorable reaction to a sexual relationship between the centurion and the Pais. It is striking how pervasive this assumption is, given how egregiously it mischaracterizes Jewish sexual practices at the turn of the era. To be sure, surviving Jewish writings of the Greek and Roman periods overwhelmingly criticize sex between men when the topic arises. Philo of Alexandria (e.g., *Abr.* 135; *Spec.* 3.36), rabbinic literature (e.g., Tg. Ps.-J. Lev 20:13), Josephus (e.g., *C.Ap.* 2.199), and many other Jewish writers disparage same-sex intercourse.[36] Indeed, a number of Jewish texts roughly contemporaneous with the New Testament assert the incompatibility of same-sex intercourse with Jewish norms. The Sibylline Oracles asserts that Jews "do not engage in impious intercourse with *paides*" (ἀρσενικοὺς παῖδας; 3.596), and the Letter of Aristeas makes similar claims (1.152). Although written centuries later, the Tosefta likewise states that "Israel are not suspected of same-sex intercourse" (e.g., t. Qidd. 5.9–10).

There are, however, clear indications that these claims cannot be taken at face value. Cotter cites two secondary sources—a book each by Robin Scroggs and Sacha Stern—as authorities for her claim that first-century Jews refrained from such intercourse, though both are more cautious in distinguishing the claims of Jewish texts from historical reality. Scroggs is careful to note that "the discussion is conducted *as if* both male and female homosexuality were possible realities within the Jewish community, although it is mostly gentiles who are specifically accused." Likewise,

---

36. E.g., Jub. 20.5–6; Rom 1:26–27; Jude 7. William Loader has written extensively on the topic: William Loader, *Sexuality in the New Testament: Understanding the Key Texts* (Louisville: Westminster John Knox, 2010); Loader, *Philo, Josephus, and the Testaments on Sexuality: Attitudes towards Sexuality in the Writings of Philo and Josephus and in the Testaments of the Twelve Patriarchs* (Grand Rapids: Eerdmans, 2011); Loader, *The Pseudepigrapha on Sexuality: Attitudes towards Sexuality in Apocalypses, Testaments, Legends, Wisdom, and Related Literature* (Grand Rapids: Eerdmans, 2011); Loader, *The Dead Sea Scrolls on Sexuality: Attitudes towards Sexuality in Sectarian and Related Literature at Qumran* (Grand Rapids: Eerdmans, 2009); Loader, *Enoch, Levi, and Jubilees on Sexuality: Attitudes towards Sexuality in the Early Enoch Literature, the Aramaic Levi Document, and the Book of Jubilees* (Grand Rapids: Eerdmans, 2007); Loader, *The New Testament on Sexuality* (Grand Rapids: Eerdmans, 2012).

Stern observes the assertion that "Israel are not suspected of same-sex intercourse" is contradicted by other rabbinic texts.[37] The cautions of Scroggs and Stern are warranted, as we will see in chapter 5; some Jewish men *did* have sex with other men around this time, and, moreover, there is little evidence that Jews mandated that gentiles abide by any of their distinctive sexual regulations.[38]

When ancient Jewish authors claimed that Jews abstained from same-sex intercourse, they engaged in rhetorical formulations that cannot be taken as descriptive of reality. Cotter, for instance, claims that it is "impossible to explain why Matthew would have preserved [the homoerotic sense of the word παῖς] in his story for this *very Jewish* Gospel and this *very Jewish* Jesus."[39] The phrase "very Jewish" implies a quantitative scale of Jewishness, one that accepts the identity-parameters delimited by specific Jewish interlocutors in their own politics of authenticity. That certain Jews were more insistent about sexual components of their identity or contested more vigorously the parameters of Jewish authenticity cannot be taken as evidence of their greater participation in an authentic Judaism. Bruce Lincoln's thirteenth thesis on method in the study of religion is pertinent: "When one permits those whom one studies to define the terms in which they will be understood … or fails to distinguish between 'truths', 'truth-claims', and 'regimes of truth', one has ceased to function as historian or scholar."[40] Following Lincoln's point, we might think of "authentic Jewishness" as a contested field, evident throughout the works of these very authors. Their claims of Jewish abstinence are clear instances

---

37. Cotter cites Robin Scroggs, *The New Testament and Homosexuality: Contextual Background for Contemporary Debate* (Philadelphia: Fortress, 1983), 66–98; Sacha Stern, *Jewish Identity in Early Rabbinic Writings*, AGJU 23 (Leiden: Brill, 1994), 23–26. The quotations to the contrary are from the very pages Cotter cites: Scroggs, *New Testament and Homosexuality*, 84 (emphasis in original); Stern, *Jewish Identity Identity in Early Rabbinic Writings*, 26.

38. For such sources see chapter 5 or the longer discussion in Christopher B. Zeichmann, "Same-Sex Intercourse Involving Jewish Men 100 BCE–100 CE: Sources and Significance for Jesus' Sexual Politics," *Religion and Gender* 10 (2020): 13–36.

39. Cotter, *Christ of the Miracle Stories*, 125, emphasis added.

40. Bruce Lincoln, "Theses on Method," *MTSR* 8 (1996): 227; cf. William E. Arnal, *The Symbolic Jesus: Historical Scholarship, Judaism and the Construction of Contemporary Identity*, Religion in Culture (London: Equinox, 2005), 20–38; James G. Crossley, *Jesus in an Age of Neoliberalism: Quests, Scholarship and Ideology*, BibleWorld (London: Equinox, 2012), 105–32.

of such authenticity politics in action. The absurdity of credulously accepting ancient claims that all Jews abhorred same-sex intercourse is all the more obvious when one considers how many Roman writers condemned same-sex intercourse with equal fervor; despite the sweeping claims of Cicero (e.g., *Rep.* 4.3–4), Plutarch (e.g., *Quaest. rom.* 274d–e), among many others, that same-sex intercourse was incompatible with Greek or Roman identity, no historian would take these claims at face value or presume such prejudices were distinctively Roman.[41] Even though sweeping condemnations of same-sex intercourse occurred throughout antiquity, only Jewish ones are credulously accepted as descriptions of reality instead of rhetorical formulations. In short, it is unhelpful to label the author of Matthew and other writers very Jewish, while assuming that Jewish men who had sex with other men would not have claimed the same about themselves. We will see in chapter 3 that this ideological investment both racializes the Jewish people and construes them as an essentially *religious* people in contrast with the whiteness of queer secularity.

The State of Affairs

The centurion bore renewed utility among gay interpreters insofar as he was functionary of the Roman state and participated its institutions of respectability as conceived in the imaginary of the late twentieth and early twenty-first centuries (e.g., patronage, patriotism, family life). The Stonewall Riots, which provided the impetus for the US gay liberation movement, protested state violence against queer bodies, but gay interpretations of the 1990s and 2000s idealized a considerably different relationship between the state and queer bodies, indeed it became common to identify queer bodies with such agents of state violence. And while not all those writing such interpretations ascribe to homonormative politics (indeed, many would disavow it), there is something about the centurion that draws them to conceptualize him in that particular register.[42]

---

41. See many other examples discussed and cited in Craig A. Williams, "Greek Love at Rome," *CQ* 45 (1995): 517–39.

42. For instance, Theodore Jennings advocated a sexual ethics that, at least within Christian theological discourse, might be characterized as radical: Jennings, *Ethic of Queer Sex* is critical of heterosexual marriage and endorses forms of sex-work, sex tourism, and pederasty. Even so, the centurion at Capernaum largely draws his discussion into the realm of respectability politics.

The surge of heteronormative reactions is also intelligible in this light, as their charges of anachronism speak to the sense that queer recognition is not only recent but intrusive. The past is conceived as a place of pervasive religiosity, religiosity that was marked by homogeneous sexual norms. Many heteronormative interpretations of the pericope simply *presume* that Jews disdained men who had sex with other men. Evidence to the contrary from the turn of the era may as well not exist, as the ideological stakes demand other ancient data be prioritized. Also striking is how some of these heteronormative interpretations reflect the recent legal distinctions between the homosexual citizen and the sexual predator. On the one hand, some stigmatize the homoerotic interpretation by associating it with sexual predation. Thus, Donald Faris: "At least one pro-homosexual ideology author argues that Jesus not only approved of pedophilia but healed the 'boy' of the centurion at Capernaum (Matthew 8:5–13) and so restored him for the sexual enjoyment of the Roman officer."[43] Others, however, clarify to their readers that Roman pederasty has nothing to do with contemporary homosexuality. In at least one instance, this is an explicitly normative distinction: Amy-Jill Levine and Ben Witherington III clarify that their objection to the homoerotic interpretation on grounds that they do not want to perpetuate a stereotype of queer people as sexual abusers.[44]

It would be easy to interpret this exegetical debate as a tug of war, representative of broader trends about the state's fluctuating acceptance or discrimination against queer bodies—with some attempting to draw the state's power in the direction of homophobia and other toward queer recognition. But there is reason to think the relationship is more complex than simple opposition. Cricket Keating argues that state actors instead rely upon a complex mixture of both homophobia and the homonormativity to mobilize consent, as they come to serve complementary purposes in contemporary statecraft, each serving as ways of consolidating power.[45] This is significant, since the state's orientation toward queer subjects is often treated as if it were "nothing more than a variable reflecting static

---

43. Donald L. Faris, *Trojan Horse: The Homosexual Ideology and the Christian Church* (Burlington: Welch, 1989), 33.

44. Levine and Witherington, *Gospel of Luke*, 198.

45. Christine (Cricket) Keating, "Conclusion: On the Interplay of State Homophobia and Homoprotectionism," in *Global Homophobia: States, Movements, and the Politics of Oppression*, ed. Meredith L. Weiss and Michael J. Bosia (Urbana: University of Illinois Press, 2013), 246–54.

religious values and traditional attitudes about sexuality."[46] In chapter 3, we will see how interpreters have critically engaged this relationship between state power and the homoerotic interpretation.

---

46. Michael J. Bosia and Meredith L. Weiss, "Political Homophobia in Comparative Perspective," in Weiss and Bosia, *Global Homophobia*, 7.

3
MILITARY OCCUPATION AND SEXUAL ABUSE IN ROMAN GALILEE: HOMOEROTIC COUNTERREADINGS, 2000–PRESENT

> Studies ... have privileged the experiences and activities of urban, white queer communities in the United States. By and large, these white, middle-class queer communities are represented as universal, and their experiences and identity claims are posited as the interpretive lens through which the lives of (often) working-class people of color are examined.
> —Marlon M. Bailey, "Gender/Racial Realness"

> If one reads the Bible identifying with ... slaves, one quickly discerns a nonliberative thread running through the Bible.
> —Delores S. Williams, "Black Theology and Womanist Theology"

The homoerotic reading of the Healing of the Centurion's Pais has gathered little traction (or even interest) outside the North Atlantic and Australasia. One notices, for instance, the dearth of such interpretations from Latin America: although a handful of publications produced there mention it,[1]

---

1. E.g., André Sidnei Musskopf, "Biblia, sanación y homosexualidad: 'Hombres sean sumisos a su propio marido. De la misma manera, mujeres sean sumisas a sus esposas,'" *RIBLA* 49 (2004): 97–99 (from Brazil); Ebel Botero, *Homofilia y homofobia: Estudio sobre la homosexualidad, la bisexualidad y la represión de la conducta homosexual* (Medellín: Lealón, 1980), 165–66 (from Colombia); Karina Berenice Bárcenas, "Iglesias para la diversidad sexual: Tácticas de inclusión y visibilización en el campo religioso en México," *Revista Cultura & Religión* 8.1 (2014): 102 (from Mexico); Eliseo Pérez Álvarez, *¿Eres o te haces? Una Probadita a la Homosexualidad y la Biblia* (Buenos Aires: GEMPRIP, 2017), 97–98 (from Mexico); Ariel Álvarez Valdés, "¿Hizo Jesús un milagro a un homosexual?," *Revista Criterio* 2412 (2015): n.p. (from Argentina); Carlos Iturra, *El discípulo amado y otros paisajes masculinos*, Narrativas (Santiago

the homoerotic interpretation in the region is almost entirely informed by English work translated into Portuguese or Spanish, as well as Latin American scholarship initially published in English for an Anglophone readership.² This is not a mere lacuna in scholarship available in these languages: even though academics from Spain have supported the homoerotic interpretation for quite some time, almost no Latin American commentators cite Spanish scholars on this particular issue.³ One observes a similar scarcity of interest in homoerotic readings from eastern Europe, Africa, and Asia.⁴ The homoerotic interpretation of the pericope, it would seem,

---

de Chile: Catalonia, 2012), 49–52 (from Chile). See also the op-eds mentioning the passage: Carlos Ernesto Sánchez, "Soy Homosexual," *La Nación*, 20 June 2011 (from Chile); Daniel Caballero, "¿Sano Jesús al amante homosexual del centurión?," *Semper Reformada Latinoamerica: Teologia para Vivir*, 4 December 2017 (from Peru).

2. For examples of the former, see, e.g., Gerd Theissen, *La Sombra del Galileo*, trans. Constantino Ruiz-Garrido (Salamanca: Sígueme, 1988), 151; Daniel Helminiak, *Lo que la Biblia realmente dice sobre la homosexualidad*, trans. Patricio Camacho Posada, 2nd ed. (Madrid: Egales, 2012), which, along with other Spanish translations of English literature, are by far the most commonly cited sources in Latin American discussions of the centurion's homoeroticism. For examples of the latter, see the work of Thomas Hanks, an American theologian who has spent most of his career in various Latin American countries: Hanks, "Matthew and Mary," 191–92; Hanks, *Subversive Gospel*, 14, 47–48.

3. Discussions by scholars from Spain are numerous, recent examples include Enric Vilà, "The Centurion's Servant in Jesus' Gospels: A Queer Love Story?," in *Queer Ways of Theology* (Warsaw: Wydawnictwo Newsroom, 2016), 41–64; Alfonso Ropero Berzosa, "Homosexualidad," in *Gran Diccionario enciclopédico de la Biblia*, ed. Alfonso Ropero Berzosa (Barcelona: Editorial CLIE, 2013), 1199; Xabier Pikaza Ibarrondo, "Centuriones," in *Gran diccionario de la Biblia*, ed. Xabier Pikaza Ibarrondo (Estella: Verbo Divina, 2015), 211–12; Raúl Zaldívar, *Técnicas de análisis e investigación de la Biblia: Un enfoque evangélico de la Crítica Bíblica* (Barcelona: Editorial CLIE, 2016), 69–71. One of the few exceptions to the disconnect between Spain and Latin America on this interpretation is Álvarez Valdés, "Hizo Jesús," which cites Xabier Pikaza Ibarrondo, *Palabras de amor: Guía de amor humano y cristiano* (Bilbao: Desclee de Brouwer, 2007), 120–23. The relationship between Spain and Latin America is complex, but this is not the place to expound upon the history of theological exchange between the two. In short, since the Second Vatican Council, there has been an increasing separation of the two, with Spanish and Portuguese theology trending ever more towards Europe and a Latin American theological identity congealing in its own right.

4. E.g., from South Korea, see the brief remark in Jae-Hyun Kim, "백부장의 πίστις: Q 복음서의 가버나움 백부장에 관한 연구" ["Centurion's πίστις: a study on the Capernaum centurion of the Q gospels"], 신학사상 [*Theological Thought*] 182 (2018): 193

is a parochial reading that has only found substantial support in the North America, Western Europe, and some Anglophone colonies in the Pacific.

One could explain away the geographic insularity of the homoerotic reading by pointing to factors such as religious demographics, denominational proclivities, and regionally specific sexual norms. Such explanations, however, overlook the fact that the homoerotic reading garners interest little among interpreters of color at all, especially those in the Global South. Or, for that matter, women and nonbinary interpreters. While there are important exceptions, this datum is hardly incidental. The present chapter will consider one set of factors limiting many interpreters' faith in the emancipatory potential of the pericope, namely, colonial and patriarchal legacies complicating the viability of a military officer—one who ostensibly had intercourse with a child—as an exemplar of Christian discipleship. In short, the social distinctions important to the homoerotic interpretation (soldier-civilian, elder-junior, occupier-occupied, etc.) prove a liability in contexts outside the overwhelmingly white domain of homophile and gay interpretation.

The relationship between the centurion and the Pais is marked by a deeply skewed power differential. One gets the sense that many queer interpreters of color, feminists, and their allies—especially those thinking with a postcolonial inflection—prioritize different concerns than those centered by homoerotic readings of this pericope. The present chapter begins by considering a handful of studies that have attempted to reconcile these issues: support for Christian queer political issues, but also the recognition that there is something troubling about the homoerotic interpretation. This chapter takes as its central example an article published by Filipino biblical scholar Revelation Velunta arguing that Jesus effectively restored an abusive relationship.[5] Velunta's interpretation is exemplary of the *counter*reading of the Healing of the Centurion's Pais, a reading marked by its

---

n. 1. E.g., from Poland, see Tlumaczyl Jerzy Jaworski, review of *What the Bible Really Says about Homosexuality*, by Daniel Helminiak, *Tęczowe Prymierzeinformacyjny* 1 (1996): 5–7. Cf. K. Renato Lings, *Holy Censorship or Mistranslation? Love, Gender and Sexuality in the Bible* (Noida: HarperCollins India, 2021), 194–209, which was written by a Danish theologian for an Indian audience, though its relevance to specifically Indian points of interest is rarely obvious.

5. Revelation E. Velunta, "The *Ho Pais Mou* of Matthew 8:5–13: Contesting the Interpretations in the Name of Present-Day *Paides*," *Bulletin for Contextual Theology in Africa* 7.2 (2000): 25–32. Velunta published a revised version as Revelation E. Velunta, "The Centurion and His 'Beloved,'" *Mission Sparks* 3 (2017): 24–47. The only

emphasis on imbalanced power and a refusal to uncritically romanticize sexuality within the pericope. This chapter then considers the conditions necessary for such counterreadings to emerge. First, it places the counterreading alongside antebellum American abolitionists' criticism of biblical slavery, as many deemed the Bible a liability due to its clear endorsement of slavery. Critical engagement with the pericope's depiction of slavery preceded the counterreading by over a century, with many abolitionists anticipating objections within the counterreading. Second, it considers how racial, sexual, colonial, and other forms of oppression converge in the homoerotic interpretation, attending in particular to the racialization of sexuality in the North Atlantic. That is to say, recent events have prompted broader thoughts about how these issues converge, particularly relating to the sexual violence of the military in the early twenty-first century. This chapter will argue that far from being a shortcoming specific to the queer hermeneutical tradition, it speaks to broader failures within New Testament scholarship.

The Pais Is an Abused Filipina Child

Velunta's powerful 2000 article, "The *Ho Pais Mou* of Matthew 8:5–13: Contesting the Interpretations in the Name of Present-Day *Paides*," argues that the Pais is a victim of exegetical amnesia. Unlike most people whom Jesus heals in the Gospel of Matthew, the Pais lacks both identity and agency: the centurion (i.e., his owner) is the Pais's sole point of identification, acting also as his voice and providing the diagnosis. Indeed, the Pais never encounters Jesus at all but "starts and ends in the background."[6] Particularly significant for Velunta is how interpretations consistently reinscribe Matthew's chauvinistic interest in the centurion at the expense of the Pais. Whether it be his faith, his military office, his benevolence to the people of Capernaum, or his ethnicity, the centurion demands attention rarely granted to the Pais.

---

time I have ever seen either article cited is in Jennings and Liew, "Mistaken Identities," 490 n. 58.

6. Velunta, "Centurion and His 'Beloved,'" 27. Velunta here invokes the analysis of John P. Meier, *The Vision of Matthew: Christ, Church, and Morality in the First Gospel* (Philadelphia: Fortress, 1979), 68–69.

More than this, most interpretations downplay the centurion's role as a multivalent agent of state violence: he is a settler, military officer, and enslaver. While it had long been customary to simply gloss over any political implications of the pericope, this is no longer possible thanks to widespread denigration of the Roman Empire in recent biblical scholarship.

Velunta identifies two hermeneutical maneuvers that interpreters commonly deploy to alleviate suspicion of the centurion, whether or not that interpretation is homoerotic. First, some interpreters acknowledge the role of social power in the story but neutralize it by downplaying its implications. In such readings, the centurion is assumed to be a politically, ideologically, or theologically neutral figure: Fritz Kunkel, for instance, claims that in this passage "two empires meet; and curiously enough, they are pleased with one another. Jesus, marvelling at the captain's faith, predicts in his excitement a vast spread of the teaching to 'many from east and west.'"[7] Whatever tensions exist between God's kingdom and the Roman Empire, the questions of politics is safely set aside. Second, many interpretations, often operating with an empire-critical hermeneutic, contend that Jesus overcomes the Roman Empire in the pericope, with God's kingdom eclipsing that of Rome. The centurion, as a representative of Rome, bows humbled before Jesus and recognizes him as holding greater authority than the emperor. Warren Carter—who expends considerable effort situating both Jesus and Matthew within the matrices of Roman imperial power—suggests the pericope is subversive in its politics: "Jesus demonstrates God's empire in healing the centurion's servant and asserts God's supremacy in accomplishing what Rome's empire cannot do despite the propaganda claims … that Rome has healed a sick world."[8] Either the centurion learns an important lesson from the incident, or he never needed reforming in the first place. In either case, Velunta notes that "both Jesus and the centurion come out smelling like roses."[9]

---

7. Fritz Kunkel, *Creation Continues: A Psychological Interpretation of Matthew* (Mahwah: Paulist, 1989), 120–21.

8. Warren Carter, *Matthew and the Margins: A Socio-political and Religious Reading*, Bible and Liberation (Maryknoll, NY: Orbis Books, 2000), 200. On the rhetoric of subversion in New Testament studies, see Robert J. Myles, "The Fetish for a Subversive Jesus," *JSHJ* 14 (2016): 52–70; Christopher B. Zeichmann, "Liberal Hermeneutics of the Spectacular in the Study of the New Testament and the Roman Empire," *MTSR* 31 (2019): 152–83.

9. Velunta, "Centurion and His 'Beloved,'" 33.

Against both of these interpretive tendencies, Velunta follows Musa Dube and others who contend that Matthew adopts an uncritical attitude toward institutions of the Roman Empire, given the evangelist's redaction in this direction is demonstrable: Matthew exonerates Pontius Pilate (27:24), removes ambiguity from the centurion's confession (27:54; cf. Mark 15:39), omits references to Legion in the tale of the Gadarene Demoniacs (8:28–34; cf. Mark 5:1–20), and so on.[10] Velunta assents and argues that Matthew's indifference toward Roman violence is especially evident in the Healing of the Centurion's Pais. Matthew's Jesus comfortably interacts with an enslaving military officer, even praising him for his faith. And although Velunta sees a homoerotic relationship implied within the pericope, his assessment of the centurion differs significantly from the homophile and gay readings discussed in earlier chapters.

> A positive reading of the pericope would have Jesus affirming a homosexual relationship with the healing of the centurion's younger lover. But the opposite is equally, if not more horrifyingly, true. Jesus' "healing" might have restored someone who was trying to break free back into a relationship of exploitation. Because of the partners' difference in age, "the nature of pederasty is inequality, and inequality always leads to domination, and domination to dehumanization and abuse."[11]

Velunta contends that the Pais's illness was an act of resistance, a refusal to partake in the labor (be it manual or sexual) that the centurion demanded of him. Jesus's friendliness to the centurion comes at the expense of the enslaved Pais, whose body was exploited in accordance with his owner's sexual whims. Consent, after all, was not part of a slave's vocabulary.[12]

---

10. Musa W. Dube, *Postcolonial Feminist Interpretation of the Bible* (Saint Louis: Chalice, 2000). See also, e.g., Dorothy Jean Weaver, "'Thus You Will Know Them by Their Fruits': The Roman Characters of the Gospel of Matthew," in *The Gospel of Matthew in Its Roman Imperial Context*, ed. John Riches and David C. Sim, LNTS 276 (London: T&T Clark, 2005), 107–27.

11. Velunta, "Centurion and His 'Beloved,'" 38, quoting Mader, "*Entimos Pais*," 232. Mader here summarizes the conclusion of Scroggs, *New Testament and Homosexuality*, 36–38, 43.

12. See the recent discussion in Anise K. Strong, "Male Slave Rape and the Victims' Agency in Roman Society," in *Slavery and Sexuality in Classical Antiquity*, ed. Deborah Kamen and C. W. Marshall, Wisconsin Studies in Classics (Madison: University of Wisconsin Press, 2021), 174–87.

But this type of abuse is not limited to antiquity. Velunta juxtaposes the centurion's use of the Pais with the sexual abuse and trafficking of Filipino children by white expatriates from the North Atlantic.

> Pagsanjan, Laguna, south of Manila, is famous for its beautiful waterfalls. The place is also a popular haven for paedophiles, mostly from Europe or the United States, that prey on the very poor and the very young. The violence of poverty that millions face every day, throughout the world, can drive people to prostitute themselves and even their children. The number of child prostitutes in the streets of Asia's metropolitan cities is staggering. The majority of them are not much older than Rosario Baluyot. Their bodies bear the ravages of beatings, malnutrition, and AIDS. I have had the opportunity to meet with some of these children. Their names, their voices, their cries offer a name, a voice, a cry for the *pais* submerged in Matthew's text.[13]

Baluyot was a Filipina girl about twelve years old whom a white sex tourist sexually abused in a manner that killed her. Baluyot lived in Olongapo City, the site of US Naval Base Subic Bay at the time of her death in 1987. White tourists (often, sex tourists) to the city usually bore a connection to the Navy, be it direct or indirect. The evidence against her abuser was overwhelming, but punishment was limited to a fine approximating $1000 US dollars. The travesty of Baluyot's death provides stark evidence of how colonial legacies continue to imbalance interactions between settler and colonized. Velunta detects leniency for colonizers within both the Philippine legal system and interpretations of this passage: just as the legal system protects the interests of white colonizers in the Philippines, so also do interpretations protect the interests of the centurion (who is usually identified as a Roman colonizer). Even if one doubts the homoerotic interpretation, there can be little doubt that the centurion was responsible for both the enslavement and health of the Pais. Thus, when Jesus healed the Pais, he restored an abusive relationship.

Although Velunta is hesitant to celebrate the pericope, several factors distinguish his project from heteronormative readings that disparage the homoerotic interpretation. First, Velunta agrees with other homoerotic interpretations that the pericope implies some kind of sexual relationship between the centurion and the Pais. This is important and perhaps the

---

13. Velunta, "Centurion and His 'Beloved,'" 39.

greatest distinguishing feature from the heteronormative interpretations: namely, that there may indeed be *something* sexual implied within the pericope. Second, while some of Velunta's apprehensions may resemble the objections of heteronormative readings,[14] his normative ethics do not presume the Bible's inherent authority. That is, Velunta deems Jesus culpable in the Pais's continued slavery and sexual abuse. This differs from the objections of many heteronormative readings, who dispute the presence of homoeroticism on grounds that it violates biblical ethics: homosexual intercourse was regarded as sinful, ergo it is impossible that Jesus would tacitly accept it. Third, and most importantly, is the centrality of Velunta's hermeneutics of suspicion.[15] Velunta has written favorably about queer theology, but his implicit argument is that queer biblical interpretation and theology *must be done better*, namely, in a manner that considers how the Bible has been racialized, figured into colonial legacies, and justified sexual violence. There is a conspicuous failure in homoerotic interpretations to consider how various forms oppression intersect in the pericope, as they instead tend toward a myopic preoccupation with what is good for (white) gays in a North Atlantic context.

Velunta is not the only one to sympathetically criticize the homoerotic interpretation. David Gowler observes that "sexual relations between owners and slaves were accepted, whether the slave was male or female.... Even if 'genuine affection' could exist between the owner and the slave,

---

14. E.g., Gagnon, "Notes": "By the reasoning of those who put a pro-homosex spin on the story, we would have to conclude that Jesus had no problem with this particularly exploitative form of same-sex intercourse inasmuch as he did not explicitly tell the centurion to stop doing it." Martin Davie, *The Church of England Evangelical Council: Studies on the Bible and Same-Sex Relationships Since 2003* (West Knapton: Gilead, 2015), 340: "Jesus' endorsement of such a relationship would have meant endorsement of an exploitative relationship involving pederasty and probably rape." These arguments differ from Velunta and other counterreadings because they not only implicate the homoerotic reading in moral wrongdoing but to discredit its historical/theological/hermeneutical plausibility as well. That is, we are to imagine it would have been impossible for Jesus to endorse such immoral activities, which is presented as a *reductio ad absurdum* of the homoerotic reading.

15. This chapter deploys the phrase *hermeneutics of suspicion* in a very limited sense. Though the phrase generally refers to the idea that texts are both "generative and constitutive of social realities that go beyond surface meaning" (to quote Robert Myles), this chapter instead limits the term to a hermeneutical posture comported to ascertain the legitimation of various violences (e.g., sexual, racial, gendered) within the biblical text itself.

this oppression was part of the wider, general exploitation of human beings as slaves. So, for modern readers, this relationship—because of the abuse of power inherently involved in an owner/slave relationship—is ethically problematic."[16] Gowler explicitly names the ethical issue at play for modern readers, namely, the power differential between owners and slaves in any such relationship. Richard Valantasis likewise poses ethical questions for readers' personal reflection after favorably discussing the homoerotic interpretation.

> How do readers/hearers react to the power and authority of Jesus after they learn of his civilized engagement with the leader of an occupying force? Can one learn from one's occupier? Will Jesus heal a beloved child in such a social, political, and possibly sexual environment?[17]

Though Valantasis never answers these questions, they encourage the reader to adopt a state of ambivalence: whatever good the pericope offers, one should not prematurely celebrate its potential homoeroticism. As early as 1989, the editor of a queer Christian newsletter appended a short piece advocating a homoerotic reading of the pericope with the following coda:

> Editor's Note: This exegesis may be criticized on the ground that it would support slavery as well as homosexual relations. Think about that. But note that the text points out that the centurion loved his servant deeply. Genuine love, going beyond self-serving lust or mere admiration, may redeem what otherwise be an exploitative relationship.[18]

Several others have made similar points.[19] These counterreadings range from the position that the narrative is more or less irredeemable (so

---

16. David B. Gowler, "Text, Culture and Ideology in Luke 7:1–10: A Dialogic Reading," in *Fabrics of Discourse: Essays in Honor of Vernon K. Robbins*, ed. David B. Gowler, L. Gregory Bloomquist, and Duane F. Watson (Harrisburg, PA: Trinity Press International, 2003), 118.

17. Richard Valantasis, *The New Q: A Fresh Translation with Commentary* (London: T&T Clark, 2005), 83–84.

18. Jim Lokken *apud* McNeill, "Positive Messages from the Bible," 11.

19. E.g., James E. Miller, "The Centurion and His Slave Boy" (paper presented at the Annual Meeting of the Society of Biblical Literature, San Francisco, 1997); Jennings and Liew, "Mistaken Identities"; Bonnie J. Flessen, *An Exemplary Man: Cornelius and Characterization in Acts 10* (Eugene: Pickwick, 2011), 57–59; Martin Forward, "A Pilgrimage of Grace: The Journey Motif in Luke-Acts," in *A Man of Many*

Velunta) to cautioning against credulous enthusiasm for the pericope (so Valantasis) to significant revision of traditional characterizations (so Jennings and Liew).

With Whom Does One Sympathize?

The counterreading is marked by simultaneous affirmation of homoeroticism in the pericope and identification of significant ethical problems within it. Counterreadings are fundamentally marked by the values they hold in tension. The values advocated among such interpretations vary significantly but overlap such that four concerns commonly recur.

Parts: Essays in Honor of John Westerdale Bowker on the Occasion of His Eightieth Birthday, ed. Eugene E. Lemcio (Eugene: Pickwick, 2015), 68–69; Joseph A. Marchal, "Pinkwashing Paul, Excepting Jesus: The Politics of Intersectionality, Identification, and Respectability," in *The Bible and Feminism: Remapping the Field*, ed. Yvonne Sherwood (Oxford: Oxford University Press, 2017), 448–49; Marchal, "LGBTIQ Strategies of Interpretation," in *The Oxford Handbook of New Testament, Gender, and Sexuality*, ed. Benjamin H. Dunning (Oxford: Oxford University Press, 2019), 191–92; Jonathan Tallon, "What Do the Gospels Say Directly about Being Gay?," 6 July 2018, https://tinyurl.com/sbl6705i; M Adryael Tong, "Gender and Sexuality in Postcolonial Perspective," in *The Oxford Handbook of New Testament, Gender, and Sexuality*, ed. Benjamin H. Dunning (Oxford: Oxford University Press, 2019), 122; Johanna Stiebert, *Rape Myths, the Bible, and #MeToo*, Rape Culture, Religion and the Bible (London: Routledge, 2020), 23–24; Reid and Matthews, *Luke 1–9*, 223–25; Caroline Blyth, *Rape Culture, Purity Culture, and Coercive Control in Teen Girl Bibles*, Rape Culture, Religion and the Bible (New York: Routledge, 2021), 58; John E. Christianson, *Matthew and the Roman Military: How the Gospel Portrays and Negotiates Imperial Power* (Lanham: Lexington/Fortress Academic, 2022), 125–152. Note also the ambivalence of Alan H. Cadwallader, "Surprised by Faith: A Centurion and a Canaanite Query the Limits of Jesus and the Disciples," in *Pieces of Ease and Grace: Biblical Essays on Sexuality and Welcome*, ed. Alan H. Cadwallader (Adelaide: ATF Theology, 2013), 89; Iturra, *Discípulo amado*, 49–52.

See also my own publications on the topic: Christopher B. Zeichmann, "Rethinking the Gay Centurion: Sexual Exceptionalism, National Exceptionalism in Readings of Matt 8:5–13//Luke 7:1–10," *BCT* 11.1 (2015): 35–54; Zeichmann, "Gender Minorities in and under Roman Power: Respectability Politics in Luke–Acts," in *Luke–Acts*, ed. James Grimshaw, Texts@Contexts (London: Bloomsbury, 2018), 61–73; Zeichmann, *The Roman Army and the New Testament* (Lanham: Lexington/Fortress Academic, 2018), 67–70. Readers might notice that the present monograph reconsiders several points argued in these earlier publications.

First is the disparity between the evangelists' casual acceptance of slavery as a morally neutral institution and more recent understandings of slavery as a heinous evil. The counterreading mitigates against efforts to rehabilitate the centurion qua slave-owner. Neither the centurion's Christian faith nor his humanitarianism undoes the evil of enslaving another human being. Even more striking is that Jesus has nothing to say about this; because he heals a slave without comment, one is left with the impression he takes no issue with slavery. This is striking and extends beyond Jesus's restoration of a slave to his owner's labor force. Rather, counterinterpretations regard enslaver-enslaved relations as inherently coercive, given the essential power imbalance. Intercourse between the centurion and the Pais (if one follows Luke in imagining him as enslaved) was exploitative.

Roman writers knew that sex between owners and their slaves was inherently coercive. One might recall the comments of Seneca the Elder, who acknowledged this type of intercourse was rarely willing: "unchastity is a crime for a free man, a duty for a slave, and an obligation owed [to his former owner] by a freedman" (*Contr.* 4 praef. 10).[20] An attendant reminds a slave-owner in the novel *Chaereas and Callirhoe*, "You are her master, with full power over her, so she must do your will whether she likes it or not" (2.62).[21] Though these are literary texts, the sense that slave's sex with their owner was often unwanted was not limited to fictional imagination, as Jennifer Glancy draws our attention to one papyrus threatening the continual abuse of a real-life slave in Roman Egypt.

> Resistance of male or female slaves to sexual overtures sanctioned by their owners was not acceptable servile behavior. A scrap of papyrus from Oxyrhynchus records a crude proposition or, more accurately, a threat from two males to a third. It reads: "Apion and Epimas proclaim to their best-loved Epaphroditus that if you allow us to bugger you it will go well for you, and we will not thrash you any longer." Epaphroditus typically appears in the papyri as a name associated with a slave. Here, a young slave, or perhaps a freedman, seems to have two "options": to

---

20. Impudicitia in ingenuo crimen est, in servo necessitas, in liberto officium.

21. κύριος γὰρ εἶ καὶ ἐξουσίαν ἔχεις αὐτῆς, ὥστε καὶ ἑκοῦσα καὶ ἄκουσα ποιήσει τὸ σοὶ δοκοῦν. For more examples from ancient literature, see the literature cited in the introduction.

submit to unwanted sexual activities or to allow two other men to (continue to) beat him.[22]

An image of the Epaphroditus papyrus is provided below (fig. 3). Thus, while Roman writers do not characterize intercourse with enslaved people as rape in a legal or moral sense (*stuprum, raptus*), they were nevertheless aware that sex with a freeborn person required a willingness that was not expected when having intercourse with an enslaved liaison. This is not to say that sex with one's owner was never desirable—though we would have little way of knowing when this might have been the case, since nearly all evidence of such intercourse during the Roman period has been filtered through enslavers' self-serving narratives (e.g., the fickle fancies of Giton in Petronius's *Satyricon*; the link between erotic desire and slavishness in other Greco-Roman novels: Xenophon of Ephesus, *Eph.* 1.4.1; Apuleius *Metam.* 3.19–22).

At best, sex between enslaver and enslaved involved unwitting participation in a broader Roman rape culture: the legal regime informing Roman sexuality centered around the delineation of inheritance lines (i.e., the parentage of freeborn children) and enforcing social hierarchies by delimiting whose body was penetrable and whose was not (i.e., acts permissible within freeborn sex). Because enslaved people were excluded from such lines of inheritance, the exact parentage of their children was of considerably less significance than those born of *conubium*. Likewise, the penetrability of slaves' bodies was a matter of course. Even when enslaved people might have characterized the intercourse as enjoyable, they were rarely in a position to refuse an encounter and had no legal recourse for any injuries that their resistance may have induced. Unwanted sex or exploitative sex may or may not fit the present reader's conception of rape, but none of these typify a relationship that one would uphold as exemplary.[23] There is no textual basis to infer the Pais's opinion of the centurion,

---

22. Jennifer A. Glancy, *Slavery in Early Christianity* (Oxford: Oxford University Press, 2002), 53, discussing P.Oxy. 3070 (first century CE); see figure 3 for the recto of the papyrus. Glancy directs readers to the discussion of the papyrus in Dominic Montserrat, *Sex and Society in Græco-Roman Egypt* (London: Routledge, 1996), 136–38.

23. See the discussion of this issue as it relates to biblical studies in Rhiannon Graybill, *Texts after Terror: Rape, Sexual Violence, and the Hebrew Bible* (Oxford: Oxford University Press, 2021), 1–29.

since the Pais never speaks, much less appears, in the gospels. He only exists off-stage and without a voice.

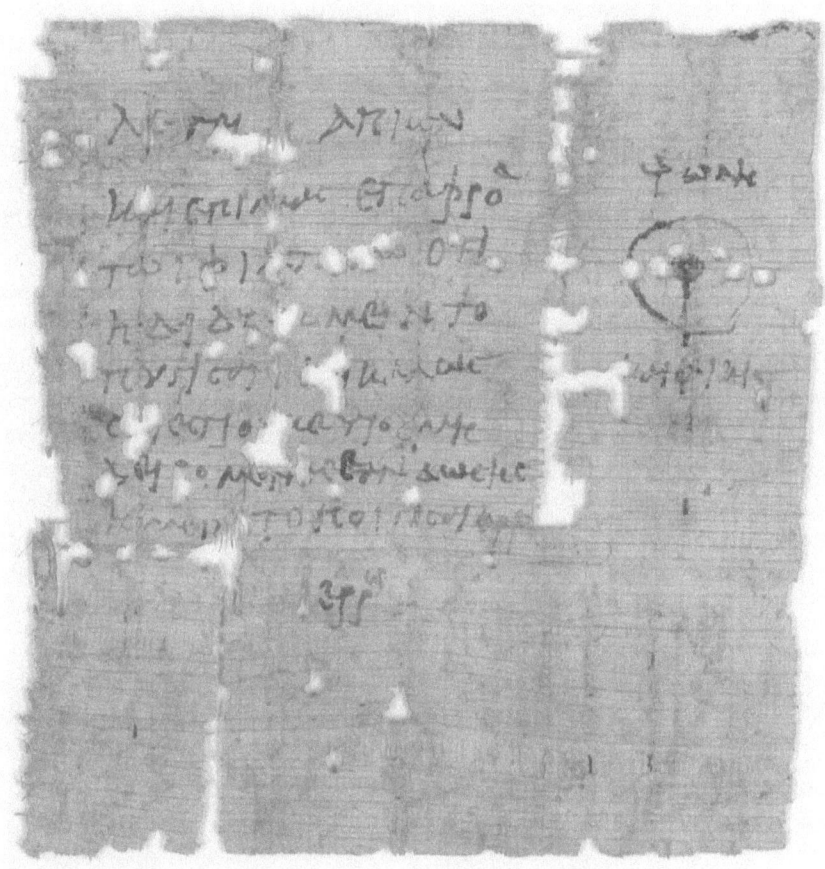

Fig. 3. P.Oxy. 3070, discussed in the block quotation of Glancy above. One excerpt omitted by Glancy is the portion of the papyrus to the far right. The top word reads "boner" (ψωλή); the bottom line reads "and butthole" (καὶ φίκις), with a crude representation of anal intercourse between the two lines of text. The papyrus implies snide threat elsewhere: the letter ends with a faux-friendly, "Farewell! Farewell!" and the papyrus' verso likewise reads, "Deliver to the most beloved [φιλτάτῳ] Epaphroditus." Note also the phrasing resembling that of an imperial edict—in satirizing the genre, do Apion and Epimas knowingly reinscribe imperial relations of power and masculinity? Photograph courtesy of The Egypt Exploration Society and the University of Oxford Imaging Papyri Project.

The matter is hardly any better if one imagines the Pais was freeborn. When discussing Matthew's version of the pericope, Jennings and Liew securely establish that sexual congress commonly occurred between soldiers and freeborn male adolescents (παῖδες) during Roman times.[24] Denis B. Saddington, however, objects that a close reading of Jennings and Liew's data presumes an asymmetrical relationship between the Roman army and the inhabitants of the regions conquered; this relationship crucially structured the conditions for soldiers' sex with young people, typically involving rape.[25] Particularly vivid is an example they quote from Tacitus: "Whenever a young woman or a handsome youth fell into their hands, they were torn to pieces by the violent struggles of those who tried to secure them" (Tacitus, *Hist.* 3.33).[26] In another instance, Tacitus recounts how handsome Batavian youth were beckoned to a Roman garrison under the pretense of recruitment; Roman soldiers instead raped the young men because the Batavians were "no longer regarded as allies ... but as slaves" (Tacitus, *Hist.* 4.14).[27] Greek and Roman literature presumes that soldiers' wartime rape of civilians was commonplace.[28] It was sufficiently pervasive that even though Roman law ascribed the status *infamia* to freeborn Romans penetrated by other men, partial exceptions were given to male victims of wartime rape.[29] Given that most soldiers' slaves were erstwhile prisoners of war, the violence undergirding of such relationships is not something one would want to replicate.

Legionaries' sexual violence has been a topic of important recent research on the Roman military. Caryn Reeder, David Mattingly, and C. R. Whittaker demonstrate that the relationship between Rome and its provinces was reinscribed in soldiers' sexual abuse of youth in conquered lands: resistance to Roman aggression was demonstrably futile and resulted in

---

24. Jennings and Liew, "Mistaken Identities," 474–77.
25. Saddington, "Centurion in Matthew."
26. Jennings and Liew, "Mistaken Identities," 475.
27. See also Quintilian, *Decl.* 3, which tells of a soldier raped by a military tribune who then killed his rapist. The soldier defended the murder of a superior by noting that the act reduced his status to one approximating a slave's.
28. Williams, *Roman Homosexuality*, 112–16 discusses several passages, including Sallust, *Bell. cat.* 51.9; Cicero, *Phil.* 3.31, *Verr.* 2.4.116, *Att.* 1.16.5; Rhet. Her. 4.12; Livy, *Ab urbe cond.* 26.13.15; Valerius Maximus, *Fact.* 9.1.7; Seneca, *Ep.* 97.2.
29. Williams, *Roman Homosexuality*, 214–15; Richlin, "Not before Homosexuality," 555–66.

broken bodies.³⁰ Palestinian rabbis often presumed as much; Benjamin Isaac observes that Jewish women held captive by Roman soldiers were assumed to have been raped, whereas those held by local bandits were not.³¹ One might observe the same assumption in the writings of Josephus (*C.Ap.* 1.35) and other Roman writers (e.g., Chariton, *Chaer.* 8.4.3).

Roman art also depicts vivid portraits of such military sexual violence. To merely note the two most famous examples, one relief found at Aphrodisias depicts the emperor Claudius preparing to rape the female personification of Britannia (see fig. 4), and another at the same site depicts Nero doing the same with a personified Armenia (see fig. 5). Legionaries held immense power over the denizens of the provinces they garrisoned, often without concern for consent as a marker for acceptable intercourse.

Fig. 4. Claudius preparing to rape Britannia. The emperor Claudius is here depicted as a soldier preparing to deliver the coup de grâce before raping a woman whose clothes have been torn off— the personified Britannia. The sculpture is a symbolic representation of his military victory in that region and its partial annexation to the Roman Empire. The sculpture was erected in 48 CE in the Asian city of Aphrodisias (now in Turkey). The accompanying inscription reads Τιβέριος Κλαύδιος Καῖσαρ—Βρεταννία (Tiberius Claudius Caesar—Britannia) (SEG 31.918). Photograph by Steve Kershaw.

---

30. Caryn A. Reeder, "Wartime Rape, the Romans, and the First Jewish Revolt," *JSJ* 48 (2017): 363–85; David J. Mattingly, *Imperialism, Power, and Identity: Experiencing the Roman Empire* (Princeton: Princeton University Press, 2011), 94–121; C. R. Whittaker, *Rome and Its Frontiers: The Dynamics of Empire* (London: Routledge, 2004), 115–43.

31. Benjamin Isaac, *The Limits of Empire: The Roman Army in the East*, rev. ed. (Oxford: Clarendon, 1992), 85–86, citing t. Ketub. 4:5; b. Ketub. 51b; y. Ketub. 2:2, 26d. Likewise, 4 Ezra 10:22 links the rape of Jewish women and children to Jews captured and enslaved by Roman soldiers. I am grateful to David Tombs, who has drawn my attention to several mishnaic texts presuming women having spent time with soldiers had been raped: m. Ketub. 1:2, 1:4, 2:5–6, 2:9.

Fig. 5. Nero preparing to rape Armenia. The emperor Nero is here depicted as a soldier as having conquered a nude female archer—the personified Armenia. This sculpture is a symbolic representation of his military victory in that province after its defection to Parthia and its return to a quasi-Roman client kingdom. The sculpture was erected in 63 CE in the Asian city of Aphrodisias (now in Turkey). The accompanying inscription reads [Νέρων] Κλαύδιος Δρούσος Καῖσαρ Σεβαστὸς Γερμανικός (Nero Claudius Drusus Caesar Augustus Germanicus) (SEG 31.920). Photograph by Steve Kershaw.

A second concern among counterinterpretations regards pederasty. Homophile interpretations often either sexualize youth or imagine relationships between adults and adolescents to be self-evidently worthy of celebration, a phenomenon particularly common within homophile readings. Gay interpretations evince greater apprehension about this issue and seek to distance homosexuality from pederasty, aware that this would be a significant blight on the legal projects such interpretations serve. In both cases, though, interpretations simply assert that this relationship was loving, rather than considering how it was inextricable from the accrual of power that comes with age in pederastic relationships. We do not know the age of the Pais, but Roman pederasty typically involved boys who had not developed full facial hair; it often entailed sex with children well below what most would consider a reasonable age of consent and thus constituted abusive or exploitative sex.

A third objection concerns the tendency to uncritically uphold an agent of state violence as exemplary. Jesus commends a military officer in a way that mitigates against a number of emancipatory hermeneutics: antiimperialism, abolitionism, antiracism, and so on. The pericope takes for granted that the centurion's role in state violence is entirely compatible with Jesus's preaching and draws upon his authority for the gospels' normative visions of the world. That Jesus was friendly with an agent of state violence and tacitly accepted slavery is not an appealing prospect for most interpreters, though few have addressed the matter directly. Particularly instructive is the counterreading of Jennings and Liew, which argues that the centurion was less a hero and more of a heel; the centurion, for instance, completely misunderstands Jesus's position within the divine hierarchy and is vaguely hostile to Jesus.[32] There is a sense that if one is to reconcile one's values to the pericope, it would require extensive reconsideration of its characters.

The fourth, and cumulative, objection is that the hermeneutical sympathies of most interpretations lie with the centurion, taking at face-value the claims of the biblical texts, namely, that the Pais is dear or important (ἔντιμος) to him. Sympathy for the centurion leads people to gloss over the issues of slavery, colonialism, and pederasty in service of their preferred exegetical project. On the one hand, this problem is intrinsic to the text itself, as noted above: the gospels partake in a chauvinism that further marginalizes already-marginal voices.[33] Matthew, Luke, and Q depict Jesus as fascinated with the centurion and only interested in the Pais insofar as his owner cares for him. Luke-Acts has a recurring interest in wealthy and respected characters. In the case of the centurion, Luke redacts his source to both make him considerably wealthier and grant him prestige within Capernaum (7:3–5). Interpreters consistently reinscribe this prejudice. One particularly egregious interpretation remarks that "Jesus healed the boy without raising a question and restored him to the *enjoyment* of the Roman officer."[34] Even the sexual pleasure is unironically imagined to be one-sided. That readers are prone to sympathize with the centurion is obvious in both homoerotic and heteronormative commentary; nearly all interpreters find reason to agree with Jesus's acclaim for the centurion.

A Text of Terror: The Developing Interpretive Situation

The claims of the counterreading are somewhat surprising. The gospels are rarely subjected to moral scrutiny, as most interpreters are more than happy

---

32. Jennings and Liew, "Mistaken Identities," 484–88.

33. Likewise Reid and Matthews, *Luke 1–9*, 225: "Because of feminist concern for the most vulnerable in society, it is unsettling that we hear nothing from the slave's point of view. We do not know if he wants to be healed. Perhaps he would prefer to die rather than be trapped in this relationship from which he has no power to escape." Cf. the remarks in Levine and Witherington, *Gospel of Luke*, 201.

34. Erwin Buck, *Studies on Homosexuality and the Church* ([Unknown location]: Evangelical Lutheran Church in Canada, 2001), 28, emphasis added.

to claim agreement with Jesus whenever possible.[35] The ethics of Jesus are presumed beyond doubt. Jesus's unimpeachability might be contrasted with the apostle Paul, a figure who often elicits ambivalence in the popular imagination (concerning, e.g., patriarchy, sexual ethics, slavery). In criticizing Jesus, counterinterpretations oppose nearly two millennia of biblical interpretation.

The counterreading arose within a broader tradition of critically engaging troublesome portions of the Bible. One recalls Phyllis Trible's work on "texts of terror," a phrase coined to designate biblical tales that accept or even laud violence against women.[36] Trible's purpose is explicitly normative, as these texts often legitimize violence today.

> Choice and chance inspire my telling these particular tales: hearing a black woman describe herself as a daughter of Hagar outside the covenant; seeing an abused woman on the streets of New York with a sign, "My name is Tamar"; reading news reports of the dismembered body of a woman found in a trash can; attending worship services in memory of nameless women; and wrestling with the silence, absence, and opposition of God. All these experiences and others have led me to a land of terror from whose bourn no traveler returns unscarred.[37]

Trible contends that misogynistic violence is often intrinsic to the text itself and not merely a later imposition by sexist interpreters who misconstrue an unimpeachable Bible. Rather than attempting to redeem these stories by drawing out hitherto-hidden messages of hope or otherwise sanitizing them, Trible directs readers' attention to the significant gap between the moral standing commonly ascribed to the Bible and the stories actually contained within it. Her project memorializes those who have suffered sexual violence.

---

35. One famous exception would be Elisabeth Schüssler Fiorenza, *Jesus and the Politics of Interpretation* (London: Continuum International, 2000).

36. Phyllis Trible, *Texts of Terror: Literary-Feminist Readings of Biblical Narratives*, OBT 13 (Philadelphia: Fortress, 1984).

37. Trible, *Texts of Terror*, 1–2. For a discussion about the limitations of the texts-of-terror approach that draws upon a robust feminist framework, see Graybill, *Texts after Terror*. The phrase *texts of terror* is used here in a less restricted manner than either Graybill or Trible do. For them, the phrase refers to a specific praxis of narrative criticism recounting biblical "sad stories." The phrase is used more loosely here to designate critical readings of the sexual violence and slavery, regardless of their conformity to Trible's strictly *descriptive* method.

While Trible focuses upon sexual violence against women, the phrase "texts of terror" has subsequently characterized biblical passages that endorse violence against other populations, including queer folk, racialized minorities, indigenous people, and those with disabilities. How, for instance, does Joshua's genocide of Canaanites legitimate settler colonialism? Or Revelation's celebration of humiliation of the whore of Babylon relate to contemporary violence against sex workers? Or Leviticus's admonition to execute men who have intercourse with other men and homophobia today? Many since Trible have argued that there is little redeeming in such passages. These and other biblical texts present ethical problems for those ascribing them authority. This is not a strictly historical or literary matter but ultimately a *theological* issue in that it concerns the normative meaning-making practices of Jewish and Christian Scriptures.[38]

Although Trible may have devised the phrase texts of terror and in doing so facilitated the spread of a certain feminist hermeneutic of suspicion within biblical scholarship, she was hardly the first to articulate grievances about biblical ethics. Particularly instructive for our purposes is how the centurion figured into debates about slavery before the US government abolished it in 1865. It is here, a context where Jesus's approbation of the centurion was commonly marshalled as support for slavery, that exegetical seeds were sown and later blossomed into the counterreading of the Healing of the Centurion's Pais. Although many commentators were happy to claim that this pericope supported their own view of slavery (whether favoring or opposing it), of particular interest here are the abolitionist interpretations that saw little redeeming in New Testament depictions of slavery, similar to the texts of terror approach. For such interpreters, the Bible was a liability to the cause of abolition and, as such, one best approached the Bible with either a pair of metaphorical scissors or

---

38. The counterreading differs from the texts-of-terror approach of Robert E. Goss and Mona West, introduction to *Take Back the Word: A Queer Reading of the Bible*, ed. Robert E. Goss and Mona West (Cleveland: Pilgrim, 2000), 5: "The whole Bible is a text of terror because of the ways in which our abuse has been justified by the misinterpretation of a few obscure passages. We believe the point of reference for a queer reading of scripture is the notion that the Bible is our friend. When we approach the Bible as a friendly text, as a text that 'does not harm,' the terror of the Scriptures is transformed into the life-giving Word of God." Whereas Shore-Goss and West focus on the terror the Bible has wrought upon queer bodies, the counterreading centralizes the terror wrought upon racialized, young, and sex-trafficked bodies.

perhaps even a box of matches. To be clear, the present section will examine interpretations that predate any homoerotic reading of the pericope.

The centurion proved a valuable ally to slavery apologists during the nineteenth century. Typical are the remarks of John Richter Jones: "Christ never alludes to the subject of emancipation in his personal teaching; but if the servant of the gentile centurion was a slave, as in all probability he was, we would have strong proof from his own mouth for the perfect compatibility of slaveholding with a high order of Christian piety."[39] Jones further observes that even if the Pais was not enslaved, the centurion nevertheless owned other people who were: "I say ... to my slave [τῷ δούλῳ μου], 'Do this' and he does it" (Matt 8:9; Luke 7:8). Jones's interpretation exemplifies a reading strategy common in proslavery literature, drawing attention to the fact that Jesus unambiguously and unconditionally extols the centurion *qua* slave-owner. Compare, for instance, South Carolina congressman Laurence Keitt's comments before the US House of Representatives from 1858.

> He heals the slave of the centurion, and has no rebuke for slavery, but praises for the officer's faith. No, sir, nothing of condemnation, nothing of even reproof from the Savior's lips, for the "vile wretch,"—the "man stealer," who, according to the approved Yankee formula "held his brother man in bondage."[40]

Numerous others made the same point.[41] The appeal of this reading is obvious, as it relies on a hermeneutics of the text's plain sense and is dif-

---

39. John Richter Jones, *Slavery Sanctioned by the Bible: A Tract for Northern Christians* (Philadelphia: Lippincott, 1861), 28. On the popularity of this pericope among proslavery advocates, see J. Albert Harrill, *Slaves in the New Testament: Literary, Social, and Moral Dimensions* (Minneapolis: Fortress, 2006), 183; Ian Boxall, *Matthew through the Centuries*, Wiley Blackwell Bible Commentaries (Oxford: Blackwell, 2019), 156–57.

40. Laurence M. Keitt, "The Origins of Slavery," in *Appendix to the Congressional Globe Containing Speeches, Important State Papers, Laws, etc. of the First Session Thirty-Fifth Congress*, ed. John C. Rives (Washington, DC: Rives, 1858), 406.

41. E.g., "Was not the best man that Christ met while He was on earth a centurion slaveholder in the army of Tiberius Cæsar?... As Christ did not require the centurion to emancipate his slave, is it not reasonable to infer that love did not require it?" from Sidney Edwards Morse, *Premium Questions on Slavery, Each Admitting of a Yes or No Answer* (New York: Harper & Brothers, 1860), 8. Likewise, William Gannaway Brownlow asserted that even though Roman slavery was far less humane than American

ficult to dispute theologically, given its syllogistic logic: if Jesus never condemned slavery and if he in fact commended a slave-owner in highest terms, then slavery is not only acceptable but can even be admirable.

Abolitionists resorted to exegetical gymnastics in their efforts to discredit this pervasive reading. William Henry Brisbane, for instance, objected:

> The servant who was sick was a child, as a Greek scholar would readily admit. "My little son," instead of "my servant," would have been a more literal translation. Luke represents him as a servant "who was dear unto him," and also as a little son.... But the centurion had at least one servant—as evident from the 9th verse. But what sort of servant was he? Was he a slave? There is no proof of it—not the slightest. The case of the centurion, therefore, cannot be used in defence of slavery.[42]

Brisbane's argument seems straightforward, but he employs some exegetical sleight of hand to mitigate against the proslavery interpretation. Brisbane harmonizes the pericope with the Healing of the Royal Official's Son (John 4:46–54), which depicts the Pais as the officer's son and thus freeborn. His appeal to the authority of "the Greek scholar" also performs significant rhetorical work, since few philologists would agree with the rigid semantic domain he ascribed to δοῦλος, let alone his stretching of παῖς past its breaking point.

Brisbane's contention that the Pais was not really enslaved exemplifies a reading strategy common among abolitionists. This approach, popularized by Albert Barnes and thus known as the "Barnes Hypothesis," initially concerned Paul's Letter to Philemon but was commonly applied to other texts as well. Barnes argued that the man named Onesimus was not enslaved, rebutting arguments that Paul returned a fugitive slave to his owner.[43] Paul did not *really* support slavery. Brisbane, Barnes, and others

---

slavery, Jesus nevertheless "established the fact that a man could be Christian and yet hold slaves," pointing to the centurion as his evidence. William Gannaway Brownlow and Abram Pryne, *Ought American Slavery to be Perpetuated? A Debate* (Philadelphia: Lippnincott, 1858), 83.

42. William Henry Brisbane, *Slaveholding Examined in the Light of the Holy Bible* (Philadelphia: Wyeth, 1847), 94. This argument was repeated nearly verbatim in George Barrell Cheever, *The Guilt of Slavery and the Crime of Slaveholding: Demonstrated from the Hebrew and Greek Scriptures* (Boston: Jewett, 1860), 367–68.

43. See its famous articulation in Albert Barnes, *An Inquiry into the Scriptural Views of Slavery* (Philadelphia: Perkins & Purves, 1846), 242–44. J. Albert Harrill,

adopted this same line of reasoning with the Healing of the Centurion's Pais. This argument undermined claims that Jesus praised the centurion *qua* slave-owner and explains why Jesus's teachings never addressed the issue of slavery directly. Aside from the passing reference to the high priest's slave (Mark 14:47 and parallels), this pericope narrates the sole instance where Jesus intervened in an owner-slave relationship. If the Pais was not enslaved, then Jesus was silent about slavery for the same reason he said nothing about rocket ships: he never encountered them. Slavery apologists, naturally, were not convinced.[44]

Although this was the most popular approach among abolitionists, there were a few other ways of reading the pericope. Some proffered a more disparaging reading of the centurion. Cyrus Grosvenor suggested that Jesus chastised the centurion behind the scenes: "Christ commended the centurion's faith, but what instructions he gave him in regard to slavery, or any other subject, we are not informed."[45] Advocates for slavery mocked Grosvenor's reasoning, as it depended on pure speculation. John Flournoy proffered a more provocative approach:

> Did not this Centurion base his unworthiness, that the Lord should come to him on the *consideration*, that he was a slave-owner and a fighting man? And when Jesus approved of his declaration, is not that approval predicated upon the truth, the Centurion uttered as to his unworthiness? He said he "was unworthy *for* that is, *because*, he had servants and soldiers under him." Jesus accredited his declaration, as he was truly *unworthy* for the *reasons he stated.*[46]

"The Use of the New Testament in the American Slave Controversy: A Case History in the Hermeneutical Tension between Biblical Criticism and Christian Moral Debate," *Religion and American Culture* 10 (2000): 149–86 provides an excellent discussion of the Barnes Hypothesis and its reception.

44. E.g., John Fletcher, *Studies on Slavery: In Easy Lessons* (Natchez: Warner, 1852), 117.

45. Cyrus P. Grosvenor, *Slavery vs. the Bible: A Correspondence Between the General Conference of Maine and the Presbytery of Tombecbee, Mississippi* (Worcester: Spooner & Howland, 1840), 90–91.

46. John J. Flournoy, *A Reply to a Pamphlet, Entitled "Bondage, a Moral Institution Sanctioned by the Scriptures and the Saviour, &c. &c." So Far as It Attacks the Principles of Expulsion with No Defence, However, of Abolitionism* (Atlanta: [unknown publisher], 1838), 15. The typography uses several unusual stylizations for emphasis, all of which have been rendered as italics in the quoted text.

To rephrase, the centurion recognized that the act of enslaving other people and military service rendered him unworthy (Matt 8:8; Luke 7:7). Jesus aided the centurion because he recognized and repented of these evils. While few find this interpretation convincing, it at least finds grounding in the biblical text, rather than emerging wholesale from the interpreter's imagination.

Because the United States' population was overwhelmingly Christian, efforts to identify an abolitionist strain within the Bible were shrewd, even if they were not always persuasive. Frederick Douglass articulated the reasoning clearly.

> It is no evidence that the Bible is a bad book, because those who profess to believe the Bible are bad. The slaveholders of the South, and many of their wicked allies at the North, claim the Bible for slavery; shall we, therefore, fling the Bible away as a pro-slavery book? It would be as reasonable to do so as it would be to fling away the Constitution.[47]

Douglass located the problem in proslavery interpretations, insisting that the Bible did not inherently endorse slavery, and instead preferred to see interpretation as a political phenomenon. It was better to reclaim the text than let slavery-advocates claim a monopoly on such an authoritative text.

A small minority of interpreters, however, took precisely the position that Douglass rejected and argued that the Bible was indeed implicated in slavery. Such abolitionists usually fell into one of two camps. First were anticlerical whites, including William Lloyd Garrison and contributors to his newspaper *The Liberator*. Such abolitionists prided themselves on their education and literacy, so their interpretations are well documented. Typical is a speech of Henry C. Wright, who put forth the following resolution at the American Anti-Slavery meeting of 1850.

> Resolved, That if the Bible sanctions slavery and is thus opposed to the self-evident truth that "all men are created equal and have an inalienable right to liberty," the Bible itself is a self-evident falsehood, and out to be, and ere long be, regarded as the enemy of Nature and Nature's God, and the progress of the human race in liberty, justness and goodness.[48]

---

47. Frederick Douglass, "Speech in Boston, Massachusetts, February 8, 1855," in *The Frederick Douglass Papers, Series One: Speeches, Debates, and Interviews*, ed. John W. Blassingame, 5 vols. (New Haven: Yale University Press, 1985), 3:6.

48. Quoted in T. D. P. Stone, "Speech of Henry C. Wright," *The Liberator (Boston)* 20.22 (1850): 3.

Christianity and its authoritative texts were partially responsible for slavery and, contrary to Douglass's suggestion, it was prudent to reject biblical authority entirely.

Second were people who prioritized their lived experience of slavery over the biblical canon.[49] Like anticlerical whites, these black abolitionists identified numerous texts of terror throughout the Bible, even if such terminology was not at hand. Biblical critique by black abolitionists—be they enslaved or free—is less well known. Antiliteracy laws meant that few enslaved people wrote anything, let alone texts that others deemed worthy of preservation. That said, a few noteworthy examples have survived. Lewis and Milton Clarke were formerly enslaved brothers who published an extensive account of their experience. Though they regard proslavery theology as a corruption of Christianity, they acknowledge that the Bible often has little to offer slaves: "What do slaves know about the Bible? They generally believe there is somewhere a real Bible, that came from God; but they frequently say the Bible now used is master's Bible; most that they hear from it being, 'Servants, obey your masters.'"[50] The Clarkes go nowhere near as far as anticlericals, but they nevertheless encourage suspicion of emphatically *biblical* discourse on slavery. Indeed, this skepticism is evident from the very title of their book, "Narratives of the Sufferings of Lewis and Milton Clarke, Sons of a Soldier of the Revolution, during a Captivity of More Than Twenty Years among the Slaveholders of Kentucky, One of the *So-Called* Christian States of North America," implying that American Christianity served as a façade for something else entirely.

---

49. There were exceptions to this typology, of course. Rabbi M. J. Raphall gave a public lecture concerning the view of slavery in the Hebrew Bible and made clear his own views: "My friends, I find, and I am sorry to find, that I am delivering a pro-slavery discourse. I am no friend to slavery in the abstract, and still less friendly to the practical working of slavery. But I stand here as a teacher in Israel; not to place before you my own feelings and opinions, but to propound to you the word of God, the Bible view of slavery. With a due sense of my responsibility, I must state to you the truth and nothing but the truth, however unpalatable or unpopular that truth may be." M. J. Raphall, "The Bible View of Slavery," in *Fast Day Sermons: Or, the Pulpit on the State of the Country* (New York: Rudd & Carleton, 1861), 239–40.

50. Lewis G. Clarke and Milton Clarke, *Narratives of the Sufferings of Lewis and Milton Clarke, Sons of a Soldier of the Revolution, During a Captivity of More Than Twenty Years among the Slaveholders of Kentucky, One of the So-Called Christian States of North America* (Boston: Marsh, 1846), 105.

Charles Colcock Jones, a white missionary whose work focused on people enslaved at plantations, encountered even greater distrust when he delivered a sermon in 1833.

> I was preaching to a large congregation on the Epistle of Philemon; and when I insisted upon fidelity and obedience as Christian virtues in servants, and upon the authority of Paul, condemned the practice of running away, one half of my audience deliberately rose up and walked off with themselves, and those that remained looked any thing but satisfied, either with the preacher or his doctrine. After dismission, there was no small stir among them; some solemnly declared that there was no such Epistle in the Bible; others, that it was not the Gospel; others, that I preached to please the masters; others, that they did not care if they never heard me preach again.[51]

The people who heard Jones's preaching rejected the authority of Philemon, identifying its alignment with owners' interests—no doubt part of the reason Jones was invited to preach. Whatever Jones was saying, it did not cohere with enslaved people's conception of a loving god.

Perhaps most famous, though, were the objections of Nancy Ambrose, the grandmother of theologian Howard Thurman. Ambrose had been enslaved until the Emancipation Proclamation and, being illiterate, asked Thurman to read the Bible out loud during his weekly visits. She never requested anything from the Pauline corpus. Thurman eventually inquired why, and her response is worth quoting at length.

> During the days of slavery … the master's minister would occasionally hold services for the slaves. Old man McGhee was so mean that he would not let a Negro minister preach to his slaves. Always the white minister used as his text something from Paul. At least three or four times a year he used as a text: "Slaves, be obedient to them that are your masters … as unto Christ." Then he would go on to show how it was God's will that we were slaves and how, if we were good and happy slaves, God would bless us. I promised my Maker that if I ever learned to read and if freedom ever came, I would not read that part of the Bible.[52]

---

51. Charles Colcock Jones, *Tenth Annual Report of the Association for the Religious Instruction of the Negroes in Liberty County, Georgia* (Savanna: Purse, 1845), 24–25; cf. Col 3:22, Eph 6:5, 1 Pet 2:18.

52. Quoted in Howard Thurman, *Jesus and the Disinherited* (New York: Abingdon-Cokesbury, 1949), 30–31.

The Pauline corpus had been banished from Ambrose's canon for its role in legitimizing slavery. The Bible is rife with texts of terror; the abolitionist cause, according to many, was best served by excising such texts from biblical authority rather than parsing them for alternative meanings that might be more congenial to their politics.[53] This approach, far from presuming that there a single authoritative meaning that underlies the biblical text (an assumption that proslavery interpreters, pious abolitionists, and even anticlerical whites shared), evinces what Vincent Wimbush calls a "thinking about thinking." Wimbush observes that these sorts of readings understand "the political constructedness of Scripture-reading and that such reading ought to result in talking and thinking about life and death, slavery and freedom."[54] The interpretation of the Bible, rather, was the product of political interests, interests that tended to align with one's social position.

While recent interpretations regard slavery as self-evidently evil, they commonly identify something redeeming within the Healing of the Centurion's Pais, such that they resemble pious abolitionist apologetics. For instance, some attempt to rehabilitate the centurion by suggesting that he manumitted the Pais after meeting Jesus, as Grosvenor argued a century and a half ago.[55] Although most commentators have aligned themselves with the centurion, several recent interlocutors identify something amiss in the pericope. Carter, for instance, notes that "the healing can be understood to support the empire, especially, as some have argued, paralysis is a psychosomatic protest against imperial power," even though Carter nevertheless maintains the pericope is "ambiguous" and ultimately subverts Roman power.[56] Elizabeth Dowling articulates similar apprehensions, linking the modern phenomenon of human trafficking to Lukan politics of

---

53. For more on abolitionist hermeneutics of suspicion, see Albert J. Raboteau, *Slave Religion: The "Invisible Institution" in the Antebellum South*, updated ed. (Oxford: Oxford University Press, 2004), 290–318; Harrill, "Use of the New Testament"; Allen Dwight Callahan, *The Talking Book: African Americans and the Bible* (New Haven: Yale University Press, 2006), 21–40; Hector Avalos, *Slavery, Abolitionism, and the Ethics of Biblical Scholarship*, Bible in the Modern World 38 (Sheffield: Sheffield Phoenix, 2011), 261–84.

54. Vincent L. Wimbush, "Interpreters—Enslaving/Enslaved/Runagate," *JBL* 130 (2011): 21.

55. E.g., Amanda C. Miller, *Rumors of Resistance: Status Reversals and Hidden Transcripts in the Gospel of Luke*, Emerging Scholars (Minneapolis: Fortress, 2014), 186. Cf. the speculations of Levine and Witherington, *Gospel of Luke*, 202.

56. Carter, *Matthew and the Margins*, 200.

slavery and concludes that the good news is "somewhat compromised" in this pericope.[57] Dube pushes the matter farther, arguing that the Gospel of Matthew adopts an accommodationist stance toward the Roman Empire, with a particularly pernicious imperialism in this pericope: Jesus and the centurion operate within similar conceptions of power (Matt 8:9) and Jesus's prediction that those from elsewhere will overtake the Jewish people's position in God's kingdom (8:11–12) both seem to eagerly anticipate Rome's imperial conquest.[58]

To be clear, many of these scholars would not designate the pericope a text of terror. The hermeneutics of suspicion they employ are nevertheless significant for present purposes in that they both contribute to and reflect a changing hermeneutical climate. These were necessary precursors to the counterreading.

Whereas the homophile interpretation presumed Jesus's moral authority and the gay interpretation aligned queer folks with the state, the counterreading does neither. That is, the preservation of biblical ethics is unnecessary within counterreadings, thanks to a variety of historical developments. This way of reading gradually found some acceptance among biblical specialists. On the one hand, the work of Paul Ricoeur and Hans-Georg Gadamer on the hermeneutics of suspicion provided a scholarly imprimatur for methods of interpretation that had already been operating outside the academy for a considerable period of time, including the abolitionist readings delineated above.[59] Undoubtedly more significant, though, have been demographic changes within the biblical academy, leading to more voices prepared to denaturalize the interpretive frames of whiteness and heteropatriarchy.

A Text of Terror: The Political Situation(s) Today

There is no single issue that determines the counterreading. Take, for instance, three seemingly disparate sets of concerns: Velunta links it with sex tourism,

---

57. Elizabeth V. Dowling, "Luke–Acts: Good News for Slaves?," *Pacifica* 24 (2011): 131.

58. Dube, *Postcolonial Feminist Interpretation*, 131–32.

59. Paul Ricoeur, *Freud and Philosophy* (New Haven: Yale University Press, 1970); Hans-Georg Gadamer, "The Hermeneutics of Suspicion," *Man and World* 17 (1984): 313–23.

Joseph Marchal contends that homoerotic interpretations often reinforce American exceptionalism, and Joanna Stiebert invokes the MeToo critique of rape culture.[60] But despite their divergence, most counterreadings recognize that the centurion is a racialized figure and that sex is inherently fraught with power. The romanticization of sex between a slave and their owner presumes a frame of patriarchal whiteness, which then informs the relationships between the pivotal categories within the interpretation: enslaver-enslaved, sex-romance-consent, senior-junior, settler-subaltern, and so on.

This merely states the obvious. But consider one of the stranger debates about the passage among abolitionists and slavery advocates: the race of the Pais. Proslavery interpreters consistently argued that the Pais was *not* white in order to suggest meaningful parallels between the racialization of slavery in biblical and antebellum contexts. By contrast, some antebellum American abolitionists—in an effort to distinguish biblical slavery from then-contemporary slavery—argued the Pais may have been white.[61] Such abolitionists assumed that the enslavement of white people was more objectionable than that of black people. However, all interpreters comfortably presumed that the centurion himself was white. While enslaving another person was itself sufficient to racially encode the centurion, his whiteness was further extrapolated from his service in the Roman army (usually rendering him Italian), Jesus's remark that he was not an Israelite (Matt 8:10–12; Luke 7:9), and the comments of the local leadership that he acted as patron to the local synagogue, despite not being Jewish himself (Luke 7:3–5).

The centurion's whiteness, though often tacit, operates in more recent interpretations, including homoerotic readings: the homophile reading of Mayer, for instance, narrated a fictionalized version of the pericope wherein the centurion Manlius was a Roman citizen and the Pais was a nameless boy from Bithynia (in modern-day Turkey).[62] Most interpretations, be they

---

60. Velunta, "Centurion and His 'Beloved'"; Marchal, "LGBTIQ Strategies of Interpretation," 191–92; Stiebert, *Rape Myths*, 23–24.

61. Proslavery argument, e.g., Augustin Verot, *A Tract for the Times: Slavery and Abolitionism, Being the Substance of a Sermon, Preached in the Church of St Augustine, Florida, on the Fourth Day of January, 1861, Day of Public Humiliation, Fasting and Prayer* (New Orleans: Catholic Propagator Office, 1861), 6. Abolitionist argument, e.g., Flournoy, *Reply to a Pamphlet*, 15; James Bennett, *Lectures on the History of Christ*, vol. 1, 2nd ed. (London: Westley & Davis, 1828), 307.

62. Mayer, "Le procurateur de Judée."

homoerotic or heteronormative, imagine the centurion to be a Roman citizen, effectively encoding him as white. Indeed, few would deny that they conceive the centurion with the visage of a white man.[63]

Most significant for our purposes is how the centurion's *homosexuality* marks him as white in homoerotic interpretations. As Jasbir Puar notes, liberal politics of inclusion since the Civil Rights era have construed the "Sexual Other" (e.g., queer people) as white by default and the "Racial Other" as cis-heterosexual.[64] Since 9/11, these sexual politics have increasingly included the Religious Other among those who are produced as cis-heterosexual. For a concrete example, one might consider discourse on the tragic Orlando massacre at the Pulse nightclub on 11 June 2016, where fifty people at a gay nightclub were killed by a gunman named Omar Mateen. The fact that the Mateen was Muslim led many to presume Islamic homophobia was his primary motivation. Consequently, many asserted the American need to protect queer populations from Muslim terrorists, especially by ramping up the war on terror. Then-presidential-candidate Donald Trump declared that "a radical Islamic terrorist targeted the nightclub, not only because he wanted to kill Americans, but in order to execute gay and lesbian citizens, because of their sexual orientation."[65] These musings were not limited to a bigoted blowhard but were widely

---

63. Much has been written about how Romanness, Roman citizenship, Greco-Roman, and similar concepts are racialized in both academic literature and the popular imagination. See, most famously Martin Bernal, *Black Athena: The Afroasiatic Roots of Classical Civilization; The Fabrication of Ancient Greece, 1785–1985i*, vol. 1 (New Brunswick: Rutgers University Press, 1987); Denise Eileen McCoskey, *Race: Antiquity and Its Legacy* (London: Taurus, 2012); Donna Zuckerberg, *Not All Dead White Men* (Cambridge: Harvard University Press, 2018). A brief comment on the *ethnos* of the centurion (presuming he was a real person) is prudent. Given that Capernaum was in Herod Antipas's tetrarchy of Galilee, the centurion was not Roman but a local gentile who served in Antipas's small royal army and almost certainly recruited from within his tetrarchy—assuming he is a historical figure. Of course, it is possible the evangelists anachronistically projected the military situation of Galilee of their time onto the pericope. See Saddington, "Centurion in Matthew"; Zeichmann, *Roman Army and the New Testament*, 1–11; see appendix 3.

64. Puar, *Terrorist Assemblages*, 231.

65. Quoted in Ryan Teague Beckwith, "Read Donald Trump's Speech on the Orlando Shooting," *Time* 13 June 2016, https://tinyurl.com/SBL6705q. Note that the shooting occurred on a Latino-themed night, with nearly all victims being Puerto Rican. Trump's glossing over this datum to characterize the victims as "American" further racializes the victims as white.

shared in news commentary, including various left-leaning queer publications. In the days following the shooting, nearly all queer publications supposed that ISIS had directed Mateen to commit murder, which conceptualized Mateen within a larger phenomenon of Islamic homophobia.[66] Being marked as both Racial and Religious Other, Mateen's motives were already intelligible as an act of homophobic Islamic terrorism against the Sexual Other. Whether or not Mateen intended to partake in antigay violence was immaterial, since Trump and others already *knew* that he, being a Muslim terrorist, *must* be homophobic.

The centurion is usually read as white, as a military officer, as a settler, as a slave owner, and—at least in homoerotic interpretations—as someone who had sex with a young person or a slave. These issues have only recently been identified as interpretive problems, let alone *intersecting* problems. This confluence of liabilities may explain the lack of a single, overarching grievance against homoerotic interpretation: any given counterinterpretation will emphasize some of these problems more than others.

What follows is a tentative account of how these problems have become meaningful in the two decades since 11 September 2001, when the connection between religious, sexual, and racial othering has become increasingly salient. What political conditions lead counterreaders to articulate their suspicion of homoerotic readings of the passage, not on the grounds of historiographic validity or heteronormativity, but because the pericope functions as a text of terror, especially for queer people of color? This context witnessed a proliferation of gay interpretations, though much of what will be argued here applies *mutatis mutandis* in antecedent periods.

Discourse on gender and sexuality has been heavily implicated in Western imperialism. Edward Said noted the matter in his era-defining monograph *Orientalism*: "Why the Orient seems still to suggest not only fecundity but sexual promise (and threat), untiring sensuality, unlimited desire, deep generative energies, is something on which one could speculate: it is not the province of my analysis here, alas, despite its frequently

---

66. Doug Meyer, "Omar Mateen as US Citizen, Not Foreign Threat: Homonationalism and LGBTQ Online Representations of the Pulse Nightclub Shooting," *Sexualities* 23 (2020): 249–68; Brett Krutzsch, *Dying to Be Normal: Gay Martyrs and the Transformation of American Sexual Politics* (Oxford: Oxford University Press, 2019), 149–66.

noted appearance."[67] While Said did not elaborate on this connection between the sexualization and the racialization of the so-called East, a number of postcolonial feminists subsequently addressed the issue at length. Leila Ahmed's discussion of "the discourse on the veil" is instructive, as she demonstrates that nascent feminist discourse contributed to British policymaking for Egypt during the Victorian era.[68] British colonizers claimed to rescue Muslim women from their culture's patriarchal oppression; the British treated the veil as a synecdoche for such patriarchy. For a woman to be free of the veil and similar symbols was to liberate herself from Islamic patriarchy. Victorian feminism not only denigrated Islam and supported the colonization of the Racial/Religious Other, but also reassured the British that their patriarchal violence was nowhere near as bad, all under the aegis of an emancipatory project. One is reminded of Gayatri Chakravorty Spivak's contention that white feminist rhetoric concerning the Global South often reduces to "white men saving brown women from brown men."[69]

The destruction wrought by the Global War on Terrorism and related campaigns has renewed critical analysis of military sexual violence. In the name of combatting terrorism abroad, members of the US Army and Central Intelligence Agency committed horrifying sexual abuses upon Iraqi civilians. One might recall the gang rape of a fourteen-year-old girl by on-duty members of the US Army, who then murdered her and her family in the Iraqi city of al-Mahmudiyah. Or one might recall how American forces photographed a woman being raped and that there is evidence that they had done so with girls as young as fifteen. Or one might recall journalist reports that children as young as twelve years old being stripped naked and beaten by occupying forces. Or any number of similar allegations, often witnessed by members of the press but never reaching trial due to apparent coverup schemes. Many abuses in Iraq were not only sexual but had a *same-sex* character as well: US soldiers attached electrodes to the genitals of an Iraqi man before returning him to his family in a vegetative state, and several photographs of simulated anal rape were taken

---

67. Edward W. Said, *Orientalism*, 25th anniv. ed. (New York: Vintage, 2003), 188.
68. Leila Ahmed, *Women and Gender in Islam: Historical Roots of a Modern Debate* (New Haven: Yale University Press, 1992), 144–68.
69. Gayatri Chakravorty Spivak, "Can the Subaltern Speak?," in *Marxism and the Interpretation of Culture*, ed. Cary Nelson and Lawrence Grossberg (Urbana: University of Illinois Press, 1988), 296.

at Abu Ghraib. Much of this could be repeated about other recent military endeavors, such as young boys being enslaved for sexual purposes by American-backed militias in Afghanistan. Yet such abuses are quickly forgotten, to the extent they were known in the first place.

Military interventions are commonly presented as efforts to bring the enlightened gender politics of liberal Judeo-Christianity to the Muslim world.[70] One thinks of Laura Bush's national address shortly after 9/11, claiming that "the fight against terrorism is also a fight for the rights and dignity of women."[71] Or the leaked campaign by the Obama administration to shore up support for the war in Afghanistan among German and French nationals by emphasizing the plight of Afghan women.[72] Or media preoccupation with Osama bin Laden's pornography collection after his assassination and speculation about his perversions. Or, again, any number of other examples. Rather than characterizing this tension between the civilizing mission of military endeavors and the sexual violence of those acting on behalf of such missions as mere hypocrisy, one might instead consider how religion, race, violence, imperialism, and sexuality are mutually constitutive such that these apparent contradictions exist within a cohesive ideological system.

Puar explores this tapestry of state and sexual violence, offering a compelling analysis of queer subject formation and its relationship to the American exceptionalism that arose after 9/11. For Puar, *exceptionalism* refers to narratives of national uniqueness that "paradoxically signals distinction from (to be unlike, dissimilar) as well as excellence (immanence,

---

70. Much has been written on "Judeo-Christianity" as Islamophobic framing device, but see the crisp articulation in Anya Topolski, "The Dangerous Discourse of the 'Judaeo-Christian' Myth: Masking the Race-Religion Constellation in Europe," *Patterns of Prejudice* 54 (2020): 71–90.

71. Laura Bush, "Radio Address by Mrs. Bush," *The White House*, 17 November 2001, https://tinyurl.com/SBL6705r.

72. Various news sources reported on the 2010 cable named "Afghanistan: Sustaining West European Support for the NATO-led Mission—Why Counting on Apathy Might Not Be Enough." On the collective amnesia surrounding these events, my experience as an educator mirrors that of Rebecca A. Adelman, "'Coffins after Coffins': Screening Wartime Atrocity in the Classroom," in *The War of My Generation: Youth Culture and the War on Terror*, ed. David Kieran (New Brunswick: Rutgers University Press, 2015), 243 n. 40: "Anecdotally, it seems that increasing numbers of my undergraduates are unfamiliar with the story of what happened at Abu Ghraib and the resultant images. At the time, however, this would have been a difficult story to miss."

superiority), suggesting a departure from yet mastery of linear teleologies of progress."[73] Numerous overlapping narratives of American exceptionalism preceded the thirteen colonies' federation, ranging from the religious to the artistic, the economic to the military, frequently understanding the United States as the biblical "city on a hill" that stands as exemplar for the rest of the world (Matt 5:14). American exceptionalism imagines the United States as a profoundly unique nation-state, particularly its normative morality: though sometimes led astray, America is especially positioned to do good in the world, acting as "a light unto the nations" (Isa 42:6).

Puar contends that queer subjects play an integral role in authorizing the United States as an exceptional antiterrorist state, a state that is marked as both racially and religiously normative. The presence of queer subjects both signifies the antiterrorist state's sexual exceptionalism and aids the formation of "homonationalism."[74] The antiterrorist state is also consistently identified as a gay-friendly state, particularly evident in its secular tolerance of the queer folk inhabiting its borders, thereby incorporating sexual norms into its exceptionalist self-understanding. Within narratives of sexual exceptionalism, the gay-friendly/antiterrorist state finds its foil in the violently homophobic terrorist. The terrorist is not only marked *racially* as a person of color, but he is also distinguished *sexually* by his perversely heterosexual masculinity, *religiously* by his refusal to comply with liberal democratic norms as manifest in his intolerance of queer sexualities, and *mortally* by his inevitable death.

Queer secularity, by locating transgressiveness as a site of proper agency, finds those who adhere to religious sexual norms as deficient. Here, we might turn to an important article by Joan W. Scott on her neologism "sexularism."[75] Scott speaks alongside others in criticizing the

---

73. Puar, *Terrorist Assemblages*, 3.

74. On the development of homonationalism as a concept since the initial publication of *Terrorist Assemblages*, see Canton Winer and Catherine Bolzendahl, "Conceptualizing Homonationalism: (Re-)Formulation, Application, and Debates of Expansion," *Sociology Compass* 15.5 (2021): e12853.

75. Joan Wallach Scott, *The Fantasy of Feminist History*, Next Wave Provocations (Durham, NC: Duke University Press, 2011), 91–116; cf. Janet R. Jakobsen and Ann Pellegrini, *Love the Sin: Sexual Regulation and the Limits of Religious Tolerance*, Sexual Cultures (New York: New York University Press, 2003); Saba Mahmood, *Politics of Piety: The Islamic Revival and the Feminist Subject*, rev. ed. (Princeton: Princeton University Press, 2012).

widespread assumption that "secularism encourages the free expression of sexuality, and that it thereby ends the oppression of women because it removes transcendence as the foundation for social norms and treats people as autonomous individuals, pleasure seeking agents capable of crafting their own destiny." This promise of gender equality is premature in its self-satisfied celebration, but—more troublingly—it serves as an alibi for progressive politics by disguising its own Islamophobia. This could be reiterated mutatis mutandis concerning additional Religious Others, including Pharisees or first-century Jews. Jesus's high regard for love-based relationships rescues him from his religious context through his liberal decency, insofar as he endorses a relationship that conforms to secular rituals of courtship.[76] That love of this sort is found among gentiles is significant.[77]

Puar's work is complex and the foregoing description may be unduly abstract, so an example of how homonationalism animates public discourse may clarify. Consider the events following the execution of two Iranian teenagers, Mahmoud Asgari (aged 16) and Ayaz Marhoni (18), for having sex with an anonymous male (13). The details of the crime are uncertain, particularly whether the intercourse was consensual or not, though Human Rights Watch identifies the latter as much more probable based on the connotation of the Farsi words used in legal documents. Regardless, when photographs of the youths' public execution via hanging emerged online, Western media quickly identified the young men as gay teenagers lynched by fundamentalist Muslim homophobes. The queer activist organization OutRage!, for instance, staged a protest where they distributed placards highlighting the religious fanaticism of the Islamic state, "Iran: Stop Killing Kids and Queers."[78] OutRage! founder Peter

---

76. I paraphrase here James G. Crossley, *Jesus in an Age of Terror: Scholarly Projects for a New American Century*, BibleWorld (London: Equinox, 2008), 104. Theologically imbued narratives of Western decency almost invariably imagine Jesus and the Bible to better represent the norms of liberal democracy than Islam; see also the excellent discussions in Crossley, *Jesus in an Age of Neoliberalism*, 38–67; Yvonne Sherwood, "Bush's Bible as a Liberal Bible (Strange though That Might Seem)," *Postscripts* 2 (2006): 47–58.

77. Gentiles are frequently linked with homosexuality in Christian theological discourse. See the overview in John Perry, "Gentiles and Homosexuals: A Brief History of an Analogy," *JRE* 38 (2010): 321–47.

78. This occurred at the one-year anniversary of the executions, on 19 July 2006. In another incident shortly before this, OutRage! distributed placards reading "No

Thatchell, who brought the executions to the attention of Western media, declared "this is just the latest barbarity by the Islamo-fascists in Iran."[79] Less subtle was a statement from the Log Cabin Republicans, a conservative American LGBT group: "In the wake of news stories and photographs documenting the hanging of two gay Iranian teenagers, Log Cabin Republicans re-affirm their commitment to the global war on terror." The Log Cabin Republicans' slide from homophobic Iranian sexual politics to the enlightened nation-building of the secular West not only lends credence to the latter's superiority, but also removes from visibility the question of how these teens would have fared had they been convicted for raping a boy in the United States. Instead, Asgari and Marhoni emerge as gay, life-worthy subjects whose wrongful execution confirms the inevitable demise of the Muslim terrorist state.

Puar confronts the widespread perception that queerness exists apart from the politics it criticizes and is singularly transgressive, since these perceptions lead people to overlook the increasing mobilization of queer populations in service of state violence.[80] Queers have been provisionally embraced as a component of the antiterrorist state, and this embrace often certifies violence against the Racial/Religious Other. Puar's work can be read as an attempt to understand what renders queer complicities with state violence possible and desirable, without presuming such collusion is intentional. She argues that queer recognition often hinges on the endorsement of state violence, as the authority to kill no longer resides solely in the

---

Occupation of Iraq. Islamists! Stop Killing Iraqi Gays" (18 March 2006). For further analysis of OutRage!'s rhetoric of colonial enlightenment, see Jin Haritaworn with Tamsila Tauqir and Esra Erdem, "Gay Imperialism: Gender and Sexuality Discourse in the 'War on Terror,'" in *Out of Place: Interrogating Silences in Queerness/Raciality*, ed. Adi Kuntsman and Esperanza Miyake (York: Raw Nerve, 2008), 71–95.

79. Quoted in Rahul Rao, "Echoes of Imperialism in LGBT Activism," in *Echoes of Empire: Memory, Identity and Colonial Legacies*, ed. Kalypso Nicolaïdis, Berny Sebe, and Gabrielle Maas (London: Taurus, 2015), 357, as is the Log Cabin Republicans quotation immediately following.

80. This topic has been discussed extensively. See, e.g., Duggan, "New Homonormativity"; Haritaworn with Tauqir and Erdem, "Gay Imperialism"; Dean Spade, "Under Cover of Gay Rights," *N.Y.U. Review of Law & Social Change* 37 (2013): 79–100; Nadeem Mahomed and Farid Esack, "The Normal and Abnormal: On the Politics of Being Muslim and Relating to Same-Sex Sexuality," *JAAR* 85 (2017): 224–43; Judith Butler, "Sexual Politics, Torture, and Secular Time," *British Journal of Sociology* 59 (2008): 1–23.

state apparatus but circulates throughout the populace. It is therefore not a question of individual responsibility or guilt but a complicity embedded within the general citizenry.[81] That queers—now subjects "hailed by the neoliberal state," as argued in chapter 2—participate in such politics is to be expected. Puar consequently holds suspect efforts to demarcate "good queer politics" apart from "bad queer politics."[82]

Returning to the gospels, we might consider William Arnal's insights about how constructions of a "very Jewish Jesus" become salient for identity claims today.[83] We saw in chapter 2 that heteronormative interpreters often object to the homoerotic interpretation on grounds that Jesus qua Jew would not have accepted a relationship between the centurion and the Pais. Because of their distinctive monotheism, among other practices (e.g., opposition to infant exposure, abstention from various foods), Jews were exceptional among the various *ethnē* of the empire. Jewish sexual norms formed an important part of this exceptionalism, being uniquely heteronormative in a Roman context where homoeroticism was pervasive, uniquely opposed to sexual intercourse with slaves where it was otherwise common, uniquely insistent upon endogamy, and so on.

Arnal notes that often implied in the notion of a "very Jewish Jesus" is an unbroken continuity between ancient and contemporary religiosity: claims about Jesus's Judaism often entail implicit claims about Judaism and Christianity today. This supposition of continuity is evident in many het-

---

81. This point is worth emphasizing. Condemnations of "the racist" (i.e., the individual, monadic bigot) are often counterproductive in that such censures render invisible structural forms of racial violence through their myopic focus on the monstrous racist qua individual. By locating racism *over there*, the accuser is implicitly freed of participation in racist norms. Sara Ahmed has discussed this issue with great nuance: Sara Ahmed, "Declarations of Whiteness: The Non-performativity of Anti-Racism," *borderlands* 3.2 (2004): n.p.; Sara Ahmed, "Problematic Proximities: Or Why Critiques of Gay Imperialism Matter," *Feminist Legal Studies* 19 (2011): 119–32.

82. Jasbir K. Puar, "Homonationalism Gone Viral: Discipline, Control, and the Affective Politics of Sensation" (paper presented at the Portland Center for Public Humanities, Portland, 21 May 2012).

83. Arnal, *Symbolic Jesus*; Arnal, "The Cipher 'Judaism' in Contemporary Historical Jesus Scholarship," in *Apocalypticism, Anti-Semitism and the Historical Jesus: Subtexts in Criticism*, ed. John S. Kloppenborg and John W. Marshall, LNTS 275 (London: T&T Clark, 2005), 24–54; Arnal, "Jesus as Battleground in a Period of Cultural Complexity," in *Jesus beyond Nationalism: Constructing the Historical Jesus in a Period of Cultural Complexity*, ed. Halvor Moxnes, Ward Blanton, and James G. Crossley, BibleWorld (London: Equinox, 2009), 99–117.

eronormative readings of the pericope. Stephen Voorwinde, for instance, objects that the centurion could not have "enjoyed such a good reputation in the Jewish community at Capernaum had he been known as a sexual predator."[84] Jewishness effectively precludes tolerance of sexual predation. Heteronormative readings tend to imagine Jesus as an essentially religious person in the vein of torah-centric Judaism. As Arnal notes:

> The label "religious" is the crux of the matter. At its heart are the debates concerning categories, idealism and the meaning of "religion." That is, the very self-evident and uncontentious statement, "Jesus was a Jew," is taken to mean, by advocates of the observant Jewish Jesus, that Jesus was a religious person in the tradition of Judaism. Jesus, as a Jew, would have participated in his religion's essence. This view is by no means self-evidently false. It conceptualizes and hence manufactures "facts," however, on the basis of a fundamental preconceived outlook. In this instance, the preconceived outlook revolves around the reality of religion as *sui generis:* religion is an entity unto itself. "Jesus was a Jew" can *only* mean "Jesus was a religious Jew."[85]

Claims that Jesus's Judaism precluded his condoning of same-sex intercourse implicitly operate with assumptions about the role of religion in society not only in antiquity but today as well. In attaching this assumption to an authoritative figure such as Jesus, it becomes normative, thereby delimiting the proper role of religion on matters sexual and political (one thinks, e.g., of how this resonates with recent religious exemptions for equal opportunity employers or how "sincerely held religious beliefs" often provide loopholes for antiqueer discrimination). Insofar as Jesus is intelligible as an essentially religious figure, he remains *un*intelligible within the context of contemporary secularity and the queer politics that have emerged from it.

We might productively understand gay and homophile readings within this same conceptual framework of Jewish religiosity, albeit with the centurion as racialized as white in part because he is the Sexual Other, whereas Jews are presented as the Racial and Religious Other. Whereas

---

84. Voorwinde, *Jesus' Emotions in the Gospels*, 18.
85. William E. Arnal, "Making and Re-making the Jesus-Sign: Contemporary Markings on the Body of Christ," in *Whose Historical Jesus?*, ed. William E. Arnal and Michel Desjardins, SCJ 7 (Waterloo: Wilfrid Laurier University Press, 1997), 310, emphasis in original.

Jesus was a Jew par excellence in heteronormative readings (i.e., Jesus opposed homoeroticism because of Jewish norms), homoerotic interpretations treat Jesus's Judaism in a diametrically opposed manner. Martignac's 1975 article began an almost uniform trend in framing Jesus as an exceptional individual *against* the background of a sexually intolerant Judaism. Martignac's reasoning is worth quoting at length.

> This pederast officer knows the country he occupies well. In his army and in his homeland, he can quite freely love a servant or a slave without anyone finding fault in it. Among the Jews, however, things are quite different: homophilia is scorned and condemned. Therefore, when it comes to saving his young lover, is it not shameless that he goes to address Jesus? While he is a Jew, [the centurion] does not realize all that separates him from the strictly legalistic tradition of his religion. Given his Roman mores, how could he not dread gravely offending Jesus by running to him, a Jew, to heal his young lover?... Fearing that Jesus would still be confined by legalistic and ecclesiastical moralism, he felt that this "Lord" was not abolishing the Law but fulfilling it by transcending it in love. He believes that Jesus can overcome all the "taboos" of his own religion and act miraculously, even at the request of a pagan, and—scandalously—a pederast pagan, without the slightest acceptance from anyone.[86]

Jesus, unlike his Jewish contemporaries, looked beyond the centurion's sexual proclivities in an enlightened act of tolerance. Jews, by contrast, were inimical to queer people. Even though Jews are still depicted as uniquely opposed to same-sex intercourse, homoerotic interpretations deem Jesus unique and sexually exceptional vis-à-vis Jews. The interpretation of Theissen quoted in chapter 2 provides another vivid example. Gamaliel's Jewishness is foregrounded: he is distinguished by his Hebrew name unlike the Hellenized, Latinized, and Anglicized "Jesus" (rather than Yeshua) and the narrator's "Andreas" (who stands in for the reader), not to mention Gamaliel shares a name with the renowned first-century rabbi (cf. Acts 5:34–40, 22:3). Gamaliel's Jewishness is loaded with religious baggage, as he alludes to torah obedience as his reason for disdaining homosexuals. The gentile centurion and the enlightened Jesus stand in stark contrast to the provincial intolerance of

---

86. Martignac, "Le centurion de Capernaüm," 126; translated by Morgan Bell. Indeed, if Crowther, "Sodom," 26 is understood as a reference to the centurion, this trend goes back even earlier.

the Jewish populace. Anglican priest Jeffrey John makes the link explicit: "The disgust that many Jews would have felt for this centurion and his particular request is the disgust that many heterosexual men can feel for the homosexual."[87] Gray Temple similarly claims that because "Jesus did not live in Jewish Judea but in pagan Galilee, he was surely aware of pagan Roman tolerance for homoerotic behavior."[88]

While Jesus is the quintessential Jew in heteronormative interpretations, many homoerotic interpretations instead depict him as transcending the limits of his Jewish culture/religion. Jesus's supersession of his Jewish context is a common theme in homoerotic interpretation. Jewish norms entailed a compulsory homophobia, albeit with the exception of Jesus and early Christians, whose sexual politics more closely resemble those of the secular nation-state.

The repressive sexual norms of Jesus's Jewish peers evoke two distinct-but-complimentary populations. First are Christians hostile toward queer people. Hanks is quite explicit about this subtext. When describing Jesus's reaction to the centurion's request, Hanks observes that "Jesus does not ... dispatch them to a priest for a bit of 'ex-gay torture,' but simply heals the youth with a word from a distance."[89] Similarly, Mel White, who served as a ghostwriter for televangelists such as Pat Robertson and Jerry Falwell before coming out as gay, presents the following portrait.

> A Gentile and a member of the occupying force, the centurion was an outcast in Jerusalem, and his "special servant", almost certainly gay, was an outcast for a whole other set of reasons; yet when that centurion cried out to Jesus to heal his young lover, Jesus said, "Right. Take me to him." The centurion, knowing that the pictures on his desk might give them away, responded, "Could you heal him long distance?" Jesus must have smiled to himself knowing that the centurion and his lover had no reason to be embarrassed or ashamed. He knew why they hid their loving relationship from the local religious authorities and the gossips on the street, but they had no reason to hide their relationship from God, who created them and loved them exactly as they were. Instead of taking that risk, Jesus healed the outcast lover on the spot. I wish I could have witnessed that moment when Jesus looked into the eyes of the centurion

---

87. Jeffrey John, *The Meaning in the Miracles* (Norwich: Canterbury, 2001), 161.
88. Gray Temple, *Gay Unions: In the Light of Scripture, Tradition, and Reason* (New York: Church Publishing, 2004), 86.
89. Hanks, *Subversive Gospel*, 14.

and without a word passing between them said, "Now, friend, let your own guilt and fear be healed as well."[90]

Jews recall homophobic Christians in White's narrative: they engender shame in queer folk, are preoccupied with the letter of the law, bear a judgmental gaze, and so on. Jesus, by contrast, resembles an open-minded healer who invites a maligned soul into the Christian flock. This reading participates in the long Christian tradition of associating Judaism (or Pharisaism) with legalism, ritual, purity-preoccupation, and self-righteous religiosity, and associating Jesus with a simple gospel devoid of such trappings. The social historical and ideological problems with such depictions of Judaism are well known.

The second figure ancient Jews evoke is the Muslim fundamentalist. James Crossley has demonstrated the interpretive predilection toward depicting Jesus's Jewish peers in terms that mirror popular stereotypes of present-day Muslims.[91] Crossley argues that although Christians had long used Jews as a foil for Jesus and Christians in biblical interpretation, such supersessionism floundered after Christians began reckoning with culpability for the Holocaust and the increasingly common racialization of Jews as "provisionally white" after the Six-Day War of 1967. A new Religious/Racial Other was necessary. In order to continue affirming the superiority of Christian values, interpreters replaced Jewish cultural inferiority with Orientalist tropes about Islamic backwardness. This Orientalism extends to sexuality: ancient Jews and contemporary Muslims are depicted as repressed but licentious, homosocial but homophobic, operate with patriarchal gender norms,

---

90. Mel White, *Religion Gone Bad: The Hidden Dangers of the Christian Right* (New York: Tarcher, 2006), 303.

91. Crossley, *Jesus in an Age of Terror*, 111–29; Crossley, *Jesus in an Age of Neoliberalism*; James G. Crossley, "Jesus the Jew since 1967," in Moxnes, Blanton, and Crossley, *Jesus beyond Nationalism*, 111–29; cf. Nasar Meer and Tariq Modood, "For 'Jewish' Read 'Muslim'? Islamophobia as a Form of Racialisation of Ethno-Religious Groups in Britain Today," *Islamophobia Studies* 1 (2012): 34–53. There is, I think, much more to be said about how urban-rural geographies play out in such queer-straight, secular-religious imaginations of the pericope—the centurion representing the capital city of Rome while living in backwater Galilee. Neither Matthew nor Luke sponsor such a reading, since both describe Capernaum as a πόλις (e.g., Matt 9:1, Luke 4:31), even though archaeologists doubt that Capernaum was so populous. Halberstam, *Queer Time and Place*, 22–46, offers helpful thoughts on the common erasure of rural queers.

and so on. Jennings, for instance, imagines that the centurion "knows that religious Jews revile … the sort of love he knows; yet he goes out into the street to find a Jewish healer and, risking rejection and ridicule, asks help for the boyfriend he loves."[92] One can simply *intuit* that ancient Jews propagated these values in the same way Trump and others could intuit Omar Mateen was a homophobic terrorist. Contemporary Islam and ancient Judaism present a shared threat to the Sexual Other.

We might consider these interpretations alongside Sara Ahmed, thinking about how the proximity of sexual liberality, the war on terror, and Christian supersessionism generates a "stickiness" between ancient Judaism and modern Islam, entailing an exchange of attributes.[93] Ahmed also notes that intolerance is regarded differently when discussing Islam: "When homophobia is attributed to Islam, it becomes *a cultural attribute*. Homophobia would then be viewed as *intrinsic* to Islam, as a cultural attribute, but homophobia in the West would be viewed as *extrinsic*, as an individual attribute."[94] A similarly hostile posture toward same-sex intercourse is assumed as intrinsic to ancient Jewish culture, itself evincing their discursive proximity. In this vein, Lilly Nortjé-Meyer wonders why Jesus failed to confront his opponents' homophobia: "was homosexuality the only issue [Jesus] was reluctant to dispute with the Pharisees and scribes?"[95] Knowledge of the Pharisees is limited and extant sources indicate nothing of their opinion on same-sex intercourse. For Nortjé-Meyer, Pharisees nevertheless occupy the role of the Religious Other *cum* Racial Other. Even though Luke represents the centurion as a man appreciated by Capernaum's Jewish leadership (7:3–5), many interpretations prefer to imagine an antagonism between liberal paganism and fundamentalist Judaism. Historical acrobatics are sometimes necessary to arrive at this conclusion; for instance, James Neill claims, "If Jesus shared the contempt for homosexuality found among Hellenistic Jews like Philo or that would have been expected from the Pharisees, it would have been inconceivable that his encounter with the centurion would have occurred without at least an admonition to the centurion about his relationship with his

---

92. Jennings, *Man Jesus Loved*, 143.
93. Ahmed, *Cultural Politics of Emotion*.
94. Ahmed, "Problematic Proximities," 126, emphasis in original.
95. Lilly Nortjé-Meyer, "The Homosexual Body without Apology: A Positive Link between the Canaanite Woman in Matthew 15:21–28 and Homosexual Interpretation of Biblical Texts," *R&T* 9 (2002): 126.

pais."[96] To repeat, there is no surviving evidence of Pharisees regulating same-sex intercourse.

Homoerotic interpretations seem to identify ancient Jews with both Christian fundamentalists and repressive Muslims. This association may seem incongruous, but the two groups seem to be sticky in their homophobia. Their shared status of the Religious Other that is hostile to the Sexual Other is explicit in Jean-Fabrice Nardelli's revealing characterization of Gagnon—a biblical scholar who has written extensively against the homoerotic reading of this pericope—as an "academic turned ayatollah."[97] That a Muslim cleric stands in for repressive perversity indicates their overlap, given their shared rejection of liberal tolerance and threat of fundamentalist theocracy. Sexual politics become constitutive of secular modernity's achievements, achievements from which the terrorist and his allies are a priori excluded.

Several interpretations have identified the Healing of the Centurion's Pais as a text of terror. The constellation of race, settler colonialism, religion, sexuality, slavery, and military violence already render it a volatile pericope. The common supposition that sex between a slave and owner was not inherently exploitative operates analogously in the sexual abuses by the US military in Iraq and Afghanistan: some were quick to dismiss these abuses as no different than, say, hazing in university fraternities or provocative art pieces, thereby eliding issues of consent, imperialism, racialization, and so on.[98] Some homoerotic readings go further, claiming

---

96. James Neill, *The Origins and Role of Same-Sex Relations in Human Societies* (Jefferson: McFarland, 2009), 216. Cf. Robinson, "Jesus, the Centurion, and His Lover," 23–24: "Did Jesus extend his compassion to one even further beyond the bounds of acceptability than a Roman centurion; namely, to a Roman centurion who engaged in sexual activity with another man? That level of openness to 'the other' on the part of Jesus would certainly have challenged first-century Palestinian Jews to rethink their prejudices."

97. Jean-Fabrice Nardelli, *Homosexuality and Liminality in Gilgameš and Samuel*, Classical and Byzantine Monographs 64 (Amsterdam: Hakkert, 2007), vii.

98. Thus, Rush Limbaugh: "This is no different than what happens at [Yale University's secret fraternity] Skull and Bones initiation, and we're going to ruin people's lives over it, and we're going to hamper our military effort, and then we are going to really hammer them because they had a good time.... You know, these people are being fired at every day. I'm talking about people having a good time, these people. You ever heard of emotional release?" Quoted in Puar, *Terrorist Assemblages*, 110. Puar is also critical of Slavoj Žižek for granting these ideas an academic intonation

that the centurion was oppressed by the occupied population. This is not to mention how this pericope has provided divine authorization for disturbing acts of violence: chattel slavery in the United States and, more recently, Parker Rossman's trafficking of boys for sexual abuse.

Queer Growing Pains

The depiction of gay and homophile interpretations in this chapter is, frankly, unflattering. Such interpretations often operated with a supersessionism or (inadvertently) fed a tacit racism that imagines Jesus and the gentile centurion as eclipsing the provincial morality of contemporaneous Jews. Linn Marie Tonstad argues that crypto-supersessionism remains a common narrative in queer theology, regardless of the writer's intent.[99] Rather than identifying this as a problem specific to queer biblical interpretation, such shortcomings might be placed alongside the growing pains experienced within various hermeneutical traditions.

Judith Plaskow famously observed that Jews are often caricatured to the point of anti-Judaism in order to demonstrate the uniqueness of Jesus's teachings on gender.[100] Christian interpreters have long cherry-picked misogynistic passages from ancient Jewish writers, depicting these particular voices as representative of a monolithic Judaism and contrasting it with the ostensive novelty of Jesus's egalitarianism. In this crypto-supersessionist framework, "Judaism equals sexism, while Christianity equals feminism," as Sarah Melcher concisely put it.[101] The comments of Plaskow and Melcher could be repeated *mutatis mutandis* regarding homoerotic interpretations of the Healing of the Centurion's Pais; the homophobic statements of Philo and Josephus cast Jesus's tolerance in a brighter light. This supersessionism does not seem to reflect any conscious bigotry against Judaism but rather is a side-effect of allegorizing Jesus's opponents

---

in Slavoj Žižek, *Violence: Six Sideways Reflections*, Big Ideas//Small Books (New York: Picador, 2008), 145–48.

99. Linn Marie Tonstad, "The Limits of Inclusion: Queer Theology and Its Others," *Theology and Sexuality* 21 (2015): 1–19.

100. Judith Plaskow, "Christian Feminism and Anti-Judaism," *CrossCurrents* 28 (1978): 306–9.

101. Sarah J. Melcher, "The Problem of Anti-Judaism in Christian Feminist Biblical Interpretation: Some Pragmatic Suggestions," *CrossCurrents* 53 (2003): 23; see also the special issue *Journal of Feminist Studies in Religion* 20.1 (2004), devoted to this problem.

as analogues to modern homophobes, be they Christian fundamentalists, conservative policymakers, Muslims, or someone else. Consider the comments of Robert Williams.

> For a high-ranking Roman soldier to have a male lover would not be unusual. The Romans wouldn't even raise an eyebrow. The Jews, on the other hand, might raise an eyebrow or two, and the centurion seems to have been aware of the Jewish distaste for homosexuality. Perhaps because he was aware of the sex-negative tendency of the Hebrews, the centurion was reluctant to invite them in too close, to share with them the true nature of his relationship with the young man he loved.[102]

Williams then pauses to note: "The anti-Semitic tendency of contemporary Christians is just as sinful and insidious as the sex-negative tendency of the Hebrews, and I am on thin ice when I make these sorts of statements. Please understand that I am not contrasting Jewish and Christian thought here, but the Judeo-Christian tradition as a whole with the Greco-Roman tradition." Williams's caveat is important and well-considered. Supersessionism remains common and anti-Jewish motifs commonly occur in other hermeneutics traditions, such as Latin American and Asian liberation theologies.[103] Such supersessionism seems to be an almost predictable growing pain in developing minoritized hermeneutical traditions.

To be clear, supersessionism is far less common among academic queer interpretation of the Bible than among lay interpretation or biblical scholarship writ large. If anything, this crypto-supersessionism represents a failure of New Testament scholarship more broadly: for all the insistence on Jesus's Jewishness in recent New Testament scholarship, academics still contribute to a larger cultural context where supersessionist readings of the New Testament remain credible to lay interpreters. Though there have been significant strides on the matter since he commented such in 1997, Arnal's observations regarding Christian preoccupation with legal observance of the torah as the sine qua non of first-century Judaism are still relevant at the level of popular reception.

---

102. Robert Williams, *Just as I Am: A Practical Guide to Being Out, Proud, and Christian* (New York: Crown, 1992), 62.

103. John Pawlikowski, *Christ in the Light of the Christian-Jewish Dialogue* (New York: Paulist, 1982), 59–73; Peter C. Phan, *Being Religious Interreligiously* (Maryknoll, NY: Orbis Books, 2004), 163–71.

The standard "quintessential Jewish religious issues" are actually questions of Jewish-Christian relations and polemic. That is, the focus (regardless of the stance taken) tends to be on the cumbersomeness (or absence thereof) of Torah and related purity requirements, something that is assumed to be the major concern of first century Jews simply because it has been, through the centuries, the major concern of Christians encountering Judaism.[104]

This continues to manifest with the homoerotic interpretation of the centurion and the Pais, where the reception of torah prohibitions of homosexual intercourse dominates the conversation. Jewish religiosity often serves as the Racialized and Religious Other vis-à-vis the liberalism of Jesus, who defends the Sexual Other.

---

104. Arnal, "Making and Re-making the Jesus-Sign," 311 n. 3.

4
Whose Interpretation Is Legitimate?

> The problem for the first generation of gay educators in the US was that they were, of necessity, largely self-taught: the academy treated with contempt both the openly gay and the study of homosexuality.
> —Amy Richlin, "Eros Underground"

> The story of the centurion at Capernaum is a favorite of mine.... Particularly ill-informed pro-homosex advocates cite it as an example of how Jesus affirmed a homosexual relationship.
> —Robert A. J. Gagnon, "Did Jesus Approve of a Homosexual Couple?"

Though the homoerotic interpretation has received widespread endorsement in nonacademic arenas, it remains marginal within biblical scholarship—as evinced in both the relative infrequency of academics' endorsement and the flippant tone of their dismissal. This interpretation is rarely mentioned in peer-reviewed biblical studies journals and only three serialized biblical commentaries even acknowledge its existence. When scholars bother to notice, their discussions are glib and rarely engage it as serious interlocution, often rejecting it on specious grounds. All of this means that the vast majority of homoerotic interpretations of the pericope we have seen produced by queer laity and their allies or perhaps ministers with modest training in biblical studies. Most of these interpretations participate in what Amy Richlin terms "shadow scholarship."[1]

Shadow scholarship comprises a loose intellectual network formed around one or another shared interest (in this case, queer theology and

---

1. Richlin, "Eros Underground." The designation *shadow scholar* is intended here to be descriptive rather than normative. As anyone who has read a bad academic monograph knows, educational credentials do not always correlate with insightful (or even credible) analysis.

queer history), often made up of autodidacts or those with modest educational specialization (e.g., MDiv, BA in theology or classics). The most definitive feature of shadow scholarship is that it exists outside the academy proper, even if contributors betray their own academic aspirations. The homophile publications discussed in chapter 1 are exemplary in this regard: such periodicals were produced on razor-thin budgets and built around an interest in exchanging insights about the place of queer folk in the world. Thus, most homophile magazines included newspaper clippings, summaries of recent lectures, directories of other homophile organizations, pen-pal listings, book summaries, and other items that brought light to issues of shared concern. San Francisco–based magazine *The Mattachine Review*, for instance, reprinted a substantial portion of the 1963 pamphlet *Toward a Quaker View of Sex*, which was noteworthy for its compassionate Christian approach to homosexuality. When one subscriber wrote a letter to the editor complaining about extensive reprinting of an inexpensive (3 shilling/50 US cent) booklet, the *Mattachine Review* editor defended the choice, noting that the *Quaker* report "has received precious little attention this country and hardly any of the praise it deserves. We believe it to be one of the significant documents of the century, and for that reason we have endeavored to give it all the publicity that our limited circulation can muster."[2] Although *Mattachine* was one of the more successful homophile periodicals, its editors regularly drew attention to its precarious financial state: readers were not only encouraged to subscribe but to donate whatever they could afford. The network of *Mattachine* subscribers, writers, and donors deemed the distribution of otherwise disparate histories, opinions, and news about homosexuality a significant cultural contribution in its own right. Several publications encourage writers to use multiple pseudonyms so as to create the impression of a larger staff size. Figure 2, which delineates the citation network for homophile readings of the passage, is also instructive: readers sought out specific periodicals or publishers to learn more about the topic of interest. The diagram hints that these networks operated in less formal ways, as it is difficult to imagine so many authors spontaneously arriving at the same conclusion on their

---

2. See the comically hot-tempered exchange about *Mattachine Review*'s reprint of Alastair Heron, ed., *Towards a Quaker View of Sex* (London: Friends Home Service Committee, 1963) in Harold L. Call, "Readers Write," *Mattachine Review* 9.8 (1963): 29. One gets the impression that *Mattachine* editors were playing loose with fair use doctrines in this case.

own. Surely, many encountered the reading through sermons, personal conversations, Bible studies, and similar means of transmitting knowledge that are difficult to cite properly. Shadow scholars give the sense that their publications are bringing hidden, forgotten, or otherwise secret knowledge to light.

Though biblical analyses produced by shadow scholars approximate those of specialists, there are numerous features that distinguish such authors from so-called academic scholars. Casual perusal of queer shadow scholarship indicates that most interlocutors lack relevant educational credentials as well as competence in ancient languages, which mitigates any credibility of their research among academics. One detects a certain anxiety about this: shadow scholars showcase instances when biblical specialists *do* endorse the homoerotic interpretation as vindication of their enterprise. A 2003 article in *The Gay and Lesbian Times* concerning Jennings's interpretation of the pericope heralded his credentials in its title: "United Church of Christ Professor Says Jesus Was Actively Gay."[3] Such emphasis on credentials can misstate someone's qualifications or academic specialization. For instance, McNeill cited a "manuscript by a Franciscan biblical scholar" by Jack Clark Robinson as one basis for his homoerotic interpretation of the centurion; Robinson, however, expressed confusion and distanced himself from McNeill's designation of "biblical scholar."[4]

With this in mind, one might look at the reception of John Boswell's famous 1980 monograph, *Christianity, Social Tolerance, and Homosexuality*, which argued that homophobia only came to prevail within Christianity more than a millennium after Jesus's death. Boswell excavates a forgotten history of Christian tolerance of homoeroticism through the thirteenth century.[5] The book was significant for queer shadow scholarship precisely because its academic legitimacy was unimpeachable: a (gay) Yale professor authored a jargon-laden monograph with extensive footnotes published by a university press.[6] Carolyn Dinshaw finds such indices of academic legitimacy a common preoccupation in fan mail Boswell received, with

---

3. Anonymous, "United Church of Christ Professor Says Jesus Was Actively Gay," 27.
4. McNeill, *Freedom, Glorious Freedom*, 201; Robinson, "Author's Reply."
5. John Boswell, *Christianity, Social Tolerance, and Homosexuality: Gay People in Western Europe from the Beginning of the Christian Era to the Fourteenth Century* (Chicago: University of Chicago Press, 1980).
6. Carolyn Dinshaw, *Getting Medieval: Sexualities and Communities, Pre- and Postmodern*, Series Q (Durham: Duke University Press, 1999).

the book's readers—mostly queer men with modest academic training—claiming an affinity with Boswell's research prowess: "I, too, have studied many languages," wrote one reader; another claimed to have a "fetish" for footnotes.[7] The imprimatur of academic research was of vital importance, as it not only legitimized specific queer-friendly conclusions but established queer historiography as a venerable enterprise in its own right. Thus, even though Randolph Trumbach determines that Boswell's book "did not ... have much of an impact on either the moral theologians or the church hierarchy," Dinshaw makes a persuasive case that it nevertheless "infiltrated church, military, courts, and schools on a more fundamental level—on the ground level."[8] Boswell's opus was seminal for many lay people's interest in queer historiography, even though it had a minor impact within the academy. Why the discrepancy?

Within biblical scholarship, works appearing to be driven by disinterest and factuality are far more likely to be granted authority than those bearing overt investment in their conclusions. Because queer and allied interpreters may have *wanted* to imagine Christianity as nonheteronormative, many are suspicious not only of their conclusions but of their arguments. For present purposes, shadow scholars might be said to adopt an activist hermeneutics, a reading strategy marked by the explicit discussion of the normative stakes for their interpretation, stakes that sprout directly from their exegetical conclusions. Although many would agree that biblical readings are inherently prescriptive and comprise efforts to enact a normative political vision regardless of the interpreter's intent, most academics nevertheless have an intuitive sense that there is a difference between activist and scholastic hermeneutics, even if the differences are sometimes blurry and the reasons for distinguishing them are vague. By way of example, contemporary biblical scholars would not read the slavery-apologetics from chapter 3 for their exegetical insights concerning biblical texts but for history-of-interpretation reasons. Academics can safely dismiss proslavery interpretations without comment, as they are clearly activist interpretations whose conclusions are predetermined to advance the author's normative politics.

This suspicion speaks to a significant fault-line between scholastic and activist hermeneutics, often mapping neatly onto academic and shadow

---

7. Quoted in Dinshaw, *Getting Medieval*, 28, 25, respectively.

8. Randolph Trumbach, review of *Same-Sex Unions*, by John Boswell, *JH* 30.2 (1995): 112; Dinshaw, *Getting Medieval*, 31–32.

scholarship. The homoerotic interpretation of the centurion at Capernaum is one among many biblical readings rarely given credence among scholars today, even though it is considered learned among lay interpreters who are invested in its prescriptive implications. Consider briefly the widespread popularity of the Jesus-myth hypothesis, which contends that there never was a historical Jesus, similar to how the deities Isis and Dionysus never walked the earth. The Jesus-myth hypothesis finds few academic supporters but has its own field of shadow scholarship, with numerous websites, blogs, and self-published books acting as venues for distributing such research. Ideas operative in academic investigations, such as "chthonic versus superlunar deities," "Hellenistic Judaism," and "Christian apocrypha," lend their arguments a scholarly tenor, even if their advocates generally lack the academic capital (and thus the access to publication venues, conferences, etc.) that might prompt biblical scholars to seriously engage their work. It does not help that most Jesus-myth shadow scholars make no qualms about their axes to grind with Christianity: most identify as secular humanists or atheists and claim their work delegitimizes Christianity by setting that axe at its root. Shadow scholarship that focuses on the Bible often proves more influential than academic scholarship: television documentaries tend to give shadow scholarship disproportionate voice, there is a sense that these are scholarly (or scholarly-adjacent) forms of knowledge in churches, and students are often better acquainted with such ideas than mainstream scholarship.

Even if rarely articulated, there is a shared, if nebulous, understanding of what differentiates activist and scholastic ways of reading. Activist hermeneutics prioritize their normative vision above all other concerns, whereas scholastic hermeneutics subordinate their normative vision to at least a secondary level. We might recall the famous aphorism of Bruce Lincoln that "scholarship is myth with footnotes."[9] Lincoln's statement is often quoted flippantly against academics who naively present themselves as disinterested. That is, Lincoln is commonly presented as asserting that scholarship is just as ideologically driven as myth, even though its citational practices give the impression of disinterest. Lincoln's point, however, is more subtle. For Lincoln, footnotes are a synecdoche, not for the (self-)authorizing mechanisms of higher education generative of academic

---

9. Bruce Lincoln, *Theorizing Myth: Narrative, Ideology, and Scholarship* (Chicago: University of Chicago Press, 1999), 207–9.

capital (educational credentials, professorships, reputations of various publication venues, etc.), but rather "the dialectic encounter between an interested inquirer, a body of evidence, and a community of other competent and interested research, past, present, and future." Lincoln further observes that "scholarship implies and depends upon debate wherein one experiences the scrutiny and criticism of others who are able to point to a check on their ideological manipulation." This check is the primary means of distinguishing activist and scholastic hermeneutics: the intuitive sense of how far one can stray from the scholarly pack before one becomes lost in the wilds of the credulous. This includes bridles like peer reviews, interaction with other scholarly works, book reviews, academic presses, and the semi-public process of testing and refining ideas at scholarly conferences. The distinction between activist and scholastic reading strategies is worth belaboring because it informs how biblical scholars engage with homoerotic readings of the centurion at Capernaum. In short, academic biblical scholars generally understand themselves to be either legitimizing or discrediting shadow scholarship on the issue.

The Heterosexual Jesus and the Secret Gospel of Mark: A Point of Comparison

The implicit directive to subordinate—even suppress—one's normative political interests pervades academic biblical scholarship. One might recall the widely quoted metaphor of George Tyrell, commenting on how Adolf Harnack's portrait of the historical Jesus misses historical truths to arrive at more ideologically convenient conclusions: "The Christ that Adolf Harnack sees, looking back through nineteen centuries of Catholic darkness, is only the reflection of a liberal Protestant face, seen at the bottom of a deep well."[10] John Dominic Crossan observes that this line is often repeated as a "cheap gibe" against interpretations that are ostensibly convenient.[11] Crossan notes that this charge implies a greater practice

---

10. George Tyrell, *Christianity at the Crossroads* (New York: Longmans, Green, 1910), 49; cf. John C. Poirier, "Seeing What Is There in Spite of Ourselves: George Tyrell, John Dominic Crossan, and Robert Frost on Faces in Deep Wells," *JSHJ* 4 (2006): 127–38.

11. John Dominic Crossan, *The Birth of Christianity: Discovering What Happened in the Years Immediately after the Execution of Jesus* (San Francisco: HarperSanFrancisco, 1998), 41.

of disinterest by the accuser than the accused, resulting in more credibly historiography. Crossan is particularly invested in this issue, as the well metaphor was deployed against him for his purported reconstruction of Jesus as the "consummate party animal," among other things.[12] Dale Allison, while not naming Crossan or quoting Tyrell directly, offers comments representative of this sort of criticism.

> Western biblical scholars have little sympathy for eschatology and asceticism and so are not much good at finding either in the Jesus tradition. We are more inclined to spot social concerns, to discover, let us say, that Jesus showed a special affection for the disadvantaged, or criticized the oppressive social structures of his time.... It also does not surprise us that certain twentieth-century scholars with a different piety and of lesser orthodoxy, at home in a world of comparative luxury, instead anachronistically envision Jesus as "the proverbial party animal." This may make him real to us. But this is not the real Jesus.[13]

---

12. E.g., Donald L. Denton, *Historiography and Hermeneutics in Jesus Studies: An Examination of the Work of John Dominic Crossan and Ben F. Meyer*, LNTS 262 (London: T&T Clark, 2004), 11; Craig A. Blomberg, *Contagious Holiness: Jesus' Meals with Sinners*, New Studies in Biblical Theology 19 (Downers Grove: InterVarsity, 2005), 97. To my knowledge, Crossan has never characterized Jesus as a "party animal" in print, though the phrase is commonly attributed to him. Actual instances of academics characterizing the historical Jesus as a party animal include Robert W. Funk, *Honest to Jesus: Jesus for a New Millenium* (San Francisco: HarperSanFrancisco, 1996), 203; Leif E. Vaage, "Q¹ and the Historical Jesus: Some Peculiar Sayings (7:33–34; 9:57–58, 59–60; 14:26–27)," *Foundations and Facets Forum* 5.2 (1989): 165; Vaage, "The Excluded One: (Un)popular Christology and the Quest for the Historical Jesus in Europe, North America, and Latin America," in *Discovering Jesus in Our Place: Contextual Christologies in a Globalised World*, ed. Sturla J. Stålsett (Delhi: ISPCK, 2003), 121–44. Crossan comments on how the Tyrell quote has been used against him to this effect. "It was cheap at the start of this century..... It is still cheap at the end of this century when a scholar asserts someone like myself looks down a deep well and sees there an Irish-Catholic peasant. The scholar, by the way, is herself a British Anglican theologian." John Dominic Crossan, "Historical Jesus as Risen Lord," in *The Jesus Controversy: Perspectives in Conflict*, ed. John Dominic Crossan, Luke Timothy Johnson, and Werner H. Kelber (Harrisburg, PA: Trinity Press International, 1999), 2; cf. Crossan, *A Long Way from Tipperary: What a Former Irish Monk Discovered in His Search for the Truth* (San Francisco: HarperSanFrancisco, 2000), 150.

13. Dale C. Allison Jr., *Jesus of Nazareth: Millenarian Prophet* (Minneapolis: Fortress, 1998), 216.

Allison contends that scholars who reconstruct early Christianity in politically or theologically convenient ways risk their academic credibility, as they often project their normative interests onto an historical subject. More direct are the remarks of Donald Denton, "Because Crossan's Jesus has this kind of relevancy, it is frequently suspected that in his portrait of Jesus Crossan is (as Harnack and the nineteenth-century liberals were so accused by George Tyrell) actually seeing his own face at the bottom of a deep well. One is inclined to think there may be something to this criticism."[14]

This is a common sentiment within the biblical academy, often directed against feminist, queer, postcolonial, and other emancipatory interpretations, which are marked as aberrant from the neutrality of scholastic hermeneutics. Alexis Waller's wonderful article, "The 'Unspeakable Teachings' of The Secret Gospel of Mark: Feelings and Fantasies in the Making of Christian Histories," discusses these issues extensively and has heavily influenced the following discussion.[15] Though the immediately foregoing examples concerned the historical Jesus's sensual pleasures in general, remarks of this sort are commonly lobbed against the homoerotic interpretation of the Healing of the Centurion's Pais more specifically. We have caught glimpses of such rebuttals, ranging from the openly hostile (as with Gagnon's quotation in this chapter's epigraph) to dismissive remarks about how naïve the homoerotic interpretation is (Ian Paul: "there is no evidence in the text and no real possibility historically").[16] Even when academic commentators do not explicitly disparage it, their refusal to engage with the homoerotic interpretation speaks to a general sense that it is not a serious interpretation.

At this point, it makes sense to take a detour from our discussion of the centurion to reflect upon another example of biblical homoeroticism and consider how these issues have played out in another queer reading of gospel literature, namely, the dismissive attitude of scholars toward the Secret Gospel of Mark. We will see that many tensions that have remained implicit about the centurion and the Pais have been drawn to the fore in the case of Secret Mark.

Morton Smith first reported the existence of the Secret Gospel of Mark in 1960, claiming to have discovered a lost letter of Clement of Alexandria

---

14. Denton, *Historiography and Hermeneutics in Jesus Studies*, 11.
15. Waller, "Unspeakable Teachings," 145–73.
16. Gagnon, "Did Jesus Approve of a Homosexual Couple"; Ian Paul, *Same-Sex Unions: The Key Biblical Texts*, Grove Biblical 71 (Cambridge: Grove, 2014), 21.

at the Greek Orthodox monastery Mar Saba in the West Bank. The Clementine letter quoted a previously unknown version of the Gospel of Mark used by a Carpocratian sect. This Secret Gospel of Mark reports that Jesus "loved" a young man (τοῦ νεανίσκου ὃν ἠγάπα αὐτόν ὁ Ἰησοῦς) and taught him the mystery of the Kingdom of God while the young man wore only a linen cloth over his naked body.

Smith tentatively conjectured this was evidence that some Carpocratian Christians included homoerotic activities as part of baptismal rites, a claim to which Crossan later assented.[17] Queer theologians (as distinct from biblical scholars) occasionally reflect upon Secret Mark to excavate an alternative to heteronormativity in early Christianity, sometimes even in the life of Jesus himself. Robert Shore-Goss claims that "the Secret Gospel of Mark represents an alternative tradition of male homodevotionalism to Jesus that has countered the dominant sexless constructions of Jesus."[18] James Neill opts for a less overtly theological stance: "In an early Christian text, the Secret Gospel of Mark, there is another version of the [raising of Lazarus] in which a sexual relationship between Jesus and the youth he raised from the dead is more strongly implied."[19] The homoerotic reading of Secret Mark is popular in queer shadow scholarship, being commonly mentioned alongside the centurion at Capernaum, Jonathan and David, Ruth and Naomi, and the Ethiopian Eunuch.[20] Indeed, shadow scholars discuss Secret Mark more frequently than academic biblical scholars in recent years.

Predictably, many have express suspicion that homoerotic subtexts are present because Secret Mark is not a fragment of an ancient gospel but a

---

17. John Dominic Crossan, *Four Other Gospels: Shadows on the Contours of Canon* (Sonoma, CA: Polebridge, 1992), 81–82. Scott Brown argues that Smith's detractors often overstate the importance and prevalence of homoeroticism within Smith's discussion of Secret Mark. Scott Brown, "The Question of Motive in the Case against Morton Smith," *JBL* 125 (2006): 351–65; cf. Charles W. Hedrick, "The Secret Gospel of Mark: Stalemate in the Academy," *JECS* 11 (2003): 135–36.

18. Robert Goss, *Queering Christ: Beyond Jesus Acted Up* (New York: Pilgrim, 2002), 122.

19. Neill, *Origins and Role of Same-Sex Relations*, 217.

20. E.g., Anonymous, "United Church of Christ Professor Says Jesus Was Actively Gay," 27; Michael Lyons and Jeremy Willard, "Body of Christ: Bible Studies for Boys," *Fab* 466 (2013): 12; Douglas Sadownick, "The Christ of the Early Christians," *Gay and Lesbian Review Worldwide* 12.6 (2005): 39; Jeff Johnson, "Pastor Jeff Johnson," *Voice and Vision* 4.3 (1992): 2; Martin F. Connell, "Who Was That Naked Man?," *Gay and Lesbian Review Worldwide* 4.2 (1997): 44–45.

modern forgery. Its convenience for the theological needs of queer Christians was far too timely to be coincidence. Javier Martínez describes the academic reaction.

> [Stephen] Carlson suggests that Morton Smith deliberately waited to publish until 1973 because it was "four years after Stonewall and the beginning of the gay rights movement." [Peter] Jeffery ... resorts to an even more lurid style of praeteritio-cum-insinuation, informing readers "I have resisted the temptation to publish any of the jaw-dropping oral traditions I have heard about Smith, even though some (if accurate) would be quite revealing." The Mar Saba letter is accordingly read not only as a forgery, but one with a gay agenda: it is clear that, to them, the legendary libertine beliefs and sexual license of the Carpocratians are merely a stand-in for the threat posed to the sanctity of Mark's Gospel by twenty-first century gay marriage.[21]

Some commentators go even further and contend that the presence of queer-congenial subtexts is precisely what attracts interpreters to Secret Mark and blinds them to its obvious forgery. Bruce Chilton dismisses Secret Mark on grounds that "the image of a homoerotic Jesus short-circuited common sense as well as sound professional judgment."[22] Chilton then claims that "Morton Smith's wishful thinking or fraud set the stage for further examples of legerdemain," citing Crossan's favorable assessment of Secret Mark as such an instance of delusion. Donald Akenson's comments on Smith's purported forgery of Secret Mark are more direct: "what we have here is a nice ironic gay joke at the expense of all the self-important scholars who not only miss the irony, but believe this alleged piece of gospel comes to us in the form of the first-known letter of the great Clement of

---

21. Javier Martínez, "Cheap Fictions and Gospel Truths," in *Splendide Mendax: Rethinking Fakes and Forgeries in Classical, Late Antique, and Early Christian Literature*, ed. Edmund P. Cuerva and Javier Martínez (Groningen: Barkhuis, 2016), 8. Although one could argue that Carlson and Jeffery were both shadow scholars at the time—Carlson being a lawyer (though he now has an New Testament PhD) and Jeffery being an expert in the tangentially related field of sacred music—I would suggest that their work is largely intelligible as academic scholarship: both published their studies with university presses and were widely cited in academic venues, and Jeffery had previously won a MacArthur "Genius" award. They were hardly at the periphery of the academy.

22. Bruce D. Chilton, review of *Gospel Hoax*, by Stephen Carlson, *Review of Rabbinic Judaism* 10 (2007): 122.

Alexandria."[23] Many, many more examples could be cited. Never mind that some of these claims are demonstrably false (e.g., Smith had published a description of the find as early as 1960, submitted his monograph manuscript to Oxford University Press in the mid-1960s and thus before the Stonewall Riots; he did not deliberately delay the announcement) and that Smith himself expressed frustration that "conservative critics were the first to claim that the new text's report of Jesus's night with a young man in a sheet suggested homosexuality."[24] Like Smith, many specialists of Secret Mark do not find it ideologically convenient for the simple reason that they do not identify homoeroticism in its text. Nevertheless, many detractors insist Secret Mark is a modern forgery on this basis.

Rather than parsing whether Secret Mark is authentic or a forgery, we might consider how such responses function rhetorically vis-à-vis the disciplinary knowledge of New Testament studies. Positioning oneself as a Secret Mark-skeptic on the basis of an agenda-free method works to contrast one's research with that of activist interpreters who only see what is convenient for them. These responses impute a distinction between the neutrality of one's own historical-critical biblical scholarship and the revisionist historiography attributed to activist interpreters (whether academic or shadow scholars). Why is queer scholarship consistently denigrated in conversations about Secret Mark forgery? And how does queer scholarship come to be understood as antithetical to neutral historiography?

To start, knowledge production in New Testament studies remains heterosexist, as evident in this distinction between historiographic neutrality of scholastic hermeneutics and queer revisionism of activist hermeneutics. Secret Mark-skeptics characterize as revisionist the mere observation that the text can be plausibly read as evidence that some Carpocratians may have engaged in homoerotic rituals; ostensibly neutral academics practice scholarship from a more detached position with little investment in imagining Christian origins without heteronormativity. This neutral-revisionist binary assumes a prior distinction between heteronormative neutrality/rationality and queer ideological advocacy: legitimate scholars were able to approach the topic without prejudice and identify Secret Mark as the fraud

---

23. Donald H. Akenson, *Surpassing Wonder: The Invention of the Bible and the Talmuds*, new ed. (Chicago: University of Chicago Press, 2001), 597; cf. Akenson, *Saint Saul: A Skeleton Key to the Historical Jesus* (Oxford: Oxford University Press, 2000), 88.

24. Morton Smith, "Regarding *Secret Mark*: A Response by Morton Smith to the Account by Per Beskow," *JBL* 103 (1984): 624.

that it is, whereas the judgement of Secret Mark-advocates was clouded by their ideology and revisionist zeal. This understanding is a caricature, but it is nevertheless symptomatic of meaningful divisions within the field, pertaining to distinctive truth-regimes in an antagonistic relationship: one truth-regime characterized as prioritizing historiographic neutrality and the other truth-regime disavowing the pretense of ideological neutrality in its methods, theories, and data preferences under the aegis of social constructionism.[25] The latter truth-regime and the knowledge produced within it are associated with postcolonial, racialized, queer, and feminist varieties of scholarship—emancipatory concerns that often overlap. Queer social constructionism tends to be formulated as criticism of epistemic neutrality, as such neutrality masks the role of power in the production of knowledge. Queer social constructionist approaches to Secret Mark highlight the contingency of compulsory heteronormativity discourse within Christianity, a discourse that has long served patriarchal interests. Social constructionism sometimes goes further than arguments for historical contingency to make normative claims about that which is socially constructed. In the case of Secret Mark, X might designate "compulsory heteronormativity" discourse in Christianity within Ian Hacking's comments.

> Social construction work is critical of the status quo. Social constructionists about X tend to hold that:

---

25. The concept of the truth regime was first developed in Michel Foucault, "Truth and Power," in *Power: Essential Works of Foucault 1954–1984*, ed. James D. Faubion, trans. Robert Hurley, vol. 3 (New York: New Press, 2000), 113–33. Lorna Weir summarizes Foucault's definition and its characteristics: "Each society has its regime of truth, its 'general politics' of truth—that is, the types of discourse it accepts and makes function as true.' Foucault sketched several criteria of truth regimes: techniques that separate true and false statements; how true and false are sanctioned; the status given those who speak that which is recognized as truth." Lorna Weir, "The Concept of Truth Regime," *Canadian Journal of Sociology* 33 (2008): 368. The general absence of this concept in mainstream biblical studies no doubt contributes to the problems addressed herein. For a concise discussion of how this relates to the academic study of the New Testament, see Tat-siong Benny Liew's comments in Susanne Scholz, et al., "Roundtable: The Institute for Signifying Scriptures and Biblical Studies," *Abeng* 3 (2019): 87–91. Cf. Tat-siong Benny Liew, "When Margins Become Common Ground: Questions of and for Biblical Studies," in *Still at the Margins: Biblical Scholarship Fifteen Years after the* Voices from the Margin, ed. R. S. Sugirtharajah (London: T&T Clark, 2008), 40–55; Kotrosits, *Lives of Objects*, 145–64; Denise Kimber Buell, "Challenges and Strategies for Speaking about Ethnicity in New Testament Studies," *SEÅ* 49 (2014): 33–51.

(1) X need not have existed, or need not be at all as it is. X, or X as it is at present, is not determined by the nature of things; it is not inevitable.

Very often they go further, and urge that:

(2) X is quite bad as it is.

(3) We would be much better off if X were done away with, or at least radically transformed.[26]

Hacking correctly notes that social constructionist analyses often make normative ethical claims, but that would be an overstatement in our case. Smith, Crossan, and most other defenders of Secret Mark do not advance the second and third points in Hacking's schema. Hacking's second and third points are worth noting because Smith, Crossan, and others are nevertheless *presumed* to claim such *by their detractors*. Many critics understand Secret Mark and related discussions as implicitly evaluative in the way Hacking suggests; supposing, that is, Smith, Crossan, and other scholars exceeded claims about the historical contingency of Christian sexual norms to criticize such sexual norms as well. To be clear, it is not obvious that Crossan and others did so in their comments on Secret Mark, but the accusation that they were rewriting history for queer purposes indicates that others understood this to be the case.

This approach also operates under the dubious assumption that this heteronormative truth regime is somehow more objective than the queer one. If an authentic Secret Mark is understood as evidence that Christian sexual practices were historically contingent and thus socially constructed, then many interlocutors are eager to advocate the opposite when they argue Secret Mark was a forgery. If Secret Mark is fake, then their arguments concerning the contingency of Christian heteronormativity are also invalid. In such a case, Secret Mark's forgery not only redeems heteropatriarchal gender norms but vindicates the truth-regime that produced and continues to legitimize such norms as well. Hence, there is no need to trouble oneself with a modern apocryphon.[27]

One might understand some of the enthusiasm for Secret Mark's forgery as a rehabilitation of heteropatriarchal knowledge against the queer

---

26. Ian Hacking, *The Social Construction of What?* (Cambridge: Harvard University Press, 1999), 6, emphasis omitted.

27. See also Tony Burke, "Heresy Hunting in the New Millenium," *SR* 39 (2010): 405–20.

knowledge that Secret Mark represents. Chilton was not alone in positing a distinction between historiographic neutrality and agenda-driven queer approaches. Peter Jeffery makes several accusations against Smith, claiming that by forging Secret Mark, Smith "sought to depict this [modern-day] anti-homosexual Christianity as morally bankrupt, and the heterosexuality it advocates as inferior to the love that occurs between men who reject the love of women."[28] As for those who were gullible enough to fall for Smith's forgery, Jeffery had the following to say:

> All the experts and eminences whose endorsements Smith claimed to have obtained, and all the other scholars who became convinced that he had discovered a genuine ancient writing, will have good reason to feel abused, more than amused, by the whole sordid mess—arguably the most grandiose and reticulated "Fuck You" ever perpetrated in the long and vituperative history of scholarship.[29]

In a less polemical vein, Craig Keener asserts that Secret Mark's "understanding of homosexuality reflects that of Smith and his twentieth-century context rather that held in the first century, and some suggest that it may have been composed precisely to advance that twentieth-century perspective."[30] Stephen Carlson suggests a direct link between the positive reception of Secret Mark and its ideological convenience; Secret Mark initially appealed to those interested in Christian apocrypha and ecclesial censorship. By 1973, these scholars would have been more open to the nascent gay rights movement.[31] Jacob Neusner asserted that Smith's "'historical' results—Jesus was 'really' a homosexual magician—

---

28. Peter Jeffery, *The Secret Gospel of Mark Unveiled: Imagined Rituals of Sex, Death, and Madness in a Biblical Forgery* (New Haven: Yale University Press, 2007), 234. More recently, Jeffery's work has received prominent endorsement in Ariel Sabar, *Veritas: A Harvard Professor, A Con Man and the Gospel of Jesus's Wife* (New York: Doubleday, 2020), 33–38. Sabar goes even farther, going through Roger Bagnall's archival correspondence with Smith to discover more purported evidence of Smith's sex-obsession-*cum*-forgeristic-tendencies. For insightful criticism of Sabar's characterization of Smith, see Tony Burke, "Some Reflections on Ariel Sabar's Veritas," *Apocryphicity*, 1 September 2020, https://tinyurl.com/sbl6705j.

29. Jeffery, *Secret Gospel of Mark Unveiled*, 242.

30. Craig S. Keener, *The Historical Jesus of the Gospels* (Grand Rapids: Eerdmans, 2009), 60. Keener draws upon Carlson but depends especially on Jeffery.

31. Stephen C. Carlson, *The Gospel Hoax: Morton Smith's Invention of Secret Mark* (Waco: Baylor University Press, 2005), 95–96.

depended upon a selective believing in whatever Smith thought was historical."³² Even vague or indirect sympathy to queer ways of understanding Christian origins renders some interpreters more susceptible to fraud than neutral interpreters. Dismissive attitudes toward Secret Mark are as much assertions about the primacy of one truth-regime over another as they are statements regarding historiographic method.³³ Although much criticism of Secret Mark employs the language of ideology critique, we note that such treatments almost exclusively criticize its convenience for queer readings. Are not other ideological dimensions noteworthy, such as the fact that homoeroticism was only deemed anachronistic at a point when gay marriage was deemed an incursion upon Judeo-Christian values?³⁴

It is, I hope, obvious how this discussion of Secret Mark relates to the Healing of the Centurion's Pais. Interpretations, whether homoerotic or heteronormative, tend to preoccupy themselves with the theological authority of Jesus and are largely concerned with how Jesus, Matthew, Luke, or Q understood same-sex intercourse. For this reason, much this discussion of Secret Mark applies *mutatis mutandis* to the homoerotic interpretation of the centurion at Capernaum; there is a widespread academic interest in reassuring readers that nothing too queer was going on in early Christianity.

This can be pushed even further. There is a tacit recognition that homoerotic readings of Secret Mark or the centurion and the Pais are in some sense a fantasy, even among their advocates. Alexis Waller suggests that "queers often know that there is rarely a 'historical' place to which one can (re)turn or authoritatively cite, and yet the longing persists, and so we resort to making creative inferences from hints, suggestions, and strange absences—to inventing things that can attest to a *felt reality*."³⁵ The

---

32. Jacob Neusner, *Are There Really Tannaitic Parallels to the Gospels? A Refutation of Morton Smith*, SFSHJ 80 (Atlanta: Scholars Press, 1993), 28; Jacob Neusner, "Who Needs 'The Historical Jesus'? An Essay-Review," *BBR* 4 (1994): 116.

33. For an early announcement of the manuscript see Morton Smith, "Ἑλληνικὰ χειρόγραφα ἐν τῇ Μονῇ τοῦ ἁγίου Σάββα" ["Greek manuscripts in the monastery of St. Saba"], *Νέα Σιών* [*Zion News*] 52 (1960): 110–25, 245–56.

34. Cf. Hershel Shanks, "'Secret Mark': A Modern Forgery? Restoring a Dead Scholar's Reputation," *BAR* 35.6 (2009): 59–61, 90–92.

35. Waller, "Unspeakable Teachings," 149, emphasis in original. See also the characterization of a certain shadow scholar in Carolyn Dinshaw, *How Soon Is Now? Medieval Texts, Amateur Readers, and the Queerness of Time* (Durham: Duke University

looseness of the historiography practiced among shadow scholars is itself evidence of this: shadow scholars rely heavily upon affective proximity, the stickiness of which Ahmed writes, sketching out the social world of the centurion and the Pais via loose allegory where the imagined heroes and heels of antiquity evoke modern counterparts. Take, for example, the earliest English discussion of the pericope: a letter to the editor in the homophile periodical *ONE Magazine*. The anonymous writer prefaces a confused version of the pericope that they attribute to a lost codex, saying, "I quote it, translating from the German, from memory, as I have not the source by me. I cannot, of course, vouch for its truth—but true or not, it enshrines Truth as I have always seen it."[36] The author's distinction between varieties of truth is pivotal, grounding their theological claims in a fantasized—even fictionalized—textual history, one whose validity is safeguarded from the historiographic siege of heteropatriarchy. It is hardly surprising that early articulations of the homoerotic reading often took the form of historical fiction.[37]

What is peculiar, by way of contrast, is how the Lincolnian footnote provides an alibi for academic scholarship, such that it is imagined to be devoid of such fantasies or, if such fantasies are present, they do not discredit the enterprise in the same way as the fantasies of shadow scholarship. There is the famous example of N. T. Wright fantasizing that Matt 27:52–53, which depicts resuscitated corpses wandering Jerusalem upon Jesus's death, may be a reliable historical reminiscence.[38] This detail of

---

Press, 2012), 43: "this amateur medievalist—precisely *as* amateur, nonscientifically refusing the putatively objective—both studies and inhabits asynchrony, a queer temporal condition that opens up other worlds of desire." Emphasis in original.

36. Crowther, "Sodom," 26. The letter's author concludes in a similar vein, "Does this Codex really exist? Where is it now? Here are questions I have long desired to find out, but do not know how to set about it. But, after all, does it matter? It is just what one would expect of the Christ—complete comprehension, the realization that the love of one man for another can be both with and without sin." See appendix 2 for the full quotation with discussion.

37. See Christianopoulos, Εποχή των ισχνών αγελάδων, 9; Gyburc-Hall, "Legende"; Mayer, "Le procurateur de Judée," 63–68; Theissen, *Der Schatten des Galiläers*, 150. For more recent examples of such fictionalizing fantasy, see White, *Religion Gone Bad*, 303; Iturra, *El discípulo*, 49–52. Iturra depicts a remarkably funny scene: when Jesus sees the centurion, he is reminded of gay pop singer Ricky Martin.

38. N. T. Wright, *The Resurrection of the Son of God*, Christian Origins and the Question of God 3 (London: SPCK, 2003), 636.

the Matthean narrative stretches credulity far beyond its limit, yet the Lincolnian footnote, reproducing and reproduced by the visage of scholastic neutrality, ensures that Wright's scholarship remains authoritative (evinced not least by frequent citation of the book where this claim was made and his continued publication in academic venues), despite such fantasizing. Yet when shadow scholars make overstated claims about, say, romance in owner-slave relationships, these are quickly marshalled to discredit the homoerotic interpretation in toto. The former is marked by the footnote and benefits from its authoritative inertia, whereas the latter (whose intellectual labor is marked by the absence of such credentials, as well as the pressures of an identifiable political agenda) is always already precluded from participation in properly *academic* scholarship.

On the one hand, none of this is exactly news. Many others have commented on this exact phenomenon, with Elisabeth Schüssler Fiorenza's neologism of the "malestream" concisely naming the problem: a portmanteau of *male* and *mainstream*, subject matter and methods of biblical studies are largely determined by a racialized patriarchy that remains dominant in the field.[39] Most major biblical studies journals are reticent to publish more than an occasional article on queer biblical interpretation (if any at all), and serialized biblical commentaries are particularly implicated in the perpetuation of such inertia. This dominance, of course, is not absolute, as attested by important but sporadic examples of queer biblical scholarship published in major venues.

For We See Now in a Mirror Dimly

When academics criticize homoerotic readings of the gospels, their criticisms commonly extend beyond bounds of historical plausibility. Rather, scholars who reject the homoerotic reading of the Healing of the Centurion's Pais (or the authenticity of Secret Mark) often do not take the issue on its merits but begin with an assessment (perhaps implicitly) of its normative conclusions. Gagnon, for instance, ridicules the homoerotic reading of the centurion even though his objections contradict each other; in the end, Gagnon claims that he only bothered to address the issue because

---

39. Elisabeth Schüssler Fiorenza, *Rhetoric and Ethic: The Politics of Biblical Studies* (Minneapolis: Fortress, 1999).

"a number of pro-homosex advocates have continued to cite this story."[40] Others flippantly dismiss it without any meaningful engagement.[41] Most common, though, is the tendency to cite Denis B. Saddington's response to Liew and Jennings's article or a similar article by Gagnon, as though they have conclusively disproven the homoerotic interpretation.[42] Rather than engage with the constructive proposal of the homoerotic reading, academics frequently identify it as an activist interpretation and point to minor problems as grounds for dismissal.

That ostensibly disinterested academics direct their attention to conclusions rather than arguments suggests that little actually differentiates scholastic and activist hermeneutics, at least as regards their orientation toward normative conclusions. Compare, for instance, how academics engage shadow scholarship on the Jesus-myth hypothesis (whose advocates often express a desire to discredit Christian theology): while scholars occasionally respond to mythicist research, they often caricature it and refrain from engaging with its more compelling arguments, instead picking low-hanging fruits as though they were representative of the argument. In short, academics understand their prerogative to be discrediting the Jesus-myth hypothesis as eccentric, activist historiography. It is hard to avoid the

---

40. Gagnon, "Notes," n. 59; cf. Gagnon, "Did Jesus Approve of a Homosexual Couple."
41. E.g., Parsons, *Luke*, 118; Wolter, *Das Lukasevangelium*, 269–70.
42. Saddington, "Centurion in Matthew." E.g., Voorwinde, *Jesus' Emotions in the Gospels*, 18: "The argument on which this understanding is based has already been soundly refuted within the scholarly literature," citing only Saddington's response. See also Heinz Giesen, "Jesus und die Nichtjuden: Aufgezeigt an der Überlieferung der Wundererzählung vom Knecht des Hauptmanns von Kafarnaum (Lk 7,1–10 par. Mt 8,5–13)," in *Erinnerung an Jesus: Kontinuität und Diskontinuität in der neuttestamentlichen Überlieferung. Festschrift für Rudolf Hoppe zum 65. Geburtstag*, ed. Ulrich Busse, Michael Reichardt, and Michael Theobald, BBB 166 (Göttingen: Bonn University Press, 2011), 62; Frank England, "The Centurion (Matthew 8:9) and the Bishop: On the Nature of Authority," *Journal of Theology for Southern Africa* 160 (2018): 69 n. 37. This seems implied in Siegfried Bergler, *Von Kana in Galiläa nach Jerusalem: Literarkritik und Historie im vierten Evangelium*, Institutum Judaicum Delitzschianum Münsteraner Judaistiche Studien 24 (Berlin: LIT, 2009), 167 n. 745; Craig A. Evans, *Matthew*, New Cambridge Bible Commentary (Cambridge: Cambridge University Press, 2012), 190 n. 245; David L. Turner, *Matthew*, BECNT (Grand Rapids: Baker Academic, 2008), 234 n. 16. The merits and problems of Saddington's response are discussed in chapter 5 of the present volume. I have experienced the frustration of my own work being construed similarly; see, e.g., Ian Paul, "Did Jesus Heal the Centurion's Gay Lover?," *Psephizo*, 7 June 2016, https://tinyurl.com/SBL6705k.

impression that academic reactions to shadow scholarship are least partially prompted by a desire to erect a wall between the two, establishing the former as legitimate historiography and the latter as incredible—essentially, acts of distancing that draw attention to discrepancies in method, theory, data, and hermeneutical practices.

This type of reaction can help us identify the *sine qua non* of scholastic hermeneutics vis-à-vis activist hermeneutics. It hardly needs to be stated that all readings of the Bible are in some way normative, even among those who disavow its theological authority. This normativity ranges from efforts to legitimize specific denominational doctrines to more subtle intimations about how the world ought to be. Even though most biblical specialists would agree that academic readings do not achieve historiographic objectivity, there is nevertheless a strong sense that biblical specialists are nevertheless *more* disinterested than shadow scholars.

I would like to argue, in short, that what marks one reading as scholastic and another as activist is essentially hermeneutical in the sense of meaning-making: activist readings are too *obviously* meaningful for academics. As José Esteban Muñoz observes, "When the historian of queer experience attempts to document a queer past, there is often a gatekeeper, representing a straight present, who will labor to invalidate the historical fact of queer lives—present, past, and future."[43] That is to say, the Lincolnian footnote not only ensures academics' adherence to a set of disciplinary practices but also serves to locate the meaning of one's findings through a particular set of hermeneutical maneuvers and implied citations. These sources of authority are most potent when invoked indirectly. Gagnon, for instance, asserts:

> The Jewish elders in Luke 7 could not have supported a homosexual relationship. Luke adds the motif that Jewish elders interceded on the centurion's behalf (7:3–5). Should we argue that these Jewish elders had no problem with same-sex intercourse, when every piece of evidence that we have about Jewish views of same-sex intercourse in the Second Temple period and beyond is unremittingly hostile to such behavior?[44]

---

43. José Esteban Muñoz, *Cruising Utopia: The Then and There of Queer Futurity* (New York: New York University Press, 2009), 65.

44. Gagnon, "Did Jesus Approve of a Homosexual Couple."

Gagnon locates his analysis within specific academic discourses via allusive citation: biblical scholars can ascertain Gagnon's invocations of E. P. Sanders's work on common Judaism, Martin Hengel's work on Jews as adopting/adapting Hellenism, the method of redaction criticism, post-Foucauldian distinctions between homosexuality as a sexual orientation and the practice of individual homoerotic acts, among other subtle gestures toward academic discourse. At no point do they need to be named. Rather, academic readers are sensitive to the delicate choices in phrasing that differentiate Gagnon's academic argument from the broad brushes used among shadow scholars.

Ward Blanton contends that "the 'truth' of any given depiction of ancient Christianity emerges only in that same moment in which an audience recognizes this depiction to be an exemplary embodiment of those distinctions in terms of which it desires to identify itself."[45] That is, a given historical reconstruction becomes compelling the moment at which the categories deployed strike a chord that resonates; that resonance must evoke for the reader their own normative vision of the world in a sufficiently realistic or credible manner. Academic readers can identify activist interpretations as incredible due to the allegoric and syllogistic character of these desired recognitions, lacking insufficient realism. Activist reasoning often approximates the following:

1. Christians should adopt Jesus's stance on issues of sexual morality.
2. Homophobia was pervasive among Jews—like the Religious Right today—by default.
3. Jesus was Jewish.
4. The centurion at Capernaum and the Pais were homosexual.
5. Jesus healed the Pais without condemnation.
6. Jesus had a positive interaction with a homosexual couple and refused to condemn them.
7. A positive interaction with a homosexual couple and refusal to condemn indicates nonhomophobia in a context of pervasive homophobia.
8. Jesus was not homophobic.
9. Jesus differed from most Jews and the Religious Right today.

---

45. Ward Blanton, *Displacing Christian Origins: Philosophy, Secularity, and the New Testament*, Religion and Postmodernism (Chicago: University of Chicago Press, 2007), 6.

10. Ergo, Christians must disavow homophobia.[46]

We might recall Hacking's comment earlier: the prescriptive claims commonly (if inaccurately) attributed to social constructionist academics are *actually* deployed by shadow scholars. The hermeneutical economy of most homoerotic readings of the pericope is lean, even as it has varied considerably over the past seventy years: "authentic Christians must support a lower age of consent"; "authentic Christians must support same-sex marriage"; "authentic Christians must support the presence of queer folk in the military"; and so on. The move from text to meaning is brisk and often explicit: activist interpreters are direct in the normative implications of their research.

Scholastic ways of reading, by contrast, abstract their meaning through sufficiently *academic* measures (incantations?) so as to impress the appearance of historical credibility or disinterest. Scholastic meaning-making differs in that it is mediated by a number of theological and philosophical categories, as well as the voluminous academic literature on each—repression hypothesis, gender practices, empire, kingdom, Second Temple Judaism, and so on—that render it perspicuous to those with ears to hear. Phrasing that looks like obfuscatory jargon to the uninitiated (e.g., shadow scholars, laity) reveals familiarity with histories of complex debates to academics attuned to that particular footnote.

There are various processes required to render a scholastic interpretation "relevant" through the "desired distinctions" that Blanton mentions. These processes are *necessarily* and *inherently* obscure. By way of example, William Loader tersely dismisses the homoerotic interpretation: "Speculation that the centurion's servant must be his slave also in a sexual sense, applicable at most only in Matthew 8.5–13 and Luke 7.1–10, but not in John 4.46–54, where the boy is described as the official's son, is most improbable, as are readings of the Jesus's relation with the beloved disciple in the Fourth Gospel as homoerotic."[47] Loader does

---

46. To be sure, this is not to suggest that all (or even most) homoerotic interpretations of the passage are simple allegories. There are many more nuanced ways of doing such history—for instance, the notion of "touching across time" (see Dinshaw, *Getting Medieval*) in a way that discards an interest in origins or direct analogies in favor of drawing out affective resonances between past and present.

47. Loader, *Sexuality in the New Testament*, 33; cf. Loader, *New Testament on Sexuality*, 336–37.

not expound upon his reasoning, instead referring readers to the writings of Gagnon, whose oeuvre is readily characterized as homophobic. One might suppose that Loader's sexual politics align with Gagnon's, but this would be mistaken. Despite deeming the homoerotic reading implausible and arguing that the New Testament and contemporaneous Jewish literature almost always condemns same-sex intercourse, Loader proffered a submission to the Australian Senate supporting the legal recognition of same-sex marriage in 2012.[48] Loader's submission argued that biblical norms of sex, marriage, and family differ greatly from those today, such that it is dangerous to extrapolate contemporary sexual ethics from the Bible; the Bible is not a viable source for modern family values, even if one is Christian. Loader appeals to a difference in cultural contexts, a difference that debilitates the utility of biblical texts for contemporary legal purposes. Though this method of interpretation may present itself as the result of scholarly disinterest, Craig Martin explains how this represents a fairly routine effort to control the meaning of the Bible.

> Although disabling contextualization suggests that some part of a text may no longer be applicable, given that our own circumstances are rather different from those of the original audience, this mode of interpretation separates out some part of the text as irrelevant or no longer applicable, in contrast from the other parts of the text that are still relevant and still applicable. The text retains its authority, but some parts of it apply only in certain circumstances. This interpretive move is necessary for those who do not want to dismiss the applicability or authority of a text altogether. For instance, many people are willing to dismiss the authority of the text—some people are free to say, 'I don't care what the Bible says about sex, marriage, gender, homosexuality, or whatever—I derive my moral norms on these matters from other sources.' Those who perform a disabling contextualization typically do so because they cannot say this. In effect, their position is usually the following: 'the Bible is still an important authority; it is just that this part of it is no longer applicable.' In doing so they get to have

---

48. William Loader, "The Senate Inquiry into the Marriage Equality Amendment Bill 2010," 1 April 2012. See also the similarly terse dismissal of the homoerotic reading of the passage in Enroth and Jamison, *Gay Church*, 56–5. While arguing for full inclusion of homosexuals (as people) within Christian life, they nevertheless contend that homosexuality (as a set of sexual activities) is sinful. They seem to adopt the approach of "love the sinner, not the sin."

their cake and eat it too—the text remains authoritative and parts of it remain applicable, but they can reject those parts they are uncomfortable with.[49]

While Loader's rejection of the homoerotic reading may appear homophobic to nonacademics, Loader's dismissive approach actually serves his support for same-sex marriage: there is little redeeming about biblical sexual norms, given its misogyny and homophobia; better to disavow biblical authority on the topic than claim there is anything of value there. Loader happily concedes this particular historical/exegetical point to Gagnon but contends that it is irrelevant for legislative sexual politics today.

There is, of course, much more going on within Loader's hermeneutical processes, but the reader is confronted with a fundamentally scholastic interpretation, marked by hermeneutical layers that need to be peeled back to indirectly reveal whatever significance lie behind the pericope—distinct from the direct experience of textual meaning found in activist interpretations. One can only make sense of scholastic interpretations if one is familiar with the multitude of discourses of which knowledge is tacitly presumed. That is, the meaning of the Bible cannot be gazed upon directly, but in the words of Blanton, "through a reflective play of mirrors."[50]

Scholastic indirectness is not merely a matter of hermeneutical prioritization of concerns: it is not as though commentators simply subordinate an easily digested meaning to academic values of "disinterest" or "credibility" to render their reading scholastic. Rather, it is the gauntlet of implied interlocutors—the recognition of and deference to those academic giants on whose shoulders we stand, whose insights are too important to go unheeded but too pervasive to be named directly—to arrive at such a meaning that marks an interpretation as scholastic. If someone feels they must explain the practice of textual criticism, key arguments of Rudolf Bultmann, or the political institutions of the Roman Principate, then either they are not writing for an audience of academic biblical interpreters, or they reveal their unfamiliarity with the expectations that academic biblical scholars have of each other (thereby giving others reason to doubt the author's credibility).

---

49. Craig Martin, "How to Read an Interpretation: Interpretive Strategies and the Maintenance of Authority," *BCT* 5.1 (2009): 6.10–11.
50. Blanton, *Displacing Christian Origins*, 6.

While some of the negative reaction to the homoerotic interpretation is grounded in normative opposition to the issues it evokes (e.g., gay marriage, affirming Christianity, transgender recognition),[51] heteronormative readings of the pericope play into this disciplinary attempt to mediate the meaning of biblical texts through a variety of academic discourses. I proffer here a few sketches that link heteronormative readings of the pericope to common quasi-ideological critiques. Though these sketches are parodic in their lack of nuance and overstated connection to prescriptive conclusions, readers might nonetheless recognize variations on the subtexts they attempt to evoke.[52]

- Observant Jews held negative opinions about same-sex intercourse in the first century. Insofar as Jesus's teachings were mostly theological in nature, he likely participated in this tradition. Christianity today should best think of itself in a similar vein: emphasizing theological matters and keeping out of those things we call political.
- Jesus was a religious man of Jewish antiquity, and he was just as homophobic as others in his culture. He was not particularly unique, and he participated in problematic practices. Christianity is built upon a deeply outdated foundation and reasonable people should abandon it.
- Jesus was a singular human. No one else like him ever lived. The incarnate God cannot be considered separate from the historical Jesus. To bring him up to contemporary norms would tarnish his uniqueness, as he is only comprehensible as the post-Easter Jesus; indeed, the gospels refuse to understand him in any other way.
- Because Jesus's teachings were grounded in a close reading of the Jewish Scriptures, he probably understood homosexual activity as

---

51. For arguments explicitly along these lines, see, e.g., Gagnon, "Did Jesus Approve of a Homosexual Couple"; Paul, "Did Jesus Heal the Centurion's Gay Lover?"; Joe Dallas, *The Gay Gospel? How Pro-Gay Advocates Misread the Bible* (Eugene: Harvest House, 2007), 194–99; Robertson McQuilkin and Paul Copan, *An Introduction to Biblical Ethics: Walking in the Way of Wisdom*, 3rd ed. (Downers Grove: IVP Academic, 2014), 288; McDowell, *CSB Apologetics Study Bible*, 1182; Paul D. Little, *Who Stole Jesus?* (Atlanta: Romans Road, 2019), 297–301.

52. On the value of such parodies, see Judith Butler, "Merely Cultural," *Social Text* 52–53 (1997): 266.

a violation of these traditions. Careful analysis of the scriptures is important for Christians today, as Jesus was a theologian (indeed, a biblical scholar!) himself.

- Jesus probably never encountered anyone who engaged in same-sex intercourse, as it was not particularly common in Galilee at the time. The cultural context was simply very different from ours today. But far from suggesting that Christians should prohibit the inclusion of queer folk, we might take this silence on the matter of homoeroticism as less important than his practices concerning a kingdom of the marginal: the poor, the unclean, the foreigner, the shameful, and the like. We might extrapolate an essence from Jesus's teachings on the matter, and insofar as queer folk are marginalized today, Christian ministry demands that we should include them to the fullest extent.
- It is unlikely that Jesus really was a glutton and drunkard concerned with other people's sexual gratification, as such worldly (even hedonistic) concerns were beneath him. Indeed, Jesus would hardly be worth the time of respectable scholars if he were a Jewish Diogenes of Sinope.
- Neither the Hebrew Bible nor New Testament have clear teaching on same-sex intercourse, being inconsistent and ambiguous. There is no possible way to recover the original intent of the gospel authors (let alone Jesus), suggesting their obsolescence for twenty-first-century readers.
- Jesus would not have condoned intercourse between the centurion and the Pais, as this would have been pederasty, an exploitative phenomenon that is abhorrent, but also not to be confused with modern homosexuality, which is grounded in a more egalitarian model of same-sex relationships. Sexuality back then was entirely different from how it is practiced today.
- Jesus probably never encountered anyone who engaged in same-sex intercourse. Just as Jesus was silent on the morality of slavery (being an institution that is certainly deplorable), so also was he silent on issues of homosexual intercourse. Thus, while the Bible is useful for many things, it is sometimes inadequate when it comes to considering contemporary issues. Christians should therefore not be too insistent about *sola scriptura* but consider other sources for thinking about sexual ethics as well.

This catalogue may give a sense for the range of methods interpreters have deployed to create meaning through a heteronormative reading of the pericope, even among academics who enthusiastically support projects of queer liberation.

There are many perfectly fine reasons one might hesitate about Secret Mark's authenticity or the homoerotic interpretation of the Healing of the Centurion's Pais. It is, I hope, clear that the present argument is *not* that everyone suspicious about one or the other is a crypto-homophobe. The central contention of this chapter is that homoerotic readings are often deemed suspicious on hermeneutical rather than historiographical grounds. Namely, activist interpretations are dismissed because they presume that that one can arrive the true meaning of these texts through means that cause biblical scholars to bristle. To suggest that same-sex marriage should be legalized because Secret Mark possibly implied that Jesus had sex with a young man is too vulgar for scholastic hermeneutics. Rather, there is a widespread supposition that whatever meaning is present in biblical texts, it is not immediate. It requires more complex maneuvers than proclaiming that Jesus tacitly authorized homosexuality by engaging in it himself. The same can be said *mutatis mutandis* about the Healing of the Centurion's Pais. If one were to poll New Testament scholars about why they support gay marriage or a similar policy, few would cite Secret Mark, the Healing of the Centurion's Pais, or another homoerotic interpretation of a biblical passage. Rather, we are more likely to invoke broader secular values (e.g., tolerance, equality, intersectionality), or, if the Bible is invoked, it is likely to involve hermeneutical moves that have been abstracted considerably (e.g., sin, grace, kingdom of nobodies, marginal populations). The Bible, if it figures in at all, requires circuitous invocations or distanciations of meaning from the text itself. That is, the *sine qua non* of the academic biblical scholar (vis-à-vis the shadow scholar) is their contention that the Bible's meaning is never just *there* but requires the text's situation within specific historical, theological, and theoretical traditions, whether ancient or modern.[53]

---

53. This abstraction of meaning is especially important among those disavowing the theological authority of the New Testament, such that their personal politics are never going to depend directly upon biblical authorization (usually, non-Christians). Even these interpreters situate the Bible within a broader hermeneutical economy, with its own configuration of text, meaning, and interpretation, even if the Bible is afforded no more special a position than other media: "We can learn something about

Academic biblical scholars' meaning-making practices need not be understood as willful obfuscation, letting conclusions determine results, or the intentional linking of theological concepts to various biblical discourses. Rather, we might follow Pierre Bourdieu in noting that the legitimation of power—in this case, the claim of authority over the interpretation of an object that is itself regarded as authoritative (i.e., the Bible)—is most effective precisely when it is misrecognized by both reader and author.[54] We have all sought to be recognized as authorities on a corpus of texts that itself holds considerable authority throughout most of the world (not to mention that we are self-appointed arbiters of which methods, theories, and credentials precede a credible interpretation of this corpus). The economy of power within biblical studies would be regarded as self-authorization to any reasonable anthropologist or social theorist. Even so, there remains a widespread perception that the field's legitimation practices are grounded in inherent goods, whether theological or secular: divine revelation, democracy, equality, history, knowledge-production, and so on.

The field of biblical scholarship is a site of social contestation, even if the precise battles are rarely named as such and when they are named, opposing interpretations are identified as activist (if too overt about the normative goals of the interpretation), merely theoretical (if too preoccupied with the analysis of scholarship rather than texts), or antiquarian (if the meaning-making processes are too obscure for fellow academics). As many have observed, the effect is conservative: the rules of the game prohibit significant deviation and those playing by other rules are often relegated to their own playground (e.g., exposure limited to journals of specialized interest, minor sections at conferences). We might recall the scholarly predilection for using Tyrell's quotation about the well to dismiss others, acting as a shallow form of ideological criticism: "I can recognize this interpretation as ideologically convenient for the author, ergo their reading is not serious history but thinly veiled politics." This strain of ideological critique offers little insight by way of social history, political

---

the queer experience by considering a certain aspect of Secret Mark/Paris Is Burning/Terrorist Assemblages/I Am A Bird Now/etc."

54. Bourdieu's writing on misrecognition was sporadic. See the concise summary in David Swartz, *Culture and Power: The Sociology of Pierre Bourdieu* (Chicago: University of Chicago Press, 1997), 89–93.

analysis, or theory. It merely serves to fetishize the disinterested scholar and the authoritative inertia they represent.

5
Did the Centurion at Capernaum Have Intercourse with the Pais?

> Anyway, how's your sex life?
>
> —Johnny, *The Room*

It is time to turn to the pericope itself and consider how the foregoing discussion might inform an assessment of possible homoeroticism in the Healing of the Centurion's Pais. What might a combination of social-historical and ideological-critical analyses of the pericope with an eye toward sexuality conclude? In short, did the centurion and the Pais have intercourse?

Even if one sets aside the speculative, nosy, and somewhat ridiculous nature of this inquiry, we will see that these questions require complicated answers. This chapter will address arguments and assumptions both favoring and opposing the homoerotic reading of the pericope. This chapter operates with a chauvinistic selectivity: rather than address the more specious arguments articulated by shadow scholars, it will focus the more commonly articulated arguments of academic biblical scholars. Despite the frustrations articulated in the previous chapter, I confess that this book would feel incomplete to me without the present chapter due to the irresistible reverence academics have for the Lincolnian footnote. This chauvinism is strictly utilitarian: it will be clear that many academic arguments engage in the type of fantasy that professional biblical scholars criticize shadow scholars for. The present chapter adopts no pretense of special insight, except by way of awareness of how various politics and laws have informed interpretation of the pericope and common gaps in interlocutors' reasoning.[1]

---

1. To briefly elaborate upon my own nonneutrality: On the one hand, whether or not Jesus healed a military officer's *eromenos* strikes me as entirely irrelevant to

This chapter addresses common arguments on a topic-by-topic basis. It is necessary to begin by distinguishing between Greek and Roman pederasty and their practice in early Roman Palestine, important for clarifying at the outset which scenarios are plausible and which are implausible. Following this, two Greek terms pivotal to the homoerotic interpretation require interpretation: παῖς and ἔντιμος. What did these words mean, and how might that further refine our consideration of plausible scenarios? It is then necessary to consider some generalizations about Jewish and

---

the legal or social recognition of queer folk today. I see few redeeming qualities in the centurion and the Pais's relationship, which bears little in common with any useful conception of queerness today. I would go so far as to say that it would probably be a very *bad* thing to try to ground queer political recognition in the Bible at all, not least because biblical ethics are often awful. I'm not sure that the battle to claim a place in the Bible is a fight that's actually worth winning, given the misogyny, genocide, settler colonialism, etc. that biblical texts consistently authorize (such things, of course, sit alongside more commendable activities). Moreover, I do not much care for the flattening of queer experiences that often comes with this type of homoerotic excavation: rather than highlight the diversity of ways people refused gender or sexual conformity in antiquity, we have seen that ancient experiences of homoeroticism are often reduced to their compatibility with life under a capitalist economy and its concomitant politics of respectability—one aspect of shadow scholarship that I find particularly frustrating.

That said, I find myself invested in the homoerotic interpretation on several grounds, four of which seem particularly significant. (1) Biblical scholarship as an academic discipline remains heteronormative to an extent that is truly embarrassing. It is, to my mind, a contribution in its own right to situate biblical texts within the commonplace homoeroticism of antiquity. (2) I realize that my own dismissive stance toward the Bible is not shared by all, and this pericope holds an important place for many seeking queer recognition in specifically Christian contexts. I have sympathy for such people and their quest, even if I do not especially care for the practice of queer exegetical excavation. (3) I find myself frustrated with academic biblical scholars' dismissiveness toward shadow scholarship. Whatever the flaws of shadow scholars' work, academic scholars' contempt for such research exhibits self-serving efforts at social differentiation (perfectly intelligible within the framework outlined in Pierre Bourdieu, *Distinction: A Social Critique of the Judgment of Taste*, trans. Richard Nice [Cambridge: Harvard University Press, 1984]). (4) I am particularly interested in the ordinariness of the Bible, ancient Judaism, and early Christianity vis-à-vis so-called pagan contemporaries. This pericope is a convenient site for doing so, as it is easily situated within mundane mores of Greco-Roman culture. This might be understood within the broader critique of the *sui generis* conception of religion, a conception dominant within biblical studies. No doubt there are a multitude of other ways that I am invested in the outcome of this study, even if many reasons are sufficiently subtle that enumerating them here would be self-indulgent or they elude my own awareness entirely.

Christian sexual norms: what were attitudes about both same-sex intercourse and intercourse with slaves? Against the dominant supposition that these groups were sexually exceptional, Christians and Jews seem to have been speaking the same sexual language as other Romans, albeit with detectable accents. Two other common arguments warrant redress. The centurion's clear concern for the Pais is often taken as evidence of his romantic investment, but how unusual was this sort of treatment? Finally, the sexual norms of the militaries of the Herodian client kings warrant consideration. Although writers commonly assume that the centurion was a *Roman* centurion, this was not the case, as he must have been an officer in the royal army of Herod Antipas. What were the sexual norms within Herodian royal forces?

After these issues have been sketched out, we will be positioned to contemplate the biblical accounts of the pericope. What is the likelihood homoeroticism is present in the individual accounts in John, Luke, Matthew, and Q? This analysis should not be mistaken for claims about historical individuals or events. Determining whether the historical centurion and historical Pais had intercourse (if they even existed) requires an entirely different methodological apparatus and is left for others to ponder. The same goes for whatever the historical Jesus may have made of their relationship. I confess that I am not particularly confident that any such incident ever happened.

Roman Versus Greek Pederasty

Greek and Roman practices of same-sex intercourse differed significantly. As noted in chapter 3, Jennings and Liew cite various suggestions that the *pais* in pederastic contexts included boys aged twelve–eighteen (so Eva Cantarella), aged fourteen–twenty-one (so A. W. Price), or "the age of a modern college undergraduate" (so Martha Nussbaum).[2] While

---

2. Jennings and Liew, "Mistaken Identities," 473 n. 16, citing Eva Cantarella, *Bisexuality in the Ancient World*, trans. Cormac Ó Cuilleanáin, 2nd ed. (New Haven: Yale University Press, 2003), 36–44; A. W. Price, "Plato, Zeno, and the Object of Love," in *The Sleep of Reason: Erotic Experience and Sexual Ethics in Ancient Greece and Rome*, ed. Martha Nussbaum and Juha Sihvola (Chicago: University of Chicago Press, 2002), 192 n. 1; Martha Nussbaum, "Platonic Love and Colorado Law: The Relevance of Ancient Greek Norms to Modern Sexual Controversies," *Virginian Law Review* 80 (1994): 1551.

Price and Cantarella suggest this term included children, albeit those who had begun puberty, all three imagine an upper limit that included people of legally consenting age. That said, Jennings and Liew's invocation of Cantarella, Price, and Nussbaum gives a misleading impression. All three discuss *Greek*, rather than *Roman*, pederasty. The age range of a typical Roman *puer delicatus* ("delightful boy") is difficult to ascertain, since preferences varied from author to author, but Paul Murgatroyd offers this generalization: "Rather than a pedantic reckoning of years, the poets were more concerned with the absence of hair on the face and elsewhere on the body as a sign of youth."[3] Epigraphic and literary evidence suggests that sexual contact with slaves as young as thirteen was acceptable among Romans, though there are reports involving children as young as nine.[4] Despite the importance of the Pais's adulthood within gay interpretations, Roman historians are not so confident that a given *pais* during this period was of mature age.

Greek homoeroticism took two different forms: Greek pederasty was predicated upon the initiation of a *pais* into citizenship of the city-state and preceded by courtship rituals, though there were other, less commendable forms of homoeroticism with slaves, sex-workers, *hetairoi*, and so on. Romans provided less space for intercourse between citizens and instead encouraged citizens to focus homoerotic attention exclusively upon the most marginal: slaves, freedmen, peregrines, sex-workers, prisoners of war, and others of low status. Roman law specifically prohibited homoerotic activities between two citizens. The sexual penetration of a male Roman citizen by another man was regarded as *stuprum*, a shameful act. Greek pederasty was part of a system presuming eventual status-equality between *erastes* and *eromenos*, whereas Romans premised their homoerotic practices

---

3. Paul Murgatroyd, "Tibullus and the Puer Delicatus," *Acta Classica* 20 (1977): 105. Murgatroyd's conclusion has been affirmed more recently in Williams, *Roman Homosexuality*, 67–136. Examples of this in ancient literature are numerous, but consider one instance involving the emperor Galba: Suetonius reports that Galba begged his *pais* to shave his body hair before sleeping together (*Galb.* 7.22).

4. See Patricia Watson, "Erotion: Puella Delicata?," *CQ* 42 (1992): 253–68, discussing Martial, *Epig.* 5.34, 5.37, 10.61; Ausonius, *de Bissula*; texts from *CIL* 6 (especially 6.5163); Crinagoras in Anth. pal. 7.643. See also Laes, "Desperately Different," 317–20, which brings many more ancient sources to the discussion. For dissent from this understanding of *delicia*, see Hanne Sigismund Nielsen, "*Delicia* in Roman Literature and the Urban Inscriptions," *Analecta Romana* 19 (1990): 79–88.

upon participants' inalterable inequality.⁵ Capernaum was located within Herod Antipas's tetrarchy of Galilee, a Roman client state, and the gospels were written under the Roman Principate, making it likely that the evangelists were operating with the values of that context.

One might retort that the specifically *Roman* sexual norms were found only in more heavily Romanized areas (e.g., Italia, provincial *colonia*) and had not yet taken hold in the frontier region of Palestine, as Rome had conquered it only recently and its inhabitants remained under the sway of Hellenism. Latin texts are virtually unknown at Jesus's time, and the gospels, after all, were written in Greek. Gospel writers sit near the fulcrum of the Hellenistic and Roman periods, producing their literature in the Greek language but under the Roman Principate.

Greek texts of the late Republic and early Principate indicate that pederastic norms quickly acquired a Roman inflection: Strato of Sardis, living during the Flavian dynasty, describes his affections for enslaved people (Anth. pal. 12.211) and sex-workers (Anth. pal. 12.237, 12.239), for instance.⁶ Although Latin remained an obscure language in Palestine until the Jewish War, this does not mean Roman culture was unfamiliar to denizens of the region. That Roman norms of pederasty had made incursions into Palestine is evident in Josephus's reporting on Herodian dynasts' propensity to have intercourse with slaves, a topic addressed at length below.⁷

---

5. See the summary of Elizabeth Manwell, "Gender and Masculinity," in *A Companion to Catullus*, ed. Marilyn B. Skinner (Malden, MA: Blackwell, 2007), 118: "The deportment of these two types of youths is distinct: the Greek youth is courted, and is expected to behave demurely, to refuse initial passes by an older man, and never to appear too eager for contact; a Roman slave boy or former slave would necessarily occupy a more vulnerable position. In both cultures the boy occupies a liminal space between youth and adulthood and between the female and the male, and, as [Marilyn] Skinner observes, the Romans are concerned with not only his physical but also his moral vulnerability." Of course, sex-work and citizen-foreigner intercourse commonly occurred in classical Greece. The point here, though, is that such types of homosexual intercourse were not intelligible as pederasty in Classical Greece, even though they came to be understood as such within the Roman Empire.

6. Though hellenophone pederasty of this period is rarely discussed in scholarly literature, see the important sources attesting the phenomenon in Andrew Lear, "Ancient Pederasty: An Introduction," in *A Companion to Greek and Roman Sexualities*, ed. Thomas K. Hubbard, Blackwell Companions to the Ancient World (London: Wiley & Sons, 2013), 116.

7. See the depiction of Herod the Great and his relatives in Josephus, *A.J.* 16.230–232; *B.J.* 1.488–489, discussed at length below.

Likewise, the Warren Cup depicts two scenes of distinctively Roman pederasty, one of which includes involves a boy that appears to be thirteen years old, which will also be discussed more below (see fig. 7).[8] There is little reason to doubt that the evangelists operated in a context where pederasty was conceptually Roman.

What does this mean for the pericope under consideration? Prerequisite for any plausible homoerotic scenario is that the Pais was enslaved by the centurion, was the centurion's freedman, or was a sex-worker (and thus likely enslaved by a brothel-keeper). It is unlikely that the Pais was freeborn and much less so that he was a Roman citizen. While Roman citizens were certainly sexually penetrated on occasion, literary texts regard such incidents as scandals, and it is unlikely that an evangelist would depict such without comment. We might recall some examples mentioned in the introduction: a centurion was reportedly executed for paying a Roman boy for intercourse. The crime was not homosexual intercourse but penetration of a Roman citizen (Valerius Maximus, *Fact.* 6.1.10). We also saw that Gaius Sempronius Gracchus, when returning from Sardinia, reassured his Roman compatriots that they need not worry about him having had intercourse with any of their (citizen) children; rather, Gracchus proudly implied that he limited his sexual adventures to his own slaves while away (Aulus Gellius, *Noc. Att.* 15.12.13). Finally, a declamation relates the story of a soldier who was raped by a superior, whom the soldier then killed; his defense was that it was unacceptable for a Roman soldier to be reduced to the status of a slave (Quintilian, *Decl.* 3).

Any plausible homoerotic scenario must assume that the centurion penetrated the Pais, who was of significantly lower social status: (1) the word παῖς in homoerotic contexts almost always designates the penetrable partner, (2) the Roman social hierarchy demanded that the centurion be the penetrator and the Pais the penetrated, and (3) there is almost no evidence of military officers during the Roman period being penetrated sexually and continuing to hold their office.[9]

---

8. On the Warren Cup and Roman sexual mores, see Dyfri Williams, *The Warren Cup*, British Museum Objects in Focus (London: British Museum Press, 2006); John R. Clarke, "The Warren Cup and the Contexts for Representations of Male-to-Male Lovemaking in Augustan and Early Julio-Claudian Art," *Art Bulletin* 75 (1993): 275–94; John Pollini, "The Warren Cup: Homoerotic Love and Symposial Rhetoric in Silver," *Art Bulletin* 81 (1999): 21–52.

9. A well-known exception on the third point can be found in Suetonius, *Dom.* 10, a passage which explicitly names the resulting disrepute of such officers; cf. Tacitus,

The Ambiguity of the Word παῖς

The single most important argument for the homoerotic reading is Matthew and Luke's use of the word παῖς, a word that Q specialists deem original to that gospel as well (see appendix 1). The introduction noted the frequently homoerotic usage of the word in Greek literature, where it designated the junior sexual partner in acts of same-sex intercourse.[10] There is extensive evidence of this usage beyond the examples cited by Jennings and Liew. One of the commonplaces in Attic pottery, for instance, is the use of the phrase ὁ παῖς καλός ("the boy is beautiful") to indicate the sexual attractiveness of young men in homoerotic art (see, e.g., fig. 6). It should be noted that καλός is generally the operative word in denoting sexual interest in the accompanying text, as παῖς denotes the youth's age. The word παῖς retained its sexual connotations during the Hellenistic and Roman periods, evident in various literary sources from the time. This connotation was shared with Latin as well, clear in the mere existence of the Greek-loanword *paedico* (to penetrate anally) and the transfer of the sexual connotations to the Latin word for boy, *puer*.

The Greek word παῖς, however, designated people in addition to an *eromenos*. Indeed, the sexual implication is absent from most uses of the word. The term typically denotes either "child" in a sexless sense or "slave" in a broad capacity. These three meanings often overlapped, further contributing to ambiguity: many children were enslaved, and masters often had sex with slaves.[11]

Luke states that the Pais is enslaved (7:2), but Matthew and Q are not explicit on the matter. The word παῖς is not determinative of homoeroticism, but it is suggestive. The fact that Matthew and Q could have used more precise words like υἱός (son) or δοῦλος (slave) itself suggests they may have operated with a homoerotic subtext, something we will return

---

Ann. 11.2 with Raimud Friedl, *Der Konkubinat im kaiserzeitlichen Rom: Von Augustus bis Septimius Severus*, Historia Einzelschriften 98 (Stuttgart: Steiner, 1996), 232 n. 35. *Pace* Amy Richlin, "Not before Homosexuality," 540, claiming "army officers could (plausibly) be passive homosexuals." Though this probably happened on occasion, all evidence indicates it was a serious scandal when word of it became public.

10. Jennings and Liew, "Mistaken Identities," 468–78; see the block quotation in the introduction.

11. For a recent discussion of this ambiguity as relates this pericope, see Love L. Sechrest, "Enemies, Romans, Pigs, and Dogs: Loving the Other in the Gospel of Matthew," *ExAud* 31 (2015): 95 n. 90.

Fig. 6. *Ho Pais Kalos* ("The Boy is Beautiful"). Attic red-figure pottery, fifth century BCE. An adult man solicits sexual favors from a *pais* in exchange for a rooster. The cock is commonly depicted as a love-gift of an older man to his (prospective) *pais* in Attic art. Photograph by Zdeněk Kratochvíl.

to below. To be sure, παῖς on its own is not as direct as other terms: if the boy had been called ἐρώμενος ("sexually beloved") or characterized as καλός ("beautiful"), a sexual subtext would be unambiguous. Due to the vagueness inherent to the word itself, the specifics of Matthean, Lukan, and Q vocabulary will need to be considered individually at the end of this chapter.

Though the homoerotic meaning of παῖς is taken for granted among classicists, biblical scholars are predictably resistant to this idea, commensurate with the field's propensity to misrepresent ancient sexual practices in preserving heteronormativity. Commentators sometimes observe that the various editions of *A Greek-English Lexicon of the New Testament and Other Early Christian Literature* (BDAG), *A Greek–English Lexicon* (LSJ),

Theological Dictionary of the New Testament (*TDNT*), among other lexica, do not include a sexual definition in their entry on παῖς.[12] This silence is naïvely taken as evidence that homoerotic readings are pure eisegesis: anachronistic connotations are projected onto the word without the support of authoritative dictionaries.

One might instead interpret this omission as further evidence of the deep heteronormative inertia within biblical scholarship, as Christian writers unambiguously *did* use the term in a sexual capacity. Consider the Acts of Andrew (ca. 250 CE), which does so repeatedly. The narrator characterizes a demon-possessed slave named Alcman as παῖς (Acts Andr. 2). Alcman's owner, Stratocles, is so distraught by his slave's illness that he wishes for his own death to avoid seeing his *eromenos* in such grave condition. Luckily for both, the apostle Andrew heals Alcman and convinces Stratocles to not only seek a Christian life but to leave behind his former indulgences (including sexual gratification from his *pais* Alcman; Acts Andr. 7–8).[13] Another pericope in the Acts of Andrew describes the titular apostle healing a Bithynian man's *eromenos*.

> Demetrius, the leader of the community of Amaseans, had an Egyptian boy [*puer Aegyptius*] whom he cherished with unparalleled love. A fever overtook the boy, and he died. Later, when Demetrius heard of the signs the blessed apostle was performing, he came to him, fell at his feet with tears, and said "I am sure that nothing is difficult for you, O servant of God. Behold, my boy, whom I cherish above all, is dead. I ask that you come to my house and restore him to me." After preaching at great length on matters pertaining to the salvation of the people, he turned to the bier and said, "Lad, I tell you in the name of Jesus Christ, the Son of God, arise and stand up, healed." Immediately the Egyptian boy arose, and

---

12. E.g., Thomas F. Eaves Sr., "Eaves' Third Negative," in *A Debate on Homosexuality*, ed. Thomas F. Eaves Sr. and Paul R. Johnson (Algood: T&P Bookshelf, 1981), 117; Caballero, "Sano Jesús"; Michael L. Brown, *Can You Be Gay and Christian? Responding with Love and Truth to Questions about Homosexuality* (Lake Mary: FrontLine, 2014), 152.

13. See, e.g., the discussion of the pericope's homoeroticism in Christy Cobb, "Madly in Love: The Motif of Lovesickness in the Acts of Andrew," in *Reading and Teaching Ancient Fiction: Jewish, Christian, and Greco-Roman Narratives*, ed. Sara Raup Johnson, Rubén Dupertuis, and Christine R. Shea, WGRWSup 10 (Atlanta: SBL Press, 2018), 27–40; Ronald Charles, *The Silencing of Slaves in Early Jewish and Christian Texts* (London: Routledge, 2020), 194.

Andrew returned him to his master. (Gregory of Tours, *Liber de Miraculis Beati Andreae* 3)[14]

Though this section of the Acts of Andrew only survives via Gregory of Tours's Latin epitome, Gregory's Latin phrase *puer Aegyptius* almost certainly translates the expression παῖς Αἰγύπτιος from the original Greek text. We will see below that the Acts of Andrew casually assumes that slaves are at the sexual disposal of their non-Christian owner and even encourages such acts of intercourse between them.

The Acts of Andrew is hardly unique in this use of the word. Various hellenophone Christians used παῖς or a compound form of the word when they refer to the junior partner in same-sex couplings. Clement of Alexandria refers to various mythological lovers thus: Zeus's παῖς Ganymede, Heracles's παῖς Hylas, Apollo's παῖς Hyacinth, Poseidon's παῖς Pelops, and king Laius's παῖς Chrysippus (*Protr.* 2.33); Clement similarly characterizes the people of Sodom as lusting after παιδικά (*Paed.* 3.8). Christian writers used such terminology to refer to historical same-sex couplings as well: Origen (*Cels.* 3.36), Athanasius (*C. Gent.* 9), and Tatian (*Or. Graec.* 10) all refer to the emperor Hadrian's *eromenos* Antinous as παῖς, whereas Eusebius alludes to Alexander the Great's purported *eromenos* Hephaestion

---

14. Translation from Dennis R. MacDonald, *Christianizing Homer: The Odyssey, Plato, and The Acts of Andrew* (New York: Oxford University Press, 1994), 115–17, also providing commentary on the pericope's homoeroticism. Heteronormative readings sometimes object that no one interpreted the Healing of the Centurion's Pais homoerotically until the twentieth century: surely if sexual subtexts were present, *someone* from antiquity would have noticed, given that they were more culturally proximate to the evangelists' literary and sexual cultures than modern interpreters. Two counterarguments come to mind. First, Christians often harmonized similar pericopae, mitigating against a homoerotic reading: John's similar story unambiguously precludes homoeroticism and it will be argued below that Luke discourages sexual inferences in its version of the story. Second, this pericope in the Acts of Andrew may provide evidence that the Healing of the Centurion's Pais *was* read homoerotically, with the Acts of Andrew retelling the gospel episode with even more pronounced homoeroticism: a gentile leader's *pais* is returned to health after the owner seeks the help of a Christian healer, who does so after an exchange—all elements held in common with the Healing of the Centurion's Pais. Given the Acts of Andrew's sexual politics, one assumes that Demetrius and his *pais* remained celibate after their conversion to Christianity, a topic almost certainly raised in Andrew's prehealing speech.

with the word παῖς (*Vit. Const.* 1.7).[15] Other examples from early Greek-language Christian writings could be discussed.[16]

Returning to the gospels, one can be certain that the author of Luke knew the term παῖς had a sexual sense: Paul's speech at the Areopagus quotes the Greek poet Aratus (Acts 17:28; Aratus, *Phaen.* 5), a poet who engaged in pederasty himself (Theocritus, *Id.* 7.96–114) and presumably used the word παῖς sexually in his lost writings (cf. Anth. pal. 12.129). The author of Luke was almost certainly familiar with other literary texts where παῖς was imbued with sexual connotations, such as the writings of Plato, Thucydides, and Homer.[17] The term can operate in a similar capacity in the Septuagint, which all evangelists relied upon. LXX Gen 37:30, for instance, uses παιδάριον of the patriarch Joseph at a context when he was enslaved and sexually vulnerable to Potiphar's wife (cf. T. Jos. 14.3).

The assumption that homoerotic use of the term παῖς was either idiosyncratic or unfamiliar to Christian writers is unfounded. This, of course, does not *necessitate* that the evangelists used it in this capacity, given its range of meanings. It is vital to consider the use of the word παῖς within the narrative texture of each gospel to ascertain any homoeroticism.

The Ambiguity of the Word ἔντιμος

According to Luke 7:2, the centurion regarded the Pais as ἔντιμος, a term that most interpretations claim connotes emotional intimacy—"dear" or

---

15. On Eusebius's allusion to Hephaestion, see Christian Thrue Djurslev, *Alexander the Great in the Early Christian Tradition: Classical Reception and Patristic Literature*, Bloomsbury Studies in Classical Reception (London: Bloomsbury Academic, 2020), 187. Regardless of whether the historical Alexander and Hephaestion ever had sex, they were regularly implied to have done so by the Roman period (e.g., Arrian, *Anab.* 1.12; Aelian, *Var. hist.* 12.7; Pseudo-Diogenes, *Ep.* 24). Their relationship became intelligible within the rubric of Roman pederasty during the Principate.

16. E.g., Theophilus of Antioch, *Autol.* 1.2; George Hamartolos, *Chron.* 1.13; John Chrysostom, *Hom. Tit.* 5.4, *Hom. Matt.* 73.

17. On Luke–Acts's use of Plato, see Dennis R. MacDonald, *Luke and Vergil: Imitations of Classical Greek Literature*, New Testament and Greek Literature 2 (Lanham, MD: Rowman & Littlefield, 2015), 67–120. On the Socratic nature of Jesus's death in Luke, see the overview of scholarship in Niels Willert, "Martyrology in the Passion Narratives of the Synoptic Gospels," in *Contextualising Early Christian Martyrdom*, ed. Jakob Engberg, Uffe Holmsgaard Eriksen, and Anders Klostergaard Petersen, Early Christianity in the Context of Antiquity (Frankfurt: Lang, 2011), 15–43.

"cherished." This is so widespread that nearly all translations read something to this effect. Even heteronormative interpretations consistently agree with such characterizations. It is just a small step for homoerotic interpretations to extrapolate an erotic subtext from the word choice.

Despite the frequency of such assertions, no evidence has been marshalled to support this understanding of the word. The term means "honored" or "valuable" in Greek texts, consistent with its etymology deriving from ἐν and τιμή ("in" and "honor," respectively). Greek epitaphs provide helpful comparanda for Luke's use of ἔντιμος. In such inscriptions, the term refers to the deceased's honor, whether in a public capacity, a household, or a specific organizational unit.[18] The term denotes a person's admirable performance in an occupation or office in the epigraphic record, such as acclaiming a rabbi, veteran, *oikonomos*, and so on. This is consistent with how Jewish literature of the period applied ἔντιμος to people. LXX Isa 3:5 pits ἄτιμος (dishonored) against ἔντιμος (noble ≈ בנכבד), whereas 2 Esdras uses the term in a substantive capacity referring to Jewish leadership (14:8, 14:13, 15:7, 16:17, 17:5; τοὺς ἐντίμους ≈ החרים). This is also the meaning offered in the only other instance of the word in Luke–Acts (Luke 14:8), where the more honorable guests (ἐντιμότερος) at a wedding feast are given prioritized seating.

The term is applied to a slave (really, a freedperson) in only one single text independent of Luke's Gospel,[19] an inscription from Thermus in the Roman province of Achaea. "Polyphron, son of Lycus, manumitted his own foundling-slave Aenesa under sanction of Zeus, the Earth, and the Sun, belonging to no one in any respect, according to the laws of the Aetolians, as *isoteles* and *entimos*" (*IG* 9.1.82c).[20] Rachel Zelnick-Abramovitz

---

18. E.g., *JIWE* 1.22 ("rabbi Abba Raris, the revered"); *TAM* 4.1.288 ("Menelaus Hierocles, the respected"); SEG 26.1214 ("born of a respected father, having a mother held in the same opinion"); *IGBulg* 1.2.390 ("Aeschrion Poseidippus, a great and respected man").

19. Most scholars deem the Codex Athous variant at Herm. Sim. 5.2.2 secondary: καὶ ἐκλεξάμενος δοῦλόν τινα πιστὸν καὶ εὐάρεστον ἔντιμον ("and he chose a certain faithful and respected slave"). Regardless, the sense of the word as applied in this codex corresponds to the semantic domain argued above; it explicitly refers to a slave capable of responsibility due to their achievements within the household's economy of honor.

20. Πολύφ(ρ)ων Λύκου Α[ἰνή]σαν τὴν ἰδίαν θρεπτ[ὴν ἀπηλ]ευθέ[ρ]ωσεν ὑπ[ὸ] Δία Γῆν Ἥλιον μηδε[νὶ μη]δὲν προσήκουσαν κατὰ τοὺς Αἰτωλῶ[ν] νόμους ἰσοτελῆ καὶ ἔντειμον.

argues that in this case ἔντιμος is probably a legal term referring to civic rights granted when she was also accorded the taxation entitlements of *isoteles*; as evidence, she points to several other Aegean inscriptions wherein ἔντιμος specifies the rights conferred upon individuals (e.g., IG 9.1.728; Ephesos 135; *IKyme* 4, 5, 7, 8).[21] In short, in this case it functions as a technical term designating a very specific legal status. Aenesa's situation differs greatly from that of Luke's Pais; with Aenesa, the term refers to a freedperson and designates privileges granted to her in a legal regime entirely foreign to Herodian Galilee. Luke's use of the term for a slave is without a known precedent.[22]

The supposition that the term ἔντιμος implies an emotional or even *romantic* connection between the centurion and the Pais probably derives from modern translations of the Bible rather than Greek lexicography.[23] Many factors have compelled translators to render the word in Luke 7:2 as "dear," but it is difficult to avoid the impression that this is a mistranslation that reassures readers of the centurion's compassion, clarifying that he cared about the Pais for reasons more virtuous than utility. This might be understood within the longer tradition of softening slavery in English translations of the Bible, going back to at least the KJV and the Geneva Bible, which render the word δοῦλος as "servant" under the auspices of free labor and its dignity.[24] In this pericope, translators further render Luke's centurion a humanitarian by imputing concern for the Pais, revealing

---

21. Rachel Zelnick-Abramovitz, *Not Wholly Free: The Concept of Manumission and the Status of Manumitted Slaves in the Ancient Greek World*, Mnemosyne Supplements 266 (Leiden: Brill, 2005), 81; cf. Francesca Rocca, "La manomissione al femminile: Sulla capacità economica delle donne in Grecia in età ellenistica: l'apporto degli atti di affrancamento," *Historika* 2 (2012): 257.

22. The term is occasionally applied to slaves in Christian literature dependent upon Luke, such as the Acts of Xanthippe 1.1–10, referring to a nameless male slave enamored with Paul's teaching; the story bears no sexual subtext. I offer my gratitude to Glancy for drawing this instance to my attention. Also noteworthy is that Ἐντ(ε)ιμος is attested as a personal name in several inscriptions from the Classical Greek period through the Roman Principate (e.g., IG 12.1.44, 12.1.55, 12.1.107, 12.8.220; SEG 52.1418; *CIL* 19.470; *ILind* 51, 88; cf. Thucydides, *P.W.* 6.4.3; Diodorus Siculus, *Bib. hist.* 8.23). I am unaware of any enslaved or freed person with this name.

23. For more on the issues discussed here, see Zeichmann, "Slave Who Was ἔντιμος."

24. See the excellent discussion in Naomi Tadmor, *The Social Universe of the English Bible: Scripture, Society, and Culture in Early Modern England* (Cambridge: Cambridge University Press, 2014), 82–118.

more about recent discomfort with slavery than the meaning of the Lukan Greek text.

The term ἔντιμος rarely takes on connotations of emotional or personal importance, and, when it does, it is consistently via metaphor: LXX Isa 13:12 compares the importance of people left behind in the Babylonian exile to the value of gold and the jewel of Souphir, for instance. This is expected, since ἔντιμος refers to financial or material value when applied to objects. It is probably best to interpret Luke's use of ἔντιμος in the sense of "honored" or "important," consistent with the inscriptions that denote the respect granted to someone for duties performed in a professional capacity.

What might Luke's use of ἔντιμος indicate about the centurion's relationship with a person who was enslaved? Roman writers were clear that the sexual use of slaves rendered them more-or-less devoid of honor. The first-century writer Columella, for instance, discouraged owners from appointing male slaves used for sexual pleasure as overseer (*Rust.* 1.8.1), presumably because they garnered little respect from their peers. The Historia Augusta operates with similar prejudices when it describes Marcus Aurelius's wife's jealousy over his sexual encounters with male slaves. The emperor defended his practice, asserting, "the wife is for honor [*dignitatis*], not pleasure," implying an inverse relationship between the offer of sexual gratification and honor accumulated (Hist. Aug. Ael. 5.11).[25] Hellenistic Jewish authors assumed the same. When LXX Genesis narrates Abram's intercourse with Hagar, Sarai finds herself shamed, whereas the incident has no real effect on Hagar's relative status (LXX Gen 16:4–5); Philo assents to this reading as well (*Congr.* 154). Josephus expressed disgust when the Parthian ruler Phraates honored his former slave Thermusa by marrying her (Josephus, *A.J.* 18.40–43).[26] As Jennifer Glancy argues, sexual utility and honor were at inherent odds for enslaved people. It is precisely the fact that their bodies were readily penetrable that marked

---

25. Although the Historia Augusta is unreliable in its depiction of historical events, the argument here does not depend on the actual episode occurring, merely that the narrative is consistent with Roman understandings of honor in owner-slave intercourse.

26. Phraates was the Parthian king of kings 2 BCE–4 CE. Phraates's marriage to Thermusa may reflect a sexual regime specific to the Parthian Empire, though Josephus characterizes the situation in a manner typical of Roman writers: a beautiful woman using her newfound power to manipulate a powerful man.

them as without honor.²⁷ Of course, owners bestowed favors upon slaves with sexual duties, as is well documented. There is, however, no indication that these favors imbued a slave with honor, respect, or anything that might render ἔντιμος a befitting characterization.

The designation of the enslaved Pais as ἔντιμος weighs *against* a homoerotic reading of Luke's pericope. That is, since penetration was a source of dishonor within the Roman sexual economy, it is hard to imagine that a slave who had been used for sexual pleasure would be characterized as ἔντιμος; the two are in tension with each another. Sandra Joshel and Sheila Murnaghan thus conclude, "the free woman is crucially distinguished from the slave by the honor that comes with her status. Her honor is bound up especially with her chastity, which assures the legitimacy of the next generation and reinforces the honor and authority of her father and husband."²⁸ Slaves' sexual activity raised no questions about generational legitimacy, and their sexual history could only cultivate honor under the aegis of celibacy.²⁹ Frederick Danker, the latest editor of BDAG, is direct in his comments on the use of the word ἔντιμος in Luke 7:2: "of any special intimacy there is no suggestion in the text."³⁰ There is no evidence that ἔντιμος connoted romantic or sexual affection.

Jewish Discourse on Sex with Slaves

This book's introduction argued that Greek and Roman slave-owners commonly had intercourse with their slaves. There is a common belief

---

27. See Glancy, *Slavery in Early Christianity*, 27–29; cf. Matthew J. Perry, "Sexual Damage to Slaves in Roman Law," *Journal of Ancient History* 3 (2015): 55–75, on how this dishonor was legally constituted.

28. Sandra R. Joshel and Sheila Murnaghan, "Introduction: Differential Equations," in *Women and Slaves in Greco-Roman Culture: Differential Equations*, ed. Sandra R. Joshel and Sheila Murnaghan (London: Routledge, 1998), 4; cf. Richard P. Saller, "Symbols of Gender and Status Hierarchies in the Roman Household," in Joshel and Murnaghan, *Women and Slaves in Graeco-Roman Culture*, 87–93.

29. See, e.g., the discussion of slaves' honor and sexual activities in Kyle Harper, *Slavery in the Late Roman World, AD 275–425* (Cambridge: Cambridge University Press, 2011), 291–304.

30. Frederick W. Danker, *Jesus and the New Age: A Commentary on St. Luke's Gospel*, rev. and exp. ed. (Philadelphia: Fortress, 1988), 158. More specifically about the homoerotic interpretation, see Janusz Kręcidło, "Obraz Jezusa w Ewangeliach kanonicznych a kwestia homoseksualna," *Verbum Vitae* 39 (2021): 217–18.

that Jews both abstained from and condemned such acts, rendering the homoerotic interpretation of the passage implausible: either Jesus or the Jewish leadership at Capernaum (Luke 7:3–5) would have objected if they knew the centurion were doing so. Thus, Andrew Perriman: "It is hard to believe that [the centurion] would have been on such good terms with the conservative elders of the synagogue in Capernaum if it was known that he used his slave for sexual gratification."[31] We might also recall the assertion of Voorwinde: "it stretches credulity to the limit to suggest that the centurion, who may have been a God-fearer, would have enjoyed such a good reputation in the Jewish community at Capernaum had he been known as a sexual predator."[32] These statements operate on untenable premises.

Sexual intercourse with slaves was not a strictly gentile phenomenon but occurred among Jews as well, as regulated within torah (e.g., Exod 21:7–11; Lev 19:20–22; Deut 21:10–14). There is no indication that it was meaningfully prohibited. Catherine Hezser contends that the practice prevailed without interruption from the biblical through the Talmudic period, as Jewish writers generally assumed the sexual availability of slaves without argument.[33] Genesis Rabbah (86:3) declares, "all slaves are suspected of unchastity," which is merely a rabbinic variation on Seneca's famous dictum that "unchastity is a crime for the freeborn,

---

31. Perriman, *End of Story*, 120.
32. Voorwinde, *Jesus' Emotions in the Gospels*, 18.
33. Hezser observes a few instances where the sexual availability was assumed and comments on how later rabbinic writers rendered this explicit: "Whereas a male freed slave is at least theoretically allowed to marry a woman from a priestly family, a female freed slave may not marry a priest (cf. M. Bikk. 1:5; T. Qid. 5:3), probably because she was suspected of sexual promiscuity, as explained in T. Hor. 2:11: 'On what account does everyone exert himself to marry a female proselyte, but everybody does not exert himself to marry a freed slave woman? Because the female proselyte is assumed to have guarded herself [sexually], but the freed slave woman is [assumed to be in the status of] one who has been freely available.'" Catherine Hezser, *Jewish Slavery in Antiquity* (Oxford: Oxford University Press, 2005), 109–10; brackets are original to Hezser. Cf. Glancy, *Slavery in Early Christianity*, 50–53; Glancy, "The Sexual Use of Slaves: A Response to Kyle Harper on Jewish and Christian *Porneia*," *JBL* 134 (2015): 215–29; David P. Wright, "'She Shall Not Go Free as Male Slaves Do': Developing Views about Slavery and Gender in the Laws of the Hebrew Bible," in *Beyond Slavery: Overcoming Its Religious and Sexual Legacies*, ed. Bernadette J. Brooten and Jacqueline L. Hazelton, Black Religion/Womanist Thought/Social Justice (New York: Palgrave Macmillan, 2010), 125–42.

a necessity for a slave, and a duty for the freedman" (*Contr.* 4 praef. 10).[34] Numerous authors accept such intercourse without condemnation or even comment: in recounting Abram's intercourse with his slave Hagar, for instance, Paul, Philo, Josephus, and other Jewish writers all presume her sexual availability as a matter of course.[35] This does not mean that such activities were encouraged, as Glancy suggests such intercourse was regarded as licit: deeds that were socially tolerated without penalty but not usually encouraged.[36]

This tolerance was not limited to heterosexual intercourse. Numerous sources report that Jewish men used enslaved men for sexual purposes. Josephus recounts an incident 24–23 BCE involving enslaved eunuchs with Herod the Great and his son Alexander.

> The king had some eunuchs of whom he was immoderately fond because of their beauty [κάλλος]. One of them was entrusted with the pouring of his wine, the second with serving his dinner, and the third with putting the king to bed [κατακοιμίζειν] and taking care of the most important matters of state. Now someone informed the king that these eunuchs had been corrupted by his son Alexander with great sums of money. When Herod asked whether they had had intimate relations [κοινωνίας καὶ μίξεως] with Alexander, they confessed to this but said that they were not aware of any other offence on his part against his father. When they were further tortured, however, and were in extremities as the attendants turned the screws ever more tightly to please Antipater, they said that Alexander felt hostility and an innate hatred toward his father. (*A.J.* 16.230–232; trans. Marcus [LCL]; cf. *B.J.* 1.488–489)

Josephus implies the occurrence of sexual intercourse in his observation of the beauty of Herod's eunuchs, use of the verb κατακοιμίζω, as well as the nouns κοινωνία and μίξις. Although translators often downplay any

---

34. impudicitia in ingenuo crimen est, in servo necessitas, in liberto officium.

35. E.g., Jub. 14.21–24; Josephus, *A.J.* 1.188–193, 1.215–219; Philo, *Abr.* 248–254; Gal 4:21–5:1; see the discussions in Jennifer A. Glancy, *Corporal Knowledge: Early Christian Bodies* (Oxford: Oxford University Press, 2010), 65–66; John A. Egger, "A Most Troublesome Text: Galatians 4:21–5:1 in the History of Interpretation" (PhD diss., University of St. Michael's College, 2015). Particularly remarkable is Philo's discussion, wherein he composes a speech for Sarah clarifying that she will not feel jealousy because Abraham does not have intercourse with Hagar due to his passions but to conceive a child.

36. Glancy, "Sexual Use of Slaves."

implied sexuality, the confluence of erotic terminology and the narrative can do little to disguise what happened; Josephus's phrasing is euphemistic as well, but the sexual subtext of the Greek phrasing is unambiguous.[37]

In a similar vein, Martial chastises an unnamed Jewish poet for sleeping with a boy (*puer*) whom Martial fancies. This love triangle got messy, as Martial also accused the poet of plagiarism.

> That you are green with jealousy and run down my little books wherever you go, I forgive: circumcised poet, you show your sense. This too leaves me indifferent, that you plunder my poems while you carp at them: circumcised poet, herein also you show your sense. What does upset me is that born in Jerusalem itself you sodomize my boy [*puerum*], circumcised poet. So! You deny it, you swear to me by the temple of the Thunderer. I don't believe you. Swear, circumcised one, by Anchialus! (*Epig.* 11.94, trans. Shackleton Bailey [LCL])

Most interpreters agree that the *pais*' name was Anchialus, a name well attested among slaves and freedmen in the city of Rome, as it makes sense of the epigram's conclusion.[38] The rival poet's Jewishness is paramount to Martial's polemic; Martial mentions his circumcision, his birthplace in

---

37. For discussion of the incident, see Aryeh Kasher, *King Herod: A Persecuted Persecutor; A Case Study in Psychohistory and Psychobiography*, trans. Karen Gold, SJ 36 (Berlin: De Gruyter, 2007), 301–4; Loader, *Philo, Josephus, and the Testaments on Sexuality*, 315–16. That a Roman client king and his son had sex with eunuchs is unsurprising. There was a widespread perception that eunuchs were not only compromised in their masculinity but that this rendered them viable *cinaedi* (i.e., men to be penetrated): the reduced presence of secondary sexual characteristics, such as facial hair and musculature, lent further credence to their purported youthfulness and thus viability for penetration. The sexual use of eunuchs seems to have been particularly popular among aristocrats: the emperor Nero wed a eunuch named Sporus (Suetonius, *Nero* 28; Dio Cassius, *Hist. rom.* 62.28.2–3), the emperor Tiberius's son Drusus had a eunuch named Lygdus who was valued for his beauty (Tacitus, *Ann.* 4.10), the emperor Domitian commissioned poetry concerning the hair of his beloved eunuch Earinus (Statius, *Silv.* 3.4; Martial, *Epig.* 9.11–13, 9.16–17, 9.36), and many other examples could be listed. See Rhiannon M. Rowlands, "Eunuchs and Sex: Beyond Sexual Dichotomy in the Roman World" (PhD diss., University of Missouri-Columbia, 2014) on Roman eunuchs and sexual intercourse more broadly.

38. Marie Roux, "A Re-interpretation of Martial, *Epigram* XI.94," *SCI* 36 (2017): 81–87; Christopher B. Zeichmann, "Martial and the *fiscus Iudaicus* Once More," *JSP* 25 (2015): 115 n. 9; Rosario Moreno Soldevila, "Anchialus," in *A Prosopography to Martial's Epigrams*, ed. Rosario Moreno Soldevila, Alberto Marina Castillo, and Juan

Jerusalem, and perhaps even alludes to the *fiscus Iudaicus*, a tax that was exacted upon Jews after the Jerusalem temple's destruction. In another epigram (*Epig.* 7.35), Martial discusses his Jewish slave's unusually large penis, knowledge that presumes some type of sexual familiarity between the two.

Particularly revealing, though, is a papyrus dated to 12 May 257 BCE, a letter from a Jewish aristocrat named Tobias to a Ptolemaic minister, presenting four slave-boys as a gift (παιδάρια; *CPJ* 4). The papyrus includes a description of the children, repeatedly emphasizing their beauty and high quality. As Campbell Edgar euphemistically observed, "these black-eyed boys from Coele-Syria were not destined to lead a life of toil in the quarries or factories of the Fayum. Slaves of this sort were luxuries for the rich."[39] Of the four *paides*, two were circumcised, which may suggest their Jewishness, though this is uncertain. Regardless, the owner of these slaves was certainly Jewish: the Tobiads were an aristocratic Jewish family known for their Hellenistic sympathies, including, it would seem, pederasty.

There was a widespread assumption that slaves provided an acceptable outlet for sexual gratification among ancient Jews. Heszer concludes in no uncertain terms: "Slaves were sexually exploited in both Jewish and Greco-Roman society. The phenomenon that masters would sleep with and produce children with their slaves is taken for granted by both Jewish and Roman writers."[40] That is, there is no reason to suppose that Jews of the time operated with unique scruples that led them to deplore the practice. Instances where ancient Jewish writers denounced the sexual use of slaves are rare, tending to be isolated voices, similar to Musonius Rufus's moralizing as an isolated instance of Roman condemnation (Musonius Rufus, *Disc.* 12.1–16).[41] Glancy observes that even when Jewish authors implicitly criticize the sexual use of male slaves (e.g., in retellings of the Potiphar's wife episode, LXX Joel 3:3), their objections largely concern the owners' out-of-control sexuality rather criticizing owner-slave sex itself.

Fernández Valverde (Berlin: De Gruyter, 2019), 38–39. For use of the name among slaves and freedpersons, see, e.g., *CIL* 6.11623, 6.14327, 6.18653, 6.21687, 6.27692.

39. Campbell Cowan Edgar, "Selected Papyri from the Archives of Zenon (Nos 73–76)," *ASAE* 23 (1923): 202.

40. Heszer, *Jewish Slavery in Antiquity*, 386.

41. Glancy ("Sexual Use of Slaves") observes how rare such objections are in Jewish literature of the Hellenistic and early Roman periods, pointing to Sir 41:22 as one proclamation against such sex.

There is little indication that anyone's moral standing was affected by sexual intercourse with their own slaves.

Christian Discourse on Sex with Slaves

It might be objected that the gospels operate with a nascent Christian ethics that prohibited sexual intercourse with slaves. After all, celibacy is promoted as a virtue beginning with the earliest Christian texts. Laurena Ann Brink, for instance, declares that Christian sexual norms preclude the homoerotic interpretation: "That slaves were used to satisfy the master's or mistress's sexual desires is well documented, but Luke is concerned with constructing a portrait of a would-be disciple, so he does not intend sexual overtones."[42] Though rarely explicit, some interpreters imply that even if some Christians had intercourse with slaves, the tendency was to denounce such sex.[43] Or, at the very least, many suppose that Christians encouraged abstention from such intercourse.

While there is evidence that some early Christians encouraged celibacy or discouraged sexual intercourse outside of husband-wife relations (e.g., 1 Cor 5–7), the question of sexual intercourse with slaves was a major point of contention. Glancy and Marchal both observe that Paul is frequently indifferent on the matter of intercourse with slaves.[44] Paul, for instance, casually assumes the sexual availability of slaves in Gal 4:21–5:1 in his allegorical interpretation of Hagar, as well as the lowliness of the resulting offspring. In 1 Thes 4:3–8, Paul instructs men in Thessalonica to find a morally neutral and nonmarital sexual outlet, a category which Glancy suggests includes slaves. More controversially, Marchal has argued that Paul himself had intercourse with Onesimus, the slave whom the epistle to Philemon concerns.

Several early Christian texts treat slaves as legitimate sexual partners. The Acts of Andrew 17–21 depicts with implied endorsement the Christian woman

---

42. Laurena Ann Brink, *Soldiers in Luke–Acts: Engaging, Contradicting and Transcending the Stereotypes*, WUNT 2/362 (Tübingen: Mohr Siebeck, 2014), 133 n. 21.

43. Though not discussing the pericope in question, see, e.g., the claims in Kyle Harper, "*Porneia*: The Making of Christian Sexual Norms," *JBL* 131 (2012): 363–83; Harper, *From Shame to Sin: The Christian Transformation of Sexual Morality in Late Antiquity* (Cambridge: Harvard University Press, 2013).

44. Glancy, *Slavery in Early Christianity*, 59–70; Marchal, "Usefulness of an Onesimus"; Marchal, *Appalling Bodies: Queer Figures before and after Paul's Letters* (Oxford: Oxford University Press, 2020), 113–56.

Maximilla as entering chastity by forcing her slave Euclia to have intercourse with her husband in her stead. Clement of Alexandria discouraged Christian men from showing sexual affections toward slaves while their wife was present (*Paed.* 12.84). Other early Christian writers assumed that intercourse between enslaver and enslaved was inevitable and sought to regulate it. Glancy notes that Trad. ap. 16.15–16 outlines the regulations for enslaved concubines and their owners to be baptized.[45] Though the Traditio apostolica hardly endorses continued intercourse with slaves, it is nonetheless taken for granted and seeks only to legitimize such sex by mandating marriage.

Christian condemnations of owner-slave intercourse only emerge with any consistency in the early fourth century (e.g., Lactantius, *Inst.* 6.23.23–30, Jerome, *Ep.* 77.3, Augustine, *Incomp. nupt.* 2.8), though these condemnations imply that Christian men continued to do so anyway. John Chrysostom, for instance, discouraged the practice on grounds that it was less honorable and less pleasurable than intercourse with one's wife (*Hom. 1 Cor 7:2* 4–5). Chrysostom's moralizing hardly prohibits such sex, since he contends that the slave is guilty of seducing their owner when such acts occur! The practice nevertheless continued as a moral right among many Christians, as Paulinus of Pella declares that his only premarital explorations were with his own slaves: "I checked my passions with this chastening rule: that I should never seek an unwilling victim, nor transgress another's rights, and, heedful to keep unstained my cherished reputation, should beware of yielding to free-born loves though voluntarily offered, but be satisfied with servile amours in my own home" (*Euch.* 162–172, trans. White [LCL]). Writing in the fifth century, Paulinus presumes others would deem this a mere fault and not tantamount to a crime (*congererem graviora meis ne crimina culpis*).

An owner's right to sexual intercourse with a slave is widely articulated in early Christian literature. Carolyn Osiek offers a reasonable assessment.

> Did earlier Christian writers not speak of sexual exploitation of one's slave because a prohibition was self-evident (unlikely), because it was not done by Christians (also unlikely given the prevailing acceptance in the culture), because it was too much of a problem to tackle (ignore it and maybe it will go away), or because they did not consider it a prob-

---

45. Jennifer A. Glancy, "Obstacles to Slaves' Participation in the Corinthian Church," *JBL* 117 (1998): 482.

lem? I would argue that this was a part of the culture that they had not yet sorted out as something to reject explicitly.[46]

There was no universal set of Christian sexual norms, much less a consensus prohibiting intercourse with slaves. Much like Jewish sexual norms, Christian sexual ethics are entirely intelligible within broader Greco-Roman discourses, and there is little evidence of either being at significant odds with pagan values.

Jewish Discourse on Same-Sex Intercourse Involving Men

We saw in chapters 2 and 3 that commentators frequently claim that Jews abstained from same-sex intercourse. Typical is Gagnon's confident declaration that "actual instances of homosexual behavior among Jews of this period are not attested."[47] This claim is simply false.

There are five sets of texts that attest such intercourse in the period 100 BCE–100 CE, two of which were discussed at length above.[48] (1) Josephus reports that Herod the Great and his son Alexander both had sexual relations with royal eunuchs (*A.J.* 16.230–232; *B.J.* 1.488–489). (2) We have already seen that Martial accused a Jewish poet of stealing a male youth's affections from him, a charge laden with sexual wordplay (*Epig.* 11.94). But even beyond this, Martial repeatedly discusses homoerotic activities of Jewish men in other epigrams: Martial may imply a sexual encounter with an unnamed Jewish slave (*Epig.* 7.35); he comments on the eventuality of a certain Chrestus performing fellatio on an anonymous Jewish man (*Epig.* 7.55); Martial also expresses his fascination with the unusually large

---

46. Carolyn Osiek, "Female Slaves, Porneia, and the Limits of Obedience," in *Early Christian Families in Context: An Interdisciplinary Dialogue*, ed. David L. Balch and Carolyn Osiek (Grand Rapids: Eerdmans, 2003), 274.

47. Robert A. J. Gagnon, *The Bible and Homosexual Practice: Texts and Hermeneutics* (Nashville: Abingdon, 2001), 159–60. Gagnon continues, "given the severe stance against homosexual intercourse in the Levitical laws, it is inconceivable that any non-apostate Jew in antiquity would argue for the legitimacy of male-male sexual intercourse." Gagnon concedes a single instance, that of the men witnessed by Judah ben Pazzi discussed below, circa 300 CE.

48. For more thorough discussion of these sources, see Zeichmann, "Same-Sex Intercourse Involving Jewish Men."

penis of a Jewish man named Menophilus (*Epig.* 7.82).[49] (3) A graffito found in Beth Guvrin, inscribed roughly 100 BCE, recounts intercourse between two men who were likely Jewish: "Here Philinus the youth buggered Papias, Craterus's stepson."[50] (4) Graffiti from Pompeii record oral sex performed by a person either named Jonah (a Jewish male name) or Ionis (a Greek female name); one Latin graffito specifically commemorates this person's performance of oral sex upon a man: "Jonah/Ionis performed fellatio upon Philetus here."[51] (5) Finally, there is the Warren Cup, a

---

49. There is the complicated issue of Martial's literary persona and the extent to which it corresponds to his own life. There are clear tensions within his corpus that indicate the two cannot be immediately equated: was Martial, for instance, married (e.g., *Epig.* 3.92, 4.24) or single (e.g., *Epig.* 2.92)? The approach of Craig Williams seems appropriate: "Martial may never have had a sexual relationship with a slave-boy named Telesphorus, but the point is that, as far as Martial's Roman readers were concerned, he *could* have. In fact, ancient writers easily made the jump from persona to person, breezily disregarding occasional protests against the practice." Williams, *Roman Homosexuality*, 10, emphasis in original, discussing *Epig.* 11.26, 11.58. Whether these characters were real humans or literary concoctions is often unclear.

50. Φιλῖνος ὁ νέαξ ἐνθάδε ἐπύγιζ{ζ}εν Παπίαν τὸν τοῦ Κρατεροῦ πρόγονον. Translation from *CIIP* 3499. There is reason to infer that both Philinus and Papias were Jewish, building upon the reasoning of Adi Erlich, Nachum Sagiv, and Dov Gera, "The Philinos Cave in the Beth Guvrin Area," *IEJ* 66 (2016): 57–60. First, the inscription was discovered in Beth Guvrin, located in Hasmonaean and Roman Judea. Given the predominance of Judaism in the area at the time, simple demographic considerations render his Jewishness probable. Second, Papias/Papius was a common name throughout the empire, and Jews used it as well (see, e.g., "Joshua son of Papius" in DMI-PERP 172–179, a Jewish Papias inhabiting Scythopolis in *CIIP* 412). Third, Philinus is a name known among Idumaeans at the time (e.g., *SB* 1.4206, with more examples in Erlich, Sagiv, and Gera, "Philinos Cave in the Beth Guvrin Area," 59). Fourth, *CIIP* observes that the name Craterus is known in Palestine or among those with Palestinian ancestry: the name Craterus is attested in Galilee (SEG 36.1291) and the also for an Idumaean man near Cyrene (SEG 9.744). Finally, Philinus used an Aramaic loanword in a nearby Greek graffito: Φιλίνου ναατομια ("the bakers [= נחתמא] of Philinus"; *CIIP* 3498). This transliteration suggests Philinus was more conversant in Aramaic than he was in Greek.

51. *CIL* 4.2402: *Ion[a/i]s cu[m] Fileto hic fellat*. Another graffito mentioning the fellatio of Jonah/Ionis is *CIL* 4.2403 (*Ion[a/i]s fellat*); cf. *CIL* 4.2406, which names Jonah/Ionis with no further details. Note that in addition to the uncertainty whether it is a Jewish or Greek name, it is unclear whether Philetus was the recipient of the oral sex or a participated alongside Jonah/Ionis in performing fellatio; see the discussion in Sarah Levin-Richardson, "*Fututa sum hic*: Female Subjectivity and Agency in Pom-

Fig. 7. Side B of the Warren Cup. Two lovers, one with longer hair, the *eromenos*, having a servile hair style typical of the Augustan period. John Pollini ("Warren Cup.") estimates the *pais* being depicted is about thirteen years old. The Warren Cup is an expertly crafted piece of silverware depicting multiple men engaged in sexual intercourse with each other. The cup is 11 cm tall and contains 125 denarii worth of silver. The cup is named after Edward Perry Warren, the first modern owner of the piece. Warren was a key participant in early twentieth-century queer shadow scholarship on Greco-Roman antiquity and amassed a substantial collection of homoerotic art from antiquity. The Warren Cup is now held in the British Museum. Photograph by Vittorio Vida.

---

peian Sexual Graffiti," *Classical Journal* 108 (2013): 330. For arguments that the name should be rendered Ionis instead of Jonah, see Jaimie Gunderson, "Inscribing Pompeii: A Reevaluation of the Jewish Epigraphic Data" (MA thesis, University of Kansas, 2013), 36–37. Some suggest that another Pompeiian graffito records the homoerotic activities of a Jewish man named Libanus or a Greek woman named Libanis—*CIL* 4.2028: *Libanis fel(l)at a(ssibus) II* "Liban(u/i)s performs fellatio for two asses." The

silver drinking implement depicting two male pairs midst intercourse. A member of Herod's court likely owned this item, as it dates to the turn of the era and was probably discovered at Bethar (fig. 7).[52]

Beyond these five examples, one could mention polemics of lesser historical value attesting to Jewish homoeroticism. To mention only two of them: (1) Tacitus, *Hist.* 5.5 accuses Jews of indiscriminate sexuality, a charge that implicitly includes same-sex intercourse. This fits the general pattern of Roman writers projecting homoeroticism onto foreign cultures—often peoples of the East—as a way of distancing it from Romans (e.g., Phaedrus, *Fab.* 4.15–16; Polybius, *Hist.* 31.25.5; Cicero, *Tusc.* 4.33.70–71, 5.20.58). (2) Josephus (*B.J.* 4.560–563) alleges the Jewish rebel John of Giscala and his soldiers partook in homoerotic activities. John was one of Josephus's primary rivals during the Jewish War, so it is little surprise that the author's homophobia informs his denigration of John and his troops; Josephus seems to draw upon a literary trope of gender-deviant tyrants for this characterization.[53] This is not to mention fictional depictions of Jewish homoeroticism, such as the Jewish freedman Trimalchio starring in chapters 26–78 of Petronius's *Satyricon*; Trimalchio served as his erstwhile owner's *puer delicatus* and shows similar affections to his own male slaves, much to his wife's chagrin.[54] Though these lesser bits of evidence are insufficient in themselves to extrapolate same-sex intercourse involving Jewish men, they nevertheless depict the act as routine or unremarkable: homoerotic activities are not presented as shocks to the readers' expectations about *Jewish* men and their sexual practices (regarding, e.g., torah viola-

---

arguments for Jewish onomastics of Libanus are tendentious, whereas Libanis is a common name among Greek women. See Gunderson, "Inscribing Pompeii," 37 n. 114 for details and criticism concerning this argument.

52. The provenance of the Warren Cup is complicated. Williams (*Warren Cup*) suggests the cup was hidden during the Jewish War and never recovered by its ancient owner. Whoever the original owner was, the Warren Cup was high-quality merchandise and probably very wealthy.

53. Jason von Ehrenkrook, "Effeminacy in the Shadow of Empire: The Politics of Transgressive Gender in Josephus's *Bellum Judaicum*," *JQR* 111 (2011): 145–63; cf. Gabriella Gelardini, "Cross-Dressing Zealots in Josephus's War Account," in *Gender and Second Temple Judaism*, ed. Kathy Ehrensperger and Shayna Sheinfeld (Lanham, MD: Lexington/Fortress Academic, 2019), 197–217.

54. On Trimalchio's Jewishness, see Ranon Katzoff, *On Jews in the Roman World: Collected Studies*, TSAJ 179 (Tübingen: Mohr Siebeck, 2019), 220–26. On his homoerotic activities as both enslaver and enslaved, see Petronius *Sat.* 74–75.

tion) but part of the customary (if unflattering) sexual practices of the Greco-Roman landscape.

Even when Jewish authors condemn same-sex intercourse, they nevertheless take for granted that an adult man may legitimately find a younger male sexually attractive. Josephus indicates some sympathy for Sodomites' attraction to the beauty of Lot's guests (*A.J.* 1.200; cf. Gen 19:1–11) and describes the young Hasmonaean dynast Aristobulus III as having superlative beauty (κάλλιστος; *A.J.* 15.23). Philo of Alexandria—who deems same-sex intercourse worthy of execution (*Spec.* 3.38)—himself finds young male slaves at symposia alluring (*Contempl.* 50).[55] Both Philo and Josephus condemn the *act* of homosexual intercourse but regard sexual *objectification* of young men as both acceptable and normal.

Even more striking are rabbinic texts on the matter. Although the Talmud and Tosefta assert that "Israel is not suspected of male-male intercourse," Michael Satlow observes that these sorts of declarations disguise their tacit permissions and loopholes. Rabbinic regulations create specific exceptions to liability regarding homoerotic pederasty (t. Sanh. 10:2; cf. b. Sanh. 54b; y. Sanh. 7:9, 25a), for instance.[56] These regulations are in tension with torah's norms, since the sages treat penetration by another man as more grievous than penetrating another, even though only the latter was prohibited in torah. It seems that these prohibitions were not necessarily observed, as Rabbi Judah ben Pazzi reportedly witnessed a pair of Jewish men midst intercourse (y. Sanh. 6:3, 23b–c). Jewish sexual norms, though a contested field, differed little from those of Romans, Greeks, Christians, or other *ethnē*: although some individuals contend that their personal values unify their *ethnos*, one need not look too hard to find evidence that such sexual unity was more aspirational than actual.

But does any of this even matter? The centurion is gentile. Perriman and Voorwinde, quoted above, presume that Jews enforced their sexual

---

55. See Holger Szesnat, "'Pretty Boys' in Philo's *De Vita Contemplativa*," SPhiloA 10 (1998): 87–107.

56. Michael L. Satlow, "Rhetoric and Assumptions: Romans and Rabbis on Sex," in *Jews in a Graeco-Roman World*, ed. Martin D. Goodman (Oxford: Clarendon, 1998), 139–43; cf. Satlow, *Tasting the Dish: Rabbinic Rhetorics of Sexuality*, BJS 303 (repr., Providence, RI: Brown Judaic Studies, 2020), 185–222. Satlow's broader and more incisive point is that rabbinic sexual norms are intelligible within the spectrum of Roman sexual norms. For the declaration that same-sex intercourse was absent from Israel (לא נחשדו ישראל על משכב זכור), see, e.g., t. Qidd. 5.2; b. Qidd. 82a.

norms upon gentiles, something that is flatly contradicted by evidence from the period. Jewish writers, to be sure, are frequently critical of the sexual behaviors they attribute to gentiles, but these are rhetorical formulations rather than descriptions of social reality.[57] When Jewish writers condemn homoerotic activities, they consistently frame such abstinence as a matter of "what is permitted for us." The rhetoric of sexual difference proved salient for writers like Philo and Paul, even if they betray limited expectations that gentiles would adopt such sexual norms. If situated within broader Greco-Roman sexual rhetoric, these characterizations might be identified as a trope, rarely grounded in anything more than derogatory stereotypes.[58] Indeed, Tacitus (*Hist.* 5.5; cf. 5.13) and Martial (*Epig.* 7.30) go so far as to contrast Roman propriety with Jewish sexual libertinism, a contrast that implies rampant homoeroticism in Tacitus's case! In short, there is little reason to suspect that Jewish homophobia would prompt hostility against a gentile centurion from Jesus, the residents of Capernaum, or Jewish evangelists.

The Centurion's Concern for the Pais's Health

Commentators commonly observe the centurion's concern for the Pais's health, concern that exceeds modern interpreters' expectations. According to homoerotic interpretations, the centurion beseeches Jesus on account of his love for the Pais. The centurion's care differs from the prevailing Greco-Roman view that sick slaves should be left to die. That he goes to such lengths to save a slave indicates that his concern may not be platonic. Even heteronormative readers observe the centurion's care, but within such a framework the centurion's worry renders him a humanitarian rather than a pederast. In either case, interpreters assume the centurion is exceptional in his treatment of his slave. Does this assumption reflect the reality of Roman slavery?

---

57. See the discussion in William Loader, "'Not as the Gentiles': Sexual Issues at the Interface between Judaism and Its Greco-Roman World," *Religions* 9 (2018): 1–22.
58. See the discussion of this stereotype throughout Benjamin Isaac, *The Invention of Racism in Classical Antiquity* (Princeton: Princeton University Press, 2004). See also the discussion of Christian construction of Jews as the sexual Other in Susanna Drake, *Slandering the Jew: Sexuality and Difference in Early Christian Texts*, Divinations (Philadelphia: University of Pennsylvania Press, 2013).

On the one hand, some owners saw their slaves' healthcare as an unnecessary expense. Suetonius (*Claud.* 25.2) and Dio Cassius (*Hist. rom.* 60.29) report that the emperor Claudius redefined murder so as to include executing a sick or weak slave. That this law was deemed necessary presumes that such killings had been occurring. One need look no farther than the Roman senator Cato the Elder for evidence that this was indeed the case. Cato encouraged owners to abandon ill slaves for the same reasons that they should dispose of work-animals no longer capable of performing their duties (*Agr.* 2.7), deeming sick slaves financial liabilities. A slave-owner was accountable for providing food, housing, and other expenses incurred when a slave fell ill, unlike the obligation-free relationship with hired laborers. Cato adopted a calculated approach, one that Claudius sought to rectify: when it became clear that the cost of keeping a slave around exceeded the any value contributed, it was best to either cut ties or end the slave's life. Jennings and Liew direct their readers' attention to Cato's comments as evidence for that the centurion's concern for the Pais's health was unusual and perhaps indicative of love.[59]

But as Claudius's legislation makes clear, this harsh approach hardly prevailed. To push the point further, we might understand Claudius as codifying existing—even dominant—norms. A more moderate view of slave's health seems to have prevailed in antiquity, as contemporaries regarded Cato as an excessively harsh slave owner: Plutarch, in his biography of Cato, characterizes this treatment of slaves as the result of an "over-rigid temper" and objects to Cato's idea that there should be no personal connection between owner and slave (*Cat. Maj.* 5). By way of contrast, Pliny the Younger manumitted terminally ill slaves, granted them informal wills, and deems "inhuman" those who do not feel sorrow when their slaves die (*Ep.* 8.16). Other Roman writers encouraged owners to keep slaves' health in mind when assigning duties. Columella, for instance, advised indoor duties for slaves on cold days (*Rust.* 12.3.6). Centuries earlier, Xenophon regarded as common sense that one would seek treatment for ill slaves (*Mem.* 2.10). Roman writers frequently refer to the sale of sick slaves, which not only indicates that they were kept around, but that they retained sufficient value so as to render them desirable to other owners.[60]

---

59. Jennings and Liew, "Mistaken Identities," 490 n. 57. Cf. Mader, "*Entimos Pais*," 229; Horner, *Jonathan Loved David*, 122; John, *Meaning in the Miracles*, 158.

60. Heszer, *Jewish Slavery in Antiquity*, 252–55, citing Plato, *Leg.* 11.916; Aulus

There were a range of opinions about how to deal with the issue of sick slaves, but writers overwhelmingly denounce abandoning ill slaves as cruel. This is not to suggest that slavery was a benign institution, only to note that hyperbole in the opposite direction reinforces narratives of Christian exceptionalism. The centurion's care for the Pais is not particularly remarkable. It does not suggest an especially humanitarian slaveowner nor does it suggest a romantic attachment to the Pais. The centurion's treatment of the Pais's health satisfies the widespread expectations of Roman slave-owners.

Sexual Norms in Herodian Royal Armies

Jennings and Liew draw upon a variety of poetic and historical writings in seeking to demonstrate that the word παῖς denoted a male youth engaged in a sexual relationship with a military officer.[61] They establish beyond doubt that sexual congress commonly occurred between soldiers and male adolescents during the Roman Republic and Principate. But Denis B. Saddington observes some major historical problems with extending this conclusion to the centurion at Capernaum. Most significant among these objections is that the centurion did not serve in the *Roman* army and was not a legionary.[62]

Saddington notes that the examples marshalled by Jennings and Liew describe Greek and Roman soldiers' sexual acts, never those of eastern client kings, let alone Herodian military forces in particular. In the first century CE, three types of military forces were present in the Roman Empire: Roman legions (i.e., citizen legionaries) stationed in major imperial provinces such as Syria, Roman auxiliary cohorts (i.e., noncitizen auxiliaries) serving primarily in minor imperial provinces or subprovinces like Judea, and royal armies of individual monarchs like Antipas's Galilee (among other principalities like Nabatea and Batanea). The complicated military history of Capernaum is diagrammed in appendix 3.

Gelius, *Noc. Att.* 4.2.1; Ulpian in Dig. 21.1.1.1; t. B. Bat. 4:5. The primary concern in such contexts was the legal requirement of disclosing *all* illnesses and defects before sale.

61. Jennings and Liew, "Mistaken Identities," 474–77.
62. Saddington, "Centurion in Matthew."

Saddington's objection might appear to be special pleading: the forces of client kings were, for some unstated reason, excepted from an otherwise prevalent practice of same-sex intercourse. This is a fair criticism of Saddington's argument, as his brief article insinuates more than it explicates. Offered here are my own extrapolations of his reasoning, along with evidence specific to Palestine that clarifies this interpretation of his arguments.

As argued in chapter 3, a close reading of Jennings and Liew's primary sources reveals that the asymmetrical relationship between the Roman citizens in the legions and the inhabitants of the regions conquered generated the conditions necessary for their intercourse with male adolescents, typically involving rape. That is, legionaries' sexual violence was itself constitutive of Roman power, as these actions viscerally manifested many of the binaries structuring the Roman social hierarchy: conqueror-conquered, enslaver-enslaved, citizen-peregrine, penetrator-penetrated, among others. Most determinative of this sexual violence, however, was the citizen-peregrine binary; legionaries were the only type of soldiers who held citizenship and their sexual violence was only acceptable if meted upon noncitizens, particularly rebel populations or in the context of battle. These instances of sexual violence were inextricably caught up in the norms into which legionaries were socialized.

Even though Galilee was a client kingdom that existed at the whims of the emperor, the difference between soldiers in legions and the Galilean royal army extended beyond which government signed their paychecks. Rather, the social systems crucially structuring the values of these military institutions differed significantly. The Roman legions and auxilia were perhaps the single most prominent index of the emperor's might and thus served a considerably different purpose from the small army of a petty king that comprised local recruits and whatever equipment that king could afford. Despite the frequent tendency to study Herodian royal armies as though they were identical with the legions, they differed in considerable ways. The examples cited by Jennings and Liew clearly resulted from the Roman military's production of citizen-warrior subjectivities: maximizing the empire's maintainable dominion, preparing frontier regions for economic integration, minimizing violence from hostile subjects, affording of legal privileges to Roman citizens, and so on. Such sexual violence would be unlikely to occur in peacetime Herodian Palestine, since *none* of these components were constitutive of the Herodian military order.

Few soldiers and noncommissioned officers (including centurions) in the Galilean royal army were Roman.⁶³ The Galilean army resembled those of its neighbors Judea and Batanea in that it was recruited from within its own borders. Josephus mentions Hesbonitis and Gaba as military colonies that Antipas inherited from Herod the Great (*A.J.* 15.294; *B.J.* 3.36); soldiers were likely recruited from Sepphoris and Tiberias too, not to mention whoever could be mustered from rural areas. These soldiers were locals in every sense of the word, almost certainly spending their entire military career in their home kingdom.⁶⁴ The fact that Herodian soldiers rarely left their homeland made it desirable to pursue sexual outlets less apt to instigate outrage among their neighbors and countrymen than the rape of civilians, a supposition confirmed in the textual record. Josephus indicates that, like soldiers elsewhere in the Roman Empire, brothels were familiar to the soldiers of the Judean king Agrippa I (*A.J.* 19.357). This is also confirmed in the epigraphic record, as the fortress at Herodium bears a graffito mocking a soldier for falling in love with a sex-worker: "He recently dwelled in the brothel. He went crazy for the pleasure of the one he took."⁶⁵ Another graffito at Herodium suggests that someone witnessed

---

63. The title ἑκατοντάρχης is unknown in prewar Herodian royal armies outside the New Testament. Other texts prefer the word λοχαγός (which Josephus treats as synonymous with the Latin *centurio* in *A.J.* 17.199; see Hugh J. Mason, *Greek Terms for Roman Institutions: A Lexicon and Analysis*, ASP 13 (Toronto: Hakkert, 1974), 66, 164). See, e.g., DMIPERP 4 with discussion in Shimon Applebaum, Benjamin Isaac, and J. H. Landau, "Varia Epigraphica," *SCI* 6 (1981–1982): 99. Several Herodian military officers, mostly those of Agrippa II, are attested epigraphically (DMIPERP 12–18, 23, 30–32, 34, 38, 139, 145, 148). However, scholars commonly overstate their Roman credentials, as argued in Christopher B. Zeichmann, "Herodian Kings and Their Soldiers in the Acts of the Apostles: A Response to Craig Keener," *JGRChJ* 11 (2015): 178–90; Jonathan P. Roth, "Jewish Military Forces in the Roman Service," in *Essential Essays for the Study of the Military in New Testament Palestine*, ed. Christopher B. Zeichmann (Eugene: Wipf & Stock, 2019), 79–94; Roth, "Jews and the Roman Army: Perceptions and Realities," in *The Impact of the Roman Army (200 BC–AD 476): Economic, Social, Political, Religious, and Cultural Aspects*, ed. Lukas de Blois and Elio Lo Cascio, Impact of Empire 6 (Leuven: Brill, 2006), 409–20.

64. See the discussion in Zeichmann, *Roman Army and the New Testament*, 3–7; Roth, "Jewish Military Forces in the Roman Service," 83–88.

65. DMIPERP 119: καινοικήσας τὸ γυναικεῖον. [ἔχων] νοσοῦ χάριν συλετοῦ [...]. It is worth noting that most sex-workers in Roman antiquity were enslaved. Rebecca Flemming, "*Quae Corpore Quaestum Facit*: The Sexual Economy of Female Prostitution in the Roman Empire," *JRS* 89 (1999): 38–61; Edward E. Cohen, "Free and Unfree

a soldier committing bestiality: "Matthew has a swine that he did the nastiest thing with!"66 Such sex seems to have been licit and certainly far more acceptable than violent rape.

Josephus indicates that soldiers' sexual infractions were taken seriously by those governing: when Agrippa I's soldiers celebrated his death by sexually gratifying themselves upon statues of the deceased king's daughters (among other things), the emperor Claudius intervened and nearly transferred the Judean royal army from their homeland to Pontus, which was widely regarded as a cesspool (A.J. 19.357–366).67 Josephus reports that in another instance the Judean governor Cumanus's failure to quickly punish a single soldier who either "flashed" or "mooned" worshippers during Passover nearly led to an insurrection (A.J. 20.105–112; B.J. 2.223–227).68 These instances of sexual misconduct within the Palestinian armies indicate serious consequences for perpetuators, whether inflicted by their superiors or the populace at large.

Antipas's Galilean army had very little combat experience and was never positioned to capture prisoners-of-war that might be repurposed as slaves. The only recorded instance of Antipas's Galilean army ever entering combat was a resounding defeat at the hands of the Nabatean royal army in 37 CE (Josephus, A.J. 18.109–119). Rather, archaeological evidence suggests that the Galilean army primarily served as a local police force, evidenced by the use of small fortlets and stations along roads to deter banditry, ensure open lines of communication, and otherwise keep order.69 For these reasons, we might question the relevance that Jennings and Liew

---

Sexual Work: An Economic Analysis of Athenian Prostitution," in *Prostitutes and Courtesans in the Ancient World*, ed. Christopher A. Faraone and Laura K. McClure (Madison: University of Wisconsin Press, 2006), 95–124.

66. DMIPERP 120: Μαθαΐῳ ὕει[α] οὗ κύντατα ἤει.

67. On Pontus's miserable reputation in antiquity, see Matthijs Den Dulk, "Aquila and Apollos: Acts 18 in Light of Ancient Ethnic Stereotypes," *JBL* 139 (2020): 177–89.

68. The soldier in question was an auxiliary rather than a royal soldier. The Judean *auxilia* at the time simply consisted of Agrippa I's royal army under the Roman banner in terms of demographics (see Josephus, A.J. 19.366). On the annexation of Palestinian royal armies to the Roman *auxilia*, see Zeichmann, *Roman Army and the New Testament*, 1–21; Christopher B. Zeichmann, "Military Forces in Judaea 6–130 CE: The *status quaestionis* and Relevance for New Testament Studies," *CurBR* 17 (2018): 95–98.

69. Fernando Bermejo-Rubio and Christopher B. Zeichmann, "Where Were the Romans and What Did They Know? Military and Intelligence Networks as a Probable Factor in Jesus of Nazareth's Fate," *SCI* 38 (2019): 83–115.

ascribe to their literary sources for establishing intercourse between Herodian military officers and youth in Galilee.

That said, some heteronormative readings go too far the other direction, claiming that Saddington has conclusively disproven the homoerotic reading.[70] This is not the case, but his brief article makes the important observation that legionary sexual norms differed from those of royal soldiers. That a centurion in Antipas's army had a *pais* with whom he had intercourse is plausible.[71] Saddington, however, calls into question whether literary accounts of legionaries' sexual violence on the battlefield is also representative of how Herodian centurions interacted with adolescent Galileans.

The Problem of Anachronism

One of the biggest problems in assessing the plausibility of the homoerotic interpretation is the discrepancy between Jesus's cultural context of prewar Galilee and the much later (and sometimes geographically distant) contexts where the canonical gospels were composed. To what extent did each of these authors accurately depict the social situation of prewar Galilee, and to what extent to did they anachronistically project their own situation onto Jesus's context? Were, for instance, the evangelists aware of differences between Antipas's royal Galilean army of Jesus's context and the legions and auxiliaries of their own? At the very least, the evangelists' knowledge of the historical Jesus's activities was mediated by their experience of similar phenomena in their own social world; mix-ups could have easily occurred. For the complicated history of military presence in Capernaum in the early Roman period, the reader can peruse appendix 3.

The historical accuracy of the gospels is a substantial question, concerning which readers will already have their own opinions. I have argued elsewhere that Luke-Acts is especially prone to anachronism and consistently misrepresents the military and administrative situation of first-century Palestine.[72] I raise this issue not to point to any specific

---

70. See chapter 4 for several examples.

71. Cf. DMIPERP 53, a centurion's epitaph found in Jerusalem, erected sometime 70–135 CE by his "freedwoman and heiress Claudia Ionice." She was likely his concubine.

72. Zeichmann, "Herodian Kings," 178–90; Zeichmann, *Roman Army and the New Testament*, 83–85, 89–91.

conclusions but to emphasize the entirely provisional nature of any conclusions drawn at the literary level. This applies tenfold to the questions of the historical Jesus and any encounters he may have had with a centurion and the ill Pais.[73]

Biblical Reflections

That a centurion in Capernaum had intercourse with his male slave or someone else he designated as his παῖς is prima facie plausible in light of what we have seen, but this hardly amounts to a certain conclusion. To what extent does the scenario remain plausible when we zoom in from the general milieu to consider the distinctive accounts in each gospel? The evangelists have their own unique renditions the story and the particularities warrant consideration. The extent to which the pericope is grounded in a specific encounter of the historical Jesus is uncertain. Rather than attempting to ascertain what in these biblical accounts might be historical and what might not be, it is expedient to proceed with a *literary* analysis. That is, rather than considering the activity of the historical Jesus, the remainder of the chapter will consider how Jesus, the centurion, and the Pais are represented in John, Luke, Matthew, and Q.[74] This section proceeds in reverse-chronological order, a manner that allows us to see a progressively stripped-down version of the pericope, drawing attention to each gospel's redactional features along the way.

There are three possible relationships each evangelist might imagine between the centurion and the Pais, corresponding to their use of the word παῖς: (1) the author uses παῖς in a strictly homoerotic sense, meaning either a free *eromenos* or a slave/freedman whose relationship to the

---

73. On the plausibility of a Herodian centurion being found in Capernaum during the reign of Antipas, see Zeichmann, *Roman Army and the New Testament*, 31–33. On the gospels' narrative depiction of Jesus's presence in Capernaum, see Christopher B. Zeichmann, "Capernaum: A 'Hub' for the Historical Jesus or the Markan Evangelist?," *JSHJ* 15 (2017): 147–65.

74. The existence of Q is hardly a consensus, though a majority of critical interlocutors support the hypothesis. The reality of Q is assumed here and proves important for two reasons: first, it provides an additional witness to the pericope, and, second, it means Luke's account depends upon and revises that of Q rather than that of Matthew. Readers have undoubtedly already formed opinions about the Synoptic Problem, and this is not the place to attempt persuasion one way or the other.

centurion is crucially sexual or romantic; (2) the author uses the word as a synonym for δοῦλος, rendering it loosely or ambiguously homoerotic in that slaves were commonly at the sexual disposal of their owner. Even if they had intercourse, this was an incidental part of their owner-slave relationship; or (3) the author uses the word in a strictly asexual sense (e.g., son, chaste slave). To be clear, this is an entirely different question from whether an evangelist treats sexuality as a *focal* point. Rather, the claims here are limited to the probability that readers would have inferred or were supposed to infer that sexual intercourse occurred between the centurion and the Pais.

The Gospel of John

Commentators have long debated whether John tells the same story as Luke, Matthew, and Q. On the one hand, the narrative beats in the Healing of the Royal Official's Son (4:46–54) are shared with the Synoptic Healing of the Centurion's Pais: an official in Capernaum asks Jesus (who is located elsewhere) to heal his παῖς, which Jesus gladly does from a distance. The differences, however, are significant and concern some of the most important details; for instance, the boy being healed is the official's son (υἱός), and it is unclear whether the official (βασιλικός) serves in a civilian or military capacity.[75]

John's story precludes homoeroticism. The matter is sufficiently obvious that it does not require discussion beyond the observation that the Pais in John is the official's son. The incest taboo obviates any such possibility.[76] Though John uses the same terms as Luke, Matthew, and Q in reference to the child (παῖς, παιδίον), these terms serve to vary John's vocabulary rather than operating in any sexual manner. No one to my knowledge has

---

75. Josephus, who lived in Galilee before the war, used the term βασιλικός frequently and with reference to different varieties of people: soldiers in Herodian armies (e.g., *B.J.* 1.45, 2.429), members of the royal family (e.g., *B.J.* 1.249), and royal administrators (*A.J.* 16.399). John could be evoking any of these meanings, though commentators tend to prefer the last of these.

76. It is unlikely that the royal official uses filial-paternal terms to express erotic affection (one thinks, e.g., of "sugar daddies"). There is little evidence for such use of the terms during the Principate. For a rare exception in an earlier period, see the *pais* Giton's reference to the lecherous old Eumolpus as "dearest father" (*pater carissime*; Petronius, *Sat.* 98).

suggested a sexual subtext in John's pericope. John unequivocally uses the term παῖς in the third (i.e., asexual) sense listed above.

The Gospel of Luke

The question of homoeroticism in the Gospel of Luke is not as straightforward as it was with the Gospel of John but nevertheless clear. Far from suggesting erotic intimacy, the centurion's designation of the Pais as ἔντιμος implies an absence of sexual activity. The term ἔντιμος probably denotes importance or honor that the Pais held within the centurion's household, consistent with the other personal applications of the word discussed above.[77] It is unlikely that Luke uses the term in a strictly utilitarian manner, as the Jewish delegation draws attention to his financial generosity and general *humanitas* (7:4–5); this is particularly evident in his patronage of the local synagogue, interpreted by locals as evidence of his love of the Jewish people (ἀγαπᾷ ... τὸ ἔθνος ἡμῶν). Rather, Luke probably imagines the Pais as a slave whose contributions to the centurion's household were regarded as valuable, being literate or acting as some sort of manager. This is consistent with Luke's use of the word παῖς elsewhere, never even ambiguously permitting any sexual connotations: the word refers to the boy Jesus (2:43) and Jairus's daughter (8:51, 8:54), for instance. In this pericope, the term probably does not denote the Pais's age, but rather adds variety Luke's vocabulary of slavery. The word commonly referred to slaves of any age, not merely those who were young. The resulting image of the Pais is one who is particularly important to the centurion's affairs. He plays a role that does not compromise his honor, presumably entailing a chaste relationship between him and his owner, as we have seen that there was a reciprocal relationship between a slave's dishonor and their sexual availability.[78]

Luke's sexual politics, particularly evident in the gospel's redactional tendencies, prompt further doubt about homoeroticism in the passage.[79]

---

77. See the more extensive discussion in Zeichmann, "Slave Who Was ἔντιμος."

78. Heszer, *Jewish Slavery in Antiquity*, 73–75, 182–86, 202–4. Exceptions are uncommon, but see the fictional Trimalchio kissing his enslaved *pais* because of the slave's "excellence" (*sed quia frugi est*; Petronius, *Sat.* 57).

79. See the concise discussion in Mary Rose D'Angelo, "Women in Luke–Acts: A Redactional View," *JBL* 109 (1990): 456–57; at greater length, see Turid Karlsen Seim, *The Double Message: Patterns of Gender in Luke and Acts* (Nashville: Abingdon, 1994).

In short, Luke promotes the renunciation of sexual intercourse. Luke redacts sayings about leaving one's family to enter the Kingdom of God so as to specifically encourage one to leave their spouse (i.e., one's primary sexual partner): Luke 18:29 redacting Mark 10:29 and possibly Luke 14:26 redacting Q (contrast Matt 10:37). Luke also omits the discussion of marriage and divorce found in Mark 10:2–12, though retaining the Q-parallel that prohibits remarriage after divorce (Luke 16:18; cf. Matt 19:9). Particularly revealing is Luke's revision of the Sadducees' question about marriage in the afterlife, which Luke reframes as Jesus's complete rejection of marriage: "The sons of this age marry and are given in marriage, but those who are accounted worthy to attain to that age and to the resurrection from the dead neither marry nor are given in marriage" (Luke 20:34–35; cf. Mark 12:25). Luke treats sexual abstinence as a virtue in several other instances: one might recall Luke's addition to the road to Golgotha ("Blessed are the barren, and the wombs that never bore, and the breasts that never nursed," 23:29; cf. Mark 15:21–22), Mary's virginal conception of Jesus (1:34), and the abstinence of the prophetess Anna (2:26–38).[80] Other examples could be cited if one wishes to include the Acts of the Apostles in the investigation (e.g., the virginity of Philip's daughters in Acts 21:9, Paul's preaching in Acts 24:25).

Luke's approach to sex is even more pronounced on the issue of extramarital intercourse. Luke 18:19 revises the order of the commandments such that the prohibition on adultery is placed first (cf. Mark 10:19), thereby emphasizing it. Lukan *Sondergüter* point a similar direction, with particular interest in sexual sinners reforming their ways: the prodigal son gives up his sinful life of carousing with sex-workers (15:30), and the author may imply that the sinful woman was reputed for her sexual wrongdoings (7:36–50).

To be clear, Luke is not absolute in its opposition to marriage and sexuality. Simon Peter was married (4:38–39 [cf. Mark 1:29–31]; but see 18:26–30), and Jesus's mother Mary does not seem to have been celibate (2:6, 8:19–21 [cf. Mark 3:31–34]), though instances of implied noncelibacy are uncommon and mostly derive from Luke's sources. The references to Peter's wife and Jesus's siblings are probably instances of redactional fatigue, wherein Luke takes over Markan material with a comparatively

---

80. See, e.g., James Hoke, "'Behold, the Lord's Whore'? Slavery, Prostitution, and Luke 1:38," *BibInt* 26 (2018): 43–67.

light editorial hand against the grain of redactional tendencies evident elsewhere in the gospel.[81]

Returning to the centurion, it is hard to imagine how a righteous gentile having extramarital intercourse could possibly cohere with these sexual politics. Luke presents the centurion as a moral and noble figure, which casts doubt on the prospect of (homo)eroticism here. It seems unlikely that that reader should infer the centurion would give into base desires, even if such sexual activity was permissible within the broader cultures he inhabited. All these factors weigh heavily against a homoerotic reading of the Lukan pericope, as it is difficult to imagine its location within Lukan interests that otherwise militate against such activities.[82] Luke's Pais seems to be a chaste slave, with παῖς operating in the third sense.

The Gospel of Matthew

Matthew's pericope, by contrast, is more easily read in a homoerotic manner. Matthew introduces the character in the centurion's dialogue as "my Pais" with a possessive genitive, phrasing commonly used in Classical Greek to refer to one's *eromenos*. It is unclear whether Matthew's Pais is a slave, freedman, or freeborn, though interpreters have long understood Matthew's use of παῖς in relation to Luke and John: there is a common assumption that the Pais must be either a son or a slave. He could just as easily be a local adolescent, a sex-worker, a freedman, or someone else.[83]

---

81. On editorial fatigue, see Mark S. Goodacre, "Fatigue in the Gospels," NTS 44 (1998): 45–58. Goodacre is interested in fatigue within individual pericopae across the gospels (e.g., inconsistent details within a given story), though here one notices the general tendency within Luke–Acts to eliminate Jesus's siblings: the author omits Mark 6:3, rewrites Mark 3:21, 15:40, 15:47, and 16:1 removing references to Jesus's siblings, conspicuously mentions no siblings during Jesus's boyhood trip to Jerusalem (2:41–51), and never characterizes James as Jesus's brother in Acts. Likewise, there is no indication of Peter's family beyond this solitary reference (contrast 1 Cor 9:5).

82. Other discussions arguing that Luke less probably depicts a homoerotic relationship than other gospels are Álvarez Valdés, "Hizo Jesús"; Pikaza Ibarrondo, "Centuriones." Jennings and Liew ("Mistaken Identities") focus on Matthew to the exclusion of Luke.

83. The most noteworthy exception in this regard is Jennings and Liew, "Mistaken Identities," 468–78. They seem to imply that the Pais was either freeborn or a freedman. They also note that the New English Bible is another exception, rendering παῖς at Matt 8:6 as "a boy of mine" and 8:8, 8:13 as "the boy."

Given the social-historical and linguistic considerations above, it is prima facie likely that Matthew's depiction of a character *introduced* as the παῖς of an adult man of relatively high status (i.e., the centurion), having specified nothing more about their relationship, was in some capacity homoerotic. That is, the relationship that Matthew accentuates is that of a παῖς and its corresponding part, whatever that part may be. Even if the Pais is enslaved, his enslavement is not a feature of the character that Matthew brings to the fore. Rather, the reader only needs to know he is a παῖς to understand the character's significance and relationship with the centurion.

Matthew uses the word παῖς inconsistently elsewhere. In two instances, the word decisively lacks sexual connotations: the infants slaughtered by Herod (2:16) and the children cheering Jesus at the triumphal entry (21:15). Matthew once uses it to vary vocabulary after having already introduced a character: the boy with a demon is introduced by the boy's father as his υἱός (17:14), but the narrator later describes him as a παῖς (17:18). The latter two examples are Matthean redaction of Markan material (the word παῖς is absent from the Markan source text) and the first is Matthean *Sondergut*—each of these likely reflects Matthew's own vocabulary. In another instance, the word appears while quoting the Septuagint, which is similarly asexual: Matt 12:18 (quoting LXX Isa 42:1) acts as a synonym for δοῦλος, though any homoeroticism is undercut by the father-son relationship that Matthew extrapolates from the passage. Matthew thus uses the word παῖς in the third sense—strictly asexual—in 2:16, 12:18, 17:18, and 21:15. To what extent is this relevant, though? The particular phrasing in Matthew's pericope (ὁ παῖς μου: 8:6, 8:8) does not really allow for a generic youth, and the word παῖς only operates as "son" after the relationship has already been literarily established.

The second sense of παῖς as rough synonym of δοῦλος (and thus ambiguous with respect to homoeroticism) operates in 14:2, in Herod Antipas's report that John the Baptist has returned. Jennings and Liew make a compelling argument in this regard.

> It is clear in its literary context that this relating or "telling" on Herod's part is one mixed with both guilt and fear. For, according to Matthew, Herod commands the beheading of John with "grief" (λυπηθείς, 14:9), and the thought that John, who had a significant following among the people (14:5), has returned from the grave cannot be either good or neutral news to his "executioner." Those to whom Herod tells, relates, or confides his guilt and fear are most unlikely to be his mere "servants,"

but some trusted or "intimate" attendants who are privy to his inner thoughts and feelings.[84]

This might be buttressed by the fact that Herodian dynasts, as noted above, were reputed to have intercourse with enslaved men.

Matthew uses the word παῖς to establish the relationship between the centurion and the Pais. Jennings and Liew ultimately opt for the first understanding, a sexual relationship between a centurion and a free youth.[85] This is certainly conceivable, but Matthew's phrasing elsewhere renders the second option more appealing: where the relationship is not otherwise clarified (as in 14:2), παῖς denotes a slave bearing an incidentally sexual relationship with their owner. That the Matthean Pais is enslaved seems implied at two points unique to Matthew's Gospel. First, the Pais is first described as being present "at home" (ἐν τῇ οἰκίᾳ; 8:6) before the centurion clarifies that the Pais is at *his* home (8:8). Readers infer that the centurion and Pais share a residence.[86] Second, the nature of the illness is not onset suddenly as in Luke, which—if the illness took some time to incapacitate him—may imply that the Pais is located at his own residence.

---

84. Jennings and Liew, "Mistaken Identities," 484 n. 46. Their argument that Matt 12:18 is homoerotic in its use of παῖς fails to convince: Jesus becomes the homoerotic παῖς of the Lord in their reading, bearing incestuous overtones that stretches credulity beyond its limit.

85. Jennings and Liew, "Mistaken Identities." Despite the social-historical strengths of the article, it can be overwhelming as a whole, given everything it attempts to accomplish: demonstrating a homoerotic relationship between centurion and Pais, reading the Pais as free rather than enslaved, arguing the centurion was a heel rather than hero, suggesting that the centurion was afraid Jesus would steal the affections of the Pais, the feminine authorship of Matthew, etc. The effect for the present reader is that many novel ideas are presented in a single article that are interdependent, albeit without sufficient space for readers to consider possible objections. How does this reading, for instance, affect Matthew's Deuteronomistic schema? How consistent is this with Matthew's many other uses of the word παῖς? What about the fact that in Roman contexts the *eromenos* was often enslaved or a freedman? If Matthew was written by a woman, how does feminine discourse represent pederastic relationships? Though the article is a significant accomplishment, I find it difficult to accept all its subarguments, and, due to their interdependency, I do not find myself convinced by it as a whole—an instance where the parts are more compelling than their sum.

86. Matthew tends to specify the homeowner in its initial references to a building (e.g., 7:24–27, 8:14, 12:29, 13:57, 23:14, 24:17, 24:43), unless the residence is shared (e.g., 2:11, 5:15, 9:28).

If the Pais is enslaved or a freedman, one would presume the potential for a sexual relationship with his (former) owner unless the relationship were otherwise clarified, as with Matt 12:18 or Luke 7:2. Matthew does no such thing in this pericope.

Furthermore, Matthew's sexual politics stand in significant contrast with Luke's asceticism. Matthew has a distinctive, if abstruse, politics of extramarital sexual intercourse that may leave space for a relationship between the centurion and the Pais. As many have noted, extramarital intercourse is a theme from the very start of Matthew's Gospel. Jesus's genealogy highlights women reputed for their atypical sexual history, namely, Tamar (who pretended to be a sex-worker and conceived children by her father-in-law), Rahab (a sex-worker), Ruth (a widow with considerable sexual agency), and Bathsheba (a woman taken in adultery).[87] The Matthean narrator never names Bathsheba directly, only referring to her by her former husband Uriah: David's sexual conspiracy is brought to mind by the mere juxtaposition of their names in Matt 1:6. These women are commonly marked as sexual figures in the early history of biblical interpretation (e.g., Tamar in T. Jud. 14.2, Jub. 41.23). Matthew may resemble the Testament of Judah in seeing genealogical patterns of extramarital intercourse:

> I charge you, therefore, my children, not to love money, nor to gaze upon the beauty of women; because for the sake of money and beauty I was led astray to Bathsheba the Canaanite. For I know that because of these two things shall you who are my race fall into wickedness; for even wise men among my sons shall they mar, and shall cause the kingdom of Judah to be diminished, which the Lord gave me because of my obedience to my father. (T. Jud. 17.1–3 [Sinker])

---

87. Some have argued that Matthew's selection of women does not concern sexuality. The most thorough of these is E. Anne Clements, *Mothers on the Margin? The Significance of Women in Matthew's Genealogy* (Eugene: Pickwick, 2014), which instead sees marginality as the shared characteristic of the women in Matthew's genealogy. Clements's argument fails to convince in large part because such marginality is itself a product of patriarchal sexual norms that limited women's access to important resources outside of marriage, proving pivotal to each woman's story. See more recently Michel Remaud, "Les femmes dans la généalogie de Jésus selon Matthieu," *NRTh* 143 (2021): 3–14.

The clear referent in the testament is king David, a descendent of Judah who married "the wife of Uriah" after gazing upon her beauty. Notably, Matthew never implies wrongdoing on the part of these women, and, rather, their inclusion in Matthew's genealogy encourages the reader to reconsider their sexual reputations: they both rehabilitate Mary's reputation, and she rehabilitates theirs through a shared contribution to Israel's epic and the lineage of Jesus.

Extramarital intercourse features even more prominently in the conception narrative. Joseph expresses fear that Mary conceived Jesus with an unknown man (1:18–25), a possibility that the omission of Jesus's biological father from the genealogy cues for the reader (1:16). The significance of such data is subject to disagreement. Did Matthew's Mary conceive Jesus with a man extramaritally, or did she conceive Jesus apart from the act of sex altogether?[88] Matthew performs extensive narrative work to reassure the reader that Mary's sexual reputation is no concern, even if she was suspected of impropriety. Indeed, only an angel's intervention ensures Mary and Joseph eventually marry. Matthew's Joseph is exemplary in the mercy he shows to Mary while she was under suspicion; Matthew Marohl argues that this leniency is evident not only in Joseph's marriage to Mary, but also by eschewing the widespread practice of honor killing.[89] Matthew's Gospel begins with an emphasis on juridical mercy in instances of sexual misconduct, whether such instances were purported or verified.

Crucial for Matthew's sexual politics are the exception clauses that the author added to the Markan and Q prohibitions of divorce. The Matthean Jesus permits divorce *only* in cases of πορνεία (5:31–32); otherwise the husband causes his ex-wife to commit adultery (μοιχεύω). R. Jarrett van Tine contends that Matt 19:9–10 makes the same argument *mutatis*

---

88. See, e.g., the dated but important discussion in Jane Schaberg, *The Illegitimacy of Jesus: A Feminist Theological Interpretation of the Infancy Narratives* (San Francisco: Harper & Row, 1987).

89. Matthew J. Marohl, *Joseph's Dilemma: "Honor Killing" in the Birth Narrative of Matthew* (Eugene: Cascade, 2008). He cites as examples from Hellenistic Jewish literature: Sus 36–41; Jub. 20.4, 30.7–8; Philo, *Decal.* 121–131, *Spec.* 3.52–58, *Hypoth.* 7.1, *Ios.* 43–44. He cites as examples from early Christian literature: John 8:1–11; Prot. Jas. 13.1–14.7; John Chrysostom, *Hom. Matt.* 4.7. In other Greco-Roman literature: Aulus Gellius, *Noc. Att.* 10.23; Livy, *Ab urbe cond.* 1.58, 3.44; Suetonius, *Aug.* 65. Marohl also suggests that Josephus advocated honor killing, but this seems unlikely; see the objections in Christopher B. Zeichmann, review of *Joseph's Dilemma*, by Matthew Marohl, *BCT* 7.1 (2011): 129.

mutandis about men: by remarrying after divorce, a man becomes an adulterer.[90] This prompts a number of questions. How does this understanding of marriage fit into the debates within first-century Jewish debates about divorce (e.g., m. Git. 9:10)? What does Matthew mean by πορνεία, a term that technically denotes sex-work but was often deployed in a broader sense of sexual misdeeds?[91] The Matthean Jesus elsewhere treats adultery (μοιχεία) as a grievous wrongdoing (5:27–29, 14:3–4), and the term is conspicuously absent from the Matthean genealogy, conception narrative, and birth narrative. Whatever Mary was suspected of and the women in the genealogy did, Matthew does not characterize it as μοιχεία. Also noteworthy is that Matthew is the only gospel stating that sex-workers can enter the kingdom of heaven (πόρνη; 21:31–32), though this is used as a shaming device that implies their repentance. It should be further noted that virginity is not depicted as inherently good throughout the Gospel of Matthew: five of the ten virgins are fools (25:1–13), and the Matthean Jesus declares that celibacy is not expected of everyone (19:10–12); indeed, the praise specifically for *eunuchs* in the latter passage seems to encourage sexual nonconformity.

All of this is rather murky. The Gospel of Matthew holds much in tension with its sexual ethics, such that its resolution is far from obvious. Rather than attempting to resolve the complex issue of Matthew's understanding of divorce and adultery, one might follow Glancy's observation that none of this precludes sexual relations with slaves. She points to a cultic inscription from Lydian Philadelphia, which mandates that "apart from his own wife, a man is not to have sexual relations with another woman, whether slave or free, who has a husband."[92] Glancy observes the peculiar sexual regulations and norms the inscription codifies.

> First, … the inscription does not take for granted that readers would understand a prohibition on sexual relations with other men's wives to include a prohibition on sexual relations with married women who are enslaved; that expectation required explication. Second, although the Philadelphian

---

90. R. Jarrett van Tine, "Castration for the Kingdom and Avoiding the αἰτία of Adultery (Matthew 19:10–12)," *JBL* 137 (2018): 399–418.

91. On these issues and Matthew's ambiguity, see David Wheeler-Reed, Jennifer W. Knust, and Dale B. Martin, "Can a Man Commit πορνεία with His Wife?," *JBL* 137 (2018): 383–98.

92. *SIG* 3.985.25–27 (approximately 100 BCE): [ἀλ]λ' ἐμφανιεῖν καὶ ἀμυνεῖσθ[αι· ἄνδρα παρὰ τὴν] ἑαυτοῦ γυναῖκα ἀλλοτρίαν ἢ [ἐλευθέραν ἢ] δούλην ἄνδρα ἔχουσαν.

inscription prohibits extramarital relations with married women who are enslaved, it does not explicitly term such relations adultery.[93]

Glancy draws attention to similarly conspicuous silences in Matthew. Despite Matthew's strong condemnations of adultery, there is nothing to imply that intercourse with an unmarried slave is prohibited.[94] As we have seen, sex with slaves was accepted among Jews, Christians, and most others in the Roman Empire at the time. The sexual availability of slaves was sufficiently pervasive that the Philadelphian inscription required an explicit statement prohibiting the practice and, even so, did not deem it adultery. Might Matthew be operating within a similar conceptual framework? Even if Matthew does conceive of sexual relations with slaves as μοιχεία or πορνεία, there is no indication that the centurion was married.[95] Moreover, being gentile, it is not clear that this prohibition would apply to him, even if he were married. This all lends credence to the second possibility outlined above, namely, an implicitly homoerotic relationship between the centurion and the Pais.

---

93. Jennifer A. Glancy, "Slavery and Sexual Availability," in *The Oxford Handbook of New Testament, Gender, and Sexuality*, ed. Benjamin H. Dunning (Oxford: Oxford University Press, 2019), 636.

94. Whether Matthew implicitly condemns the sexualization of youth is unclear. The matter is bound up with Matthew's depiction of Antipas's birthday celebration (14:3–12), where Salome is described as a κοράσιον (14:11), a term which Mark 5:42 had used to denote a twelve-year-old girl in wording that Matt 9:24–25 adopts (admittedly, Matthew may imagine the girl to be a different age). Even so, it is not clear how it fits into Matthew's sexual politics: (1) a minority of commentators doubt Matthew depicts Antipas as sexualizing his stepdaughter/niece; (2) it is not clear that Matthew condemns such sexualization if it is indeed present; and (3) if Matthew does condemn the sexualization, it is not obvious which aspects of such sexualization the author deems inappropriate (e.g., age discrepancy, incest, extramarital lust, public display of lust, the feeling of lust itself).

95. It is not clear whether active soldiers in Antipas's royal army were permitted to marry, though it intuitively seems likely, given that auxiliary soldiers could (albeit without *conubium* until receiving their diploma). It is commonly observed that active legionaries were not allowed to marry, though there is no reason to think there were any legionaries stationed in Antipas's Galilee, let alone that this centurion was a legionary (of course, this did not stop legionaries from having nonmarital intercourse). It is unlikely Matthew was conversant in the specific policies of Antipas's army, more likely projecting at least some of the policies from his own context onto Jesus's situation.

The Sayings Gospel Q

There persists a widespread misconception that Q was a loose collection of sayings, what John P. Meier has characterized as a "grab bag" of logia without a coherent narrative, theology, or ideology.[96] This section proceeds on the assumption shared among most Q specialists, namely, that it was a literary text of modest sophistication, evincing a clear structure, thematic developments, and distinctive politics.[97] That is, Q was a gospel in its own right, rather than an informal collection of oral traditions, absent authorial interests and literary features. Experts are, of course, uncertain about the wording of the Sayings Gospel Q, but we will tentatively proceed with the *Critical Edition of Q* (see appendix 1), as it is the most authoritative reconstruction of the text.[98] It will be assumed that the Pais was healed, even if the editors declined to conjecture its wording at Q 7:10.[99]

As in Matthew, the Pais's relationship with the centurion is never named explicitly, implied only with the word παῖς.[100] Q's characterization of the Pais with that word cannot be attributed to inertia, as with Matthew and Luke, where one might object that they lazily took over wording found in their source. Some of Matthew's literary features suggestive of homoeroticism are present in Q: the centurion introduces him as "my Pais" via genitive of possession, and there is no indication that the Pais is enslaved. Thus, like Matthew, the relationship that Matthew accentuates between the centurion and Pais is that of παῖς and its corresponding part (as with Matthew, that corresponding part requires inference). The discussion of Matthew's version could be repeated *mutatis mutandis* on those points. There are, moreover, fewer reasons for inferring that Q's

---

96. See, e.g., John P. Meier, *A Marginal Jew: Rethinking the Historical Jesus. Mentor, Message, and Miracles*, ABRL (New York: Doubleday, 1994), 179–81.

97. Particularly compelling against this conception of Q is John S. Kloppenborg, *Excavating Q: The History and Setting of the Sayings Gospel* (Edinburgh: T&T Clark, 2000).

98. James M. Robinson, Paul Hoffmann, and John S. Kloppenborg, eds., *The Critical Edition of Q: Synopsis Including the Gospels of Matthew and Luke, Mark and Thomas with English, German, and French Translations of Q and Thomas*, Hermeneia (Minneapolis: Fortress, 2000).

99. Johnson, *Q 7:1–10*, 375–400.

100. Nearly all scholars agree that Matthew's phrasing of παῖς more accurately reflects Q than Luke's δοῦλος in this pericope. Johnson, *Q 7:1–10*, 167–84. The word παῖς is found only here in Q, being otherwise absent from the Double Tradition.

Pais is enslaved, at least compared to his depiction in Matthew and Luke. The ambiguity of the Greek word παῖς and the fact that the centurion owns at least one slave (7:8) are the only factors possibly hinting that the Pais might be enslaved. The fact that there is so little reason to suppose Q's Pais was enslaved may indicate that his relationship with the centurion was between two free men; this in itself is suggestive of a sexual relationship. The pericope can viably read the pericope as homoerotic in isolation. But how does this interpretation cohere with Q's narrative and moral universe?

The pericope occupies a peculiar place in Q. Although it is the only miracle narrated (cf. Q 11:14), Jesus's description of his own wonders in Q 7:22 conspicuously omits it: the blind regain sight, the disabled walk, skin diseases are healed, the deaf hear, the dead are raised, and the poor receive good news. Only the last of these is actually narrated in Q (6:22), though this hardly amounts to a supernatural event comparable to the healings enumerated in the list. Also baffling is how Capernaum is singled out for condemnation among Galilean towns. Q's Jesus saves his worst invective for the village where the centurion resides: "And you, Capernaum, will you be raised up into heaven? You will descend into Hades!" (10:15) This is difficult to reconcile with the centurion's demonstration of faith in that very village. Indeed, it is the only named locale where Q's Jesus has any positive reception![101] There are other bizarre issues. How does the centurion know that Jesus can heal at all, since there have been no prior healings? Does not the surprise that Jesus can heal at a distance assume prior familiarity with Jesus's miracles occurring in-person? Though the pericope fits well with Q's various themes (e.g., use of gentiles to shame Israel for its disbelief, emphasis on the power of Jesus's word, preoccupation with mediating figures) and has strong verbatim agreement in the Double Tradition, it is almost as though the pericope never occurred within Q's larger narrative world.[102] At most, it provides an imprecise precedent for the type of miracles presumed in Q 7:22, acting as shorthand for both a mostly unnarrated

---

101. Contrast, for instance, Q's condemnation of Chorazin and Bethsaida for their failure to recognize the wonders performed in them (10:13), even though Q never mentions any such miracles.

102. *Literary project* is deployed here to distinguish from the social-historical issue of the author's allusion to histories of real-life rejection, hostility, or frustration at Capernaum. Whatever vexations Q 10:15 articulates from the author's personal experiences, it leads to an inconsistent characterization of the village of Capernaum.

healing ministry and the failure of Israel to recognize Jesus presumed in 10:13–15 and 13:28–29.

Q's sexual politics are difficult to ascertain, given the gospel's fragmentary nature and obscurity when the topic does arise. Though Q 17:27 links marriage and drinking to antediluvian obliviousness, this hardly amounts to a negative assessment of sexual intercourse. The dissolution of the home is a theme in Q 9:59–60, 12:53, and 14:26; unlike Luke 14:26, the Q passage does not imagine sexually linked pairs (i.e., husband and wife) to be pitted against each other. Q 16:18 prohibits marriage after divorce on sexual grounds, "Everyone who divorces his wife and marries another commits adultery and the one who marries a divorcée commits adultery." Q 7:34 presumes a depiction of Jesus in line with a *bon vivant* although the charge of Jesus's drunkenness and consorting with sinners is framed as a rhetorical overstatement. "The son of man came, eating and drinking, and you say, 'Look! A person who is a glutton and a drunkard, a friend of tax-collectors and sinners!'" That some of those sinners were reputed for sexual wrongdoings is a reasonable inference.[103] When Sodom and Gomorrah are mentioned (10:12), no sexual connotations are present. Rather, their punishment for inhospitality anticipates the punishment of those not accepting Jesus's followers.

Given that the centurion seems to function less as Q's vision of a good disciple and more as a rhetorical means of shaming Galilean Jews—"even *this guy* gets it better than Israel!"[104]—there is little reason to infer that the centurion adhered to Jewish ritual norms (cf. Q 16:13, 16:17) or even had an affinity for Judaism broadly construed. All of this to say, Q is particularly difficult to decipher in this regard, given the opacity of its sexual politics. Even so, it is entirely feasible to read the *Critical Edition of Q*'s reconstruction of the pericope in either the first or second sense of the word παῖς—that the Pais's relationship was either exclusively or incidentally sexual.

---

103. Q never clarifies its understanding of "sin" (cf. Q 15:8–10, 17:3–4), let alone what marks someone as a "sinner" (ἁμαρτωλός). Though the word ἁμαρτωλός in Luke 7:37 is often thought to indicate sin of a sexual nature, rarely do commentators cite their lexical basis for inferring that the word was used in such a way.

104. On Q's gentiles as a rhetorical construction to shame Israel and the absence of a mission to the gentiles in Q, see William E. Arnal, "The Q Document," in *Jewish Christianity Reconsidered: Rethinking Ancient Groups and Texts*, ed. Matt Jackson-McCabe (Minneapolis: Fortress, 2007), 117–54.

Conclusion

The gospels are not uniform in their narration of the pericope. John imagines a father-son relationship entirely devoid of sex, whereas Luke depicts the Pais as a high-ranking slave who is likely free from any sexual duties. Both Matthew and Q, by contrast, are more ambiguous—it is not clear whether the Pais was enslaved or free—and can be plausibly read as presuming a homoerotic relationship. While John and Luke depict a relationship that precludes intercourse, Matthew and Q have an ambiguity that may be suggestive (perhaps even euphemistic) of a sexual relationship. One might compare the pericope in Matthew and Q with other stories using the unqualified and unclarified word παῖς to evoke its sexual sense, such as the Acts of Andrew.

Neither interpreters favoring a homoerotic interpretation nor those opposing it have a monopoly on the pericope, as the results are ambiguous and split. This is not a particularly satisfying conclusion, which might lead some to seek resolution by appealing to an underlying historical incident—the historical centurion and the historical Pais, as well as how the historical Jesus reacted to them. Such efforts veer into far less certain grounds. It is unclear whether the centurion and the Pais existed at all, let alone how one would navigate the tensions in the surviving sources: Is John dependent upon the Synoptic Gospels here? Was this pericope attested in a pre-Johannine Signs Gospel? If so, how does one navigate the differences in the Signs Gospel and the Sayings Gospel Q here? What details should one attribute to the evangelists' creativity? The questions are too extensive to be addressed here, and, frankly, I suspect that any hypothesis about an historical episode would be little more than wishful speculation. The sources are too fragmentary for historical claims and even the literary conclusions proffered here are far from certain.

A Disappointing Conclusion

One can read the present book as an attempt to grapple with a set of disappointments. Disappointment that the textual grounds for queer recognition in this pericope are uncertain. Disappointment that its homoeroticism is predicated upon pederasty. Disappointment that queer social movements often trend toward opportunistic respectability politics. Disappointment that slavery apologists were likely correct that the gospels depict Jesus's attitude toward slavery as somewhere between tacit acceptance and straightforward endorsement. Disappointment in sexual norms throughout Jewish and Christian history. Disappointment in the casual racism of abolitionist biblical interpreters. Disappointment in the academy for habituating specialists into disregarding the insights of outsiders. Disappointment in the field of biblical studies for failing to hold sexual predators accountable. Disappointment that this book feels like it is taking something important away from people like Noah Hepler, for whom the pericope holds importance. Disappointment that this book could not take the form of a celebration.

I find myself thinking about *Hunger* (2008), a movie about the Irish prison protests 1980–1981 led by Bobby Sands. Stripped of Special Category Status that had entailed de facto prisoner-of-war rights, Sands and other Irish republican inmates protested with the limited means at hand, namely, their bodies. After engaging in various dirty protests, such as smearing excrement on the walls of their prison cells and pouring urine into the hallways, they began a hunger strike that resulted in the deaths of ten prisoners. The elimination of Special Category Status had been a minor issue for the Irish republican leadership, who encouraged Sands to instead negotiate with prison administrators. Prison justice became an end in itself for Sands, coming into conflict with republican leaders over the issue. Willing to withhold necessary nutrition for their bodies to a point that risked permanent loss of bodily functions and death, the hunger-strikers pressed provocatively at the nexus of illness and state violence. The prisoners and their priests insisted that hunger-strikers' deaths were not suicides but the fault of the British government for refusing to meet protesters' demands. This dramatic shift in responsibility is vital to the political efficacy of any hunger strike. Whereas the dirty protest, by marking the prisoners as recalcitrant and even violent, produces them as subjects in need of discipline, the hunger strike had the opposite effect: the prisoners' confrontational foregrounding of their own vulnerability was precisely what rendered the hunger strike effective. To rephrase, for better or worse, protests most readily characterized as nonviolent are those most likely to evoke wider sympathy, which has the effect of shifting obligations; dirty protests marked the prisoners as barely human in their refusal to engage in some of the most basic so-called civilized behaviors, whereas hunger strikes afforded them an infant-like helplessness.[1] The effect of such reframing is readily visible in *Hunger*, reflecting the experience of many other hunger-strikers: guards engage in casual acts of violence upon the prisoners without fear of reprimand during the dirty protest, but the prisoners' treatment transforms dramatically during the hunger strike, as they are given clean rooms, offered high-quality food, provided individual orderlies to help them bathe, visited by loved ones without supervision, and so on. Once on hunger strike, the prisoners' bodies are strictly at the mercy of the British penal system, recusing themselves of their own autonomy. Britain lay exclusive claim to what happens to the strikers' bodies.

The hunger strike counterintuitively worked against the supposition that freedom from disability is a self-evident desideratum.[2] It is common to presume that, when imagining one's own desired future, that version of oneself does not include a disabled body. Within this popular wisdom is an apolitical conception of disability, a sense that disabled bodies are doubly helpless: limited in their capacities but also limited by external factors imposed upon them, far beyond their own control. Hunger strikes demonstrate that this is not always the case.

The Pais can be read as possessing a similarly disruptive body, especially if situated within the long tradition of slaves' passive resistance (e.g.,

---

1. Situating the hunger strike within a broader Irish legal tradition, see Kieran McEvoy, *Paramilitary Imprisonment in Northern Ireland: Resistance, Management, and Release*, Clarendon Studies in Criminology (Oxford: Oxford University Press, 2001), 72–107.

2. See especially Alison Kafer, *Feminist, Queer, Crip* (Bloomington: Indiana University Press, 2013).

feigning illness, deliberate slowness, sabotage) or more active forms of rebellion that disregarded their own well-being (e.g., revolts, suicide). In such light, it does not matter whether the Pais feigned or actually experienced illness.[3] His condition not only provided respite from labor but reconfigured the structures of responsibility within the household: no longer was the Pais responsible for satisfying the centurion, but the centurion now bore absolute responsibility for the Pais (lest acquaintances deem him cruel, as others did Cato the Elder). It is one of the few instances where enslaved people might have any meaningful power relative to their enslavers. Perhaps only because of the social demands it imposed upon the owner, slaves elicited sympathy when their vulnerability was brought to the fore. Slaves gained considerable political agency in their lack of autonomy, with their bodies taking on a newly troublesome character.

To press the matter further, it is not obvious that the Pais desired wellness over the alternatives of a disabled or deceased body. There are reports of self-mutilation among Greek and Roman slaves as acts of defiance. Galen, for instance, recounts an instance when a slave boy repeatedly rubbed his skin with thapsia to intentionally cause a rash in order that he might get out of work (*Hipp. Epid.* 2.1).[4] Many regarded death as preferable to continued enslavement. For example, Lam. Rab. 1:16 and b. Git. 57b describe a ship of Jewish boys and girls drowning themselves to avoid being sold to Roman brothels as slaves. This sentiment is echoed in Josephus's account of the siege of Masada, wherein Jewish rebels kill themselves, along with their own children and wives, to avoid enslavement as prisoners-of-war (*B.J.* 7.320).[5] This is not to mention the Roman Servile Wars, where many died for their freedom.

---

3. On malingering among Roman slaves, see Galen, *Hipp. Epid.* 2.1; Columella, *Rust.* 12.3.7. See also the discussions in Peter Hunt, *Ancient Greek and Roman Slavery* (London: Wiley Blackwell, 2018), 142; Keith Bradley, "Servus Onerosus: Roman Law and the Troublesome Slave," *Slavery and Abolition* 11 (1990): 148–50.

4. For comparable examples of slaves' self-mutilation from antebellum America, see Raymond A. Bauer and Alice H. Bauer, "Day to Day Resistance to Slavery," *Journal of Negro History* 27 (1942): 414–17. See also tales of freeborn Romans self-mutilating to avoid military conscription: Suetonius, *Aug.* 24.1; Ammianus Marcellinus, *Res gest.* 15.12.3.

5. Reeder, "Wartime Rape," 377. Reeder points to other prisoners of war committing suicide to avoid being sold into slavery: Livy, *Ab urbe cond.* 26.15.14, 28.22.9–11; Valerius Maximus, *Fact.* 6.1.10, 6.1e.1, 6.1e.3; Pausanias, *Descr.* 10.22.3–4. Cf. the further examples discussed in Pasi Loman, "No Woman No War: Women's Participation

Regardless of whether one assents to this reading of the Pais's resistance (a reading that is hardly necessitated by any of the gospels), it is difficult to understand Jesus as a benevolent or even benign figure in this pericope. At best, Jesus unintentionally returned the Pais to the exploitations that defined the life of a slave. Whatever respite the illness (real or feigned) lent the Pais was brought to an end, and his enslavement could continue unabated. At worst, following Velunta, Jesus restored a sexually abusive relationship. It would be strange *not* to feel disappointment.

I also find myself thinking about Jack Halberstam's reflections on "the queer art of failure," namely, the virtues of failure to succeed under the current economic-cum-social situation of heteropatriarchal capitalism. This might include failures to conform to expected gender practices. Failures to produce properly academic biblical scholarship. Failures to inhabit respectable bodies. Failures to live up to the demands of compulsory happiness. The present world does not exist such that all bodies can experience the joy or success that they might desire or might otherwise be expected to achieve. Halberstam suggests that such failings might be reconceived as an unwillingness—a willful *refusal* even—to accept the expectations imposed upon them. "Relieved of the obligation to keep smiling through chemotherapy or bankruptcy, the negative thinker can use the experience of failure to confront the gross inequalities of everyday life."[6] These failures hint at the possibility of alternative worlds. Worlds where efforts to achieve political recognition are not dependent upon the authorization of the Bible. Worlds where "sincerely held beliefs" have no bearing upon the acceptability of violence one enacts upon queer bodies. Worlds where contributions to scholarly knowledge production are not foreclosed by one's failure to adhere to the aesthetics of academic professionalism.[7]

---

in Ancient Greek Warfare," *G&R* 51 (2004): 43–44. Note also the practice of infanticide among Roman slaves: Chariton, *Chaer.* 2.8.6–7; Dio Chrysostom, *Or.* 15.8; Cod. Iust. 8.51.1.

6. Jack Halberstam, *The Queer Art of Failure*, John Hope Franklin Center (Durham, NC: Duke University Press, 2011), 4.

7. On which, see, e.g., Fred Moten and Stefano Harney, "The University and the Undercommons: Seven Theses," *Social Text* 22 (2004): 101–15. On how this might relate to the study of the Bible, see Vincent L. Wimbush, "Interrupting the Spin: What Might Happen If African Americans Were to Become the Starting Point for the Academic Study of the Bible," *UTQ* 52 (1998): 61–76; Wimbush, "In Search of a Usable Past: Reorienting Biblical Studies," in *Toward a New Heaven and New Earth: Essays in*

I would like to conclude by imagining with some specificity one of the more modest worlds, a world the readers of the present book are particularly well-positioned to help realize, even acknowledging our field's propensity for self-importance.[8] There has yet to be a thorough reckoning of the issues raised at the end of chapter 1, namely, the biblical academy's role in the sexual violation of children. The conviction of Hebrew Bible scholar Jan Joosten for possessing child pornography has at least prompted a realization that this is a more pressing issue than many had suspected. There is, of course, no easy or obvious solution. The citation policy of the present book has been to avoid favorably or neutrally citing the work of scholars who have been convicted of sexual crimes or condone the practice of pedophilia, preferring other voices when possible. However, some interpreters who played an important role in the history of the passage were convicted of crimes involving the sexual violation of children or explicitly advocate similar activities. In such cases, these are not treated as neutral discussions but excavated for their attempts at legitimizing the practices they discuss. Consider, by analogy, the similarly complicated case of Karl-Günther Heimsoth, who coined the word *homophile* and had a complicated relationship with the Nazi Party: though deeply anti-Semitic for most of his life, he seems to have disavowed the ideology and attempted to remedy his collaboration by acting as an anti-Nazi informant; this espionage led to his execution. It is insufficient to simply *identify* wrongdoings or name an interpretation's prescriptive politics. Rather, drawing upon the ideology-critical framework of others—especially analyses of Martin Heidegger, Walter Grundmann, Gerhard Kittel, and other influential scholars aligned with the Third Reich—it was necessary to discuss in explicit terms how their scholarship *authorized* their sexual practices and politics. That is, in the same way Heidegger, Grundmann, Kittel, and others gave anti-Semitic politics a veneer of legitimacy by grounding them in the academic practices like those discussed in chapter 4 (e.g., academic scholarship, scholastic hermeneutics), so also was it necessary to elaborate on how Mader and Rossman attempted to legitimize their own sexual politics.

Honor of Elisabeth Schüssler Fiorenza, ed. Fernando F. Segovia (Maryknoll, NY: Orbis Books, 2003), 179–98; Wimbush, "TEXTureS, Gestures, Power."

8. E.g., N. T. Wright, *Jesus and the Victory of God*, Christian Origins and the Question of God 2 (London: SPCK, 1997), xv: "If what I write could help in any way towards the establishment of justice and peace there [i.e., in Israel and Palestine], or indeed anywhere else, I would be deeply grateful."

In imagining this possible world, recall the field's treatment of Richard Pervo, a New Testament scholar who pled guilty to possessing more than 4,200 pornographic images of minors on his computer in 2001.[9] His conviction seems to have had no discernable effect on his standing in the field. Though already a senior scholar, Pervo's postconviction life proved to be his most prolific, publishing monographs on a roughly annual basis and even receiving the honor of a Festschrift, one that bears the unfortunate title *Delightful Acts*.[10] When he died in 2017, the Society of Biblical Literature website posted a fawning obituary that glossed over his crimes. It was not until 2020, following Joosten's conviction for possessing child pornography, that a reckoning began at the periphery of biblical scholarship. Largely beginning on Twitter accounts of individual biblical scholars or Facebook groups, frustrations with the Society's slow reaction to the Joosten conviction led others to express frustration about the continued memorialization of Pervo. Ellen Muehlberger, for instance, alluded to Pervo when she tweeted, "we make an effort to bolster those men—even *Festschrift* them! We go to great lengths to rehabilitate their reputations, and we write long, dare I say haughty, emails to those who question it."[11] Annette Yoshiko Reed was more explicit in her reply to Muehlberger: "Indeed, I think part of [the] reason it's important to speak out now about Jan Joosten is that this isn't the first such case in recent memory in Biblical Studies—and in the case of Richard Pervo, concern for his reputation outweighed any horror at his conviction for child pornography."[12] Only after an outcry through unofficial channels did the Society remove Pervo's obituary from its site, but it did so without acknowledgment or comment.

Important in all this is that attempts at accountability were largely limited to non-peer-reviewed venues: social media, webinars in newer scholarly societies (especially the Bible and Religion in the Ancient Near East Collective), blog posts, petitions, and so on. Despite a statement from

---

9. Tim Sturrock, "Pervo Pleads Guilty, Sentenced in Porn Case," *The Minnesota Daily*, 1 June 2001, https://tinyurl.com/sbl6705m.

10. Harold W. Attridge, Dennis R. MacDonald, and Clare K. Rothschild, eds., *Delightful Acts: New Essays on Canonical and Non-Canonical Acts*, WUNT 1/391 (Tübingen: Mohr Siebeck, 2017).

11. Ellen Muehlberger, Twitter comment, 22 June 2020, https://tinyurl.com/SBL6705n.

12. Annette Yoshiko Reed, Twitter comment, 22 June 2020, https://tinyurl.com/SBL6705p.

the Society of Biblical Literature Council following Joosten's conviction that the "SBL has procedures in place to address such issues and we ask for your patience as we strengthen these," there was no public discussion of what these policies might be or how they were ultimately strengthened.[13] What good, after all, are strengthened policies if no one knows what they are? The effect is noteworthy, as Pervo's work continues to be afforded neutrality in the most important (i.e., influential and visible) arenas of the field and thus maintain its position within the realm of respectable biblical scholarship. The biblical academy is particularly prone to memorialization, which, whatever its merits of such reverence for the past, often serves to codify and sanitize such legacies. How one might bring about a more accountable biblical academy, unfortunately, remains entirely theoretical.

---

13. The Society of Biblical Literature Council, "Statement regarding SBL and Former Member Jan Joosten," Society of Biblical Literature, 25 June 2020, https://www.sbl-site.org/assets/pdfs/Joosten_Statement.pdf.

APPENDIX 1
Text and Translation of the Passage in Matthew, Luke, John, and Reconstruction of Q

The text of Matthew, Luke, and John is the SBL Greek text with some changes to capitalization, with my own English translation for each. The text of Q is *The Critical Edition of Q*'s reconstruction with my own translation.[1] I have removed some of the more technical sigla from Q's Greek text and rendered Q 7:3 a statement rather than a question. For documentation on the International Q Project's sources and reasoning, see the *Documenta Q* volume devoted to this pericope.[2]

The Gospel of Matthew

[8:5] εἰσελθόντος δὲ αὐτοῦ εἰς Καφαρναοὺμ προσῆλθεν αὐτῷ ἑκατόνταρχος παρακαλῶν αὐτὸν [6] καὶ λέγων· κύριε, ὁ παῖς μου βέβληται ἐν τῇ οἰκίᾳ παραλυτικός, δεινῶς βασανιζόμενος. [7] καὶ λέγει αὐτῷ· ἐγὼ ἐλθὼν θεραπεύσω αὐτόν. [8] καὶ ἀποκριθεὶς ὁ ἑκατόνταρχος ἔφη· κύριε, οὐκ εἰμὶ ἱκανὸς ἵνα μου ὑπὸ τὴν στέγην εἰσέλθῃς· ἀλλὰ μόνον εἰπὲ λόγῳ, καὶ ἰαθήσεται ὁ παῖς μου· [9] καὶ γὰρ ἐγὼ ἄνθρωπός εἰμι ὑπὸ ἐξουσίαν, ἔχων ὑπ᾽ ἐμαυτὸν στρατιώτας, καὶ λέγω τούτῳ· πορεύθητι, καὶ πορεύεται, καὶ ἄλλῳ· ἔρχου, καὶ ἔρχεται, καὶ τῷ δούλῳ μου· ποίησον τοῦτο, καὶ ποιεῖ. [10] ἀκούσας δὲ ὁ Ἰησοῦς ἐθαύμασεν καὶ εἶπεν τοῖς ἀκολουθοῦσιν· ἀμὴν λέγω ὑμῖν, παρ᾽ οὐδενὶ τοσαύτην πίστιν ἐν τῷ Ἰσραὴλ εὗρον. [11] λέγω δὲ ὑμῖν ὅτι πολλοὶ ἀπὸ ἀνατολῶν καὶ δυσμῶν ἥξουσιν καὶ ἀνακλιθήσονται μετὰ Ἀβραὰμ καὶ Ἰσαὰκ καὶ Ἰακὼβ ἐν τῇ βασιλείᾳ τῶν οὐρανῶν· [12] οἱ δὲ υἱοὶ τῆς βασιλείας ἐκβληθήσονται εἰς τὸ σκότος τὸ ἐξώτερον· ἐκεῖ ἔσται ὁ κλαυθμὸς καὶ ὁ βρυγμὸς τῶν ὀδόντων. [13] καὶ εἶπεν ὁ

---

1. Robinson, Hoffmann, and Kloppenborg, *Critical Edition of Q*, 102–17.
2. Johnson, *Q 7:1–10*.

Ἰησοῦς τῷ ἑκατοντάρχῃ· ὕπαγε, ὡς ἐπίστευσας γενηθήτω σοι· καὶ ἰάθη ὁ παῖς ἐν τῇ ὥρᾳ ἐκείνῃ.

[Matt 8:5] When he entered Capernaum, a centurion approached him, pleading to him [6] and saying, "Sir, my Pais is laying at home paralyzed, suffering horribly!" [7] And he said to him, "I'll come and heal him." [8] The centurion answered him, saying, "Sir, I am not worthy to have you come under my roof. But only speak the word and let my Pais be healed. [9] For I am also a man under authority, having soldiers under me. I say to this one, 'Go,' and he goes; and to another, 'Come,' and he comes; and to my slave, 'Do this,' and he does it." [10] When Jesus heard, he was amazed and said to those following, "Truly, I'm telling you, among no one in Israel have I found such faith! [11] I'm telling you, many from the east and west will come and recline with Abraham, Isaac, and Jacob in the kingdom of heaven. [12] But the sons of the kingdom will be thrown out into the outer darkness—where there's wailing and grinding teeth." [13] Jesus said to the centurion, "Go. Just as you believed, it will happen for you." And the Pais was healed in that hour.

The Gospel of Luke

[7:1] ἐπειδὴ ἐπλήρωσεν πάντα τὰ ῥήματα αὐτοῦ εἰς τὰς ἀκοὰς τοῦ λαοῦ, εἰσῆλθεν εἰς Καφαρναούμ. [2] ἑκατοντάρχου δέ τινος δοῦλος κακῶς ἔχων ἤμελλεν τελευτᾶν, ὃς ἦν αὐτῷ ἔντιμος. [3] ἀκούσας δὲ περὶ τοῦ Ἰησοῦ ἀπέστειλεν πρὸς αὐτὸν πρεσβυτέρους τῶν Ἰουδαίων, ἐρωτῶν αὐτὸν ὅπως ἐλθὼν διασώσῃ τὸν δοῦλον αὐτοῦ. [4] οἱ δὲ παραγενόμενοι πρὸς τὸν Ἰησοῦν παρεκάλουν αὐτὸν σπουδαίως λέγοντες ὅτι ἄξιός ἐστιν ᾧ παρέξῃ τοῦτο, [5] ἀγαπᾷ γὰρ τὸ ἔθνος ἡμῶν καὶ τὴν συναγωγὴν αὐτὸς ᾠκοδόμησεν ἡμῖν. [6] ὁ δὲ Ἰησοῦς ἐπορεύετο σὺν αὐτοῖς. ἤδη δὲ αὐτοῦ οὐ μακρὰν ἀπέχοντος ἀπὸ τῆς οἰκίας ἔπεμψεν φίλους ὁ ἑκατοντάρχης λέγων αὐτῷ· κύριε, μὴ σκύλλου, οὐ γὰρ ἱκανός εἰμι ἵνα ὑπὸ τὴν στέγην μου εἰσέλθῃς· [7] διὸ οὐδὲ ἐμαυτὸν ἠξίωσα πρὸς σὲ ἐλθεῖν· ἀλλὰ εἰπὲ λόγῳ, καὶ ἰαθήτω ὁ παῖς μου. [8] καὶ γὰρ ἐγὼ ἄνθρωπός εἰμι ὑπὸ ἐξουσίαν τασσόμενος, ἔχων ὑπ' ἐμαυτὸν στρατιώτας, καὶ λέγω τούτῳ· πορεύθητι, καὶ πορεύεται, καὶ ἄλλῳ· ἔρχου, καὶ ἔρχεται, καὶ τῷ δούλῳ μου· ποίησον τοῦτο, καὶ ποιεῖ. [9] ἀκούσας δὲ ταῦτα ὁ Ἰησοῦς ἐθαύμασεν αὐτόν, καὶ στραφεὶς τῷ ἀκολουθοῦντι αὐτῷ ὄχλῳ εἶπεν· λέγω ὑμῖν, οὐδὲ ἐν τῷ Ἰσραὴλ τοσαύτην πίστιν εὗρον. [10] καὶ ὑποστρέψαντες εἰς τὸν οἶκον οἱ πεμφθέντες εὗρον τὸν δοῦλον ὑγιαίνοντα.

[Luke 7:1] After he finished saying all his teachings for people to hear, he entered Capernaum. [2] But a centurion had a certain slave whom he held in esteem, that was sick and nearing death. [3] And hearing about Jesus, he sent elders from among the Jews, asking that he might come and save his slave. [4] When Jesus arrived, they pled to him with haste, saying, "He is worthy for you to do this, [5] for he loves our people and he build the synagogue for us." [6] And Jesus went with them. But already, when he wasn't far from the house, the centurion sent friends who said to him, "Sir, don't bother, since I am not worthy to have you come under my roof, [7] and so I wasn't worthy to come to you. But speak the word and let my Pais be healed. [8] For I am also a man under practicing authority, having soldiers under me. I say to this one, 'Go,' and he goes; and to another, 'Come,' and he comes; and to my slave, 'Do this,' and he does it." [9] When Jesus heard these things, he marveled at him and turned to the crowd following him and said, "I'm telling you, not even in Israel have I found such faith." [10] And when they returned to the house, the ones who'd been sent found the slave in good health.

The Gospel of John

[4:46] ἦλθεν οὖν πάλιν εἰς τὴν Κανὰ τῆς Γαλιλαίας, ὅπου ἐποίησεν τὸ ὕδωρ οἶνον. καὶ ἦν τις βασιλικὸς οὗ ὁ υἱὸς ἠσθένει ἐν Καφαρναούμ. [47] οὗτος ἀκούσας ὅτι Ἰησοῦς ἥκει ἐκ τῆς Ἰουδαίας εἰς τὴν Γαλιλαίαν ἀπῆλθεν πρὸς αὐτὸν καὶ ἠρώτα ἵνα καταβῇ καὶ ἰάσηται αὐτοῦ τὸν υἱόν, ἤμελλεν γὰρ ἀποθνῄσκειν. [48] εἶπεν οὖν ὁ Ἰησοῦς πρὸς αὐτόν· ἐὰν μὴ σημεῖα καὶ τέρατα ἴδητε, οὐ μὴ πιστεύσητε. [49] λέγει πρὸς αὐτὸν ὁ βασιλικός· κύριε, κατάβηθι πρὶν ἀποθανεῖν τὸ παιδίον μου. [50] λέγει αὐτῷ ὁ Ἰησοῦς· πορεύου· ὁ υἱός σου ζῇ. ἐπίστευσεν ὁ ἄνθρωπος τῷ λόγῳ ὃν εἶπεν αὐτῷ ὁ Ἰησοῦς καὶ ἐπορεύετο. [51] ἤδη δὲ αὐτοῦ καταβαίνοντος οἱ δοῦλοι αὐτοῦ ὑπήντησαν αὐτῷ λέγοντες ὅτι ὁ παῖς αὐτοῦ ζῇ. [52] ἐπύθετο οὖν τὴν ὥραν παρ' αὐτῶν ἐν ᾗ κομψότερον ἔσχεν· εἶπαν οὖν αὐτῷ ὅτι ἐχθὲς ὥραν ἑβδόμην ἀφῆκεν αὐτὸν ὁ πυρετός. [53] ἔγνω οὖν ὁ πατὴρ ὅτι ἐκείνῃ τῇ ὥρᾳ ἐν ᾗ εἶπεν αὐτῷ ὁ Ἰησοῦς· ὁ υἱός σου ζῇ, καὶ ἐπίστευσεν αὐτὸς καὶ ἡ οἰκία αὐτοῦ ὅλη. [54] τοῦτο δὲ πάλιν δεύτερον σημεῖον ἐποίησεν ὁ Ἰησοῦς ἐλθὼν ἐκ τῆς Ἰουδαίας εἰς τὴν Γαλιλαίαν.

[John 4:46] He went again into Cana of Galilee, where he made the water into wine. And there was a certain royal officer whose son lay sick was in Capernaum. [47] This man heard that Jesus had come out of Judaea into

Galilee, went to him, and asked that he might come down to heal his son, for he was about to die. [48] Jesus said to him, "Unless you see signs and wonders, you will never believe." [49] The royal officer said to him, "Sir, come down before my Pais dies." [50] Jesus said to him, "Go, your son lives!" The man believed the words Jesus said and went. [51] And already when he was heading down, his slaves went to meet him, saying that his Pais was living. [52] He then asked them the hour when he became better. They said to him, "The fever left him yesterday in the seventh hour." [53] The father knew that was the hour when Jesus said to him, "Your son lives," and he himself and his whole house believed. [54] This was the second sign Jesus did when he came out of Judaea into Galilee.

The Sayings Gospel Q

7:1 ⟦καὶ ἐγένετο ὅτε⟧ ἐ⟦πλήρω⟧σεν τοὺς λόγους τούτους, εἰσῆλθεν εἰς Καφαρναούμ. 3 <>ἦλθεν αὐτῷ ἑκατόνταρχ⟦ο⟧ς παρακαλῶν αὐτὸν ⟦καὶ λέγων⟧· ὁ παῖς ⟦μου κακῶς ἔχ<ει>. καὶ λέγει αὐτῷ· ἐγὼ⟧ ἐλθὼν θεραπεύσ⟦ω⟧ αὐτόν. 6 καὶ ἀποκριθεὶς ὁ ἑκατόνταρχος ἔφη· κύριε, οὐκ εἰμὶ ἱκανὸς ἵνα μου ὑπὸ τὴν στέγην εἰσέλθῃς, 7 ἀλλὰ εἰπὲ λόγῳ, καὶ ἰαθή⟦τω⟧ ὁ παῖς μου. 8 καὶ γὰρ ἐγὼ ἄνθρωπός εἰμι ὑπὸ ἐξουσίαν, ἔχων ὑπ' ἐμαυτὸν στρατιώτας, καὶ λέγω τούτῳ· πορεύθητι, καὶ πορεύεται, καὶ ἄλλῳ· ἔρχου, καὶ ἔρχεται, καὶ τῷ δούλῳ μου· ποίησον τοῦτο, καὶ ποιεῖ. 9 ἀκούσας δὲ ὁ Ἰησοῦς ἐθαύμασεν αὐτόν, καὶ εἶπεν τῷ ἀκολουθοῦσιν· λέγω ὑμῖν, οὐδὲ ἐν τῷ Ἰσραὴλ τοσαύτην πίστιν εὗρον. 10 <..>

[7:1] And when he finished these sayings, he entered Capernaum. [3] A centurion came to him, pleading to him, saying, "My Pais is sick." And he said to him, "I'll come and heal him." [6] The centurion answered him, saying, "Sir, I am not worthy to have you come under my roof. [7] But only speak the word and let my Pais be healed. [8] For I am also a man under authority, having soldiers under me. I say to this one, 'Go,' and he goes; and to another, 'Come,' and he comes; and to my slave, 'Do this,' and he does it." [9] When Jesus heard, he marveled at him and said to those following, "I'm telling you, not even in Israel have I found such faith." [10] [The Pais's healing seems implied, but the wording is uncertain.]

Appendix 2
Chronology of Homoerotic Readings 1950–1989

Appendix 2 attempts a chronology of homoerotic readings until 1990, a chronology that gestures towards completeness but inevitably falls short. Whenever the relevant discussion of the centurion and The Pais is brief enough, I have included the relevant excerpt. The excerpts here are not cleaned up the way they have been in the body of the present book, so there may be some peculiarities. All emphasis is found in the original publication. Footnotes are usually omitted. Those interested in the genealogy of citations can refer either to the original text or figure 2.

There is some selectivity in what to include. Omitted are discussions of Dinos Christianopoulos's poem, as these tend to concern the poetry itself, often entirely sidestepping its relationship to the Bible.[1] Likewise, even when authors have clearly encountered the homoerotic reading but do not explicitly mention the interpretation of this particular passage, their publication is omitted—for example, annotated bibliographies or book reviews.[2] 1990 marks a convenient and round ending point, especially since the number of publications on the topic quickly explodes, becoming a relatively frequent point of reference in queer theological discourse by 1994, even if it still remains neglected by most academics.

---

1. E.g., Friar, "Poetry of Dinos Christianopoulos," 60: "if the centurion Cornelius prays to the Lord to save his beloved slave Andonios, it is, as he confesses, because 'love dictates my faith,' and in final desperation he declares that 'if need be, I can even turn Christian.'" One would hardly get the impression that this poem is based on a biblical text from Friar's very brief discussion. Likewise, John Taylor, "The Poetry of Dinos Christianopoulos," *The Cabirion/Gay Books Bulletin* 12 (1985): 11, which may be the source of Mader's ("*Entimos Pais*," 233 n. 6) knowledge of the poem.

2. E.g., Horner, *Homosexuality in Biblical Times*, 3, 8; but see its discussion with regards to Rossman in chapter 1.

Finally, it is worth noting that as archives become digitized, there will inevitably be readings from this period that are uncovered after publication of this monograph. Updates regarding appendix 2 will be posted at http://armyofromanpalestine.com/centurion-pais/. Moreover, some of the readings too long to include in this appendix can be found on this webpage as well, along with any original-language versions of the texts cited below and any corrigenda related to the book's content.

1950

Christianopoulos, Dinos. Εποχή των ισχνών αγελάδων [*Season of the Lean Cows*]. Thessaloniki: Kochlias, 1950.
Page 9: The Greek-language poem is titled "Εκατόνταρχος Κορνήλιος" ("Centurion Cornelius"). For full English translation by Kimon Friar, see chapter 1.

1955

Crowther, R. H. "Sodom: A Homosexual Viewpoint." *ONE Magazine* 3.1 (1955): 24–28.

> Recently a European correspondent, who wished to remain anonymous, wrote to ONE, in part, as follows:
> In one copy of a predecessor of WEG ... was printed something which was of infinite help to me and which I have used over and over again in writing and to my friends. I quote it, translating from the German, from memory, as I have not the source by me. I cannot, of course, vouch for its truth—but true or not, it enshrines Truth as I have always seen it.
> "In some remote monastery in Asia Minor was discovered part of a lost Codex of the Gospels which throws a vivid light on Jesus' attitude towards homosexuals. Here is the relevant extract:
>> As Jesus and His disciples walked through Galilee there came to Him a man weeping and crying—'Master, have mercy upon me, for men curse and revile me because of my love for a young man, my servant, with whom I live.' And Jesus answering, said unto him, 'Why doest thou this?' And he said, 'Because my heart burns with love for this young man, my servant.'
>> And Jesus said unto him, 'If your love be with sin, it shall be cursed; but if your love be without sin, it shall be blessed. Go in peace.'"

Does this Codex really exist? Where is it now? Here are questions I
have long desired to find out, but do not know how to set about it.
But, after all, does it matter? It is just what one would expect of the
Christ – complete comprehension, the realization that the love of
one man for another can be both with and without sin (and the best
definition I know of 'sin' is 'anything that comes between God and
myself'). (26)

"R. H. Crowther" was a pseudonym of ONE Institute board member Julian
Underwood.[3] "WEG" refers to the German homophile publication, *Weg
zu Freundschaft*, commonly known as *Der Weg*; during the first two years
of publication (1951–1952), *Der Weg* went by the name *Die Insel: Monats-
blätter für Freundschaft und Toleranz*, the likely "precursor" that the letter
referred to. The article mentioned here does not seem to exist, at least not
in *Die Insel*. No such codex has been found in Asia Minor. Though this
story lacks both a healing and a military officer, there is reason to think the
author offers a muddled interpretation of the Healing of the Centurion's
Pais: themes of being reviled (by Jews?), the beloved's status as a slave, its
occurrence in Galilee, the shared household, the implied use of παῖς in the
designation "young man," Jesus's commendation of a homosexual man,
and so on. There is reason to doubt that any letter detailing such a find was
ever published in a German homophile magazine, given the meaning the
author assigns to truth.

1959

Kepner, James, Jr. "World Religions and the Homophile: An Introduction."
ONE Institute Quarterly 7 (1959): 124–32.

> Luke 7:2 uses a term that was used for the boy love-slaves of well-to-do
> Roman soldiers. (130 n. 35)

Syllabi indicate that the homoerotic interpretation of the passage was regularly featured in the various classes that Kepner taught at ONE Institute,
including introductions to studies in homosexuality, religion and homo-

---

3. See *January–June 1948*. Vol. 2.1a.1 of *Catalog of Copyright Entries*, 3rd series
(Washington, DC: Copyright Office, 1948), 646.

sexuality, and the history of homosexuality. It is not clear when, precisely, he began including discussion of the pericope.

1960

Martin, Thomas, and B. Newman. "Guilt and the Homosexual." *ONE Magazine* 8.12 (1960): 12–13.

> Let us look into the incident of the Centurion's "servant" as is related in two of the Gospels: St. Matthew VIII, verses 5–13, and again in St. Luke VII, verses 2–10. This records one of the miracles the Savior performed in healing the Centurion's servant. St. Matthew uses the Greek word "pais"—meaning a youth. This word was so often used in relation to the youthful lover of a Roman soldier, especially an officer of the armies. Even the Centurion, knowing the hatred of the homophile by all the Jewish authorities, said that he was not worthy for Christ to enter under his roof—still, Jesus said: "I have not found so great a faith, no not in Israel." Take this and the fact that not once did Jesus make a statement against any homophile practice, how then can a Christian stand up and condemn what Christ did not? (13)

1963

Gyburc-Hall, Larion. "Legende." *Der Kreis* 31.4 (1963): 14–22.

German narrative story too long to translate in full here. "Larion Gyburc-Hall" was a pseudonym of Werner Schmitz.[4] The story tells of a man named Utaj Ben Ammichur whose jealous slave Jarib murdered Utaj's *eromenos* Chobab. Jarib is nearly beaten to death in an act of mob vengeance, but Jesus heals him at the request of a forgiving Utaj. The story is not a straightforward retelling of the Healing of the Centurion's Pais; for example, Utaj resides in Shechem, and there is no indication he is a military man. However, like Crowther, "Sodom: A Homosexual Viewpoint" (1955), the parallels are distinct enough that it is clear the pericope is in mind. This is most evident in Utaj's insistence that Jesus not come under his roof, leading Jesus to heal Utaj's slave Jarib at a distance.

---

4. Hubert Kennedy, *The Ideal Gay Man: The Story of Der Kreis* (Binghamton: Haworth, 1999), 60.

Various. "Zur 'Legende' von Larion Gyburc-Hall." *Der Kreis* 31.5 (1963): 2–3.
Three German letters to the editor praising Gyburc-Hall's short story that are too long to translate in full here. Letters are from "Dr. med. Wolfgang E. Bredtschneider," "Dr. iur. C.," and "H. B."

1965

Mayer, Michel. "Le procurateur de Judée: Suite à la manière d'Anatole France." *Arcadie* 134 (1965): 63–71.
French article too long to translate in full here; the entire article is devoted to the homoerotic reading of the passage.

Morgan, W. L. D. "The Homosexual and the Church: A Historical Survey and Assessment." Unpublished manuscript, 1965(?).

> Accordingly, we must state that there are no references to homosexuality in the Gospels: explicitly, Jesus had nothing to say about it. There may be some implied reference to it in the story of the healing of the centurion's servant, for certain MSS use terms suggesting that she servant was in fact the centurion's boy-friend, rather than his highly regarded batman. (7)

The reference to text-critical variations in the manuscripts is incorrect; there are no significant variations with the nouns referring to the Pais: it is consistently δοῦλος and παῖς in both Matthew and Luke. The unpublished manuscript is undated, though it describes a 1965 article from the magazine *New Christian* as "recent," though this label is not applied to other articles from earlier in the decade. From this we might infer that the manuscript was probably written in 1965 or 1966.

1966

Eck, Marcel. *Sodome: Essai sur l'homosexualité*. Paris: Fayard, 1966.

> That Christ does not explicitly mention homosexuality does not mean that he does not condemn it. Too often, homosexuals have a vested interest in one-sided interpretation: have we not read a learned exegesis by one of them demonstrating that the centurion's servant was, in fact, his *eromenos*? (266, translated from French by Morgan Bell)

Eck almost certain refers to the work of Mayer published in 1965, as he regularly cites articles in *Arcadie* throughout the pages of his book.

Christianopoulos, Dinos. "The Centurion Cornelius." Pages 267–68 in *Modern European Poetry*. Edited by Willis Barnstone. Translated by Kimon Friar. New York: Bantam, 1966.
English Translation of Christianopoulos, "Εκατόνταρχος Κορνήλιος" (1950); see chapter 1.

Martin, Thomas, and B. Newman. "Guilt and the Homosexual." *ONE Magazine* 14.11 (1966): 12–13.
Reprint of Martin and Newman, "Guilt and the Homosexual" (1960), coincidentally with the same pagination. See above entry for excerpt.

1967

Crowther, R. H. "Sodom: A Homosexual Viewpoint." *ONE Magazine* 15.6 (1967): 11–15.
Page 13: Reprint of Crowther, "Sodom: A Homosexual Viewpoint" (1955). See above entry for relevant excerpt.

1968

Van de Spijker, A. M. J. M. Herman. *Die gleichgeschlechtliche Zuneigung; Homotropie: Homosexualität, Homoerotik, Homophilie, und Die katholische Moraltheologie*. Olten: Walter, 1968.

> One does no real service to the homotropic man if, based on the idea that *pais* can also mean a boy-toy, the story of the centurion at Capernaum in Mt 8:5–13 is interpreted in such a way that the sick servant is his lover. With special emphasis on the centurion's sense of sin in Mt 8:8 and on the servant's recovery in Mt 8:13, one wants to conclude that Jesus is mild and good towards the homotropic. It is clear that such interpretations must be rejected. The mercy of God towards every human being, also towards the androtropic man or the gynecotropic woman, cannot be "substantiated" or "proved" with such an untrue exegesis, as it happens too often in magazines for homotropes. (93–94, translated from German by Christopher B. Zeichmann)

APPENDIX 2: CHRONOLOGY OF HOMOEROTIC READINGS 1950-1989   235

"Homotrope" and its derivatives androtrope and gynotrope, though no longer used at all today, encompass a broad meaning: not only people sexually attracted to those of their same gender, but also those with non-sexual feelings of romance or tenderness toward their own gender.

1970

Davidson, Alex. *The Returns of Love: Letters of a Christian Homosexual.* London: InterVarsity, 1970.

> So I have come painfully through to the stage of Trust, and am learning the hardest lesson of all—that where your well-being is concerned I am not indispensable. I'm learning to keep my hands off, to stop interfering, to love you enough to let you go. If you want me, you know where to find me, and whenever you need my help it will be yours for the asking, but I will no longer force myself upon you.
> A strange bond, this, whose permanence depends on the *loosening* of knots! I think it is really possible for none but those who believe in Christ, since among unbelievers Trust can only mean trust in each other. The best they can say is, "I love you so much that I will cease to smother you with my attentions, trusting that you will manage quite successfully without them." But the loved one might not be able to manage; and the lover, seeing him wallow helplessly, might conclude in despair that he is indispensable after all, and so the relationship would be driven into a vicious spiral. For the Christian, though, Trust means primarily trust in God, and *His* reliability is guaranteed. As a Christian, what I can say is, "I love you so much that I will see to smother you with my attentions, trusting that *He* will manage you quite successfully without them." I must learn to be like the centurion in the Gospel story, who was so sure of the power and love of Christ that he asked for (and got) a blessing for the sick servant "who was dear to him" even without invading the privacy of the sick-room. It was done at a distance, unobtrusively, without fuss: "only say the word, and my boy shall be healed." I'm trying by the grace of god to maintain my relationship to you on that level. If it ever slips back, and I forget myself, be brutal and tell me. (86)

The book collects conversations the author had with a real-life friend ("Peter"), putting them in a fictional epistolary form. The letters concern the author's own homosexuality and eventual decision to remain celibate. The centurion is invoked ambiguously here, but the scare-quotes surrounding "who was dear to him" may imply an attraction paralleling the one that Alex holds for Peter. The book's cover incorrectly names its own subtitle as "A Contemporary Christian View of Homosexuality."

1973

Derrett, J. Duncan M. "Law in the New Testament: The Syro-Phoenician Woman and the Centurion of Capernaum." *NovT* 15 (1973): 161–86.

> The query as to whether the sufferer was the centurion's son or servant/slave remains unsolved. We were intended to be in doubt! The intense concern of the Centurion for the boy suggests a deep emotional attachment; if it was a son he might have been illegitimate (were Herodian centurions allowed to marry?); if it was a slave he could have been a 'dolly boy' whom the centurion loved the more deeply for having conquered desire. We do not know. The adolescent or youth was highly disturbed with a complaint thought to be susceptible of spirit healing. (174)

> His servant or slave was in a state of complete disobedience, perhaps as a defensive response. What do we know of a slave's mentality; how would their contemporary counterparts to our psychiatrists deal with disturbed ex-dolly-boys, for example? But we do know that both adults were convinced, to the point of utter want of self-consciousness, that a 'man of God' held their answer. (186)

1974

Enroth, Ronald M., and Gerald E. Jamison. *The Gay Church*. Grand Rapids: Eerdmans, 1974.

> An equally interesting relationship centers around the New Testament figure who has come to be known as "the gay centurion." In Matthew 8:5-13, one of Jesus' healings is described as performed on a centurion's "servant." Some state that this is a direct reference to the youthful lover of an officer in the Roman army, a common situation in biblical days. The story continues to show how Jesus, astounded by the faith of this Roman homosexual, not only did not condemn the gay condition, but went out of his way to heal his young lover. The validity of such an interpretation is based on the Greek word Matthew uses for "servant"—*pais*, meaning either "youth" or "servant," with the context determining the ore accurate connotation. An examination of the same story in the Lucan account, however, leaves no room for doubt that "servant" is the correct

reading here. In Luke 7:2-10, the Greek word is *doulos*, simply meaning "servant." Thus the possible reference "youth," a word that triggers the imaginations of gay Christians, is eliminated. (56-57)

Birchard, Roy. Review of *The Gay Church*, by Ronald M. Enroth and Gerald E. Jamison. *Gay Christian* 3 (1974): 10-11.

So too, in their chapter on the Bible, they mix serious exegesis by gay theologians with a recounting of a gay Cain-Abel story they picked up somewhere and the supposed healing of a "gay centurion." One is reminded of the genteel, romantic Bible novels of one's youth—Ben Hur, Dear and Glorious Physician, etc. From what further shore of the gay world did they gather in these daydreams? (for at this point their scholarly apparatus of footnotes quite disappears). (11)

Kepner, James, Jr. "The Oldest Gay Stories in the World." *In Touch* 2.3 (1974): 61-65.

There are scores of other cryptic stories in the Old Testament and a few in the New (the raising of Lazarus from the dead, and also of the Centurion's boy-lover) which find their explanation in the addition of such background information. (65)

Christianopoulos, Dinos. Ποιήματα *1949-1970* [*Poems 1949-1970*]. Thessaloniki: Diagonos, 1974.
Page 11: Reprint of the Greek poem Christianopoulos, "Εκατόνταρχος Κορνήλιος" (1950). See chapter 1 for English translation.

1975

Martignac, J. "Le centurion de Capernaüm." *Arcadie* 255 (1975): 117-28.
The French article is too long to quote or translate in full here; the entire article is devoted to the homoerotic reading of the passage. It was previously presented as a paper at Groupe des Chrétiens Homophiles de Marseille in May 1974.

Anonymous. "How Dare You Presume These Are Heterosexual!" *Oregon Liberator* 5.1 (1975?): 6.

Cornelius the Centurion and his 'Friend' (also translates 'Lover') (6)

No year is listed for this volume of *Oregon Liberator*, and its publishing schedule was irregular.

1976

Rossman, Parker. *Sexual Experience between Men and Boys: Exploring the Pederast Underground*. New York: Association, 1976.
  Page 99: summarizing the musings of a "Gnostic pederast monk"; see quotation of the excerpt in chapter 1.

Ortleb, Charles. "God and Gays: A New Team." *Christopher Street* 1.4 (1976): 25–31.

> "There is one curious story of the Roman centurion whose boy servant is ill. Jesus is asked to cure him. It is said that the centurion loved the boy very deeply; one could read into it a homosexual relationship." (27, quoting John J. McNeill in an interview)

1977

Derrett, J. Duncan M. *Glimpses of the Legal and Social Presuppositions of the Authors*. Vol. 1 of *Studies in the New Testament*. Biblical Studies 1. Leiden: Brill, 1977.
  Pages 156 and 168: Reprints Derrett, "Law in the New Testament" (1973) with updates. See above entry for relevant excerpts, both of which remain unchanged in this reprint.

Anonymous. *The Rebel, Jesus*. Hollywood: The People's Church Collective—Jesuene Ek-klesia, 1977(?).

> He took his cause directly to Gays (the Centurion, John the Beloved, Lazarus), Women (Mary & Martha, Mary his mother), those of "bad repute" (The Samaritan woman, Mary of Magdala, publicans, wine-bibbers), Black people (Simon of Cyrene), workers (Luke 4:30–2) and other victims of the world empire (Matt.21:31) (3)

No author or date is found on this publication, but it may be authored mostly by Mikhail F. Itkin, bishop of the church. Nearly identical wording is found in another anonymous and undated publication of the church:

Anonymous. *Manifesto*. Hollywood: The People's Church-Community of the Love of Christ, 1977(?). Page 3.

1978

Horner, Tom M. "The Centurion's Servant." *Insight* 2.3 (1978): 9.
Entire article devoted to the topic, too long to quote here.

Horner, Tom M. *Jonathan Loved David: Homosexuality in Biblical Times*. Philadelphia: Westminster John Knox, 1978.

> There are, in fact, two hints in the Gospels which indicate that he [Jesus] would not have been hostile. The first is the possible homosexual motif in the story of the healing of the centurion's servant (Matthew 8:5–13 and Luke 7:1–10). It has always seemed to me that it was more than an ordinary concern that this Roman official displayed in this case for a mere slave. Luke uses here the word *doúlos*, "slave." This has not at all the same connotation as in Matthew. In either case, however, Jesus made no note of it, which means that if the homosexual element were present, he was not disturbed by it. Instead, he was overwhelmed by the man's faith, which is clearly the paramount element in the story. (122)

Christianopoulos, Dinos. Ποιήματα *1949–1970* [*Poems 1949–1970*]. 2nd ed. Thessaloniki: Diagonos, 1978.
Page 11: Reprint of the Greek poem Christianopoulos, "Εκατόνταρχος Κορνήλιος" (1950). See chapter 1 for English translation.

Pritchard, Richard E. *A Contribution to the Discussion on the Homosexual Lifestyle and Its Legalization in Madison*. Madison: Self-Published, 1978.

> Frequent comments are made, and at least one book was written saying that homosexuality was common in the Bible, and accepted. Gay writers have said that Cain and Abel were "probably" homosexuals, Ruth and Noami, David and Jonathan, Jesus and John, Jesus and Lazarus, the centurion and his healed servant, Paul and Timothy. Where they don't say "probably," they suggest "possibly." (12)

1980

Botero, Ebel. *Homofilia y homofobia: Estudio sobre la homosexualidad, la bisexualidad y la represión de la conducta homosexual*. Medellín: Lealón, 1980.
Pages 165–66: Spanish excerpt too long for quotation here.

Hocquenghem, Guy. *Le gay voyage: Guide et regard homosexuels sur les grandes métropoles*. Paris: Michel, 1980.

> The Bible does not condemn Sodom for homosexuality, but for the sole crime that the desert society, the nomadic society, cannot allow: the crime against hospitality. And Saint Paul? My knowledgeable exegetes have a response to everything. St. Paul's text was the victim of poor translations. If one returns to the original text in Aramaic, one discovers what Paul condemns: it is not homosexuality [as such], but only the homosexual prostitution in the temples encouraged by the pagan bourgeoisie. As regards Christ, remember the episode of the Roman centurion who asked the Son of God to save his servant: for anyone who knows the habits of the Roman armies, this servant is evidently his lover. (48, in the entry on New York [*New York jour et nuit*]; translated from French by Morgan Bell)

1981

Horner, Tom M. *Homosexuality and the Judeo-Christian Tradition: An Annotated Bibliography*. Philadelphia: American Theological Library Association, 1981.

> [Bibliographic entry number] 283. Horner, Tom. "The Centurion's Servant." Insight: A Quarterly of Gay Catholic Opinion. Vol. 2, No. 3 (Summer 1978), p. 9.
> A sermon on Matthew 8:5–13 as a possible homosexual reference. Horner uses the translations of The New English Bible and The New American Bible, both of which render pais as "boy" and suggests that Luke, in 7:1–10, changed pais to doulos, "slave," because of the particularly humanitarian emphasis that is found throughout his Gospel. (69)
>
> Group Two: Homosexual References According to Some Critics
> [Readers should note that there is no general agreement that the references listed below are definite homosexual references. They are listed

here because some critics allege them to be definite homosexual references, or at least to contain some homosexual connotations. Again, commentaries should be consulted.]…
Matthew 8:5–13 ("boy" here appears as "slave" in Luke 7:1–10; but see translations of The New English Bible and The New American Bible) (113)

Christianopoulos, Dinos. Ποιήματα 1949–1970 [Poems 1949–1970]. 3rd ed. Thessaloniki: Diagonos, 1981.
Page 11: Reprint of the Greek poem Christianopoulos, "Εκατόνταρχος Κορνήλιος" (1950). See chapter 1 for English translation.

Taylor, Robert R., Jr. "A Triumph for Truth." Pages 7–8 in *A Debate on Homosexuality*. Edited by Thomas F. Eaves Sr. and Paul R. Johnson. Algood: T&P Bookshelf, 1981.

> Those who revere the beautiful and pure Biblical friendships between David and Jonathan, between David and Mephibosheth, between the aged Eli and the youthful Samuel, between the aged Naomi and the gentle Ruth, between the honorable centurion and his dying servant in Luke 7 and Matthew 8, between Joseph and Potiphar or even between Jesus and John will be repelled to read the homosexual accusations that Johnson reads into these friendship and fellowship frameworks. Johnson appears to be wearing his homosexual goggles every time he reads of two males or two females who were friends. He wishes they were homosexual and the wish fathers the thought that they were in his perverted mind. To Johnson it appears there can be neither friendship nor fellowship between those of the same sex without homosexual tendencies as major motivations. Like Freud he sees sex—perverted as far as he is concerned—as about the only drawing power between human beings. (7–8)

Johnson, Paul R. "Johnson's Third Affirmative." Pages 105–12 in *A Debate on Homosexuality*. Edited by Thomas F. Eaves Sr. and Paul R. Johnson. Algood: T&P Bookshelf, 1981.

> Jesus approved of the centurion and his male companion in St. Matthew 8 where the Greek word *pais* is used to describe this same-sex relationship. Pais is the word that any gay male in Greek culture would use in referring to his younger lover. (108)

Eaves, Thomas F., Sr. "Eaves' Third Negative." Pages 113–20 in *A Debate on Homosexuality*. Edited by Thomas F. Eaves Sr. and Paul R. Johnson. Algood: T&P Bookshelf, 1981.

> Matthew 8:4, Again Johnson assigns his meaning to words as he stated, "Jesus approved the Centurion and his male companion in Matthew 8 where the Greek word *pais* is used to describe the same sex relationship." The word *pais* is defined as: "With relationship between one human being and another—1) From the viewpoint of age boy, youth, 2) from the view point of descent son, 3) from the view point of social position servant." (Greek-English Lexicon, Arndt and Gingrich, p. 609). (Word *pais* is also used by Isaiah of Jesus in Matthew 12:18). (117)

Johnson, Paul R. "Johnson's Fourth Affirmative." Pages 121–29 in *A Debate on Homosexuality*. Edited by Thomas F. Eaves Sr. and Paul R. Johnson. Algood: T&P Bookshelf, 1981.

> Rev. Eaves castigates me for using sources which he, himself introduced, demanding that I use only the Bible. Yet time and again, the Dean "quotes" as his only proof, Arndt and Gingrich, a limited German work, rarely accepted by conservatives. Arndt and Gingrich ramble on for a page or two trying to define *pais*, not once mentioning the regular and popular definition of this gay term found everywhere in Greek literature. Even the Dean would find little creedal agreement with this outdated, homophobic source. Why is the Dean so afraid to investigate more direct, more complete and more knowledgeable sources? Rev. Eaves refuses to even discuss the Aramaic (the very language Jesus spoke) to find out what Jesus really believed about gays in St. Matthew 5:23.
>
> Jesus healed the Centurion's lover (*pais*) in Luke 7:7. The greatest modern scholar of Greek sexuality writes, "In many contexts and almost invariably in poetry the passive (gay) partner is called *pais* ..." (K. J. Dover, *Greek Homosexuality*, p. 16). Luke was a Greek Historian and knew what meaning the Greeks placed on the term. The Bible uses other Greek terms to denote regular servants or sons. The Greek term (*pais*) in the Bible is either used to denote a physical union between two humans or a spiritual union (marriage) between God and a human. Jesus, David and the prophets were married to God and were called *pais* because they were the more passive. Anderson, p. 8. (124)

Eaves, Thomas F., Sr. "Eaves' Fourth Negative." Pages 130–37 in *A Debate on Homosexuality*. Edited by Thomas F. Eaves Sr. and Paul R. Johnson. Algood: T&P Bookshelf, 1981.

> Isaiah referred to Jesus as servant (*pais*), Isaiah 42:1 quoted in Matthew 12:18. In Johnson's own example (Luke 7:7) the sick man is referred to as servant (*pais*—v. 7) and servant (*doulon*—v. 10). Furthermore in John 4 the nobleman's ill child is referred to as son (*huion*—v. 47); child (*paidion*—infant, v. 49); son (*huios*—v. 50), and son (*pais*—v. 51). According to Johnson every male child two years and under were united in a physical union. Herod killed all the children (*paidas*—accusative plural form of *pais*). Matthew 2:16. (Other passages where same form appears—Acts 20:12; Luke 8:5; 8:54; 12:45, etc.). (135)

Johnson, Paul R. "Affirmative Rejoinder." Pages 138–39 in *A Debate on Homosexuality*. Edited by Thomas F. Eaves Sr. and Paul R. Johnson. Algood: T&P Bookshelf, 1981.

> According to the Greeks, *pais* meant "gay" when describing a union between an older and younger male. Between any two humans it always meant a physical union in the Bible.... Infants were *pais* if they sucked their mother's breast (physical union). An adult was *pais* (gay) for obvious parallel reasons. St. Paul embraced a *pais* at Troas several young gays staged a protest in the temple and eunuch overseers were often gay (Acts 20:9, 10; Matt. 21:15ff; Lk. 12:45; Dn. 9:9). (138–39)

The book from which these passages are excerpted is titled *Gays and the New Right: A Debate* in some printings. The second paragraph in Johnson's fourth affirmative is indented as though it were a block quotation, though its origination is unclear—if it indeed is a quote. It is possible that this is what "Anderson, p. 8" refers to, though this is also uncertain: the author's full name is never given, the title is never mentioned at all, and it is not provided a bibliographic entry.

1982

Christianopoulos, Dinos. "The Centurion Cornelius." *Gay Sunshine Journal* 47 (1982): 170.

Reprint of the English translation Dinos Christianopoulos, "The Centurion Cornelius" (1966), which translates Christianopoulos, "Εκατόνταρχος

Κορνήλιος" (1950). It is appended with the following note from Kimon Friar:

> See Luke 7:1–10, where it is told how Jesus healed the servant of a centurion 'who was dear unto him, was sick, and ready to die.' The poet has given the arbitrary names Cornelius and Andónios to centurion and servant respectively. See also Matthew 8:5–13. (170)

1983

Kepner, James, Jr. *Becoming a People: A Four Thousand Year Gay and Lesbian Chronology*. 1st ed. Hollywood: National Gay Archives, 1983.

> 28 A.D.: Jesus of Nazareth healed a Roman officer's dead love-servant (Matt 8). (4)

1984

Kepner, James, Jr. *A Brief Chronology of Gay/Lesbian History from Earliest Times*. Hollywood: National Gay Archives, 1984(?).

> 28 A.D.: Jesus of Nazareth healed a Roman officer's dead love-servant (Matt 8). (6)

This publication is undated, but based on internal references it seems to be a distillation of Kepner, *Becoming a People* (1983).

1986

Lambert, James. Review of *Sexual Experience*, by Parker Rossman. *Gay Christian* 41 (1986): 31.

> The gem of the book is a report of the early Christian view that the Roman centurion who pleads with Jesus for help in curing his slave was apparently a pederast. (31)

Theissen, Gerd. 1986. *Der Schatten des Galiläers: Historische Jesusforschung in erzählender Form*. Munich: Kaiser.
Page 150: For English translation of this German text, see chapter 2 for excerpt. The author is credited as Gerd Theißsen for this edition.

Gray-Fow, Michael. "Pederasty, the Scantinian Law and the Roman Army." *Journal of Psychohistory* 13 (1986): 449–60.

> By the end of the first century A.D. it was apparently considered quite normal for a centurion to have such a boy (Mar. 1.31.1), and genuine affection which could exist for these boys probably lies behind the Gospel story of the centurion and his sick 'servant' (Luke 7.2–10). (457)

1987

Theissen, Gerd. *The Shadow of the Galilean*. Translated by John Bowden. Minneapolis: Augsburg Fortress, 1987.
Page 106: See chapter 2 for excerpt. English translation of Theissen, *Der Schatten des Galiläers* (1986).

Mader, Donald. "The *Entimos Pais* of Matthew 8:5–13 and Luke 7:1–10." *Paidika* 1.1 (1987): 27–39.
The entire article is devoted to the homoerotic reading of the passage, too long for quotation here.

Kepner, James, Jr. *Gay Spirit: The Cord of Many Strands*. Hollywood: International Gay & Lesbian Archives, 1987(?).

> The word translated harlot is said to be pornoi, Greek word for **male** whore, also used of the Prodigal son, and the terms describing the Centurion's "servant" in Matthew is thought by some to give a homophile turn to two of Jesus' resurrecting acts. (9)

The publication is undated, though various archives date it to 1987 or 1988. Pagination varies depending on the version in-hand.

1988

Theissen, Gerd. *La Sombra del Galileo*. Translated by Constantino Ruiz-Garrido. Salamanca: Sígueme, 1988.
Page 151: Spanish translation of Theissen, *Der Schatten des Galiläers* (1986). For English translation of the excerpt, see chapter 2.

1989

McNeill, John J. "Positive Messages from the Bible." *Advent: Lutherans Concerned/San Francisco* 11.4 (1989): 10–11.

Pages 10–11: Excerpt too long for quotation but concludes with an editor's note from Jim Lokken, which is quoted in full in Chapter 3.

Lawrence, Raymond J., Jr. *The Poisoning of Eros: Sexual Values in Conflict.* New York: Augustine Moore, 1989.

Pages 69–71: Excerpt too long for quotation.

Faris, Donald L. *Trojan Horse: The Homosexual Ideology and the Christian Church.* Burlington: Welch, 1989.

> At least one pro-homosexual ideology author argues that Jesus not only approved of pedophilia but healed the "boy" of the centurian at Capernaum (Matthew 8:5–13) and so restored him for the sexual enjoyment of the Roman officer. Most Christians would not only be surprised but very offended by this suggestion.
> The fact that adult/adult homosexual acts were consistently and widely condemned in the Greco-Roman world does not imply they did not exist. They certainly did and we have no reason to believe that they were thought of as any less noble, tender, caring, or long-term than such relationships in modern times. The fact is, such relationships were considered to be wrong, *per se*, in the same way the Judeo-Christian Scriptures and tradition condemned adulterous relationships, no matter how noble, tender, caring or long-term they were thought to be. (33)

Maranger, Keith. "Annual Richmond Dignity/Integrity Banquet Features Evangelical Feminist." *Our Own Community Press* 13.6 (1989): 2–3.

> "the biblical authors knew nothing of homosexual orientation and nothing about covenanted same-sex love, unless we're thinking of David and Jonathan, or Ruth and Naomi, or the centurion and the beloved servant boy." (2, quoting the speaker, Virginia Ramey Mollenkott)

Noncitations

Sometimes, commentators mistakenly claim that a publication discusses the homoerotic interpretation where no such discussion takes place. The following are sometimes cited so as to give the incorrect impression that they discuss the pericope in a way they do not. There is no discussion of the centurion at Capernaum in any homoerotic capacity in these publications, despite occasional assertions to the contrary.

Boswell, John. *Christianity, Social Tolerance, and Homosexuality: Gay People in Western Europe from the Beginning of the Christian Era to the Fourteenth Century* Chicago: University of Chicago Press, 1980.

Dover, Kenneth James. *Greek Homosexuality*. Cambridge: Harvard University Press, 1978.

Gillabert, Émile. *Saint Paul: Ou Le Colosse aux pieds d'argile*. Marsanne: Métanoïa, 1974.

Wegner, Uwe. *Der Hauptmann von Kafarnaum (Mt 7,28a; 8,5–10.13 par Lk 7,1–10): Ein Beitrag zur Q-Forschung*. WUNT 2/14. Tübingen: Mohr Siebeck, 1985.

Appendix 3
Military Presence in Capernaum

The military and administrative history of Palestine is extremely complicated, especially during the early Roman period. The following table outlines the type of military units present in Galilee, Judea, and Batanea from the period 66 BCE–135 CE, as well as when these regions were politically independent and which region Capernaum was administratively run by. Thus, although a centurion at Capernaum in the time of Jesus would almost certainly have been a royal soldier in Herod Antipas's royal army, it would be easy for ancient writers (like the evangelists) and modern writers (like many scholars) to get mixed up and assume he served in another army.

[Administrative status]. [Head of military]: [his title]. [Troops present]: [troops' origination, if noteworthy]; [external aid, if applicable].

Abbreviations:

    CK: client kingdom allied with Rome.
    EP: equestrian subprovince of Roman Syria.
    IK: independent kingdom not allied with Rome.
    RA: royal army.
    Shaded cell indicates the kingdom or province governing Capernaum.

	Judea	Galilee	Batanea
66 BCE civil war	IK. Aristobulus II: king. RA; aid from mercenaries.		IK. Ptolemy son of Mennaeus: king. RA.
63 BCE Pompey's conquest	CK. Hyrcanus II: ethnarch. RA; aid from Roman legions during conquest.		CK. Ptolemy son of Mennaeus: tetrarch. RA.
57 BCE 5 Synods	Synods. Synedria at Jerusalem and Jericho. Legions.	Synod. Synedrion at Sepphoris. Legions.	
47 BCE return to monarchy	CK. Hyrcanus II: ethnarch; Antipater: procurator. RA.	CK. Hyrcanus II: ethnarch; Herod: governor. RA.	
44 BCE Antipater dies	CK. Hyrcanus II: ethnarch; Phasael: governor. RA.		
42 BCE	CK. Hyrcanus II: ethnarch; Phasael: tetrarch. RA.	CK. Hyrcanus II: ethnarch; Herod: tetrarch. RA.	
40 BCE Uprising	IK. Antigonus: king. RA; aid from IK of Parthia and RA of Batanaea during conquest.		CK. Lysanias: tetrarch. RA.
37 BCE	CK. Herod the Great: king. RA; aid from Roman legions during conquest.		CK. Cleopatra: queen; Zenodorus: lessee. RA.
30 BCE			CK. Zenodorus: tetrarch. RA.
23 BCE Batanea split	CK. Herod the Great: king. RA.		
4 BCE Herod dies	CK. Archelaus: ethnarch. RA: inherited most of Herod's RA; aid from legions and Nabataea's RA during revolts.	CK. Antipas: tetrarch. RA: inherited some of Herod's RA.	CK. Philip: tetrarch. RA: inherited some of Herod's RA.
6 CE Archelaus ousted	EP. Coponius: prefect. Local *auxilia*: formed from Archelaus's RA.		
34 CE Philip dies	EP. Pilate: prefect. Judean *auxilia*.		Syria: Consular Roman province. Vitellius: legate. Legions and *auxilia*.
37 CE	EP. Marullus: prefect. Judean *auxilia*.		CK. Agrippa I: king. RA.
39 CE Antipas banished	CK. Agrippa I: king. RA.		

APPENDIX 3: MILITARY PRESENCE IN CAPERNAUM 251

41 CE Judea reunified	CK. Agrippa I: king. RA: formed from Judean *auxilia*.		
44 CE Agrippa I dies	EP. Fadus: procurator. Judean *auxilia*: formed from Agrippa I's RA.		
53 CE	EP. Felix: procurator. Judean *auxilia*.		CK. Agrippa II: king. RA.
55 CE Batanea expanded	EP. Felix: procurator. Judean *auxilia*.		CK. Agrippa II: king. RA.
66 CE Galilee revolts	EP. Antonius Julianus: procurator. Legions and various *auxilia*.	IK. Josephus: governor. Galilean rebel army.	CK. Agrippa II: king. RA.
67 CE Galilee subdued	EP. Marcus Antonius Julianus: legate. Legions and various *auxilia*; aid from RAs of Batanaea, Commagene, and Emesa.		
70 CE Judea promoted	Praetorian Roman province. Sextus Vettulenus Cerialis: legate. Legions and foreign *auxilia*.		CK. Agrippa II: king. RA.
96 CE Agrippa II dies	Praetorian Roman province. Sextus Hermidius Campanus: legate. One legion and foreign *auxilia*.		Syria: Consular Roman province. Lucius Junius Caesennius Paetus: legate. Legions and *auxilia*.
120 CE Judea promoted	Consular Roman province. Lucius Cossonius Gallus: legate. Two legions and foreign *auxilia*.		
132 CE Bar Kokhba War	Israel: IK. Simon Bar Kokhba: prince. RA.	Judea: Consular Roman province. Quintus Tineius Rufus: legate. Legions and foreign *auxilia*.	
135 CE Roman victory	Syria Palaestina: Consular Roman province. Cnaeus Minicius Faustinus Sextus Iulius Severus: legate. Legions and foreign *auxilia*.		

Bibliography

Adelman, Rebecca A. "'Coffins after Coffins': Screening Wartime Atrocity in the Classroom." Pages 223–45 in *The War of My Generation: Youth Culture and the War on Terror*. Edited by David Kieran. New Brunswick: Rutgers University Press, 2015.

Ahmed, Leila. *Women and Gender in Islam: Historical Roots of a Modern Debate*. New Haven: Yale University Press, 1992.

Ahmed, Sara. *The Cultural Politics of Emotion*. Edinburgh: Edinburgh University Press, 2004.

———. "Declarations of Whiteness: The Non-performativity of Anti-Racism." *borderlands* 3.2 (2004): n.p.

———. "Problematic Proximities: Or Why Critiques of Gay Imperialism Matter." *Feminist Legal Studies* 19 (2011): 119–32.

Akenson, Donald H. *Saint Saul: A Skeleton Key to the Historical Jesus*. Oxford: Oxford University Press, 2000.

———. *Surpassing Wonder: The Invention of the Bible and the Talmuds*. New ed. Chicago: University of Chicago Press, 2001.

Allison, Dale C., Jr. *The Intertextual Jesus: Scripture in Q*. Harrisburg, PA: Trinity Press International, 2000.

———. *Jesus of Nazareth: Millenarian Prophet*. Minneapolis: Fortress, 1998.

Álvarez Valdés, Ariel. "¿Hizo Jesús un milagro a un homosexual?" *Revista Criterio* 2412 (2015): n.p.

Anastasios, Nikolaides. "Πάθος και Ήθος στο έργο του Ντίνου Χριστιανόπουλου" [Pathos and ethos in the work of Dinos Christianopoulos]. PhD diss., Aristotle University of Thessaloniki, 2011.

Andelman, David A. "8 Indicted in 'Boys-for-Sale' Ring." *New York Times*, May 4 1973, p. 44.

Anonymous. "À propos d'un procès." *Le Monde*, 26 January 1977.

———. "Expositie Mader volgens hof geen kinderporno." *De Volkskrant* 31 March 1992, p. 9.

———. "Foto's van Don Mader als pornografisch in beslag genomen." *Nieuwsblad van het Noorden*, 3 June 1994, p. 13.

———. "How Dare You Presume These Are Heterosexual!" *Oregon Liberator* 5.1 (1975?): 6.

———. "James Kirkup." *The Telegraph* 12 May 2009. https://www.telegraph.co.uk/news/obituaries/culture-obituaries/books-obituaries/5314221/James-Kirkup.html.

———. "Kinderfoto's Mader: Kunst of Porno?" *Nieuwsblad van het Noorden* 17 March 1992, p. 19.

———. *Manifesto*. Hollywood: The People's Church-Community of the Love of Christ, 1977(?).

———. "Minister Denies Vice Ring Guilt." *Bridgeport Telegram*, 22 November 1972, p. 10.

———. "Ο Ντίνος Χριστιανόπουλος αρνήθηκε το Μεγάλο Βραβείο Γραμμάτων" [Dinos Christianopoulos refused the Grand State Prize for Literature]. *Naftemporiki*, 23 January 2012. https://tinyurl.com/sbl6705a.

———. "Pedophilia Accusations Haunt Green Politician." *Deutsche Welle*, 4 May 2013.

———. "'Porno-foto's' retour." *Nieuwsblad van het Noorden*, 15 June 1994, p. 13.

———. "Pornograaf vrijgesproken." *Nieuwsblad van het Noorden*, 31 March 1992, p. 7.

———. "Probation Set in Morals Case." *Bridgeport Post*, 16 February 1974, p. 25.

———. *The Rebel, Jesus*. Hollywood: The People's Church Collective—Jesuene Ek-klesia, 1977(?).

———. "Un appel pour la révision du code pénal à propos des relations mineurs-adultes." *Le Monde* 23 May 1977.

———. "United Church of Christ Professor Says Jesus Was Actively Gay." *Gay and Lesbian Times* 805 (2003): 27.

———. "Words of the Centurion." *Integrator: The Newsletter of Integrity Toronto* 93.5 (1993): 1.

Applebaum, Shimon, Benjamin Isaac, and J. H. Landau. "Varia Epigraphica." *SCI* 6 (1981–1982): 98–118.

Armstrong, Elizabeth A. *Forging Gay Identities: Organizing Sexuality in San Francisco, 1950–1994*. Chicago: University of Chicago Press, 2002.

Arnal, William E. "The Cipher 'Judaism' in Contemporary Historical Jesus Scholarship." Pages 24–54 in *Apocalypticism, Anti-Semitism and the*

Historical Jesus: Subtexts in Criticism. Edited by John S. Kloppenborg and John W. Marshall. LNTS 275. London: T&T Clark, 2005.

———. "Jesus as Battleground in a Period of Cultural Complexity." Pages 99–117 in *Jesus beyond Nationalism: Constructing the Historical Jesus in a Period of Cultural Complexity*. Edited by Halvor Moxnes, Ward Blanton, and James G. Crossley. BibleWorld. London: Equinox, 2009.

———. "Making and Re-making the Jesus-Sign: Contemporary Markings on the Body of Christ." Pages 308–19 in *Whose Historical Jesus?* Edited by William E. Arnal and Michel Desjardins. SCJ 7. Waterloo: Wilfrid Laurier University Press, 1997.

———. "The Q Document." Pages 119–54 in *Jewish Christianity Reconsidered: Rethinking Ancient Groups and Texts*. Edited by Matt Jackson-McCabe. Minneapolis: Fortress, 2007.

———. *The Symbolic Jesus: Historical Scholarship, Judaism and the Construction of Contemporary Identity*. Religion in Culture. London: Equinox, 2005.

Attridge, Harold W., Dennis R. MacDonald, and Clare K. Rothschild, eds. *Delightful Acts: New Essays on Canonical and Non-Canonical Acts*. WUNT 1/391. Tübingen: Mohr Siebeck, 2017.

Avalos, Hector. *Slavery, Abolitionism, and the Ethics of Biblical Scholarship*. Bible in the Modern World 38. Sheffield: Sheffield Phoenix, 2011.

Bailey, Marlon M. "Gender/Racial Realness: Theorizing the Gender System in Ballroom Culture." *Feminist Studies* 37 (2011): 365–86.

Barnes, Albert. *An Inquiry into the Scriptural Views of Slavery*. Philadelphia: Perkins & Purves, 1846.

Barnstone, Willis, ed. *Modern European Poetry*. New York: Bantam, 1966.

Bartram, Jerry. "A Sacred Gift from God." *The Globe and Mail*, 11 June 1994, p. D4.

Baudry, André. "Comiques ou martyrs." *Arcadie* 69 (1959): 465–68.

———. "L'homophile catholique." *Arcadie* 142 (1965): 419–26.

Bauer, Raymond A., and Alice H. Bauer. "Day to Day Resistance to Slavery." *Journal of Negro History* 27 (1942): 388–419.

Beckwith, Ryan Teague. "Read Donald Trump's Speech on the Orlando Shooting." *Time*, 13 June 2016. https://tinyurl.com/SBL6705q.

Bennett, James. *Lectures on the History of Christ*. Vol. 1. 2nd ed. London: Westley & Davis, 1828.

Bentham, Jeremy. *Doctrine*. Vol. 3 of *Not Paul, but Jesus*. London: Bentham Project, 2013.

Bérard, Jean, and Nicolas Sallé. "The Ages of Consent: Gay Activism and the Sexuality of Minors in France and Quebec (1970–1980)." *Clio* 42 (2015): 99–124.

Berenice Bárcenas, Karina. "Iglesias para la diversidad sexual: Tácticas de inclusión y visibilización en el campo religioso en México." *Revista Cultura & Religión* 8.1 (2014): 83–108.

Bergler, Siegfried. *Von Kana in Galiläa nach Jerusalem: Literarkritik und Historie im vierten Evangelium*. Institutum Judaicum Delitzschianum Münsteraner Judaistiche Studien 24. Berlin: LIT, 2009.

Bermejo-Rubio, Fernando, and Christopher B. Zeichmann. "Where Were the Romans and What Did They Know? Military and Intelligence Networks as a Probable Factor in Jesus of Nazareth's Fate." *SCI* 38 (2019): 83–115.

Bernal, Martin. *Black Athena: The Afroasiatic Roots of Classical Civilization; The Fabrication of Ancient Greece, 1785–1985*. Vol. 1. New Brunswick: Rutgers University Press, 1987.

Bersani, Leo. "Is the Rectum a Grave?" *AIDS* 43 (1987): 197–222.

Bérubé, Allan. *Coming Out under Fire: The History of Gay Men and Women in World War II*. 20th anniv. ed. Chapel Hill: University of North Carolina Press, 2010.

Blanton, Ward. *Displacing Christian Origins: Philosophy, Secularity, and the New Testament*. Religion and Postmodernism. Chicago: University of Chicago Press, 2007.

Blomberg, Craig A. *Contagious Holiness: Jesus' Meals with Sinners*. New Studies in Biblical Theology 19. Downers Grove: InterVarsity, 2005.

Blyth, Caroline. *Rape Culture, Purity Culture, and Coercive Control in Teen Girl Bibles*. Rape Culture, Religion and the Bible. New York: Routledge, 2021.

Bock, Darrell L. *Luke*. BECNT. 2 vols. Grand Rapids: Baker Academic, 1996.

Boroughs, Rod. "Oscar Wilde's Translation of Petronius: The Story of a Literary Hoax." *English Literature in Translation* 38 (1995): 9–49.

Borrillo, Daniel. *L'homophobie*. Que sais-je? Paris: Presses Universitaires de France, 2001.

Bosia, Michael J., and Meredith L. Weiss. "Political Homophobia in Comparative Perspective." Pages 1–29 in *Global Homophobia: States, Movements, and the Politics of Oppression*. Edited by Meredith L. Weiss and Michael J. Bosia. Urbana: University of Illinois Press, 2013.

Bosman, Frans. "Rechtszaak om naaktfoto's van jongens." *Het Parool*, 13 December 1990, p. 7.

Boswell, John. *Christianity, Social Tolerance, and Homosexuality: Gay People in Western Europe from the Beginning of the Christian Era to the Fourteenth Century*. Chicago: University of Chicago Press, 1980.

———. *Same-Sex Unions in Premodern Europe*. New York: Vintage, 1994.

Botero, Ebel. *Homofilia y homofobia: Estudio sobre la homosexualidad, la bisexualidad y la represión de la conducta homosexual*. Medellín: Lealón, 1980.

Bourdieu, Pierre. *Distinction: A Social Critique of the Judgment of Taste*. Translated by Richard Nice. Cambridge: Harvard University Press, 1987.

Bourg, Julian. *From Revolution to Ethics: May 1968 and Contemporary French Thought*. 2nd ed. Montreal: McGill-Queen's University Press, 2017.

Boxall, Ian. *Matthew through the Centuries*. Wiley Blackwell Bible Commentaries. Oxford: Blackwell, 2019.

Bradley, Keith. "Servus Onerosus: Roman Law and the Troublesome Slave." *Slavery and Abolition* 11 (1990): 135–57.

Brentlinger, Rick. *Gay Christian 101: Spiritual Self-Defense for Gay Christians; What the Bible Really Says about Homosexuality*. Pace: Salient, 2007.

Brink, Laurena Ann. *Soldiers in Luke–Acts: Engaging, Contradicting and Transcending the Stereotypes*. WUNT 2/362. Tübingen: Mohr Siebeck, 2014.

Brisbane, William Henry. *Slaveholding Examined in the Light of the Holy Bible*. Philadelphia: Wyeth, 1847.

Brown, Michael L. *Can You Be Gay and Christian? Responding with Love and Truth to Questions about Homosexuality*. Lake Mary: FrontLine, 2014.

Brown, Scott. "The Question of Motive in the Case against Morton Smith." *JBL* 125 (2006): 351–83.

Brownlow, William Gannaway, and Abram Pryne. *Ought American Slavery to be Perpetuated? A Debate*. Philadelphia: Lippnincott, 1858.

Buck, Erwin. *Studies on Homosexuality and the Church*. [Unknown location]: Evangelical Lutheran Church in Canada, 2001.

Buell, Denise Kimber. "Challenges and Strategies for Speaking about Ethnicity in New Testament Studies." *SEÅ* 49 (2014): 33–51.

Buisson-Fenet, Hélène. *Un sexe problématique: L'église et l'homosexualité masculine en France, 1971–2000*. Culture et Société. Saint-Denis: Presses universitaires de Vincennes, 2004.
Burke, Tony. "Heresy Hunting in the New Millenium." *SR* 39 (2010): 405–20.
———. "Some Reflections on Ariel Sabar's Veritas." *Apocryphicity*, 1 September 2020. https://tinyurl.com/sbl6705j.
Bush, Laura. "Radio Address by Mrs. Bush." *The White House*, 17 November 2001. https://tinyurl.com/SBL6705r.
Butler, Judith. "Merely Cultural." *Social Text* 52–53 (1997): 265–77.
———. "Sexual Inversions." Pages 81–98 in *Foucault and the Critique of Institutions*. Edited by John Caputo and Mark Yount. Greater Philadelphia Philosophy Consortium. University Park: Pennsylvania State University Press, 1993.
———. "Sexual Politics, Torture, and Secular Time." *British Journal of Sociology* 59 (2008): 1–23.
Caballero, Daniel. "¿Sano Jesús al amante homosexual del centurión?" *Semper Reformada Latinoamerica: Teologia para Vivir*, 4 December 2017.
Cadwallader, Alan H. "Surprised by Faith: A Centurion and a Canaanite Query the Limits of Jesus and the Disciples." Pages 85–100 in *Pieces of Ease and Grace: Biblical Essays on Sexuality and Welcome*. Edited by Alan H. Cadwallader. Adelaide: ATF Theology, 2013.
Call, Harold L. "Readers Write." *Mattachine Review* 9.8 (1963): 28–29.
Callahan, Allen Dwight. *The Talking Book: African Americans and the Bible*. New Haven: Yale University Press, 2006.
Campbell, Matthew. "French Philosopher Michel Foucault 'Abused Boys in Tunisia.'" *The Sunday Times*, 28 March 2021.
Cantarella, Eva. *Bisexuality in the Ancient World*. Translated by Cormac Ó Cuilleanáin. 2nd ed. New Haven: Yale University Press, 2003.
Carlier, François. *Études de Pathologie Sociale: Les Deux Prostitutions*. Paris: Dentu, 1887.
Carlson, Stephen C. *The Gospel Hoax: Morton Smith's Invention of Secret Mark*. Waco: Baylor University Press, 2005.
Carter, Warren. *Matthew and the Margins: A Socio-political and Religious Reading*. Bible and Liberation. Maryknoll, NY: Orbis Books, 2000.
Cassidy, Ron. "The Clear Teaching of the Bible on Homosexual Practice: A Response to Ian K. Duffield." *ExpTim* 115 (2004): 298–301.

Cerutti, Franco. "L'homosexualité dans les lettres italiennes contemporaines." *Arcadie* 67–68 (1959): 406–15.
Charles, Ronald. *The Silencing of Slaves in Early Jewish and Christian Texts*. London: Routledge, 2020.
Cheever, George Barrell. *The Guilt of Slavery and the Crime of Slaveholding: Demonstrated from the Hebrew and Greek Scriptures*. Boston: Jewett, 1860.
Cheng, Patrick S. "Domine, Non Sum Dignus: Theological Bullying and the Roman Catholic Church." Pages 164–73 in *Inquiry, Thought, and Expression*. Vol. 2 of *More than a Monologue: Sexual Diversity and the Catholic Church*. Edited by J. Patrick Hornbeck II and Michael A. Norko. Catholic Practice in North America. New York: Fordham University Press, 2014.
Chilton, Bruce D. Review of *Gospel Hoax*, by Stephen Carlson. *Review of Rabbinic Judaism* 10 (2007): 122–28.
Christianopoulos, Dinos. "The Centurion Cornelius." *Gay Sunshine Journal* 47 (1982): 170.
———. "The Centurion Cornelius." Pages 267–68 in *Modern European Poetry*. Edited by Willis Barnstone. Translated by Kimon Friar. New York: Bantam, 1966.
———. "The Centurion Cornelius." Page 673 in *Gay Roots: Twenty Years of Gay Sunshine; An Anthology of Gay History, Sex, Politics, and Culture*. Edited by Winston Leyland. Vol. 1. San Francisco: Gay Sunshine, 1991.
———. Εποχή των ισχνών αγελάδων [Season of the lean cows]. Thessaloniki: Kochlias, 1950.
———. *The Naked Piazza: Poems*. Translated by Nicholas Kostis. Peania: Bilieto, 2000.
———. "The Poetry of Dinos Christianopoulos: A Selection." *Journal of the Hellenic Diaspora* 6 (1979): 68–83.
———. *Poems*. Translated by Nicholas Kostis. Athens: Odysseas, 1995.
———. Ποιήματα *1949–1970* [*Poems 1949–1970*]. Thessaloniki: Diagonos, 1974.
———. "Συνέντευξη" [Interview]. Διαγώνιος 79.11 (1979): 3–4.
Christianson, John E. *Matthew and the Roman Military: How the Gospel Portrays and Negotiates Imperial Power*. Lanham, MD: Lexington/Fortress Academic, 2022.
Clarke, John R. "The Warren Cup and the Contexts for Representations of Male-to-Male Lovemaking in Augustan and Early Julio-Claudian Art." *Art Bulletin* 75 (1993): 275–94.

Clarke, Lewis G., and Milton Clarke. *Narratives of the Sufferings of Lewis and Milton Clarke, Sons of a Soldier of the Revolution, During a Captivity of More Than Twenty Years among the Slaveholders of Kentucky, One of the So-Called Christian States of North America*. Boston: Marsh, 1846.

Clements, E. Anne. *Mothers on the Margin? The Significance of Women in Matthew's Genealogy*. Eugene: Pickwick, 2014.

Cobb, Christy. "Madly in Love: The Motif of Lovesickness in the Acts of Andrew." Pages 27–40 in *Reading and Teaching Ancient Fiction: Jewish, Christian, and Greco-Roman Narratives*. Edited by Sara Raup Johnson, Rubén Dupertuis, and Christine R. Shea. WGRWSup 10. Atlanta: SBL Press, 2018.

Cohen, Edward E. "Free and Unfree Sexual Work: An Economic Analysis of Athenian Prostitution " Pages 95–124 in *Prostitutes and Courtesans in the Ancient World*. Edited by Christopher A. Faraone and Laura K. McClure. Madison: University of Wisconsin Press, 2006.

Connell, Martin F. "Who Was That Naked Man?" *Gay and Lesbian Review Worldwide* 4.2 (1997): 44–45.

Corriveau, Patrice. *Judging Homosexuals: A History of Gay Persecution in Quebec and France*. Translated by Käthe Roth. Sexuality Studies. Vancouver: University of British Columbia Press, 2011.

Cotter, Wendy. *The Christ of the Miracle Stories: Portrait through Encounter*. Grand Rapids: Baker Academic, 2010.

Crossan, John Dominic. *The Birth of Christianity: Discovering What Happened in the Years Immediately after the Execution of Jesus*. San Francisco: HarperSanFrancisco, 1998.

———. *Four Other Gospels: Shadows on the Contours of Canon*. Sonoma, CA: Polebridge, 1992.

———. "Historical Jesus as Risen Lord." Pages 1–47 in *The Jesus Controversy: Perspectives in Conflict*. Edited by John Dominic Crossan, Luke Timothy Johnson, and Werner H. Kelber. Harrisburg, PA: Trinity Press International, 1999.

———. *A Long Way from Tipperary: What a Former Monk Discovered in His Search for the Truth*. San Francisco: HarperOne, 2000.

Crossley, James G. *Jesus in an Age of Neoliberalism: Quests, Scholarship and Ideology*. BibleWorld. London: Equinox, 2012.

———. *Jesus in an Age of Terror: Scholarly Projects for a New American Century*. BibleWorld. London: Equinox, 2008.

———. "Jesus the Jew since 1967." Pages 111–29 in *Jesus beyond Nationalism: Constructing the Historical Jesus in a Period of Cultural Complexity*. Edited by Halvor Moxnes, Ward Blanton, and James G. Crossley. BibleWorld. London: Equinox, 2009.
Crowther, R. H. "Sodom: A Homosexual Viewpoint." *ONE Magazine* 3.1 (1955): 24–28.
Cvetkovich, Ann. *An Archive of Feelings: Trauma, Sexuality, and Lesbian Public Cultures*. Series Q. Durham, NC: Duke University Press, 2003.
D'Angelo, Mary Rose. "Women in Luke-Acts: A Redactional View." *JBL* 109 (1990): 441–61.
Dallas, Joe. *The Gay Gospel? How Pro-Gay Advocates Misread the Bible*. Eugene: Harvest House, 2007.
———. *Speaking of Homosexuality: Discussing the Issues with Kindness and Clarity*. Grand Rapids: Baker, 2016.
Danker, Frederick W. *Jesus and the New Age: A Commentary on St. Luke's Gospel*. Rev. and exp. ed. Philadelphia: Fortress, 1988.
Davidson, Alex. *The Returns of Love: Letters of a Christian Homosexual*. London: InterVarsity, 1970.
Davie, Martin. *The Church of England Evangelical Council: Studies on the Bible and Same-Sex Relationships Since 2003*. West Knapton: Gilead, 2015.
Deamer, Geoffrey. "The Dead Turk." Page 166 in *Lads: Love Poetry from the Trenches*. Edited by Martin Taylor. London: Constable, 1989.
Den Dulk, Matthijs. "Aquila and Apollos: Acts 18 in Light of Ancient Ethnic Stereotypes." *JBL* 139 (2020): 177–89.
Denton, Donald L. *Historiography and Hermeneutics in Jesus Studies: An Examination of the Work of John Dominic Crossan and Ben F. Meyer*. LNTS 262. London: T&T Clark, 2004.
Derrett, J. Duncan M. *Glimpses of the Legal and Social Presuppositions of the Authors*. Vol. 1 of *Studies in the New Testament*. Biblical Studies 1. Leiden: Brill, 1977.
———. "Law in the New Testament: The Syro-Phoenician Woman and the Centurion of Capernaum." *NovT* 15 (1973): 161–86.
Dinshaw, Carolyn. *Getting Medieval: Sexualities and Communities, Pre- and Postmodern*. Series Q. Durham, NC: Duke University Press, 1999.
———. *How Soon Is Now? Medieval Texts, Amateur Readers, and the Queerness of Time*. Durham, NC: Duke University Press, 2012.

Djurslev, Christian Thrue. *Alexander the Great in the Early Christian Tradition: Classical Reception and Patristic Literature*. Bloomsbury Studies in Classical Reception. London: Bloomsbury Academic, 2020.

Douglass, Frederick. "Speech in Boston, Massachusetts, February 8, 1855." Pages 5–14 in vol. 3 of *The Frederick Douglass Papers, Series One: Speeches, Debates, and Interviews*. Edited by John W. Blassingame. New Haven: Yale University Press, 1985.

Doundoulakis, Emmanouil. "Saints and Sanctity in the Poems of Greek 'Unconventional' Poets during the Twentieth and Twenty-First Century: The Cases of C. P. Cavafy and D. Christianopoulos." Pages 12–18 in *The 2015 West East Institute International Academic Conference Proceedings: Prague*. Prague: West East Institute, 2015.

Dover, Kenneth James. *Greek Homosexuality*. Cambridge: Harvard University Press, 1978.

Dowling, Elizabeth V. "Luke–Acts: Good News for Slaves?" *Pacifica* 24 (2011): 123–40.

Drake, Susanna. *Slandering the Jew: Sexuality and Difference in Early Christian Texts*. Divinations. Philadelphia: University of Pennsylvania Press, 2013.

Dube, Musa W. *Postcolonial Feminist Interpretation of the Bible*. Saint Louis: Chalice, 2000.

Duffield, Ian K. "The Clear Teaching of the Bible? A Contribution to the Debate about Homosexuality and the Church of England." *ExpTim* 115 (2004): 109–15.

Duggan, Lisa. "The New Homonormativity: The Sexual Politics of Neoliberalism." Pages 175–94 in *Materializing Democracy: Toward a Revitalized Cultural Politics*. Edited by Russ Castronovo and Dana D. Nelson. New Americanists. Durham, NC: Duke University Press, 2002.

Durand, Mickaël. "From Tension to Reconciliation: A Look at the History and Rituals of the French Organization David et Jonathan." Pages 155–80 in *Diversidad sexual y sistemas religiosos: Diálogos trasnacionales en el mundo contemporáneo*. Edited by Martín Jaime Ballero. Lima: Centro de la Mujer Peruana Flora Tristán, 2017.

Eaves, Thomas F., Sr. "Eaves' Third Negative." Pages 113–20 in *A Debate on Homosexuality*. Edited by Thomas F. Eaves Sr. and Paul R. Johnson. Algood: T&P Bookshelf, 1981.

———. "Eaves' Fourth Negative." Pages 130–37 in *A Debate on Homosexuality*. Edited by Thomas F. Eaves Sr. and Paul R. Johnson. Algood: T&P Bookshelf, 1981.

Eck, Marcel. *Sodome: Essai sur l'homosexualité*. Paris: Fayard, 1966.
Edgar, Campbell Cowan. "Selected Papyri from the Archives of Zenon (Nos 73–76)." *ASAE* 23 (1923): 73–98.
Edmondson, Jonathan. "Slavery and the Roman Family." Pages 337–61 in *The Ancient Mediterranean World*. Vol. 1 of *The Cambridge World History of Slavery*. Edited by Keith Bradley and Paul Cartledge. Cambridge: Cambridge University Press, 2011.
Egger, John A. "A Most Troublesome Text: Galatians 4:21–5:1 in the History of Interpretation." PhD diss., University of St. Michael's College, 2015.
Eng, David L. *The Feeling of Kinship: Queer Liberalism and the Racialization of Intimacy*. Durham, NC: Duke University Press, 2010.
England, Frank. "The Centurion (Matthew 8:9) and the Bishop: On the Nature of Authority." *Journal of Theology for Southern Africa* 160 (2018): 58–74.
Enroth, Ronald M., and Gerald E. Jamison. *The Gay Church*. Grand Rapids: Eerdmans, 1974.
Eribon, Didier. *Michel Foucault et ses contemporains*. Paris: Fayard, 1994.
Erlich, Adi, Nachum Sagiv, and Dov Gera. "The Philinos Cave in the Beth Guvrin Area." *IEJ* 66 (2016): 55–69.
Evans, Craig A. *Matthew*. New Cambridge Bible Commentary. Cambridge: Cambridge University Press, 2012.
Falsch, J. "Gay Love." *Wisconsin Light* 10.22 (1997): 4.
Faris, Donald L. *Trojan Horse: The Homosexual Ideology and the Christian Church*. Burlington: Welch, 1989.
Fell, Gordon. "Is It Better to Do What's Right or What's Wrong in Our Own Eyes?" *The Journal: News of the Churches of God* 157 (2013): 3, 7.
Fischel, Joseph J. *Sex Harm in the Age of Consent*. Minneapolis: University of Minnesota Press, 2016.
Flemming, Rebecca. "*Quae Corpore Quaestum Facit*: The Sexual Economy of Female Prostitution in the Roman Empire." *JRS* 89 (1999): 38–61.
Flessen, Bonnie J. *An Exemplary Man: Cornelius and Characterization in Acts 10*. Eugene: Pickwick, 2011.
Fletcher, John. *Studies on Slavery: In Easy Lessons*. Natchez: Warner, 1852.
Flournoy, John J. *A Reply to a Pamphlet, Entitled "Bondage, a Moral Institution Sanctioned by the Scriptures and the Saviour, &c. &c." So Far as It Attacks the Principles of Expulsion with No Defence, However, of Abolitionism*. Atlanta: [unknown publisher], 1838.

Forward, Martin. "A Pilgrimage of Grace: The Journey Motif in Luke-Acts." Pages 62–75 in *A Man of Many Parts: Essays in Honor of John Westerdale Bowker on the Occasion of His Eightieth Birthday*. Edited by Eugene E. Lemcio. Eugene: Pickwick, 2015.
Foucault, Michel. *The History of Sexuality: An Introduction*. Translated by Robert Hurley. New York: Pantheon, 1978.
———. "Sexual Morality and the Law." Pages 271–85 in *Politics, Philosophy, Culture: Interviews and Other Writings 1977–1984*. Edited by Lawrence D. Kritzman. Translated by Alan Sheridan. London: Routledge, 1988.
———. *"Society Must Be Defended": Lectures at Collège de France 1975–76*. Translated by David Macey. New York: Picador, 2003.
———. "Truth and Power." Pages 111–33 in vol. 3 of *Power: Essential Works of Foucault 1954–1984*. Edited by James D. Faubion. Translated by Robert Hurley. New York: New Press, 2000.
Fredrick, David. "Reading Broken Skin: Violence in Roman Elegy." Pages 172–93 in *Roman Sexualities*. Edited by Judith P. Hallett and Marilyn B. Skinner. Princeton: Princeton University Press, 1997.
Friar, Kimon. "The Poetry of Dinos Christianopoulos: An Introduction." *Journal of the Hellenic Diaspora* 6 (1979): 59–67.
Friedl, Raimud. *Der Konkubinat im kaiserzeitlichen Rom: Von Augustus bis Septimius Severus*. Historia Einzelschriften 98. Stuttgart: Steiner, 1996.
Füller, Christian. "Danys Phantasien und Träume." *Frankfurter Allgemeine Zeitung*, 29 April 2013.
Funk, Robert W. *Honest to Jesus: Jesus for a New Millenium*. San Francisco: HarperSanFrancisco, 1996.
Gadamer, Hans-Georg. "The Hermeneutics of Suspicion." *Man and World* 17 (1984): 313–23.
Gagnon, Robert A. J. *The Bible and Homosexual Practice: Texts and Hermeneutics*. Nashville: Abingdon, 2001.
———. "Did Jesus Approve of a Homosexual Couple in the Story of the Centurion at Capernaum?" April 24 2007. http://www.robgagnon.net/articles/homosexCenturionStory.pdf.
———. "Notes to Gagnon's Essay in the Gagnon-Via *Two Views* Book." 2 October 2003. http://www.robgagnon.net/2Views/HomoViaResp NotesRev.pdf.
Gamson, Joshua. "Messages of Exclusion: Gender, Movements, and Symbolic Boundaries." *Gender and Society* 11 (1997): 178–99.
Gelardini, Gabriella. "Cross-Dressing Zealots in Josephus's War Account." Pages 197–217 in *Gender and Second Temple Judaism*. Edited by Kathy

Ehrensperger and Shayna Sheinfeld. Lanham, MD: Lexington/Fortress Academic, 2019.

Giesen, Heinz. "Jesus und die Nichtjuden: Aufgezeigt an der Überlieferung der Wundererzählung vom Knecht des Hauptmanns von Kafarnaum (Lk 7,1–10 par. Mt 8,5–13)." Pages 51–69 in *Erinnerung an Jesus: Kontinuität und Diskontinuität in der neuttestamentlichen Überlieferung: Festschrift für Rudolf Hoppe zum 65. Geburtstag*. Edited by Ulrich Busse, Michael Reichardt, and Michael Theobald. BBB 166. Göttingen: Bonn University Press, 2011.

Gillabert, Émile. *Saint Paul: Ou Le Colosse aux pieds d'argile*. Marsanne: Métanoïa, 1974.

Glancy, Jennifer A. *Corporal Knowledge: Early Christian Bodies*. Oxford: Oxford University Press, 2010.

———. "Obstacles to Slaves' Participation in the Corinthian Church." *JBL* 117 (1998): 481–501.

———. "The Sexual Use of Slaves: A Response to Kyle Harper on Jewish and Christian *Porneia*." *JBL* 134 (2015): 215–29.

———. "Slavery and Sexual Availability." Pages 627–44 in *The Oxford Handbook of New Testament, Gender, and Sexuality*. Edited by Benjamin H. Dunning. Oxford: Oxford University Press, 2019.

———. *Slavery in Early Christianity*. Oxford: Oxford University Press, 2002.

Goodacre, Mark S. "Fatigue in the Gospels." *NTS* 44 (1998): 45–58.

Goss, Robert E. "Luke." Pages 526–47 in *The Queer Bible Commentary*. Edited by Deryn Guest, Robert E. Goss, Mona West, and Thomas Bohache. London: SCM, 2006.

———. *Queering Christ: Beyond Jesus Acted Up*. New York: Pilgrim, 2002.

Goss, Robert E. and Mona West. Introduction to *Take Back the Word: A Queer Reading of the Bible*. Edited by Robert E. Goss and Mona West. Cleveland: Pilgrim, 2000.

Gowler, David B. "Text, Culture and Ideology in Luke 7:1–10: A Dialogic Reading." Pages 89–125 in *Fabrics of Discourse: Essays in Honor of Vernon K. Robbins*. Edited by David B. Gowler, L. Gregory Bloomquist, and Duane F. Watson. Harrisburg, PA: Trinity Press International, 2003.

Gray-Fow, Michael. "Pederasty, the Scantinian Law and the Roman Army." *Journal of Psychohistory* 13 (1986): 449–60.

Graybill, Rhiannon. *Texts after Terror: Rape, Sexual Violence, and the Hebrew Bible*. Oxford: Oxford University Press, 2021.

Grosvenor, Cyrus P. *Slavery vs. the Bible: A Correspondence Between the General Conference of Maine and the Presbytery of Tombecbee, Mississippi*. Worcester: Spooner & Howland, 1840.

Gunderson, Jaimie. "Inscribing Pompeii: A Reevaluation of the Jewish Epigraphic Data." MA thesis, University of Kansas, 2013.

Gunther, Scott. *The Elastic Closet: A History of Homosexuality in France, 1942–Present*. Basingstoke: Palgrave Macmillan, 2009.

Gunthorp, Dale. *I'm Gay and God Loves Me: What the Bible Says*. London: Metropolitan Community Church of East London, 2003.

Gyburc-Hall, Larion. "Legende." *Der Kreis* 31.4 (1963): 14–22.

Hacking, Ian. *The Social Construction of What?* Cambridge: Harvard University Press, 1999.

Halberstam, Jack. *In a Queer Time and Place: Transgender Bodies, Subcultural Lives*. Sexual Cultures. New York: New York University Press, 2006.

———. *The Queer Art of Failure*. John Hope Franklin Center. Durham, NC: Duke University Press, 2011.

Haller, Tobias Stanislas. *Reasonable and Holy: Engaging Same-Sexuality*. New York: Seabury, 2009.

Halperin, David M. *One Hundred Years of Homosexuality and Other Essays on Greek Love*. New York: Routledge, 1990.

Hanks, Tom. "Matthew and Mary of Magdala: Good News for Sex Workers." Pages 185–95 in *Take Back the Word: A Queer Reading of the Bible*. Edited by Robert E. Goss and Mona West. Cleveland: Pilgrim, 2000.

———. *The Subversive Gospel: A New Testament Commentary of Liberation*. Translated by John P. Doner. Cleveland: Pilgrim, 2000.

Harding, James E. *The Love of David and Jonathan: Ideology, Text, Reception*. BibleWorld. London: Routledge, 2016.

Haritaworn, Jin, with Tamsila Tauqir and Esra Erdem. "Gay Imperialism: Gender and Sexuality Discourse in the 'War on Terror.'" Pages 71–95 in *Out of Place: Interrogating Silences in Queerness/Raciality*. Edited by Adi Kuntsman and Esperanza Miyake. York: Raw Nerve, 2008.

Harper, Kyle. *From Shame to Sin: The Christian Transformation of Sexual Morality in Late Antiquity*. Cambridge: Harvard University Press, 2013.

———. "*Porneia*: The Making of Christian Sexual Norms." *JBL* 131 (2012): 363–83.

———. *Slavery in the Late Roman World, AD 275–425*. Cambridge: Cambridge University Press, 2011.

Harrill, J. Albert. "The Use of the New Testament in the American Slave Controversy: A Case History in the Hermeneutical Tension between Biblical Criticism and Christian Moral Debate." *Religion and American Culture* 10 (2000): 149–86.

———. *Slaves in the New Testament: Literary, Social, and Moral Dimensions*. Minneapolis: Fortress, 2006.

Harvey, Keith. *Intercultural Movements: American Gay in French Translation*. Encounters 3. London: Routledge, 2014.

Hedrick, Charles W. "The Secret Gospel of Mark: Stalemate in the Academy." *JECS* 11 (2003): 133–45.

Heimsoth, Karl-Günther. "Freundesliebe oder Homosexualität: Ein Versuch einer anregenden und scheidenden Klarstellung." *Der Eigene* 10 (1925): 415–25.

———. "Hetero- und Homophilie: Eine neuorientierende An- und Einordnung der Erscheinungsbilder, der 'Homosexualität' und der 'Inversion' in Berücksichtigung der sogenannten 'normalen Freundschaft' auf Grund der zwei verschiedenen erotischen Anziehungsgesetze und der bisexuellen Grundeinstellung des Mannes." PhD diss., Universität Rostock, 1924.

Helminiak, Daniel. "Jesus and the Centurion's Slave Boy." *White Crane Journal* 47 (2000): 7–8.

———. *Lo que la Biblia realmente dice sobre la homosexualidad*. Translated by Patricio Camacho Posada. 2nd ed. Madrid: Egales, 2012.

———. "Scripture, Sexual Ethics, and the Nature of Christianity." *Pastoral Psychology* 47 (1999): 261–71.

Heron, Alastair, ed. *Towards a Quaker View of Sex*. London: Friends Home Service Committee, 1963.

Heszer, Catherine. *Jewish Slavery in Antiquity*. Oxford: Oxford University Press, 2005.

Higginbotham, Evelyn Brooks. *Righteous Discontent: The Women's Movement in the Black Baptist Church, 1880–1920*. Cambridge: Harvard University Press, 1993.

Hocquenghem, Guy. *Le gay voyage: Guide et regard homosexuels sur les grandes métropoles*. Paris: Michel, 1980.

Hoke, James. "'Behold, the Lord's Whore'? Slavery, Prostitution, and Luke 1:38." *BibInt* 26 (2018): 43–67.

Hopkins, Keith. "Novel Evidence for Roman Slavery." *Past and Present* 138 (1993): 3–27.

Hopper, George S. E. *Reluctant Journey: A Pilgrimage of Faith from Homophobia to Christian Love.* Leeds: University Printing Services, 1997.

Horner, Tom M. "The Centurion's Servant." *Insight* 2.3 (1978): 9.

———. *Homosexuality in Biblical Times: An Annotated Bibliography.* [Location unknown]: Self-published, 1977.

———. "Jesus." Pages 635–39 in *Encyclopedia of Homosexuality.* Edited by Wayne R. Dynes. New York: Garland, 1990.

———. *Jonathan Loved David: Homosexuality in Biblical Times.* Philadelphia: Westminster John Knox, 1978.

———. *Sex in the Bible.* Rutland: Tuttle, 1974.

Huber, Lynn R. "Interpreting as Queer or Interpreting Queerly?" Pages 311–321 in *Bodies on the Verge: Queering the Pauline Epistles.* Edited by Joseph A. Marchal. SemeiaSt 93. Atlanta: SBL Press, 2019.

Hughes, Aaron W. *From Seminary to University: An Institutional History of the Study of Religion in Canada.* Toronto: University of Toronto Press, 2020.

Hunt, Peter. *Ancient Greek and Roman Slavery.* London: Wiley Blackwell, 2018.

Independent Gay Forum. "About IGF CultureWatch," 1998. *Independent Gay Forum.* https://tinyurl.com/sbl6705c.

Isaac, Benjamin. *The Invention of Racism in Classical Antiquity.* Princeton: Princeton University Press, 2004.

———. *The Limits of Empire: The Roman Army in the East.* Rev. ed. Oxford: Clarendon, 1992.

Iturra, Carlos. *El discípulo amado y otros paisajes masculinos.* Narrativas. Santiago de Chile: Catalonia, 2012.

Jablonski, Olivier. "The Birth of a French Homosexual Press in the 1950s." *JH* 41.3–4 (2001): 233–48.

Jackson, Julian. *Living in Arcadia: Homosexuality, Politics, and Morality in France from Liberation to AIDS.* Chicago: University of Chicago Press, 2009.

Jakobsen, Janet R., and Ann Pellegrini. *Love the Sin: Sexual Regulation and the Limits of Religious Tolerance.* Sexual Cultures. New York: New York University Press, 2003.

James, Simon. "Engendering Change in Our Understanding of the Structure of Roman Military Communities." *Archaeological Dialogues* 13 (2006): 31–36.

January–June 1948. Vol. 2.1a.1 of *Catalog of Copyright Entries.* 3rd series. Washington, DC: Copyright Office, 1948.
Jaworski, Tlumaczyl Jerzy. Review of *What the Bible Really Says about Homosexuality,* by Daniel Helminiak. *Tęczowe Prymierzeinformacyjny* 1 (1996): 5–7.
Jeffery, Peter. *The Secret Gospel of Mark Unveiled: Imagined Rituals of Sex, Death, and Madness in a Biblical Forgery.* New Haven: Yale University Press, 2007.
Jennings, Theodore W., Jr. *An Ethic of Queer Sex: Principles and Improvisations.* Chicago: Exploration, 2013.
———. *The Man Jesus Loved: Homoerotic Narratives from the New Testament.* Cleveland: Pilgrim, 2003.
Jennings, Theodore W., Jr., and Tat-siong Benny Liew. "Mistaken Identities but Model Faith: Rereading the Centurion, the Chap, and the Christ in Matthew 8:5–13." *JBL* 123 (2004): 467–94.
John, Jeffrey. *The Meaning in the Miracles.* Norwich: Canterbury, 2001.
Johnson, Jeff. "Pastor Jeff Johnson." *Voice and Vision: The Newsletter of the Lutheran Lesbian and Gay Ministry* 4.3 (1992): 2.
Johnson, Paul R. "Affirmative Rejoinder." Pages 138–39 in *A Debate on Homosexuality.* Edited by Thomas F. Eaves Sr. and Paul R. Johnson. Algood: T&P Bookshelf, 1981.
———. "Johnson's Fourth Affirmative." Pages 121–29 in *A Debate on Homosexuality.* Edited by Thomas F. Eaves Sr. and Paul R. Johnson. Algood: T&P Bookshelf, 1981.
———. "Johnson's Third Affirmative." Pages 105–12 in *A Debate on Homosexuality.* Edited by Thomas F. Eaves Sr. and Paul R. Johnson. Algood: T&P Bookshelf, 1981.
Johnson, Steven R., ed. *Q 7:1–10: The Centurion's Faith in Jesus' Word.* Documenta Q. Leuven: Peeters, 2002.
Johnson, William Stacy. "Finding Our Way Forward." *SJT* 62 (2009): 81–90.
Jones, Charles Colcock. *Tenth Annual Report of the Association for the Religious Instruction of the Negroes in Liberty County, Georgia.* Savanna: Purse, 1845.
Jones, John Richter. *Slavery Sanctioned by the Bible: A Tract for Northern Christians.* Philadelphia: Lippincott, 1861.
Jordan, Deborah. *Centenary of Queensland Women's Suffrage 2005.* Brisbane: University of Queensland Press, 2005.
Jordan, Mark D. *Recruiting Young Love: How Christians Talk about Homosexuality.* Chicago: University of Chicago Press, 2011.

Josephus. *16–17*. Vol. 7 of *Jewish Antiquities*. Translated by Ralph Marcus. LCL 410. Cambridge: Harvard University Press, 1963.

Joshel, Sandra R., and Sheila Murnaghan. "Introduction: Differential Equations." Pages 1–21 in *Women and Slaves in Greco-Roman Culture: Differential Equations*. Edited by Sandra R. Joshel and Sheila Murnaghan. London: Routledge, 1998.

Junior, Nyasha. *Reimagining Hagar: Blackness and Bible*. Biblical Refigurations. Oxford: Oxford University Press, 2019.

Kafer, Alison. *Feminist, Queer, Crip*. Bloomington: Indiana University Press, 2013.

Kasher, Aryeh. *King Herod: A Persecuted Persecutor; A Case Study in Psychohistory and Psychobiography*. Translated by Karen Gold. SJ 36. Berlin: De Gruyter, 2007.

Katzoff, Ranon. *On Jews in the Roman World: Collected Studies*. TSAJ 179. Tübingen: Mohr Siebeck, 2019.

Kaye, Richard A. "Losing His Religion: Saint Sebastian as Contemporary Gay Martyr." Pages 86–105 in *Outlooks: Lesbian and Gay Sexualities and Visual Cultures*. Edited by Peter Horne and Reina Lewis. New York: Routledge, 1996.

Keating, Christine (Cricket). "Conclusion: On the Interplay of State Homophobia and Homoprotectionism." Pages 246–54 in *Global Homophobia: States, Movements, and the Politics of Oppression*. Edited by Meredith L. Weiss and Michael J. Bosia. Urbana: University of Illinois Press, 2013.

Keener, Craig S. *The Historical Jesus of the Gospels*. Grand Rapids: Eerdmans, 2009.

Keitt, Laurence M. "The Origins of Slavery." Pages 404–9 in *Appendix to the Congressional Globe Containing Speeches, Important State Papers, Laws, etc. of the First Session Thirty-Fifth Congress*. Edited by John C. Rives. Washington, DC: Rives, 1858.

Kennedy, Hubert. *The Ideal Gay Man: The Story of Der Kreis*. Binghamton: Haworth, 1999.

Kepner, James, Jr. *Becoming a People: A Four Thousand Year Gay and Lesbian Chronology*. 3rd ed. Hollywood: National Gay Archives, 1996.

———. *A Brief Chronology of Gay/Lesbian History from Earliest Times*. Hollywood: National Gay Archives, 1984(?).

———. *Gay Spirit: The Cord of Many Strands*. Hollywood: International Gay & Lesbian Archives, 1987(?).

———. "The Oldest Gay Stories in the World." *In Touch* 2.3 (1974): 61–65.

———. "World Religions and the Homophile: An Introduction." *ONE Institute Quarterly* 7 (1959): 124–32.

Kim, Jae-Hyun. "백부장의 πίστις: Q 복음서의 가버나움 백부장에 관한 연구" ["Centurion's πίστις: a study on the Capernaum centurion of the Q gospels"]. 신학사상 [*Theological Thought*] 182 (2018): 193–221.

Kirchick, James. "The Struggle for Gay Rights Is Over." *The Atlantic*, 28 June 2019. https://tinyurl.com/sbl6705e.

Kirkup, James. "The Love That Dares to Speak Its Name." *Gay News* 96 (1976): 26.

Kloppenborg, John S. *Excavating Q: The History and Setting of the Sayings Gospel*. Edinburgh: T&T Clark, 2000.

Koepnick, Erik. "The Historical Jesus and the Slave of the Centurion: How the Themes of Slavery, Sexuality, and Military Service Intersect in Matthew 8:5–13." *Oshkosh Scholar* 3 (2008): 82–92.

Kolendo, Jerzy. "L'esclavage et la vie sexuelle des hommes libres à Rome." *Index* 10 (1981): 288–97.

Kotrosits, Maia. *The Lives of Objects: Material Culture, Experience, and the Real in the History of Early Christianity*. Class 200. Chicago: University of Chicago Press, 2020.

———. "Penetration and Its Discontents: Greco-Roman Sexuality, the *Acts of Paul and Thecla*, and Theorizing Eros without the Wound." *JHSex* 27 (2018): 343–66.

Kręcidło, Janusz. "Obraz Jezusa w Ewangeliach kanonicznych a kwestia homoseksualna." *Verbum Vitae* 39 (2021): 201–22.

Krutzsch, Brett. *Dying to Be Normal: Gay Martyrs and the Transformation of American Sexual Politics*. Oxford: Oxford University Press, 2019.

Kunkel, Fritz. *Creation Continues: A Psychological Interpretation of Matthew*. Mahwah: Paulist, 1989.

Laes, Christian. "Desperately Different? *Delicia* Children in the Roman Household." Pages 298–324 in *Early Christian Families in Context: An Interdisciplinary Dialogue*. Edited by David L. Balch and Carolyn Osiek. Grand Rapids: Eerdmans, 2003.

Lambert, James. Review of *Sexual Experience*, by Parker Rossman. *Gay Christian* 41 (1986): 31.

Lawrence, Raymond J., Jr. "The Fish: A Lost Symbol of Sexual Liberation?" *Journal of Religion and Health* 30 (1991): 311–19.

———. *The Poisoning of Eros: Sexual Values in Conflict*. New York: Augustine Moore, 1989.

Lear, Andrew. "Ancient Pederasty: An Introduction." Pages 102–27 in *A Companion to Greek and Roman Sexualities*. Edited by Thomas K. Hubbard. Blackwell Companions to the Ancient World. London: Wiley & Sons, 2013.

Levin-Richardson, Sarah. "*Fututa sum hic*: Female Subjectivity and Agency in Pompeian Sexual Graffiti." *Classical Journal* 108 (2013): 319–45.

Levine, Amy-Jill, and Ben Witherington III. *The Gospel of Luke*. New Cambridge Bible Commentary. Cambridge: Cambridge University Press, 2018.

Lewis, Holly. *The Politics of Everybody: Feminism, Queer Theory, and Marxism at the Intersection*. London: Zed, 2016.

Liew, Tat-siong Benny. "When Margins Become Common Ground: Questions of and for Biblical Studies." Pages 40–55 in *Still at the Margins: Biblical Scholarship Fifteen Years after the* Voices from the Margin. Edited by R. S. Sugirtharajah. London: T&T Clark, 2008.

Lincoln, Bruce. "Theses on Method." *MTSR* 8 (1996): 225–27.

———. *Theorizing Myth: Narrative, Ideology, and Scholarship*. Chicago: University of Chicago Press, 1999.

Lings, K. Renato. *Holy Censorship or Mistranslation? Love, Gender and Sexuality in the Bible*. Noida: HarperCollins India, 2021.

Little, Paul D. *Who Stole Jesus?* Atlanta: Romans Road, 2019.

Loader, William. *The Dead Sea Scrolls on Sexuality: Attitudes towards Sexuality in Sectarian and Related Literature at Qumran*. Grand Rapids: Eerdmans, 2009.

———. *Enoch, Levi, and Jubilees on Sexuality: Attitudes towards Sexuality in the Early Enoch Literature, the Aramaic Levi Document, and the Book of Jubilees*. Grand Rapids: Eerdmans, 2007.

———. *The New Testament on Sexuality*. Grand Rapids: Eerdmans, 2012.

———. "'Not as the Gentiles': Sexual Issues at the Interface between Judaism and Its Greco-Roman World." *Religions* 9 (2018): 1–22.

———. *Philo, Josephus, and the Testaments on Sexuality: Attitudes towards Sexuality in the Writings of Philo and Josephus and in the Testaments of the Twelve Patriarchs*. Grand Rapids: Eerdmans, 2011.

———. *The Pseudepigrapha on Sexuality: Attitudes towards Sexuality in Apocalypses, Testaments, Legends, Wisdom, and Related Literature*. Grand Rapids: Eerdmans, 2011.

———. "The Senate Inquiry into the Marriage Equality Amendment Bill 2010." 1 April 2012.

———. *Sexuality in the New Testament: Understanding the Key Texts*. Louisville: Westminster John Knox, 2010.
Loman, Pasi. "No Woman No War: Women's Participation in Ancient Greek Warfare." *G&R* 51 (2004): 34–54.
Long, Ronald E. "Introduction: Disarming Biblically Based Queer Bashing." Pages 1–18 in *The Queer Bible Commentary*. Edited by Deryn Guest, Robert E. Goss, Mona West, and Thomas Bohache. London: SCM, 2006.
Lyons, Michael, and Jeremy Willard. "Body of Christ: Bible Studies for Boys." *Fab* 466 (2013): 12.
MacDonald, Dennis R. *Christianizing Homer: The Odyssey, Plato, and The Acts of Andrew*. New York: Oxford University Press, 1994.
———. *Luke and Vergil: Imitations of Classical Greek Literature*. New Testament and Greek Literature 2. Lanham, MD: Rowman & Littlefield, 2015.
Macey, David. *The Lives of Michel Foucault: A Biography*. New York: Pantheon, 1994.
Mader, Donald H. "The *Entimos Pais* of Matthew 8:5–13 and Luke 7:1–10." *Paidika* 1.1 (1987): 27–39.
———. "The *Entimos Pais* of Matthew 8:5–13 and Luke 7:1–10." Pages 223–35 in *Homosexuality and Religion and Philosophy*. Edited by Wayne R. Dynes and Stephen Donaldson. Studies in Homosexuality 12. New York: Garland, 1992.
———. "To the Editor." *Gay and Lesbian Review Worldwide* 15.1 (2008): 6.
Mahmood, Saba. *Politics of Piety: The Islamic Revival and the Feminist Subject*. Rev. ed. Princeton: Princeton University Press, 2012.
Mahomed, Nadeem, and Farid Esack. "The Normal and Abnormal: On the Politics of Being Muslim and Relating to Same-Sex Sexuality." *JAAR* 85 (2017): 224–43.
Manwell, Elizabeth. "Gender and Masculinity." Pages 111–28 in *A Companion to Catullus*. Edited by Marilyn B. Skinner. Malden, MA: Blackwell, 2007.
Maranger, Keith. "Annual Richmond Dignity/Integrity Banquet Features Evangelical Feminist." *Our Own Community Press* 13.6 (1989): 2–3.
Marchal, Joseph A. *Appalling Bodies: Queer Figures before and after Paul's Letters*. Oxford: Oxford University Press, 2020.
———. "Bottoming Out: Rethinking the Reception of Receptivity." Pages 209–38 in *Bodies on the Verge: Queering Pauline Epistles and Interpre-*

tations. Edited by Joseph A. Marchal. SemeiaSt 93. Atlanta: SBL Press, 2019.

———. "LGBTIQ Strategies of Interpretation." Pages 177–96 in *The Oxford Handbook of New Testament, Gender, and Sexuality*. Edited by Benjamin H. Dunning. Oxford: Oxford University Press, 2019.

———. "Pinkwashing Paul, Excepting Jesus: The Politics of Intersectionality, Identification, and Respectability." Pages 432–53 in *The Bible and Feminism: Remapping the Field*. Edited by Yvonne Sherwood. Oxford: Oxford University Press, 2017.

———. "The Usefulness of an Onesimus: The Sexual Use of Slaves and Paul's Letter to Philemon." *JBL* 130 (2011): 749–70.

Marohl, Matthew J. *Joseph's Dilemma: "Honor Killing" in the Birth Narrative of Matthew* Eugene: Cascade, 2008.

Martel, Frédéric. *The Pink and the Black: Homosexuals in France Since 1968*. Translated by Jane Marie Todd. Stanford: Stanford University Press, 1999.

Martial. *Books 1–5*. Vol. 1 of *Epigram,*. Translated by D. R. Shackleton Bailey. LCL 94. Cambridge: Harvard University Press, 1993.

———. *Books 11–14*. Vol. 3 of *Epigrams*. Translated by D. R. Shackleton Bailey. LCL 480. Cambridge: Harvard University Press, 1993.

Martignac, J. "Le centurion de Capernaüm." *Arcadie* 255 (1975): 117–28.

Martin, Craig. "How to Read an Interpretation: Interpretive Strategies and the Maintenance of Authority." *BCT* 5.1 (2009): 6.1–26.

Martin, Thomas, and B. Newman. "Guilt and the Homosexual." *ONE Magazine* 8.12 (1960): 12–13.

———. "Guilt and the Homosexual." *ONE Magazine* 14.11 (1966): 12–13.

Martínez, Javier. "Cheap Fictions and Gospel Truths." Pages 3–20 in *Splendide Mendax: Rethinking Fakes and Forgeries in Classical, Late Antique, and Early Christian Literature*. Edited by Edmund P. Cuerva and Javier Martínez. Gronigen: Barkhuis, 2016.

Mason, Hugh J. *Greek Terms for Roman Institutions: A Lexicon and Analysis*. ASP 13. Toronto: Hakkert, 1974.

Mattingly, David J. *Imperialism, Power, and Identity: Experiencing the Roman Empire*. Princeton: Princeton University Press, 2011.

Mayer, Michel. "Le procurateur de Judée: Suite à la manière d'Anatole France." *Arcadie* 134 (1965): 63–71.

McClure, Michael. "Is the Homosexual Movement to Be Condemned?" *Month* 27 (1994): 431–35.

———. "The Sermon." *Lesbian and Gay Christian Movements's Roman Catholic Caucus: Newsletter* 16 (1994): 5–7.
McCoskey, Denise Eileen. *Race: Antiquity and Its Legacy.* London: Taurus, 2012.
McDowell, Sean. *CSB Apologetics Study Bible for Students.* Nashville: Holman, 2017.
McEvoy, Kieran. *Paramilitary Imprisonment in Northern Ireland: Resistance, Management, and Release.* Clarendon Studies in Criminology. Oxford: Oxford University Press, 2001.
McNeill, John J. *The Church and the Homosexual.* Boston: Beacon, 1976.
———. *Freedom, Glorious Freedom: The Spiritual Journey of Fullness of Life for Gays, Lesbians, and Everybody Else.* Boston: Beacon, 1995.
———. "Positive Messages from the Bible." *Advent: Lutherans Concerned/San Francisco* 11.4 (1989): 10–11.
———. *Sex as God Intended: Reflection on Human Sexuality as Play.* Maple Shade: Lethe, 2008.
McQuilkin, Robertson, and Paul Copan. *An Introduction to Biblical Ethics: Walking in the Way of Wisdom.* 3rd ed. Downers Grove: IVP Academic, 2014.
Meeker, Martin. "Behind the Mask of Respectability: Reconsidering the Mattachine Society and Male Homophile Practice, 1950s and 1960s." *JHSex* 10 (2001): 78–116.
Meer, Nasar, and Tariq Modood. "For 'Jewish' Read 'Muslim'? Islamophobia as a Form of Racialisation of Ethno-Religious Groups in Britain Today." *Islamophobia Studies* 1 (2012): 34–53.
Meier, John P. *A Marginal Jew: Rethinking the Historical Jesus. Mentor, Message, and Miracles.* Vol. 2. ABRL. New York: Doubleday, 1994.
———. *The Vision of Matthew: Christ, Church, and Morality in the First Gospel.* Philadelphia: Fortress, 1979.
Melcher, Sarah J. "The Problem of Anti-Judaism in Christian Feminist Biblical Interpretation: Some Pragmatic Suggestions." *CrossCurrents* 53 (2003): 22–31.
Meyer, Doug. "Omar Mateen as US Citizen, Not Foreign Threat: Homonationalism and LGBTQ Online Representations of the Pulse Nightclub Shooting." *Sexualities* 23 (2020): 249–68.
Miller, Amanda C. *Rumors of Resistance: Status Reversals and Hidden Transcripts in the Gospel of Luke.* Emerging Scholars. Minneapolis: Fortress, 2014.

Miller, James E. "The Centurion and His Slave Boy." Paper presented at the Annual Meeting of the Society of Biblical Literature. San Francisco, 1997.
———. "Letters." *The Door* 136 (1994): 4–5.
Miller, Neil. *Out of the Past: Gay and Lesbian History from 1869 to the Present*. New York: Vintage, 1995.
Miner, Jeff, and John Tyler Connoley. *The Children Are Free: Reexamining the Biblical Evidence on Same-Sex Relationships*. Indianapolis: Jesus Metropolitan Community Church, 2002.
Moore, Clive. *Sunshine and Rainbows: The Development of Gay and Lesbian Culture in Queensland*. Saint. Lucia: University of Queensland Press, 2001.
Moore, Paul. *Take a Bishop Like Me*. New York: Harper & Row, 1979.
Montserrat, Dominic. *Sex and Society in Græco-Roman Egypt*. London: Routledge, 1996.
Morgan, W. L. D. "The Homosexual and the Church: A Historical Survey and Assessment." Unpublished manuscript, 1965(?).
Moreno Soldevila, Rosario. "Anchialus." Pages 38–39 in *A Prosopography to Martial's Epigrams*. Edited by Rosario Moreno Soldevila, Alberto Marina Castillo, and Juan Fernández Valverde. Berlin: De Gruyter, 2019.
Morris III, Charles E. "Archival Queer." *Rhetoric and Public Affairs* 9 (2006): 145–51.
Morse, Sidney Edwards. *Premium Questions on Slavery, Each Admitting of a Yes or No Answer*. New York: Harper & Brothers, 1860.
Moten, Fred, and Stefano Harney. "The University and the Undercommons: Seven Theses." *Social Text* 22 (2004): 101–15.
Muñoz, José Esteban. *Cruising Utopia: The Then and There of Queer Futurity*. New York: New York University Press, 2009.
Murgatroyd, Paul. "Tibullus and the Puer Delicatus." *Acta Classica* 20 (1977): 105–19.
Murray, Theresa, and Michael McClure. *Moral Panic: Exposing the Religious Right's Agenda on Sexuality*. Listen Up! London: Cassell, 1995.
Musskopf, André Sidnei. "Biblia, sanación y homosexualidad: 'Hombres sean sumisos a su propio marido. De la misma manera, mujeres sean sumisas a sus esposas.'" *RIBLA* 49 (2004): 88–100.
Myles, Robert J. "The Fetish for a Subversive Jesus." *JSHJ* 14 (2016): 52–70.
Nair, Yasmin. "The Secret History of Gay Marriage." 25 June 2015. https://tinyurl.com/sbl6705d.

Nardelli, Jean-Fabrice. *Homosexuality and Liminality in Gilgameš and Samuel.* Classical and Byzantine Monographs 64. Amsterdam: Hakkert, 2007.
Nedra, Pierre. "'L'amour grec' et 'Eros socraticus.'" *Arcadie* 84 (1960): 706–13.
Neill, James. *The Origins and Role of Same-Sex Relations in Human Societies.* Jefferson: McFarland, 2009.
Neusner, Jacob. *Are There Really Tannaitic Parallels to the Gospels? A Refutation of Morton Smith.* SFSHJ 80. Atlanta: Scholars, 1993.
———. "Who Needs 'The Historical Jesus'? An Essay-Review." *BBR* 4 (1994): 113–26.
Nielsen, Hanne Sigismund. "*Delicia* in Roman Literature and the Urban Inscriptions." *Analecta Romana* 19 (1990): 79–88.
Nolland, John. *Luke 1–9:20.* WBC 35A. Dallas: Word, 1989.
Nortjé-Meyer, Lilly. "The Homosexual Body without Apology: A Positive Link between the Canaanite Woman in Matthew 15:21–28 and Homosexual Interpretation of Biblical Texts." *R&T* 9 (2002): 118–34.
Nunokawa, Jeff. "*In Memoriam* and the Extinction of the Homosexual." *ELH* 58 (1991): 427–38.
Nussbaum, Martha. "Platonic Love and Colorado Law: The Relevance of Ancient Greek Norms to Modern Sexual Controversies." *Virginian Law Review* 80 (1994): 1515–651.
Ortleb, Charles. "God and Gays: A New Team." *Christopher Street* 1.4 (1976): 25–31.
Osiek, Carolyn. "Female Slaves, Porneia, and the Limits of Obedience." Pages 255–74 in *Early Christian Families in Context: An Interdisciplinary Dialogue.* Edited by David L. Balch and Carolyn Osiek. Grand Rapids: Eerdmans, 2003.
Page, Alan. "Jesus Was Not Anti-Gay." *Gay and Lesbian Humanist* 13.4 (1994): 30.
Parsons, Mikeal C. *Luke.* Paideia. Grand Rapids: Baker Academic, 2015.
Paul, Ian. "Did Jesus Heal the Centurion's Gay Lover?" *Psephizo*, 7 June 2016. https://tinyurl.com/SBL6705k.
———. *Same-Sex Unions: The Key Biblical Texts.* Grove Biblical 71. Cambridge: Grove, 2014.
Paulinus Pellaus. *Eucharisticus.* Translated by Hugh G. Evelyn White. LCL 115. Cambridge: Harvard University Press, 1921.
Pawlikowski, John. *Christ in the Light of the Christian-Jewish Dialogue.* New York: Paulist, 1982.

Perez, Mark, dir. *Queer Eye: More Than a Makeover.* Season 5, episode 1, "Preaching Out Loud." Aired 5 June 2020 on Netflix.
Pérez Álvarez, Eliseo. *¿Eres o te haces? Una Probadita a la Homosexualidad y la Biblia.* Buenos Aires: GEMPRIP, 2017.
Perriman, Andrew. *End of Story? Same-Sex Relationships and the Narratives of Evangelical Mission.* Eugene: Cascade, 2019.
Perry, John. "Gentiles and Homosexuals: A Brief History of an Analogy." *JRE* 38 (2010): 321–47.
Perry, Matthew J. "Sexual Damage to Slaves in Roman Law." *Journal of Ancient History* 3 (2015): 555–75.
Phan, Peter C. *Being Religious Interreligiously.* Maryknoll, NY: Orbis Books, 2004.
Phang, Sara Elise. *The Marriage of Roman Soldiers (13 B.C.–A.D. 235): Law and Family in the Imperial Army.* Columbia Studies in the Classical Tradition 24. Leiden: Brill, 2001.
Pikaza Ibarrondo, Xabier. "Centuriones." Pages 211–13 in *Gran diccionario de la Biblia.* Edited by Xabier Pikaza Ibarrondo. Estella: Verbo Divina, 2015.
———. *Palabras de amor: Guía de amor humano y cristiano.* Bilbao: Desclee de Brouwer, 2007.
Plaskow, Judith. "Christian Feminism and Anti-Judaism." *CrossCurrents* 28 (1978): 306–9.
Plautus. *The Little Carthaginian, Pseudolus, The Rope.* Translated by Wolfgang De Melo. LCL 260. Cambridge: Harvard University Press, 2012.
Poirier, John C. "Seeing What Is There in Spite of Ourselves: George Tyrell, John Dominic Crossan, and Robert Frost on Faces in Deep Wells." *JSHJ* 4 (2006): 127–38.
Pollini, John. "The Warren Cup: Homoerotic Love and Symposial Rhetoric in Silver." *Art Bulletin* 81 (1999): 21–52.
Posner, Richard A., and Katharine B. Silbaugh. *A Guide to America's Sex Laws.* Chicago: University of Chicago Press, 1996.
Price, A. W. "Plato, Zeno, and the Object of Love." Pages 170–99 in *The Sleep of Reason: Erotic Experience and Sexual Ethics in Ancient Greece and Rome.* Edited by Martha Nussbaum and Juha Sihvola. Chicago: University of Chicago Press, 2002.
Pritchard, Richard E. *A Contribution to the Discussion on the Homosexual Lifestyle and Its Legalization in Madison.* Madison: Self-Published, 1978.

Puar, Jasbir K. "Homonationalism Gone Viral: Discipline, Control, and the Affective Politics of Sensation." Paper presented at the Portland Center for Public Humanities. Portland, 2012.

———. *The Right to Maim: Debility, Capacity, Disability*. Anima. Durham, NC: Duke University Press, 2017.

———. *Terrorist Assemblages: Homonationalism in Queer Times*. 10th anniversary ed. Next Wave. Durham, NC: Duke University Press, 2017.

Raboteau, Albert J. *Slave Religion: The "Invisible Institution" in the Antebellum South*. Updated ed. Oxford: Oxford University Press, 2004.

Rao, Rahul. "Echoes of Imperialism in LGBT Activism." Pages 353–70 in *Echoes of Empire: Memory, Identity and Colonial Legacies*. Edited by Kalypso Nicolaïdis, Berny Sebe, and Gabrielle Maas. London: Taurus, 2015.

Raphall, M. J. "The Bible View of Slavery." Pages 227–46 in *Fast Day Sermons: Or, the Pulpit on the State of the Country*. New York: Rudd & Carleton, 1861.

Rawcliffe, Derek. "The Centurion's Faith." *The Pink Paper*, 23 December 1994, p. 6.

Reeder, Caryn A. "Wartime Rape, the Romans, and the First Jewish Revolt." *JSJ* 48 (2017): 363–85.

Reid, Barbara E., and Shelly Matthews. *Luke 1–9*. Wisdom Commentary 43A. Collegeville: Liturgical, 2021.

Reilly, Elinor. "New Ways in Theology at Holy Cross." *Fenwick Review* 25.5 (2018): 5–7.

Reinhard, Wilhelm. *Lenchen im Zuchthause*. Karlsruhe: Bielefeld, 1840.

———. *Nell in Bridewell: Description of the System of Corporal Punishment (Flagellation) in the Female Prisons of South Germany*. Translated by W. Charles Costello and Alfred R. Allinson. Paris: Society of British Bibliophiles, 1900.

Remaud, Michel. "Les femmes dans la généalogie de Jésus selon Matthieu." *NRTh* 143 (2021): 3–14.

Richlin, Amy. "Eros Underground: Greece and Rome in Gay Print Culture 1953–65." *JH* 49.3–4 (2005): 421–61.

———. "Not before Homosexuality: The Materiality of the *Cinaedus* and the Roman Law against Love between Men." *JHSex* 3 (1993): 523–73.

Ricoeur, Paul. *Freud and Philosophy*. New Haven: Yale University Press, 1970.

Robinson, Jack Clark. "Author's Reply." *Gay and Lesbian Review Worldwide* 15.1 (2008): 6.

———. "Jesus, the Centurion, and His Lover." *Gay and Lesbian Review Worldwide* 14.6 (2007): 22–24.

Robinson, James M., Paul Hoffmann, and John S. Kloppenborg, eds. *The Critical Edition of Q: Synopsis Including the Gospels of Matthew and Luke, Mark and Thomas with English, German, and French Translations of Q and Thomas*. Hermeneia. Minneapolis: Fortress, 2000.

Rocca, Francesca. "La manomissione al femminile: Sulla capacità economica delle donne in Grecia in età ellenistica: l'apporto degli atti di affrancamento." *Historika* 2 (2012): 247–72.

Ropero Berzosa, Alfonso. "Homosexualidad." Pages 1198–1202 in *Gran Diccionario enciclopédico de la Biblia*. Edited by Alfonso Ropero Berzosa. Barcelona: Editorial CLIE, 2013.

Rossman, Parker. *Pirate Slave*. Nashville: Nelson, 1977.

———. Review of *Adolescent Sexuality*, by Robert Sorensen. *Journal of Sex Research* 10 (1974): 165–71.

———. *Sexual Experience between Men and Boys: Exploring the Pederast Underground*. New York: Association, 1976.

Roth, Jonathan P. "Jewish Military Forces in the Roman Service." Pages 79–94 in *Essential Essays for the Study of the Military in New Testament Palestine*. Edited by Christopher B. Zeichmann. Eugene: Wipf & Stock, 2019.

———. "Jews and the Roman Army: Perceptions and Realities." Pages 409–20 in *The Impact of the Roman Army (200 BC–AD 476): Economic, Social, Political, Religious, and Cultural Aspects*. Edited by Lukas de Blois and Elio Lo Cascio. Impact of Empire 6. Leuven: Brill, 2006.

Roux, Marie. "A Re-interpretation of Martial, *Epigram* XI.94." *SCI* 36 (2017): 81–104.

Rowlands, Rhiannon M. "Eunuchs and Sex: Beyond Sexual Dichotomy in the Roman World." PhD diss., University of Missouri-Columbia, 2014.

Sabar, Ariel. *Veritas: A Harvard Professor, A Con Man and the Gospel of Jesus's Wife*. New York: Doubleday, 2020.

Saddington, Denis B. "The Centurion in Matthew 8:5–13: Consideration of the Proposal of Theodore W. Jennings, Jr., and Tat-Siong Benny Liew." *JBL* 125 (2006): 140–42.

Sadownick, Douglas. "The Christ of the Early Christians." *Gay and Lesbian Review Worldwide* 12.6 (2005): 39.

Said, Edward W. *Orientalism*. 25th anniv. ed. New York: Vintage, 2003.

Saller, Richard P. "Symbols of Gender and Status Hierarchies in the Roman Household." Pages 87–93 in *Women and Slaves in Graeco-Roman Cul-*

ture: *Differential Equations*. Edited by Sandra R. Joshel and Sheila Murnaghan. London: Routledge, 1998.

Sánchez, Carlos Ernesto. "Soy Homosexual." *La Nación*, 20 June 2011.

Sanders, James A. "God's Work in the Secular World." *BTB* 37.4 (2007): 145–52.

Sartre, Jean-Paul. "Qu'est-ce qu'un collaborateur." *Situations* 3 (1949): 43–60.

Satlow, Michael L. "Rhetoric and Assumptions: Romans and Rabbis on Sex." Pages 135–44 in *Jews in a Graeco-Roman World*. Edited by Martin D. Goodman. Oxford: Clarendon, 1998.

———. *Tasting the Dish: Rabbinic Rhetorics of Sexuality*. BJS 303. Repr., Providence, RI: Brown Judaic Studies, 2020.

Schaberg, Jane. *The Illegitimacy of Jesus: A Feminist Theological Interpretation of the Infancy Narratives*. San Francisco: Harper & Row, 1987.

Schipper, Aldert. "Rechter buigt zich over pornografisch karakter van foto's Amerikaan Mader." *Trouw*, 12 December 1990, p. 9.

Scholz, Susanne, Timothy J. Sandoval, Francisco Lozada, Jr., and Tat-Siong Benny Liew. "Roundtable: The Institute for Signifying Scriptures and Biblical Studies." *The Abeng* 3 (2019): 71–94.

Schüssler Fiorenza, Elisabeth. *Jesus and the Politics of Interpretation*. London: Continuum International, 2000.

———. *Rhetoric and Ethic: The Politics of Biblical Studies*. Minneapolis: Fortress, 1999.

Scott, Joan Wallach. *The Fantasy of Feminist History*. Next Wave Provocations. Durham, NC: Duke University Press, 2011.

Scroggs, Robin. *The New Testament and Homosexuality: Contextual Background for Contemporary Debate*. Philadelphia: Fortress, 1983.

Scullin, Sarah. "Making a Monster." *Eidolon*, 24 March 2016. https://tinyurl.com/https-tinyurl-com-SBL0699e/.

Sechrest, Love L. "Enemies, Romans, Pigs, and Dogs: Loving the Other in the Gospel of Matthew." *ExAud* 31 (2015): 71–105.

Sedgwick, Eve Kosofsky. *Epistemology of the Closet*. Berkeley: University of California Press, 1990.

Seim, Turid Karlsen. *The Double Message: Patterns of Gender in Luke and Acts*. Nashville: Abingdon, 1994.

Shanks, Hershel. "'Secret Mark': A Modern Forgery? Restoring a Dead Scholar's Reputation." *BAR* 35.6 (2009): 59–61, 90–92.

Sherwood, Yvonne. "Bush's Bible as a Liberal Bible (Strange though That Might Seem)." *Postscripts* 2 (2006): 47–58.

Shore-Goss, Robert E. "Gay Liberation." Pages 257–64 in *The Oxford Encyclopedia of the Bible and Gender Studies.* Edited by Julia O'Brien. Oxford: Oxford University Press, 2014.
Shorter, Edward. *Written in the Flesh: A History of Desire.* Toronto: University of Toronto Press, 2005.
Sibalis, Michael. "Homophobia, Vichy France, and the 'Crime of Homosexuality': The Origins of the Ordinance of 6 August 1942." *GLQ* 8 (2002): 301–18.
Sinker, Robert, trans. "The Testaments of the Twelve Patriarchs." *ANF* 8:1–38
Skinner, Marilyn B. "*Ego Mulier*: The Construction of Male Sexuality in Catullus." Pages 129–50 in *Roman Sexualities.* Edited by Judith P. Hallett and Marilyn B. Skinner. Princeton: Princeton University Press, 1997.
Skordi, Ioanna. "The 'Regiment of Pleasure': Cavafy and His Homoerotic Legacy in Greek Writing." PhD diss., King's College London, 2018.
Smith, Jonathan Z. *Drudgery Divine: On the Comparison of Early Christianity and the Religions of Late Antiquity.* Jordan Lectures in Comparative Religion 14. Chicago: University of Chicago Press, 1990.
Smith, Morton. "Ἑλληνικὰ χειρόγραφα ἐν τῇ Μονῇ τοῦ ἁγίου Σάββα" ["Greek manuscripts in the monastery of St. Saba"]. *Νέα Σιών* [*Zion News*] 52 (1960): 110–25, 245–56.
———. "Regarding *Secret Mark*: A Response by Morton Smith to the Account by Per Beskow." *JBL* 103 (1984): 624.
The Society of Biblical Literature Council. "Statement regarding SBL and Former Member Jan Joosten." Society of Biblical Literature. 25 June 2020, https://www.sbl-site.org/assets/pdfs/Joosten_Statement.pdf.
Soler-Gallart, Marta. *Achieving Social Impact: Sociology in the Public Sphere.* SpringerBriefs in Sociology. Berlin: Springer, 2017.
Spade, Dean. "Under Cover of Gay Rights." *N.Y.U. Review of Law & Social Change* 37 (2013): 79–100.
Sphero, M. W. *The Gay Faith: Christ, Scripture, and Sexuality.* New Orleans: Herms, 2011.
Spivak, Gayatri Chakravorty. "Can the Subaltern Speak?" Pages 271–313 in *Marxism and the Interpretation of Culture.* Edited by Cary Nelson and Lawrence Grossberg. Urbana: University of Illinois Press, 1988.
Stayton, William R. "Pederasty in Ancient and Early Christian History." Pages 438–39 in *Human Sexuality: An Encyclopedia.* Edited by Vern L.

Bullough and Bonnie Bullough. Garland Reference Library of Social Science 68. New York: Garland, 1994.
Stern, Sacha. *Jewish Identity in Early Rabbinic Writings.* AGJU 23. Leiden: Brill, 1994.
Stiebert, Johanna. *Rape Myths, the Bible, and #MeToo. Rape Culture, Religion and the Bible.* London: Routledge, 2020.
Stone, T. D. P. "Speech of Henry C. Wright." *The Liberator (Boston)* 20.22 (1850): 3.
Strong, Anise K. "Male Slave Rape and the Victims' Agency in Roman Society." Pages 174–87 in *Slavery and Sexuality in Classical Antiquity.* Edited by Deborah Kamen and C. W. Marshall. Wisconsin Studies in Classics. Madison: University of Wisconsin Press, 2021.
Stuart, Elizabeth. "For God's Sake Stop Pretending!" *LGCM News* June 1993, pp. 4–7.
Sturrock, Tim. "Pervo Pleads Guilty, Sentenced in Porn Case." *The Minnesota Daily.* 1 June 2001. https://tinyurl.com/sbl6705m.
Stychin, Carl F. *Governing Sexuality: The Changing Politics of Citizenship and Law Reform.* Oxford: Hart, 2003.
Sullivan, Andrew. "The End of Gay Culture." *The New Republic.* 24 October 2005. https://tinyurl.com/sbl6705f.
Swartz, David. *Culture and Power: The Sociology of Pierre Bourdieu.* Chicago: University of Chicago Press, 1997.
Szesnat, Holger. "'Pretty Boys' in Philo's *De Vita Contemplativa*." *SPhiloA* 10 (1998): 87–107.
Tadmor, Naomi. *The Social Universe of the English Bible: Scripture, Society, and Culture in Early Modern England.* Cambridge: Cambridge University Press, 2014.
Tallon, Jonathan. "What Do the Gospels Say Directly about Being Gay?" 6 July 2018. https://tinyurl.com/sbl6705i.
Tardieu, Ambroise. *Étude médico-légale sur les attentats aux moeurs.* 6th ed. Paris: Baillère, 1873.
Taylor, Charles. "The Politics of Recognition." Pages 25–74 in *Multiculturalism: Examining the Politics of Recognition.* Edited by Amy Gutmann. Princeton: Princeton University Press, 1994.
Taylor, John. "The Poetry of Dinos Christianopoulos." *The Cabirion/Gay Books Bulletin* 12 (1985): 11–13.
Taylor, Robert R., Jr. "A Triumph for Truth." Pages 7–8 in *A Debate on Homosexuality.* Edited by Thomas F. Eaves Sr. and Paul R. Johnson. Algood: T&P Bookshelf, 1981.

Temple, Gray. *Gay Unions: In the Light of Scripture, Tradition, and Reason*. New York: Church Publishing, 2004.
Theissen, Gerd. *Der Schatten des Galiläers: Historische Jesusforschung in erzählender Form*. Munich: Kaiser, 1986.
———. *Erlösungsbilder: Predigten und Meditationen*. Kaiser: Gütersloh, 2002.
———. *La Sombra del Galileo*. Translated by Constantino Ruiz-Garrido. Salamanca: Sígueme, 1988.
———. *The Shadow of the Galilean*. Translated by John Bowden. Minneapolis: Augsburg Fortress, 1987.
Thurman, Howard. *Jesus and the Disinherited*. New York: Abingdon-Cokesbury, 1949.
Tong, M Adryael. "Gender and Sexuality in Postcolonial Perspective." Pages 117–35 in *The Oxford Handbook of New Testament, Gender, and Sexuality*. Edited by Benjamin H. Dunning. Oxford: Oxford University Press, 2019.
Tonstad, Linn Marie. "The Limits of Inclusion: Queer Theology and Its Others." *Theology and Sexuality* 21 (2015): 1–19.
Topolski, Anya. "The Dangerous Discourse of the 'Judaeo-Christian' Myth: Masking the Race-Religion Constellation in Europe." *Patterns of Prejudice* 54 (2020): 71–90.
Trible, Phyllis. *Texts of Terror: Literary-Feminist Readings of Biblical Narratives*. Overtures to Biblical Theology 13. Philadelphia: Fortress, 1984.
Trumbach, Randolph. Review of *Same-Sex Unions*, by John Boswell. *JH* 30.2 (1995): 111–17.
Turner, David L. *Matthew*. BECNT. Grand Rapids: Baker Academic, 2008.
Tyrell, George. *Christianity at the Crossroads*. New York: Longmans, Green, 1910.
Vaage, Leif E. "The Excluded One: (Un)popular Christology and the Quest for the Historical Jesus in Europe, North America, and Latin America." Pages 121–44 in *Discovering Jesus in Our Place: Contextual Christologies in a Globalised World*. Edited by Sturla J. Stålsett. Dehlhi: ISPCK, 2003.
———. "Q^1 and the Historical Jesus: Some Peculiar Sayings (7:33–34; 9:57–58, 59–60; 14:26–27)." *Foundations and Facets Forum* 5.2 (1989): 159–76.
Valantasis, Richard. *The New Q: A Fresh Translation with Commentary*. London: T&T Clark, 2005.

Van de Spijker, A. M. J. M. Herman. *Die gleichgeschlechtliche Zuneigung; Homotropie: Homosexualität, Homoerotik, Homophilie, und die katholische Moraltheologie*. Olten: Walter, 1968.
Van Driel-Murray, Carol. "Gender in Question." *Theoretical Roman Archaeology Journal* 1992 (1995): 3–21.
Van Tine, R. Jarrett. "Castration for the Kingdom and Avoiding the αἰτία of Adultery (Matthew 19:10–12)." *JBL* 137 (2018): 399–418.
Velunta, Revelation E. "The Centurion and His 'Beloved.'" *Mission Sparks* 3 (2017): 24–47.
———. "The *Ho Pais Mou* of Matthew 8:5–13: Contesting the Interpretations in the Name of Present-Day *Paides*." *Bulletin for Contextual Theology in Africa* 7.2 (2000): 25–32.
Verot, Augustin. *A Tract for the Times: Slavery and Abolitionism, Being the Substance of a Sermon, Preached in the Church of St Augustine, Florida, on the Fourth Day of January, 1861, Day of Public Humiliation, Fasting and Prayer*. New Orleans: Catholic Propagator Office, 1861.
Verstraete, Beert C. "Slavery and the Social Dynamics of Male Homosexual Relations in Ancient Rome." *JH* 5 (1980): 227–36.
Via, Dan O., and Robert A. J. Gagnon. *Homosexuality and the Bible: Two Views*. Minneapolis: Fortress, 2003.
Vilà, Enric. "The Centurion's Servant in Jesus' Gospels: A Queer Love Story?" Pages 41–64 in *Queer Ways of Theology*. Warsaw: Wydawnictwo Newsroom, 2016.
Von Ehrenkrook, Jason. "Effeminacy in the Shadow of Empire: The Politics of Transgressive Gender in Josephus's *Bellum Judaicum*." *JQR* 111 (2011): 145–63.
Voorwinde, Stephen. *Jesus' Emotions in the Gospels*. London: T&T Clark, 2011.
Walker, Iain. "Scandal of Gay Clergy." *Mail on Sunday*, 10 July 1988, pp. 12–15.
Waller, Alexis G. "The 'Unspeakable Teachings' of The Secret Gospel of Mark: Feelings and Fantasies in the Making of Christian Histories." Pages 145–73 in *Religion, Emotion, Sensation: Affect Theories and Theologies*. Edited by Karen Bray and Stephen D. Moore. Transdisciplinary Theological Colloquia. New York: Fordham University Press, 2020.
Warner, Michael. "Normal and Normaller: Beyond Gay Marriage." *GLQ* 5 (1999): 119–71.
Watson, John. *Lessons on the Miracles and Parables of Our Lord*. London: Church of England Sunday School Institute, 1882.

Watson, Patricia. "Erotion: Puella Delicata?" *CQ* 42 (1992): 253–68.
Weaver, Dorothy Jean. "'Thus You Will Know Them by Their Fruits': The Roman Characters of the Gospel of Matthew." Pages 107–27 in *The Gospel of Matthew in Its Roman Imperial Context*. Edited by John Riches and David C. Sim. LNTS 276. London: T&T Clark, 2005.
Wegner, Uwe. *Der Hauptmann von Kafarnaum (Mt 7,28a; 8,5–10.13 par Lk 7,1–10): Ein Beitrag zur Q-Forschung*. WUNT 2/14. Tübingen: Mohr Siebeck, 1985.
Weigel, George. "Defending the Indefensible at Holy Cross." *The National Review*, 5 April 2018. https://tinyurl.com/sbl6705h.
———. "March Madness at the College of the Holy Cross." *The National Review*, 29 March 2018. https://tinyurl.com/sbl6705g.
Weir, Lorna. "The Concept of Truth Regime." *Canadian Journal of Sociology* 33 (2008): 367–89.
Wheeler-Reed, David, Jennifer W. Knust, and Dale B. Martin. "Can a Man Commit πορνεία with His Wife?" *JBL* 137 (2018): 383–98.
White, Mel. *Religion Gone Bad: The Hidden Dangers of the Christian Right*. New York: Tarcher, 2006.
Whittaker, C. R. *Rome and Its Frontiers: The Dynamics of Empire*. London: Routledge, 2004.
Wilde, Oscar. *Le Chant du cygne: Contes parlés d'Oscar Wilde*. Paris: Mercure de France, 1942.
Willert, Niels. "Martyrology in the Passion Narratives of the Synoptic Gospels." Pages 15–43 in *Contextualising Early Christian Martyrdom*. Edited by Jakob Engberg, Uffe Holmsgaard Eriksen, and Anders Klostergaard Petersen. Early Christianity in the Context of Antiquity. Frankfurt: Lang, 2011.
Williams, Craig A. "Greek Love at Rome." *CQ* 45 (1995): 517–39.
———. *Roman Homosexuality*. 2nd ed. Oxford: Oxford University Press, 2010.
Williams, Delores S. "Black Theology and Womanist Theology." Pages 58–72 in *The Cambridge Companion to Black Theology*. Edited by Dwight N. Hopkins and Edward P. Antonio. Cambridge: Cambridge University Press, 2012.
Williams, Dyfri. *The Warren Cup*. British Museum Objects in Focus. London: British Museum Press, 2006.
Williams, Robert. *Just as I Am: A Practical Guide to Being Out, Proud, and Christian*. New York: Crown, 1992.

Wilson, Nancy. *Homosexuality: Our Story Too; Lesbians and Gay Men in the Bible*. San Francisco: UFMCC, 1992.
Wimbush, Vincent L. "In Search of a Usable Past: Reorienting Biblical Studies." Pages 179–98 in *Toward a New Heaven and New Earth: Essays in Honor of Elisabeth Schüssler Fiorenza*. Edited by Fernando F. Segovia. Maryknoll, NY: Orbis Books, 2003.
———. "Interpreters—Enslaving/Enslaved/Runagate." *JBL* 130 (2011): 5–24.
———. "Interrupting the Spin: What Might Happen If African Americans Were to Become the Starting Point for the Academic Study of the Bible." *UTQ* 52 (1998): 61–76.
———. "TEXtureS, Gestures, Power: Orientation to Radical Excavation." Pages 1–20 in *Theorizing Scriptures: New Critical Orientations to a Cultural Phenomenon*. Edited by Vincent L. Wimbush. Signifying (on) Scriptures. New Brunswick: Rutgers University Press, 2008.
Winer, Canton, and Catherine Bolzendahl. "Conceptualizing Homonationalism: (Re-)Formulation, Application, and Debates of Expansion." *Sociology Compass* 15.5 (2021): e12853.
Wiseau, Tommy, dir. *The Room*. Wiseau-Films, 2003.
Witte, John, Jr. "Honor Thy Father and Thy Mother? Child Marriage and Parental Consent in Calvin's Geneva." *JR* 86 (2006): 580–605.
Wolter, Michael. *Das Lukasevangelium*. HNT 5. Tübingen: Mohr Siebeck, 2008.
Wright, David P. "'She Shall Not Go Free as Male Slaves Do': Developing Views about Slavery and Gender in the Laws of the Hebrew Bible." Pages 125–42 in *Beyond Slavery: Overcoming Its Religious and Sexual Legacies*. Edited by Bernadette J. Brooten and Jacqueline L. Hazelton. Black Religion/Womanist Thought/Social Justice. New York: Palgrave Macmillan, 2010.
Wright, N. T. *Jesus and the Victory of God*. Christian Origins and the Question of God 2. London: SPCK, 1997.
———. *The Resurrection of the Son of God*. Christian Origins and the Question of God 3. London: SPCK, 2003.
Wyke, Maria. "Herculean Muscle! The Classicizing Rhetoric of Bodybuilding." *Arion* 3/4.3 (1997): 51–79.
Xiao, An. "On the Origins of 'They Tried to Bury Us, They Didn't Know We Were Seeds.'" *Hyperallergic*, 3 July 2018. https://tinyurl.com/sbl6705b.
Zaldívar, Raúl. *Técnicas de análisis e investigación de la Biblia: Un enfoque evangélico de la Crítica Bíblica*. Barcelona: Editorial CLIE, 2016.

Zeichmann, Christopher B. "Capernaum: A 'Hub' for the Historical Jesus or the Markan Evangelist?" *JSHJ* 15 (2017): 147–65.

———. "Gender Minorities in and under Roman Power: Respectability Politics in Luke-Acts." Pages 61–73 in *Luke-Acts*. Edited by James Grimshaw. Texts@Contexts. London: Bloomsbury, 2018.

———. "Herodian Kings and Their Soldiers in the Acts of the Apostles: A Response to Craig Keener." *JGRChJ* 11 (2015): 178–90.

———. "Liberal Hermeneutics of the Spectacular in the Study of the New Testament and the Roman Empire." *MTSR* 31 (2019): 152–83.

———. "Martial and the *fiscus Iudaicus* Once More." *JSP* 25 (2015): 111–17.

———. "Military Forces in Judaea 6–130 CE: The *status quaestionis* and Relevance for New Testament Studies." *CurBR* 17 (2018): 86–120.

———. "Rethinking the Gay Centurion: Sexual Exceptionalism, National Exceptionalism in Readings of Matt 8:5–13//Luke 7:1–10." *BCT* 11.1 (2015): 35–54.

———. Review of *Joseph's Dilemma*, by Matthew Marohl. *BCT* 7.1 (2011): 128–29.

———. *The Roman Army and the New Testament*. Lanham, MD: Lexington/Fortress Academic, 2018.

———. "Same-Sex Intercourse Involving Jewish Men 100 BCE–100 CE: Sources and Significance for Jesus' Sexual Politics." *Religion and Gender* 10 (2020): 13–36.

———. "The Slave Who Was ἔντιμος: Translation and Characterization in Luke 7:2." *BT* 74 (forthcoming).

Zelnick-Abramovitz, Rachel. *Not Wholly Free: The Concept of Manumission and the Status of Manumitted Slaves in the Ancient Greek World*. Mnemosyne Supplements 266. Leiden: Brill, 2005.

Ziegert, Thomas C. "Blessed and Challenged by Jesus: Where We Get the Chutzpah to Do Our Own Ethics." *Open Hands* 13.4 (1998): 14.

Žižek, Slavoj. *Violence: Six Sideways Reflections*. Big Ideas//Small Books. New York: Picador, 2008.

Zuckerberg, Donna. *Not All Dead White Men*. Cambridge: Harvard University Press, 2018.

Ancient Sources Index

Hebrew Bible/Old Testament		Daniel	
		9:9	243
Genesis			
16:4–5 (LXX)	182	2 Esdras = LXX Nehemiah	
19:1–11	194	14:8	180
37:30 (LXX)	179	14:13	180
		15:7	180
Exodus		16:17	180
21:7–11	7, 184	17:5	180
Leviticus		Deuterocanonical Books	
18:22	88		
19:20–22	7, 184	Sirach	
20:13	88	41:22	187
Numbers		Susannah	
31:7–8	7	36–41	210
Deuteronomy		4 Ezra	
21:10–14	7, 184	10:22	109
Judges		Ancient Jewish Literature	
21:10–24	7		
		Josephus, *Antiquitates judaicae*	
Isaiah		1.188–193	185
3:5 (LXX)	180	1.200	194
13:12 (LXX)	182	1.215–219	185
42:1 (LXX)	207, 243	15.23	194
42:6	127	15.294	199
		16.230–232	173, 185, 190
Joel		16.399	203
3:3 (LXX)	187	17.199	199
		18.40–43	182
		18.109–119	200

Josephus, Antiquitates judaicae (cont.)
19.357 199
19.357-366 200
20.105-112 200

Josephus, Bellum judaicum
1.45 203
1.249 203
1.488-489 173, 185, 190
2.223-227 200
2.429 203
3.36 199
4.560-563 193
7.320 219

Josephus, Contra Apionem
1.35 109
2.199 89

Jubilees
14.21-24 185
20.4 210
20.5-6 89
30.7-8 210
41.23 209

Letter of Aristeas
1.152 89

Philo of Alexandria, De Abrahamo
135 89
248-254 185

Philo of Alexandria, De congressu eruditionis gratia
154 182

Philo of Alexandria, De decalogo
121-131 210

Philo of Alexandria, De Iosepho
43-44 210

Philo of Alexandria, De specialibus legibus
3.36 89

3.38 194
3.52-58 210

Philo of Alexandria, De vita contemplativa
50 194

Philo of Alexandria, Hypothetica
7.1 210

Sibylline Oracles
3.596 89

Testament of Joseph
14.3 179

Testament of Judah
14.2 209
17.1-3 209

New Testament

Matthew
1:6 209
1:16 210
1:18-25 210
2:11 208
2:16 207, 243
5:14 127
5:15 208
5:23 242
5:27-29 211
5:31-32 210
5:40-41 64
7:24-27 208
8:6 3, 41, 206-8
8:8 3, 18, 41, 117, 206-8, 234
8:9 3, 30, 114, 121
8:10-12 122
8:11-12 121
8:13 3, 41, 206, 234
8:14 208
8:28-34 100
9:1 134
9:24-25 212
9:28 208

10:37	205	Luke	
12:18	207–9, 242–43	1:34	205
12:29	208	2:6	205
13:57	208	2:26–38	205
14:2	207–8	2:41–51	206
14:3–4	211	2:43	204
14:3–12	212	4:30–32	238
14:5	207	4:31	134
14:9	207	4:38–39	205
14:11	212	7:2	3, 7, 38, 175, 179–83, 209, 231
17:14	207	7:3	3
17:18	207	7:3–5	87, 111, 122, 135, 159, 184
19:9	205	7:4–5	204
19:9–10	210–11	7:6	18
19:10–12	211	7:7	3, 41, 117, 242–43
19:12	2	7:8	3, 30, 114
21:15	207, 243	7:9	9, 122
21:31	238	7:10	3, 243
21:31–32	211	7:36–50	205
23:14	208	7:37	215
24:17	208	8:5	243
24:43	208	8:19–21	205
25:1–13	211	8:51	204
27:24	100	8:54	204, 243
27:52–53	156	12:45	243
27:54	36, 100	14:8	180
		14:26	205, 215
Mark		15:30	205
1:29–31	205	16:18	205
2:16	87	18:19	205
3:21	206	18:26–30	205
3:31–34	205	18:29	205
5:1–10	100	20:34–35	205
5:42	212	23:29	205
6:3	206	23:47	36
10:2–12	205		
10:19	205	Sayings Gospel Q	
10:29	205	6:22	214
12:25	205	7:3	225
14:47	116	7:8	214
15:21–22	205	7:10	213
15:39	36, 100	7:22	214
15:40	206	7:34	215
15:47	206	9:59–60	215
16:1	206	10:12	215

Sayings Gospel Q (cont.)		Colossians	
10:13	214	3:22	119
10:13–15	215		
10:15	214	1 Thessalonians	
11:14	214	4:3–8	188
12:53	215		
13:28–29	215	Philemon	115, 119, 188
14:26	205, 215		
15:8–10	215	1 Peter	
16:13	215	2:18	119
16:17	215		
16:18	205, 210, 215	Jude	
17:3–4	215	7	89
17:27	215		

		Rabbinic Works	
John			
4:46–54	3, 22, 87, 115, 161, 203–4, 227–28, 243	b. Gittin	
		57b	219
8:1–11	210		
		b. Ketubbot	
Acts		51b	109
5:34–40	132		
17:28	179	b. Qiddushin	
20:9	243	82a	194
20:10	243		
20:12	243	b. Sanhedrin	
21:9	205	54b	194
22:3	132		
24:25	205	Genesis Rabbah	
		86:3	184
Romans			
1:26–27	89	Lamentations Rabbah	
		1:16	219
Galatians			
4:21–5:1	185, 188	m. Bikkurim	
		1:5	184
1 Corinthians			
5–7	188	m. Gittin	
9:5	206	9:10	211
13:12	157		
		m. Ketubbot	
Ephesians		1:2	109
6:5	119	1:4	109
		2:5–6	109
		2:9	109

t. Bava Batra		Clement of Alexandria, *Paedagogus*	
4:5	197	3.8	178
		12.84	189
t. Horayot			
2:11	184	Clement of Alexandria, *Protrepticus*	
		2.33	178
t. Ketubbot			
4:5	109	Eusebius, *Vita Constantini*	
		1.7	178–79
t. Qiddushin			
5:2	194	George Hamartolos, *Chronicle*	
5:3	184	1.13	179
5:9–10	89		

Gregory of Tours, *Liber de Miraculis Beati Andreae*

t. Sanhedrin
10:2 194

3 177–78

Targum Pseudo-Jonathan Leviticus
20:13 89

Jerome, *Epistulae*
77.3 189

y. Ketubbot
2:2, 26d 109

John Chrysostom, *Homiliae in epistulam ad Titum*
5.4 179

y. Sanhedrin
6:3, 23b–c 194
7:9, 25a 194

John Chrysostom, *Homiliae in Matthaeum*
4.7 210
73 179

Early Christian Writings

John Chrysostom, *In illud: Propter fornicationes autem unusquisque suam uxorem habeat*

Acts of Andrew
2 177
7–8 177
17–21 188–89

4–5 189

Acts of Xanthippe
1.1–10 181

Lactantius, *Divinarum institutionum*
6.23.23–30 189

Athanasius, *Contra gentes*
9 178

Origen, *Contra Celsum*
3.36 178

Augustine, *De incompetentibus nuptiis*
2.8 189

Paulinus of Pella, *Eucharisticus*
162–172 189

Clement of Alexandria, *Ad Theodorum*
148–51

Protevangelium of James
13.1–14.7 210

Salvian, *De gubernatione Dei*		Chariton, *Chaereas and Callirhoe*	
7.88	9	2.8.6–7	220
		2.62	105
Secret Gospel of Mark 2, 148–55, 157, 166–67		8.4.3	108
		Cicero, *De Republica*	
Shepherd of Hermas, *Similitudes*		4.3–4	91
5.2.2	180		
		Cicero, *Epistulae ad Atticum*	
Tatian, *Oratio ad Graecos*		1.16.5	108
10	178		
		Cicero, *In Verrum*	
Theophilus of Antioch, *Ad Autolycum*		2.4.116	108
1.2	179		
		Cicero, *Orationes philippicae*	
Traditio apostolica		3.31	9, 108
16.15–16	189		
		Cicero, *Tusculanae disputationes*	
Greco-Roman Literature		4.33.70–71	193
		5.20.58	193
Aelian, *Varia Historia*			
12.7	179	Codex Iustinianus	
		8.51.1	220
Ammianus Marcellinus, *Res Gestae*			
15.12.3	219	Columella, *De re rustica*	
		1.8.1	182
Apuleius, *Metamorphoses*		12.3.6	196
3.19–22	106	12.3.7	219
Aratus, *Phaenomena*		Cynic Epistles, *Diogenes*	
5	179	24	179
Arrian, *Anabasis*		Digesta	
1.12	179	17.2.63 (Paulus)	73
		21.1.1.1 (Ulpian)	197
Aulus Gellius, *Noctes Atticae*		28.5.59 (Paulus)	73
4.2.1	196–97		
10.23	210	Dio Cassius, *Historiae romanae*	
15.12	6, 174	60.29	196
		62.28.2–3	186
Callimachus, *Epigrams*			
31	4	Dio Chrysostom, *Orationes*	
		15.8	220
Cato the Elder, *De agricultura*			
2.7	196		

ANCIENT SOURCES INDEX

Diodorus Siculus, *Bibliotheca historica*		11.94	186, 190
8.23	181		
31.24	9	Musonius Rufus, *Discourses*	
37.3.6	9	12.1–16	187

Galen, *Hippocratic Epidemics*		Palatine Anthology	
2.1	219	7.643 (Crinagoras)	172
		12.129 (Aratus)	179
Historia Augusta, *Aelius*		12.211 (Strato of Sardis)	173
5.11	182	12.237 (Strato of Sardis)	173
		12.239 (Strato of Sardis)	173
Horace, *Carmina*			
1.7.54–55	73	Pausanias, *Graeciae descriptio*	
		10.22.3–4	219
Horace, *Satirae*			
1.2.116–119		Petronius, *Satyricon*	106
		26–78	193
Juvenal, *Satirae*		57	204
1.2.116–119	5–6	74–75	193
		75.11	5
Livy, *Ab urbe condita*		98	203
1.58	210		
3.44	210	Phaedrus, *Fabulae*	
26.13.15	108	4.15–16	
26.15.14	219		
28.22.9–11	219	Plato, *Leges*	
		11.916	196
Martial, *Epigrams*			
1.31	8, 245	Plautus, *Miles gloriosus*	
2.92	191	1102–1114	9
3.92	191		
4.24	191	Plautus, *Pseudolus*	
5.34	172	1180–1181	8
5.37	172		
5.48	8	Pliny the Younger, *Epistulae*	
7.30	195	8.16	196
7.35	187, 190		
7.55	190	Plutarch, *Cato Major*	
7.82	191	5	196
9.11–13	186	8.2	9
9.16–17	186		
9.36	186	Plutarch, *Quaestiones romanae et graecae*	
10.61	172	274d–e	91
11.26	191		
11.58	191		

Plutarch, *Quaestionum convivialum libri IX*
668b–c   9

Polybius, *Historiae*
31.25.5   9, 193

Quintilian, *Declamationes*
3   108, 174

Rhetorica ad Herrenium
4.12   108

Sallust, *Bellum catalinae*
51.9   9, 108

Seneca the Elder, *Controversiae*
4 praef. 10   105, 184–85

Seneca the Younger, *Epistulae*
97.2   108

Suetonius, *Augustus*
65   210
24.1   219

Suetonius, *Claudius*
25.2   196

Suetonius, *Domitianus*
10   174

Suetonius, *Galba*
7.22   172

Suetonius, *Nero*
28   186

Statius, *Silvae*
3.4   186

Tacitus, *Annales*
4.10   186
11.2   175

Tacitus, *Historiae*
3.33   108
3.40   9
4.14   108
5.5   193, 195
5.13   195

Theocritus, *Idylls*
7.96–114   179

Thucydides, *Peloponnesian War*
1.132.5   4
6.4.3   181

Valerius Maximus, *Facta et dicta memorabilia*
6.1.10   8, 174, 219
6.1e.1   219
6.1e.3   219
9.1.7   108

Vergil, *Eclogae*
2   6

Xenophon, *Agesilaus*
5.4–5   5

Xenophon, *Anabasis*
4.1.14   4
4.6.1–3   4
5.8.4–5   4
7.4.7–11   4

Xenophon, *Hellenica*
5.4.57   4

Xenophon, *Memorabilia*
2.10   196

Xenophon of Ephesus, *Ephesian Tale*
1.4.1   106

ANCIENT SOURCES INDEX   297

Papyri and Inscriptions

AE
  1929.106   9
  1929.193   9
  1977.762   9

CIIP
  412   191
  3498   191
  3499   191

CIL
  2.498   73
  4.1863   6
  4.2028   192
  4.2402   191
  4.2403   191
  4.2406   191
  6.3221   9
  6.5163   172
  6.11623   187
  6.14327   187
  6.18653   187
  6.21687   187
  6.27692   187
  19.470   181

CPJ
  4   187

CPL
  120   9

DMIPERP
  4   199
  12–18   199
  23   199
  30–32   199
  34   199
  38   199
  53   201
  119   199
  120   200
  139   199

  145   199
  148   199
  172–179   191

Ephesos
  135   181

IG
  9.1.82c   180
  9.1.728   181
  12.1.44   181
  12.1.55   181
  12.1.107   181
  12.8.220   181

IGBulg
  1.2.390   180

IKyme
  4   181
  5   181
  7   181
  8   181

I.Lind.
  51   181
  88   181

JIWE
  1.22   180

P.Oxy.
  3070   105–7

SB
  1.4206   191

SEG
  9.744   191
  26.1214   180
  31.918   109
  31.920   109
  36.1291   191
  52.1418   181

SIG
  3.985.25–27 211

Tab. Vindol.
  2.255 9

TAM
  4.1.288 180

Modern Authors Index

Adelman, Rebecca A.	126	Bolzendahl, Catherine	127
Ahmed, Leila	125	Boroughs, Rod	29
Ahmed, Sara	16, 130, 135, 156	Borrillo, Daniel	44
Akenson, Donald H.	150–51	Bosia, Michael J.	93
Allison, Dale C., Jr.	87, 147–48	Bosman, Frans	61
Álvarez Valdés, Ariel	95–96, 206	Boswell, John	73, 143–44, 247
Anastasios, Nikolaides	36	Botero, Ebel	58, 95, 240
Andelman, David A.	63	Bourdieu, Pierre	167, 170
Applebaum, Shimon	199	Bourg, Julian	45, 51–52
Armstrong, Elizabeth A.	31	Boxall, Ian	114
Arnal, William E.	90, 130–31, 138–39, 215	Bradley, Keith	74, 219
		Brentlinger, Rick	85
Avalos, Hector	120	Brink, Laurena Ann	188
Bailey, Marlon M.	95	Brisbane, William Henry	115
Barnes, Albert	115	Brown, Michael L.	177
Barnstone, Willis	37	Brown, Scott	149
Bartram, Jerry	86	Brownlow, William Gannaway	114–15
Baudry, André	49–52	Buck, Erwin	111
Bauer, Raymond A.	219	Buell, Denise Kimber	152
Bauer, Alice H.	219	Buisson-Fenet, Hélène	49
Bennett, James	122	Burke, Tony	153–54
Bentham, Jeremy	12, 27	Bush, Laura	126
Bérard, Jean	45	Butler, Judith	78, 129, 164
Berenice Bárcenas, Karina	95	Campbell, Matthew	52
Bergler, Siegfried	158	Caballero, Daniel	96, 177
Bermejo-Rubio, Fernando	200	Cadwallader, Alan H.	104
Bernal, Martin	123	Call, Harold L.	142
Bersani, Leo	78	Callahan, Allen Dwight	120
Bérubé, Allan	76	Cantarella, Eva	171–72
Birchard, Roy	237	Carlier, François	44
Blanton, Ward	160–61, 163	Carlson, Stephen C.	150, 154
Blomberg, Craig A.	147	Carter, Jimmy	67
Blyth, Caroline	104	Carter, Warren	99, 120
Bock, Darrell L.	7	Cassidy, Ron	75

Cerutti, Franco	49	Eaves, Thomas F., Sr.	58, 177, 242–43
Charles, Ronald	177	Eck, Marcel	39, 42, 56, 58, 233–34
Cheever, George Barrell	115	Edgar, Campbell Cowan	187
Cheng, Patrick S.	18	Edmondson, Jonathan	74
Chilton, Bruce D.	150, 154	Egger, John A.	185
Christianopoulos, Dinos	12, 19, 32–37, 58, 156, 229–30, 234, 237, 239, 241, 243	Eng, David L.	83
		England, Frank	158
		Enroth, Ronald M.	39, 58, 162, 236
Christianson, John E.	104	Eribon, Didier	52
Clarke, John R.	174	Erlich, Adi	191
Clarke, Lewis G.	118	Esack, Farid	129
Clarke, Milton	118	Evans, Craig A.	158
Clements, E. Anne	209	Falsch, J.	86
Cobb, Christy	177	Faris, Donald L.	92, 246
Cohen, Edward E.	199–200	Fell, Gordon	85
Connell, Martin F.	149	Fischel, Joseph J.	13
Connoley, John Tyler	69	Flemming, Rebecca	199
Copan, Paul	164	Flessen, Bonnie J.	103
Corriveau, Patrice	44, 45	Fletcher, John	116
Cotter, Wendy	87, 89, 90	Flournoy, John J.	116, 122
Crossan, John Dominic	146–50, 153	Forward, Martin	103
Crossley, James G.	90, 128, 134	Foucault, Michel	19, 23, 52, 55, 78, 152
Crowther, R. H.	38, 58, 78, 132, 156, 230, 232, 234	Fredrick, David	4,
		Friar, Kimon	32, 34–35, 229, 244
Cvetkovich, Ann	10,	Friedl, Raimud	175
D'Angelo, Mary Rose	204	Füller, Christian	54
Dallas, Joe	87, 164	Funk, Robert W.	147
Danker, Frederick W.	183	Gadamer, Hans-Georg	121
Davidson, Alex	58, 235	Gagnon, Robert A. J.	87, 102, 136, 141, 148, 157–60, 162–64, 190
Davie, Martin	102		
Den Dulk, Matthijs	200	Gamson, Joshua	71
Deamer, Geoffrey	36	Gelardini, Gabriella	193
Denton, Donald L.	147–48	Gera, Dov	191
Derrett, J. Duncan M.	39, 58, 74, 236, 238	Giesen, Heinz	158
		Gillabert, Émile	43, 247
Dinshaw, Carolyn	143–44, 155, 161	Glancy, Jennifer A.	105–7, 182–85, 187–89, 211–12
Djurslev, Christian Thrue	179		
Douglass, Frederick	117–18	Goodacre, Mark S.	206
Doundoulakis, Emmanouil	34	Goss, Robert E. See Shore-Goss, Robert E.	
Dowling, Elizabeth V.	120–21		
Drake, Susanna	195	Gowler, David B.	102–3
Dube, Musa W.	100, 121	Gray-Fow, Michael	39, 58, 60, 245
Duffield, Ian K.	75	Graybill, Rhiannon	106, 112
Duggan, Lisa	67, 81, 129	Grosvenor, Cyrus P.	116, 120
Durand, Mickaël	49	Gunderson, Jaimie	192–93

Gunther, Scott 44–46
Gunthorp, Dale 85
Gyburc-Hall, Larion 39, 58, 78, 232–33
Hacking, Ian 152–53, 161
Halberstam, Jack 10, 44, 134, 220
Haller, Tobias Stanislas 77
Halperin, David M. 45
Hanks, Thomas 10, 77–78, 96, 133
Harding, James E. 15
Haritaworn, Jin 129
Harney, Stefano 220
Harper, Kyle 183, 188
Harrill, J. Albert 114–16, 120
Harvey, Keith 51
Hedrick, Charles W. 149
Heimsoth, Karl-Günther 31
Helminiak, Daniel 75, 85, 96
Heron, Alastair 142
Heszer, Catherine 184, 187, 196, 204
Higginbotham, Evelyn Brooks 82
Hocquenghem, Guy 43, 56, 58, 240
Hoke, James 205
Hopkins, Keith 6
Hopper, George S. E. 85
Horner, Tom M. 2, 38–39, 43, 58–59, 63, 70, 196, 229, 239–41
Huber, Lynn R. 65
Hughes, Aaron W. 17
Hunt, Peter 219
Independent Gay Forum 81
Isaac, Benjamin 109, 195, 199
Iturra, Carlos 95, 104, 156
Jablonski, Olivier 27
Jackson, Julian 44–45, 47, 49–50
Jakobsen, Janet R. 127
James, Simon 9
Jamison, Gerald E. 39, 58, 162, 236
Jaworski, Tlumaczyl Jerzy 97
Jeffery, Peter 150, 154
Jennings, Theodore W. 4–5, 8, 10–12, 38, 70, 75, 86–87, 91, 98, 103–4, 108, 111, 135, 143, 158, 171–72, 175, 196–98, 200, 206–8
John, Jeffrey 133
Johnson, Jeff 149

Johnson, Paul R. 58, 241–43
Johnson, Steven R. 5, 213, 225
Johnson, William Stacy 75
Jones, Charles Colcock 119
Jones, John Richter 114
Jordan, Deborah 30
Jordan, Mark D. 64
Joshel, Sandra R. 183
Junior, Nyasha 15
Kafer, Alison 218
Kasher, Aryeh 186
Katzoff, Ranon 193
Kaye, Richard A. 34
Keating, Christine (Cricket) 92
Keener, Craig S. 154
Keitt, Laurence M. 114
Kennedy, Hubert 232
Kepner, James, Jr. 12, 38, 40, 58, 85, 231, 237, 244–45
Kim, Jae-Hyun 96
Kirchick, James 84
Kirkup, James 36
Kloppenborg, John S. 213
Knust, Jennifer W. 211
Koepnick, Erik 70
Kolendo, Jerzy 6
Kotrosits, Maia 25, 152
Kręcidło, Janusz 183
Krutzsch, Brett 124
Kunkel, Fritz 99
Laes, Christian 6, 172
Lambert, James 58, 62–63, 244
Landau, J. H. 199
Lawrence, Raymond J., Jr. 39, 58, 60, 75, 246
Lear, Andrew 173
Levin-Richardson, Sarah 191–92
Levine, Amy-Jill 11, 88, 92, 111, 120
Lewis, Holly 81
Liew, Tat-siong Benny 4–5, 8, 10–12, 38, 70, 75, 86–87, 98, 103–4, 108, 111, 152, 158, 171–72, 175, 196–98, 200, 206–8
Lincoln, Bruce 90, 145–46
Lings, K. Renato 97

Little, Paul D.	164	Moore, Clive	30
Loader, William	89, 161–63, 186, 195	Moore, Paul	25
Loman, Pasi	219–20	Montserrat, Dominic	106
Long, Ronald E.	11	Morgan, W. L. D.	58, 233
Lyons, Michael	149	Moreno Soldevila, Rosario	186
MacDonald, Dennis R.	178–79	Morris, Charles E., III	10
Macey, David	52	Morse, Sidney Edwards	114
Mader, Donald H.	7, 37–39, 41, 43, 58–62, 72, 87, 100, 196, 229, 245	Moten, Fred	220
		Muehlberger, Ellen	222
Mahmood, Saba	127	Muñoz, José Esteban	159
Mahomed, Nadeem	129	Murray, Theresa	12
Manwell, Elizabeth	173	Murgatroyd, Paul	172
Maranger, Keith	246	Murnaghan, Sheila	183
Marchal, Joseph A.	6, 24, 104, 122, 188	Musskopf, André Sidnei	95
Marlowe, Christopher	27	Myles, Robert J.	99, 102
Marohl, Matthew J.	210	Nair, Yasmin	83–84
Martel, Frédéric	51–52	Nardelli, Jean-Fabrice	136
Martignac, J.	38–39, 41–43, 48–49, 52–54, 56, 58–59, 68–69, 132, 237	Nedra, Pierre	49
		Neill, James	135–36, 149
Martin, Craig	162–63	Neusner, Jacob	154–55
Martin, Dale B.	211	Newman, B.	39–40, 58, 232, 234
Martin, Thomas	39–40, 58, 232, 234	Nielsen, Hanne Sigismund	172
Martínez, Javier	150	Nolland, John	7
Mason, Hugh J.	199	Nortjé-Meyer, Lilly	135
Matthews, Shelly	11, 104, 111	Nussbaum, Martha	171–72
Mattingly, David J.	108–9	Nunokawa, Jeff	79
Mayer, Michel	12, 39–42, 48–49, 53, 56, 58, 122, 156, 233–34	Ortleb, Charles	59, 238
		Osiek, Carolyn	189–90
McClure, Michael	12, 85	Page, Alan	85
McCoskey, Denise Eileen	123	Parsons, Mikeal C.	11, 158
McDowell, Sean	11, 164	Paul, Ian	148, 158, 164
McEvoy, Kieran	218	Pawlikowski, John	138
McNeill, John J.	9–10, 18, 38, 58–59, 69–70, 77, 103, 143, 238, 246	Pellegrini, Ann	127
		Pérez Álvarez, Eliseo	95
McQuilkin, Robertson	164	Perriman, Andrew	88, 184, 194
Meeker, Martin	50	Perry, John	128
Meer, Nasar	134	Perry, Matthew J.	183
Meier, John P.	98, 213	Phan, Peter C.	138
Melcher, Sarah J.	137	Phang, Sara Elise	8
Meyer, Doug	124	Pikaza Ibarrondo, Xabier	96, 206
Miller, Amanda C.	120	Plaskow, Judith	137
Miller, James E.	78, 103	Poirier, John C.	146
Miller, Neil	48	Pollini, John	174, 192
Miner, Jeff	69	Posner, Richard A.	67
Modood, Tariq	134	Price, A. W.	171–72

Pritchard, Richard E. 239
Puar, Jasbir K. 79–80, 123, 126–27, 129–30, 136
Raboteau, Albert J. 120
Rao, Rahul 129
Raphall, M. J. 118
Rawcliffe, Derek 86
Reed, Annette Yoshiko 222
Reeder, Caryn A. 108–9, 219
Reid, Barbara E. 11, 104, 111
Reinhard, Wilhelm 28–30
Reilly, Elinor 86
Remaud, Michel 209
Richlin, Amy 21, 23, 38, 48, 108, 141, 175
Ricoeur, Paul 121
Robinson, Jack Clark 38, 86, 136, 143
Rocca, Francesca 181
Ropero Berzosa, Alfonso 96
Rossman, Parker 38–39, 41–43, 56, 58–59, 62–64, 137, 238
Roth, Jonathan P. 199
Roux, Marie 186
Rowlands, Rhiannon M. 186
Sabar, Ariel 154
Saddington, Denis B. 11, 75, 108, 123, 158, 197–98, 201
Sadownick, Douglas 149
Sagiv, Nachum 191
Said, Edward W. 124–25
Sallé, Nicolas 45
Saller, Richard P. 183
Sánchez, Carlos Ernesto 96
Sanders, James A. 75
Sartre, Jean-Paul 19, 47
Satlow, Michael L. 194
Schaberg, Jane 210
Schipper, Aldert 61
Schüssler Fiorenza, Elisabeth 112, 157
Scott, Joan Wallach 127
Scroggs, Robin 89–90, 100
Scullin, Sarah 65
Sechrest, Love L. 175
Sedgwick, Eve Kosofsky 79
Seim, Turid Karlsen 204

Shanks, Hershel 155
Sherwood, Yvonne 104, 128
Shore-Goss, Robert E. 18, 38, 113, 149
Shorter, Edward 28
Sibalis, Michael 47
Skinner, Marilyn B. 4, 173
Skordi, Ioanna 36
Smith, Jonathan Z. 18
Smith, Morton 148–51, 153–55
Szesnat, Holger 194
Soler-Gallart, Marta 52
Spade, Dean 129
Sphero, M. W. 73
Spivak, Gayatri Chakravorty 125
Stayton, William R. 39, 58, 60
Stern, Sacha 89–90
Stiebert, Johanna 104, 122
Strong, Anise K. 100
Stuart, Elizabeth 85
Stychin, Carl F. 13
Sullivan, Andrew 84
Swartz, David 167
Tadmor, Naomi 181
Tallon, Jonathan 104
Tardieu, Ambroise 46
Taylor, Charles 12
Taylor, John 229
Taylor, Robert R., Jr. 241
Temple, Gray 133
Theissen, Gerd 74, 96, 132, 156, 244–45
Thurman, Howard 119
Tong, M Adryael 104
Tonstad, Linn Marie 137
Topolski, Anya 126
Trible, Phyllis 112–13
Trumbach, Randolph 144
Trump, Donald J. 123–24, 135
Turner, David L. 158
Tyrell, George 146–48, 167
Vaage, Leif E. 147
Valantasis, Richard 103–4
Van de Spijker, A. M. J. M. Herman 58, 234
Van Driel-Murray, Carol 9
Van Tine, R. Jarrett 210–11

Velunta, Revelation E. 97–102, 104, 122, 220
Verot, Augustin 122
Verstraete, Beert C. 6
Vilà, Enric 96
Von Ehrenkrook, Jason 193
Voorwinde, Stephen 88, 131, 158, 184, 194
Walker, Iain 63
Waller, Alexis G. 10, 148, 155
Warner, Michael 83–84
Watson, John 27
Watson, Patricia 172
Weaver, Dorothy Jean 100
Weigel, George 86
Weir, Lorna 152
Weiss, Meredith L. 93
West, Mona 113
Wheeler-Reed, David 211
White, Mel 133–34, 156
Whittaker, C. R. 108–9
Wilde, Oscar 12, 27
Willard, Jeremy 149
Willert, Niels 179
Williams, Craig A. 6, 91, 108, 172, 191
Williams, Delores S. 95
Williams, Dyfri 174, 193
Williams, Robert 138
Wilson, Nancy 85
Wimbush, Vincent L. 15, 120, 220–21
Winer, Canton 127
Witte, John, Jr. 64
Witherington, Ben, III 11, 88, 92, 111, 120
Wolter, Michael 88, 158
Wright, David P. 184
Wright, Henry C. 117
Wright, N. T. 156–57, 221
Wyke, Maria 48
Xiao, An 35
Zaldívar, Raúl 96
Zelnick-Abramovitz, Rachel 180–81
Ziegert, Thomas C. 73
Žižek, Slavoj 136–37
Zuckerberg, Donna 123

Subject Index

academic biblical scholarship
  acceptance of the homoerotic interpretation, 10–15, 74–75
  rejection of the homoerotic interpretation, 2, 75, 157–68
activist and scholastic hermeneutics, 144–68
anti-Semitism, 16, 31, 133–39, 221
Arcadie, 38–42, 48–51
definitions, 22–24
disappointment, 217–23
entimos (ἔντιμος), 7, 179–183
feminism, 14, 51–52, 97, 111–13, 125, 137, 148
footnote (Bruce Lincoln), 145–46, 156–57, 169
heteronormative interpretation of the pericope, 22–23, 86–93, 101–2, 130–33, 161–66, 178, 201
  homophobia and interpretation of the pericope, 22–23, 86, 161–63, 166
HIV/AIDS, 78–80, 83–84
homoeroticism, acceptance
  among Jews, 185–87, 190–95
  among Romans, 4–9, 23–24, 88–89, 91, 105–10
  in the American military, 76–78, 80, 83
homoeroticism, practice of
  in the Roman military, 8–9, 108–10, 174, 197–98
  in Palestinian armies, 197–201
homoerotic interpretation of the pericope
  among Catholics, 18

homoerotic interpretation of the pericope (*cont.*)
  in East Asia, 96–97
  in Australia, 30–31, 161–63
  in Denmark, 97
  in Eastern Europe, 96–97
  in France, 39–57
  in Germany, 28–30, 58, 74–75, 231–34, 244
  in Greece, 32–37
  in India, 97
  in Latin America, 58, 95–96, 240
  in Spain, 96, 188
  in the Netherlands, 60–62
  in the Philippines, 98–102
  in the United States, 67–85
homonationalism, 127–30
homonormativity, 67, 81–83, 91–92
homophile, 27–65, 142–43, 156
  origins and meaning of the term, 22–23, 31
homophobia. *See also* heteronormative interpretation of the pericope
  in Roman antiquity, 91
  in Christianity, 157–58, 161–66
  in Islam, ostensibly, 80, 123–24, 127–29, 134–35
  in Judaism, ostensibly, 86–91, 130–39
Irish republicanism, 217–18
Islamophobia, 127–28, 134–36
Jesus
  as exceptional among Jews, 131–39
  as party animal, 147–48, 215
  as quintessential Jew, 86–91, 138–39

Jesus-myth hypothesis, 145, 158
law and biblical interpretation, 12–15, 91–93
Log Cabin Republicans, 129
Nazis, 31, 46–47, 221
pais (παῖς), 3–7, 69–71, 175–79
pederasty, 5, 110, 171–74. *See also* pedophilia, rape
pedophilia, 47–48, 59–65, 68–72, 221–23. *See also* pederasty, rape
queer archive, 10, 12
Queer Eye, 1, 12, 217
queer soldiers
  in antiquity, 8–9, 77, 197–201
  in the United States, 76–85
rape, 51–54, 98–113, 125, 174, 198–201
respectability politics, 12, 14, 50–51, 68, 78–83, 91. *See also* homonormativity
Roman treatment of slaves, 195–97
same-sex marriage, 13, 67–76, 78–85, 150, 155, 161–63, 166
sex-workers, 9, 63–64, 91, 172–74, 199, 205–6, 209, 211
sexual exceptionalism, 127–35, 171
sexual intercourse with slaves
  among Christians, 188–90
  among Greeks, 174
  among Jews, 183–88
  among Romans, 3–9, 105–7, 174, 183–84
  among Roman soldiers, 8–9, 219
sexual orientation, 22–24, 44–47, 74–75, 77, 123, 160
shadow biblical scholarship
  acceptance of the homoerotic interpretation, 9–12, 141–68
  as fantasy, 155–56, 169
slaves, sexual intercourse with. *See* sexual intercourse with slaves
social differentiation, 14–15, 50, 71, 141–68, 170
Society of Biblical Literature, 65, 222–23
stickiness, 16, 135–36, 156
Stonewall Riots, 17, 31, 91, 150–51
texts of terror, 111–14

translation of the Bible, 7, 115, 179–81
truth regimes, 90, 152–55
United States of America
  interpretation of the pericope in, 67–140
  military's abuses against civilians in the Middle East, 125–26
  slavery in, 114–21
whiteness, 122–24, 131, 134

www.ingramcontent.com/pod-product-compliance
Lightning Source LLC
Chambersburg PA
CBHW021935290426
44108CB00012B/844